REVIEWS OF WARREN BLAND'S FIRST BOOK

RETIRE IN STYLE
50 AFFORDABLE PLACES ACROSS AMERICA

"*Retire in Style* provides economic and lifestyle information on the author's choices of good retirement spots."

Fred Brock, **The New York Times**

"If you're a few years away from retirement, *Retire in Style* is a good place to begin your search for the ideal, affordable retirement haven."

Robert J. Bruss, **Los Angeles Times**

"But geographer Warren Bland of California State University–Northridge says living less expensively doesn't have to mean living less well. While Boulder, CO. rates No. 1 in his guide *Retire in Style*, it's a costly place to call home. He also suggests more affordable housing places such as Gainesville, FL and Hot Springs, AR. And though housing in Naples, FL can be high, moving inland from the Gulf uncovers "perfectly nice neighborhoods without the premium price", says Bland."

Leonard Wiener, **US News & World Report** (June 2003)

"*Retire in Style* can let you zero in on what retiring Baby Boomers want . . ."

National Association of Realtors

"Bland ranks his choices on 12 criteria, from climate to transportation and the availability of retail services and health care. He suggests Boomers use the book as a starting point in the quest for a permanent retirement home or seasonal retreat."

Eileen Alt Powell, **Associated Press** (April 2003)

"Everyone likes a deal. So at our request, Warren Bland, author of *Retire in Style: 50 Affordable Places Across America* came up with half a dozen retiree-friendly bargains. Bland looked at hard data and at cultural, recreational, and educational opportunities, architectural charms, and natural surroundings. You'll be tempted."

US News & World Report Retirement Guide 2004

"It's likely that Bland's book will entice more retirees to take a closer look at Colorado Springs: The book has been Amazon.com's top seller on retirement for 45 days since its publication."

Jeanne Davant, **The Gazette** (Colorado Springs)

"Bland is right on target with many of the things he says about the area and why it is a wonderful place to live."

Karen Baker, **Times–Picayune**, Louisiana

"His study yielded 50 top communities in 23 states. These are five of the best: Gainesville, FL; Henderson, NC; Fayetteville, AR; Tucson, AZ; Chico, CA."

L.A Justice, **National Examiner**

"Devoting the last three years to seeking out ideal retirement towns—rating everything from air quality and crime to shopping and cultural happenings—the Cal State University Northridge geography professor wrote a book on where to live the good life in one's sunset years."

Caroline Dipping, **San Diego Tribune**

"*Retire in Style: 50 Affordable Places Across America* . . . attempts to predict where the nation's 76 million Baby Boomers born between 1946 and 1964 will want to spend their golden years."

Adolfo Pesquera, **San Antonio Express News**

"Bland . . . drew on 20 years of research to scout out communities with amenities important to baby boomer retirees."

Dana Bartholomew, **Los Angeles Daily News**

"Bland gave Naples a top score of five for its recreational activities and retail services."

John Henderson, **Naples Daily News**

"Bland, who specializes in regional geography of the United States, has selected 50 of the most desirable retirement places in the county."

Plus Magazine

"On my scale of one to 10, this superb new book rates a 10."

Robert J. Bruss, **Tribune Media Services**

Bland's conclusion: "If you like a desert climate and landscape and vibrancy of a major city, give Tucson a careful look."

Macario Juarez, Jr., **Arizona Daily Star**

"Bland . . . rates 50 US communities based upon criteria such as climate, cost of living, transportation, health care, cultural and recreational offerings, crime rates, and volunteer opportunities."

Book News, Inc.

"In his new book, *Retire in Style* (Next Decade, Inc.), California State University geography professor Warren Bland lists what he considers the Top 50 affordable places to retire."

Vic Roberts, **The Christian Science Monitor**

"Whether you are serious about impending retirement or reading for future use, this is a well-designed book with information on many retirement locations."

Orlando Sentinel

" . . . the book is a great resource to use to start the screening process because it makes it easy to quickly evaluate each location."

E. Thomas Wetzel, **Retirement Living News**

" . . . this handy sourcebook guides retirees toward safe, friendly communities that are rich in amenities."

Seniorcitizens.com

"In his recent book *Retire in Style: 50 Affordable Places Across America*, California State University geography professor Warren Bland ranks Annapolis 41st on his list."

Jay Livingston, **Chesapeake Life Magazine**

"In this year alone, Oxford . . . was also named in Dr. Warren Bland's popular book *Retire in Style: 50 Affordable Places Across America*."

Jack Criss, Executive Editor, **Delta Business Journal**

"Bland spent time talking to people who had lived in the area a long time, rather than basing his data on statistics alone."

Kim Lamb Gregory, **Ventura County Star**

"Bland, in his book, *Retire in Style, 50 Affordable Places Across America* . . . identifies communities that can meet budget needs."

Loretta Kalb, **Sacramento Bee**

"The single best resource currently available on US retirement communities."

Seniorjournal.com

"If you like daydreaming about where to move, this book is a great resource. It is aimed at those who might continue to work part-time during retirement, and those who seek an active lifestyle."

Miriam Sagan, **New Mexico Magazine**

"He rates communities on hard facts such as quality of health care, public transportation and cost of living, with a 10-step plan for choosing where to move."

New York Newsday (March 2003)

"There is nothing better than being there. The mix of information that is gleaned from fieldwork and from secondary sources provides a particularly insightful perspective not normally found in books of this kind."

Hubert B. Stroud, **The Professional Geographer**

"*Retire in Style* crunches the numbers and comes up with . . . Boulder, Colorado as the top-rated place to retire in the United States."

NEA Retired (July 2003)

" . . . start shopping for sunglasses. And grab a copy of Warren Bland's book *Retire in Style: 50 Affordable Places Across America*."

Jim Thompson, Kentucky Living Magazine (January 2004)

"Warren Bland, author *Retire in Style: 50 Affordable Places Across America*, says most retirees are chiefly concerned with the taxes they'll pay themselves, not what their estates will pay after they're gone or what their heirs will inherit. They're worried about the here and now."

Dallas Morning News (August 2004)

Retire in Style

60 Outstanding Places Across the USA and Canada

Retire in Style

60 Outstanding Places Across the USA and Canada

By Warren R. Bland, Ph.D.

Published by:

 **Next Decade**
books that simplify complex subjects

39 Old Farmstead Road
Chester, New Jersey 07930-2732 USA
www.nextdecade.com

Published by:

Next Decade, Inc.
39 Old Farmstead Road
Chester, New Jersey 07930-2732 USA
www.nextdecade.com

© 2005 by Warren R. Bland, Ph.D.
Printed in the United States of America

Library of Congress Cataloging-in-Publication Data

Bland, Warren R., 1941-
    Retire in style: 60 outstanding places across the USA and Canada /
    by Warren R. Bland.-
    - 2nd ed.
          p.cm.
    ISBN 1-932919-19-8 (alk. paper)
       1. Retirement, Places of--United States. 2. Retirement, Places of--Canada.
       I. Title: 60 outstanding places across the USA and Canada. II. Title.

HQ1063.B53 2005
646.7'9'0973--dc22   2004025299

$22.95 Softcover

To my wife Sarah, whose talent, hard work, and
loving support made this book possible.

About the Author

Dr. Warren Bland has spent the last thirty-six years teaching college-level geography. Educated in Canada and the United States, Dr. Bland earned a BA at Wilfrid Laurier University in Waterloo, Ontario and MA and Ph.D. degrees at Indiana University, Bloomington. He is currently a Full Professor in the Department of Geography at California State University, Northridge. His department is rated as one of the best academic geography departments in the United States.

During his long career, Dr. Bland has served as a Visiting Professor at the University of Winnipeg, organized major conferences in the United States and China, and delivered lectures at academic conferences in Canada, the United States, China and India. For twenty years he has specialized in the regional geography of the United States and Canada. Throughout this period he has traveled extensively and done geographical research all over North America, meanwhile developing a strong interest in and knowledge of the towns and cities most suitable for retirement.

Dr. Bland is a member of the Association of American Geographers, the National Council for Geographic Education, and several other professional organizations. He is the author of numerous academic articles and has served as primary reviewer for several major textbooks in economic and regional geography.

Dr. Bland has lived in Los Angeles with his wife Sarah for over thirty years. They look forward to eventually relocating to one of the splendid retirement towns discussed in his book.

Disclaimer

The purpose of this book is to provide interested individuals with an overview of upscale and affordable retirement towns. The author has spent many years researching this topic. It is presented with the understanding that the publisher and author are not engaged in rendering legal, financial, travel, real estate or other professional services in this book. When expert assistance is required, the services of a competent professional should be sought.

This book was not written to provide all the information that is available to the author and/or publisher, but to complement, amplify and supplement other texts and available information. While every effort has been made to ensure that this book is as complete and accurate as possible, there may be mistakes, either typographical or in content. Therefore, this text should be used as a general guide only, and not as the ultimate source of retirement town information. Furthermore, this book contains current information only up to the printing date.

Information herein was obtained from various sources whose accuracy is not guaranteed. Opinions expressed and information are subject to change without notice.

The author and Next Decade, Inc. shall not be held liable, nor be responsible to any person or entity with respect to any loss or damage caused, or alleged to be caused, directly or indirectly by the information contained in this book.

If you do not wish to be bound by the above, you may return this book to the publisher for a full refund.

Acknowledgments

This book is a logical outgrowth of *Retire in Style: 50 Affordable Places Across America*, which was published by Next Decade, Inc. in October 2001. That book, my first effort on retirement places, was very well received. Indeed, shortly after publication Robert Bruss, the noted real estate writer for Inman News Features, wrote me that he hoped I would "write a follow-up book on the same topic in a year or so to keep your retirement area reviews up to date." To Robert and the others who encouraged me to update and expand the coverage of *Retire in Style*, I express sincere thanks for their encouragement and advice.

I want to express my appreciation to a many people without whose help I could not have completed this project. The staff of chambers of commerce, visitors bureaus and economic development departments of more than 60 places visited during many months of travel across the United States and Canada were generous with their time and very helpful in providing useful information and in conveying their perceptions of what it is like to live in their towns. Many others contributed data and editorial assistance by mail and email. Friendly people that we had the good fortune to meet and chat with while walking streets and campuses and checking out amenities provided additional valuable insights.

Special thanks are due California State University, Northridge and its Geography Department. A sabbatical leave granted by the university allowed me to devote full attention to research and writing during a critical six-month period. My colleague and friend Antonia Hussey, chair of the Geography Department, was unflagging in her support. Departmental cartographer and colleague David Deis produced the Retirement Places map and the 50 illustrations featured in the write-ups of the top 50 retirement places. The book would not be the same without David's excellent contributions. I am also indebted to Nancy Derrico for her insightful editorial assistance and to Lisa Garbutt and Cynthia Pena for their fine work on the book cover and layout.

I owe most to Sarah, my wife, best friend and frequent traveling companion. Her assistance with field research, brainstorming about places visited, editing and her strong encouragement in difficult moments were invaluable.

Finally, I must again thank my publisher, Barbara Brooks Kimmel, whose vision, skills, good judgment, hard work and unwavering support enabled us to complete a second book together.

1 Introduction

There is good news for people contemplating retirement in the first decade of the new millennium. Americans and Canadians are living longer and healthier lives than their grandparents and parents could have imagined. A growing number of today's retirees can look forward to spending 20 or 30 years in active, fulfilling retirement. The problem, though a pleasant one, is deciding how and where to enjoy your "golden years." This book will make your task a little easier.

Making the Decision to Relocate

There is much to be said for staying put. You already know the community where you live and you probably feel connected to it. You may be reluctant to leave the neighborhood where you raised your children, even though they may now be living half a continent away. Familiarity doesn't always breed contempt. It is convenient to know your local doctor, bank manager and retail stores and it is comfortable to be in your old neighborhood.

But there are also compelling reasons to consider relocating. At retirement you are entering a new and different chapter of your life. For many, staying in familiar surroundings and not working is vaguely discomforting. On the other hand, settling into a different community that is safe, friendly and rich in opportunities for shopping, recreation and culture provides an exciting new beginning in an atmosphere free of the stresses of the workaday world. Even if you are psychologically comfortable in familiar surroundings, you may wish to relocate to a place with sunnier and warmer weather. Research indicates that mild temperatures (around 66 degrees F/19 degrees C), moderate relative humidity (around 55 percent), and fairly constant barometric pressure are ideal for human health. In contrast, extreme heat and cold and, to a lesser extent, very high and very low relative humidity and drastic changes in barometric pressure can adversely stress the body. Not surprisingly, migration to the Sunbelt and Pacific Coast has been a long-term demographic trend in North America. Finally and perhaps most importantly for those of moderate means, many retirement places offer lower costs of living, especially for housing, than do most major metropolitan areas. The ability to recoup and profitably invest some of your home equity by relocating to comparable but less expensive housing in a more affordable area increases your disposable income. For many retirees, such additional income could mean the difference between living modestly and retiring in style.

Retire in Style is not just a catchy title—it is the central concept of this book. It does not connote a cloistered existence in a gated retirement or resort community. The retirement places described here are real towns and cities that are special and highly livable. They are the kinds of places where you can enjoy an active or relaxed retirement in a safe, clean, friendly and uncrowded community rich in services and amenities. In brief, they offer a stimulating lifestyle and a high quality of life. Whether you are considering relocating within the United States or within Canada or contemplating a seasonal or permanent move across the U.S.–Canada border, *Retire in Style* will help you select the place that is best for you.

A *tropical savanna climate* is found near the tip of the Florida peninsula. Essentially a two-season climate with hot, humid and rainy summers and warm and comparatively dry winters, this sunny and virtually frost-free climate has helped lure permanent residents and winter visitors to Boca Raton and other South Florida cities.

A *semi-arid (steppe) climate* is characteristic in the Southern Rockies Retirement Region, at elevations between 4,500 and 8,000 feet in the Desert Southwest, and at locations east of the Cascade Range in the Pacific Northwest. A sunny, moderately dry, four-season climate with low relative humidity, this crisp, invigorating climate has great appeal to the outdoors oriented. Although each winter sees several snow storms, most snow melts within a few days as average daily high temperatures are above freezing even in mid-winter.

A true *desert climate* is found at elevations below 4,500 feet in the Desert Southwest Retirement Region and in interior southern California. Walled off from the moisture and moderating influence of the Pacific Ocean by California's Sierra Nevada and Coast Ranges, the entire region is very sunny and dry although not uniformly so. Average daily high temperatures exceed 95 degrees F (35 degrees C) in summer but are generally bearable thanks to low relative humidity. Spring and autumn weather is nearly ideal with warm days and cool nights; winters are mild to warm, sunny and pleasant. Although frosts are common on winter nights, little snow falls at lower elevations.

The *Mediterranean (dry-summer subtropical) climate* is found in coastal areas of central and southern California, in the state's Central Valley, and in the Medford–Ashland area of southern Oregon. There are really only two seasons here. A mild, fairly wet winter is balanced by a warm to hot, dry summer. Coastal locations like San Luis Obispo are sunnier and warmer in winter and cooler and somewhat cloudier in summer than Central Valley locations like Chico. Many people regard the sunny, mild, virtually frost-free coastal variant of the Mediterranean climate as the best in the world, a true paradise climate.

The *marine climate* is characteristic west of the Cascade Range in the Pacific Northwest Retirement Region. Winters here are mild, cloudy and wet; summers are warm, sunny and relatively dry. Spring and autumn weather is variable with cool to warm days and cool nights. Upwards of 70 percent of annual precipitation occurs between October and March. Cloudy to partly cloudy skies are more typical than clear skies except in summer. There is very little snow at lower elevations and it seldom persists on the ground for more than a few days.

Quality of Life

 Quality of life is sometimes defined very broadly to include virtually all factors influencing the standard of living of a place. Because many of these factors (for example, retail and community services, health care and cultural and recreational activities) are treated individually in this book, my definition is focused more narrowly on the livability and style of each community.

Livability and style are enhanced by the absence of some things and the presence of others. Freedom from aircraft, highway, railroad and industrial noise; from traffic congestion and tight parking; from noxious industries and tacky neighborhoods cluttered with boat trailers and recreational vehicles parked on streets and in yards translates into a superior quality of life. Conversely, the presence of clean air and attractive parks, neighborhoods and downtown shopping districts are essential to one's well-being. Clean air is especially important to older people as lung capacity diminishes with advancing age. Aesthetically appealing and well-equipped parks, attractive—well-landscaped and maintained—residential neighborhoods, and charming and viable downtown shopping districts are also vital. The city should be well planned and managed efficiently, and the community should manifest a peaceful and friendly ambiance.

Cost of Living

 Local living costs measure the relative affordability of places. Based on cost-of-living estimates from ACCRA (formerly called the American Chamber of Commerce Researchers Association) and local sources, I describe the composite (overall) cost of living and costs of housing, goods and services including groceries, health care, transportation, utilities and miscellaneous goods and services according to their percentage deviation from national norms. Because ACCRA does not report on state–provincial and local tax burdens, it was necessary to turn to state–provincial and local sources for tax information. For the United States, I rely heavily on *Who Pays?* This excellent source is available online from the Institute of Taxation and Economic Policy in Washington, D.C. Canadian tax data were obtained from the Canadian and provincial governments. For U.S. locations, I report the overall state and local tax burden for each place as a percentage of average income of middle–upper middle income taxpayers and compare that percentage to the U.S. average of 9.7 percent. I also note whether state income, sales and excise taxes and local property taxes are above or below national norms. For Canadian locations, I report to what extent the overall tax burden (federal, provincial and local) of each place is above or below the Canadian average and estimate by what percentage it exceeds the U.S. average for middle–upper middle income residents. I also report to what extent income tax rates, the combined federal–provincial sales tax on goods and services, and property taxes in particular places deviate from Canadian and American averages for each type of tax.

Transportation

 Although the private automobile dominates travel within and between American and Canadian cities, there is much to be said for places offering a range of transportation alternatives. Not everyone wants or will be able to continue driving into their seventies, yet in a community where good roads are supplemented by excellent public transit, sidewalks and trails for walking and biking, and good intercity transportation, one could remain mobile for years after giving up driving. For that reason, I evaluate local public transit in terms of frequency and quality of service, adequacy of route network and cost. I also describe intercity transportation options including air, bus and rail passenger service.

Retail Services

 Shopping is a favorite pastime; therefore, convenient access to a good variety of retail services is an important consideration. Even the smallest places discussed in this book can provide for the basic wants and needs of their residents and many offer much more. At minimum, I describe the major regional shopping centers in terms of their anchor (department)

Ratings at a Glance

Legend: 5 = Excellent / 4 = Very good / 3 = Good / 2 = Fair / 1 = Poor	Landscape	Climate	Quality of Life	Cost of Living	Transportation	Retail Services	Health Care	Community Services	Cultural Educational Activities	Recreational Activities	Work/Volunteer Activities	Crime Rates and Public Safety	Total
ATLANTIC CANADA													
Halifax, Nova Scotia	5	2	5	4	5	4	5	5	4	4	3	2	48
Fredericton, New Brunswick	5	2	5	4	3	2	5	4	4	4	3	4	45
NORTHEAST													
Burlington, Vermont	5	2	4	2	4	3	4	4	4	5	2	4	43
Ithaca, New York	5	2	5	3	3	3	3	5	4	4	4	4	45
State College, Pennsylvania	5	2	5	3	3	3	3	3	4	4	3	5	43
Pittsburgh, Pennsylvania	4	2	4	3	5	5	5	4	5	5	3	3	48
Kingston, Ontario	5	2	5	5	5	3	5	4	3	3	3	4	47
Owen Sound, Ontario	5	2	5	5	2	3	3	4	3	4	4	4	44
Stratford, Ontario	4	2	5	5	4	3	3	5	4	3	5	5	48
London, Ontario	3	2	5	5	5	5	5	5	5	4	4	3	51
MIDWEST													
Madison, Wisconsin	5	2	5	3	4	4	5	5	4	4	3	4	48
Bloomington, Indiana	4	3	4	4	2	3	3	3	5	5	3	4	43
UPPER SOUTH													
Charlottesville, Virginia	5	3	5	2	3	4	5	4	4	5	3	3	46
Lexington, Virginia	5	3	5	4	2	2	2	3	3	5	3	5	42
Chapel Hill, North Carolina	4	3	5	2	5	3	5	5	5	5	3	3	48
Pinehurst–Southern Pines, NC	4	3	5	3	2	2	4	4	3	4	4	4	42
Asheville, North Carolina	5	4	4	3	3	5	5	4	4	5	4	3	49
Hendersonville, North Carolina	5	4	5	3	2	3	4	4	4	5	3	5	47
Brevard, North Carolina	5	4	5	3	2	3	3	3	5	5	3	5	46
SOUTHEAST COAST													
Boca Raton, Florida	4	3	4	2	4	5	5	4	5	5	4	4	49
Naples, Florida	4	3	5	1	2	5	4	3	3	5	4	3	42
Sarasota, Florida	4	3	3	3	3	5	5	4	5	5	5	2	47
Gainesville, Florida	4	3	5	3	5	3	5	4	4	5	4	2	47
Tallahassee, Florida	4	3	4	3	4	3	4	5	5	5	3	1	44
Thomasville, Georgia	4	3	5	4	2	2	5	3	3	4	3	3	41
Covington, Louisiana	4	3	5	3	2	3	4	3	3	5	3	5	43
INTERIOR SOUTH													
Oxford, Mississippi	4	3	5	3	3	4	4	4	4	4	4	5	47
Hot Springs, Arkansas	4	3	4	4	3	3	3	3	3	4	4	3	41
Fayetteville, Arkansas	5	4	5	3	3	4	4	3	4	4	4	3	46

Ratings at a Glance

	Landscape	Climate	Quality of Life	Cost of Living	Transportation	Retail Services	Health Care	Community Services	Cultural Educational Activities	Recreational Activities	Work/Volunteer Activities	Crime Rates and Public Safety	Total
HEART OF TEXAS													
Austin, Texas	4	3	4	3	5	5	4	4	5	5	5	2	49
San Antonio, Texas	4	3	4	4	5	5	5	4	5	5	4	2	50
SOUTHERN ROCKIES													
Fort Collins, Colorado	4	3	5	3	4	4	4	4	5	5	4	3	48
Boulder, Colorado	5	4	5	1	5	3	4	5	5	5	5	4	51
Colorado Springs, Colorado	5	3	4	3	4	4	4	4	5	5	4	3	48
Santa Fe, New Mexico	4	4	5	1	4	4	4	4	5	5	2	2	44
DESERT SOUTHWEST													
Tucson, Arizona	5	3	3	3	4	4	5	4	5	5	4	1	46
Prescott, Arizona	4	4	5	3	2	3	3	3	3	4	3	3	40
Boulder City, Nevada	4	3	5	1	4	4	4	4	4	5	3	5	46
Las Vegas, Nevada	3	3	3	3	4	5	5	4	5	5	4	2	46
Carson City, Nevada	5	4	5	3	2	3	3	3	2	4	3	3	40
St. George, Utah	5	4	5	4	3	3	3	5	2	4	4	4	46
CALIFORNIA													
San Luis Obispo, California	5	5	5	1	3	4	3	4	4	4	3	4	45
Chico, California	4	4	5	3	3	3	3	3	3	3	2	3	39
PACIFIC NORTHWEST													
Medford–Ashland, Oregon	5	4	5	2	3	3	4	4	5	5	4	3	47
Eugene, Oregon	4	3	4	2	5	4	4	5	5	5	3	2	46
Portland, Oregon	5	4	5	2	5	5	5	5	5	5	3	2	51
Olympia, Washington	4	3	4	3	4	3	4	4	3	4	3	3	42
Bellingham, Washington	5	4	5	2	4	3	3	4	4	5	3	3	45
Victoria, British Columbia	5	4	5	4	5	4	5	5	4	4	4	3	52
Vernon, British Columbia	5	3	5	5	3	3	3	4	3	4	2	2	42

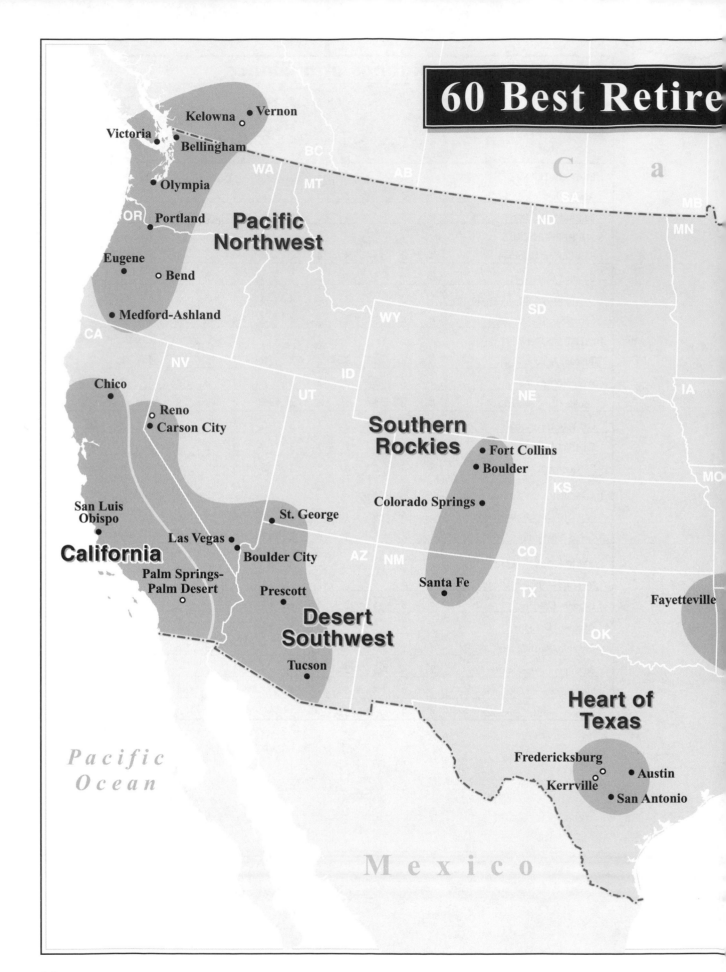

60 Best Retire

Kelowna ○ Vernon
Victoria ●
Bellingham ●
BC
WA
AB
C a
SA
MB
MN
Olympia ●
OR
Portland ●
Pacific Northwest
MT
ND
Eugene ●
○ Bend
SD
Medford-Ashland ●
CA
WY
NV
Chico ●
ID
UT
NE
○ Reno
● Carson City
Southern Rockies
● Fort Collins
● Boulder
IA
San Luis Obispo ●
St. George ●
Colorado Springs ●
KS
MO
California
Las Vegas ●
Boulder City ●
AZ
NM
CO
Palm Springs-Palm Desert ○
Prescott ●
Santa Fe ●
TX
Fayetteville
Desert Southwest
OK
Tucson ●

Heart of Texas

Fredericksburg ○
Austin ●
Kerrville ○
San Antonio ●

Pacific Ocean

M e x i c o

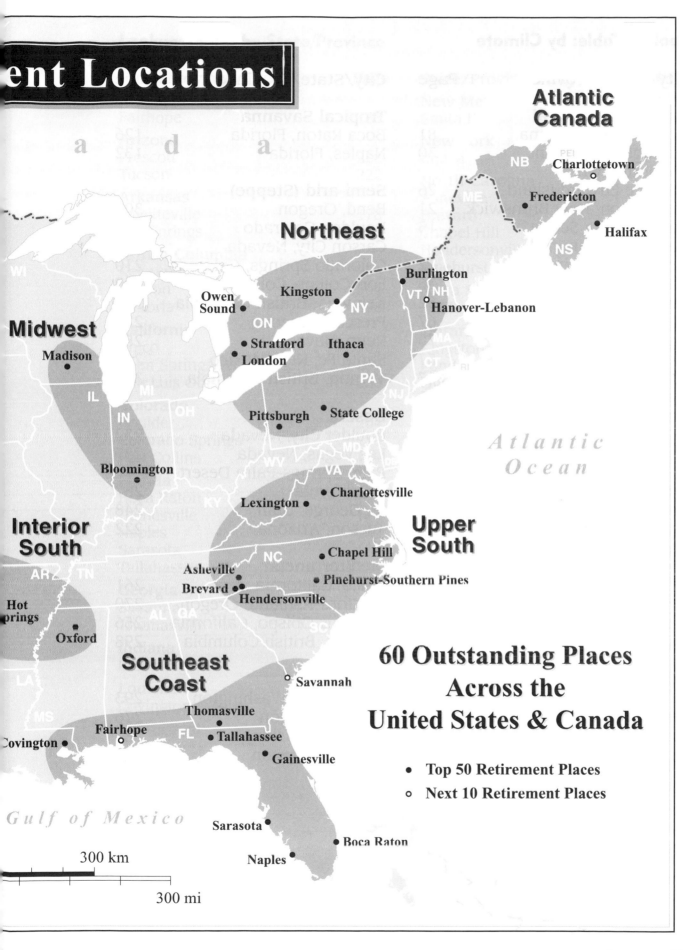

Atlantic Canada

NB
PEI
● Charlottetown

ME
● Fredericton
NS
● Halifax

Northeast

● Burlington
VT NH
Owen Sound ● Kingston
● Hanover-Lebanon
NY
ON
Midwest
● Stratford
● Ithaca
● London
Madison ●
PA
IL
MI
NJ
IN OH
Pittsburgh ● ● State College
● Bloomington
MD

WV
VA
● Charlottesville
KY
Lexington ●

Interior South
Upper South
● Chapel Hill
NC
Asheville ●
● Pinehurst-Southern Pines
AR TN
Brevard ●
Hot Springs ● ● Hendersonville
● Oxford
SC

Atlantic Ocean

Southeast Coast
○ Savannah
Thomasville ●
AL GA
Fairhope ○
LA FL
Covington ● ● Tallahassee
MS ● Gainesville

60 Outstanding Places Across the United States & Canada

● **Top 50 Retirement Places**
○ **Next 10 Retirement Places**

Gulf of Mexico

Sarasota ●
● Boca Raton
Naples ●

300 km

300 mi

Overall Ratings

Following are the overall ratings of our 60 Outstanding Places Across the U.S.A. and Canada. For ratings of the 12 individual criteria and the accompanying detailed written descriptions of each community, please turn to chapters 2 through 12. Happy reading!

Top 50 Retirement Towns
(ties are listed alphabetically)

Points	City /State/Province	Page
52	Victoria, British Columbia	298
51	Boulder, Colorado	204
51	London, Ontario	67
51	Portland, Oregon	281
50	San Antonio, Texas	191
49	Asheville, North Carolina	109
49	Austin, Texas	186
49	Boca Raton, Florida	126
48	Chapel Hill, North Carolina	98
48	Colorado Springs, Colorado	210
48	Fort Collins, Colorado	199
48	Halifax, Nova Scotia	15
48	Madison, Wisconsin	75
48	Pittsburgh, Pennsylvania	47
48	Stratford, Ontario	62
47	Gainesville, Florida	143
47	Hendersonville, North Carolina	114
47	Kingston, Ontario	52
47	Medford–Ashland, Oregon	270
47	Oxford, Mississippi	167
47	Sarasota, Florida	137
46	Boulder City, Nevada	232
46	Brevard, North Carolina	119
46	Charlottesville, Virginia	88
46	Eugene, Oregon	276
46	Fayetteville, Arkansas	178

Points	City/State/Province	Page
46	Las Vegas, Nevada	237
46	St. George, Utah	248
46	Tucson, Arizona	222
45	Bellingham, Washington	293
45	Fredericton, New Brunswick	21
45	Ithaca, New York	36
45	San Luis Obispo, California	256
44	Owen Sound, Ontario	57
44	Santa Fe, New Mexico	215
44	Tallahassee, Florida	148
43	Bloomington, Indiana	81
43	Burlington, Vermont	30
43	Covington, Louisiana	159
43	State College, Pennsylvania	41
42	Lexington, Virginia	93
42	Naples, Florida	132
42	Olympia, Washington	287
42	Pinehurst–Southern Pines, North Carolina	103
42	Vernon, British Columbia	304
41	Hot Springs, Arkansas	173
41	Thomasville, Georgia	154
40	Carson City, Nevada	243
40	Prescott, Arizona	228
39	Chico, California	261

Next 10 Retirement Towns
(unrated; listed alphabetically)

City/State/Province	Page
Bend, Oregon	309
Charlottetown, Prince Edward Island	26
Fairhope, Alabama	165
Fredericksburg, Texas	197
Hanover–Lebanon, New Hampshire	72
Kelowna, British Columbia	308
Kerrville, Texas	197
Palm Springs–Palm Desert, California	267
Reno, Nevada	252
Savannah, Georgia	164

2 The Atlantic Canada Retirement Region

Climate: Humid continental

Place Description	Overall Rating	Page
Halifax, Nova Scotia	**48**	**15**
If you enjoy a four-season climate and are attracted by the advantages of city life but repelled by the problems associated with excessive urban growth, Halifax may be just the place for you.		
Fredericton, New Brunswick	**45**	**21**
Fredericton is an undiscovered gem among Canadian retirement places. It is not perfect for everyone; some might find its winters too severe and its retail services marginal.		
Charlottetown, Prince Edward Island	**not rated**	**26**
Charlottetown, Prince Edward Island (P.E.I.) is also worth considering for retirement, especially by those hardy souls who prefer a climate with a real winter and who enjoy summer and winter outdoor activities.		

The Atlantic Canada Retirement Region consists of the three provinces of Nova Scotia, New Brunswick and Prince Edward Island along Canada's Atlantic coast. Part of the Canadian Appalachians, these small provinces have suffered from industrial decline for decades and their population of 1.8 million has grown only slowly in recent decades. Nonetheless, attracted by beautiful coastal and hill and valley landscapes, clean air and water, comparatively mild (for Canada) weather, livable towns and cities and low living costs, retirees from the United States and other parts of Canada have been moving in a steady stream into the region in search of the good life at affordable prices.

The best places to retire in style are the three provincial capitals: Halifax, Fredericton and Charlottetown. All are less than 300 miles (480 kilometers) from each other by road and only an hour or so apart by air. Halifax lies astride a magnificent natural harbor on the south shore of Nova Scotia. By far the largest city in Atlantic Canada, Halifax has a strong economy, a unique style and many amenities. Fredericton, New Brunswick, is a moderately upscale government and university town in the fertile and scenic Saint John River Valley. And across Northumberland Strait (now bridged) amidst the rich farmland of Prince Edward Island is Charlottetown, the island province's charming and historic capital city.

Halifax, Nova Scotia

Because of its large natural harbor, the British chose the site of Halifax for development of a new town and military base in 1749. After Britain conquered Canada in 1763, Halifax served as Atlantic headquarters in British North America for the Royal Navy and the British Army. During the two world wars, the port was the western terminus of the Canada–to–Europe convoy route that

Halifax, Nova Scotia

CLIMATE

Month	Average Daily Temperature High F	High C	Low F	Low C	Average Monthly Precipitation in	mm
January	32	0	16	-9	5.9	151
February	32	0	17	-8	4.5	114
March	38	4	24	-4	5.3	134
April	47	8	33	1	4.8	121
May	57	14	42	6	4.7	119
June	67	19	52	11	4.3	108
July	73	23	58	14	4.2	106
August	73	23	59	15	3.9	98
September	66	19	52	11	4.2	107
October	55	13	43	6	5.3	135
November	46	8	33	1	6.1	154
December	37	3	23	-5	6.3	160

Annual Averages

Precipitation		Snowfall	
Inches	59.4	Inches	59.8
Millimeters	1508	Centimeters	152

RATINGS

Category	poor 1	fair 2	good 3	very good 4	excellent 5
Landscape					●
Climate		●			
Quality of Life					●
Cost of Living				●	
Transportation					●
Retail Services				●	
Health Care					●
Community Services					●
Cultural Activities				●	
Recreational Activities				●	
Work/Volunteer Activities			●		
Crime	●				

Total Points: 48

carried supplies to Britain and the U.S.S.R. Today, Halifax remains Canada's principal East Coast naval base but it has also matured into a large and vital urban complex. Capital of Nova Scotia and center of operations for the federal government in Atlantic Canada, the city is a center of commerce, education and culture as well as a major port and tourist destination. With 120,000 residents in the former city of Halifax and 360,000 in the new Halifax Regional Municipality, Halifax seems destined to remain economically dominant in the region and able to offer the amenities required for stylish retirement.

Landscape   Rating: 5

 Halifax occupies a splendid site on hilly terrain overlooking Halifax Harbour. The oldest part of town—including the downtown business district, the historic waterfront, the universities, major cultural centers, older residential neighborhoods and parks—rests on a peninsula bounded by Halifax Harbour, Bedford Basin and the Northwest Arm. Halifax Harbour is devoted mainly to naval and marine freight activities, whereas Bedford Basin and the Northwest Arm are mostly utilized by pleasure craft. Outlying areas rise rather steeply to an upland surface offering outstanding views of the old town and its several waterways. The entire city is well wooded in broad-leafed and coniferous trees, and the city's many parks are especially beautiful when flowers are in bloom in summer.

Climate   Rating: 2

 Halifax has a humid continental climate with four distinct seasons. Summers are pleasantly warm; winters are cold and damp. The weather changes quickly in all seasons. Precipitation is heavy throughout the year with cold rain or snow occurring frequently in winter. On average, Halifax is sunny 50 percent of the time, varying from 40 percent in winter to 60 percent in summer. The frost free period averages 140 days, long enough to permit an excellent flower show in area parks in summer.

Quality of Life   Rating: 5

 Halifax offers an excellent quality of life. Halifax International Airport is 21 miles (35 kilometers) outside of town so there is little aircraft noise in the city. No freeways enter the central city and traffic on local streets moves slowly and fairly quietly. You can drive across town in half an hour and generally find parking. Public transit is excellent around town and is well patronized, thereby reducing automobile traffic. Halifax has a good mix of modest and upscale neighborhoods and the city boasts a fine network of parks. Point Pleasant Park and the Public Gardens, both on the peninsula east of downtown, are especially noteworthy. The revived and refurbished downtown is a pleasant place to walk, shop and dine and the city's parks are a delight to the senses as you walk, jog or bike their trails.

Cost of Living   Rating: 4

The cost of living in Halifax is evaluated as follows:

- *Composite.* ACCRA data are unavailable for Halifax. I estimate that the overall cost of living approximates the Canadian average and is 20 percent below the American average.

- *Housing.* Housing costs are near the Canadian average and 20 percent below the American average. Prices of single-family residences vary widely across the metropolitan area. Older homes in good neighborhoods on the peninsula sell for upwards of $300,000 ($225,000 U.S.). A greater variety of housing in

star-shaped Halifax Citadel offers historic re-enactments, museums and splendid views of downtown and the harbor.

Water sports are understandably popular in Halifax's marine environment. Several provincial parks and municipal beaches along the coast and on inland lakes offer supervised swimming in July and August. When the water is too cold, you can choose among 11 public pools for indoor swimming. Sailing, canoeing, kayaking and fishing are popular among the islands and picturesque coves along the coast. If you are water averse, golf, tennis, bicycling and hiking may have greater appeal. The Halifax golf experience ranges from links with magnificent harbor views to layouts along scenic rivers. You have 22 courses to choose from in the Halifax area. If tennis is your game, you will find numerous public tennis courts available at no charge. For easy biking, try Dartmouth's Trans Canada Trail. More than four miles (seven kilometers) of hard-surfaced trail winds from Sullivan's Pond along the lakes to Shubie Park. Also check out the trails of Point Pleasant Park, available on weekdays for bicycling.

Weather permitting, excellent natural ice surfaces are available for ice skating in winter on area lakes. When the weather is too mild, 17 local arenas and ice rinks provide a handy substitute. During much of the winter season, cross-country skiing can be enjoyed on groomed trails in Point Pleasant, Shubie and several other parks in the Halifax area. The nearest downhill ski facility is Ski Martock, on the edge of the Annapolis Valley about a one-hour drive from the city.

Spectator sports, movie theaters, restaurants and nightspots provide additional diversions. Intercollegiate basketball and hockey are played at Dalhousie and St. Mary's Universities. There are about 30 movie screens, a good selection of restaurants featuring Canadian, continental, ethnic and seafood entrees, and countless nightspots ranging from dinner theaters to pubs, lounges and cabarets in Halifax. If all else fails, you can always gamble away your worldly assets at Casino Nova Scotia, downtown at the waterfront.

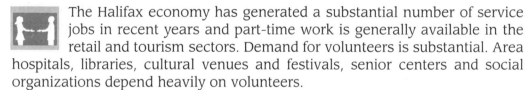

Work and Volunteer Activities — Rating: 3

The Halifax economy has generated a substantial number of service jobs in recent years and part-time work is generally available in the retail and tourism sectors. Demand for volunteers is substantial. Area hospitals, libraries, cultural venues and festivals, senior centers and social organizations depend heavily on volunteers.

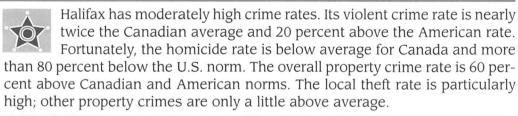

Crime Rates and Public Safety — Rating: 2

Halifax has moderately high crime rates. Its violent crime rate is nearly twice the Canadian average and 20 percent above the American rate. Fortunately, the homicide rate is below average for Canada and more than 80 percent below the U.S. norm. The overall property crime rate is 60 percent above Canadian and American norms. The local theft rate is particularly high; other property crimes are only a little above average.

Conclusion

Overall Rating 48 If you enjoy a four-season climate and are attracted by the advantages of city life but repelled by the problems associated with excessive urban growth, Halifax may be just the place for you. With a population of 360,000 in the Halifax Regional Municipality, Halifax is a Goldilocks city: not too big, not too small, just right. And since it is growing slowly, it is likely to remain of manageable size for a long time.

Located on hilly terrain along Canada's scenic Atlantic coast, Halifax has a beautiful setting and offers an excellent quality of life unspoiled by congestion, pollution or urban ugliness. Downtown and the waterfront are lively, pedestrian-friendly areas and the city's parks and residential areas are appealing. Transportation, health care and community services are exceptional; retail services and cultural and educational opportunities are very good. The city and its surrounding area provide outdoor recreation galore in lovely surroundings. Rather unusual for an Atlantic Canada city, Halifax provides decent opportunities for obtaining part-time work.

Only in climate and crime does Halifax score below average. The climate, though, is not unduly severe and the low cost of housing makes it easy to buy into one of the better neighborhoods where potential exposure to crime is minimal. All in all, Halifax ranks as one of Canada's outstanding cities. It is worth a careful look.

Fredericton, New Brunswick

Fredericton has a long history. Long before European settlement of the St. John River Valley, the site of Fredericton was inhabited by Maliseet and Mic Mac Indians. Named St. Anne's Point by its Acadian founders, the settlement was burned and its inhabitants expelled by the British during the Seven Year's War. Loyalists fleeing the American Revolution revived the settlement in 1783 and renamed it Fredericton for the second son of King George III. The town was chosen as capital of the new province of New Brunswick in 1785. Because of its importance as capital and its proximity to the American border, it soon became an important British military base. The Guard House, Barracks and Officers' Quarters still survive downtown.

Fredericton was incorporated as a city in 1848 even though it lacked the 10,000 people required for city status. A visit to the city today reveals that Fredericton is still a favored place. It has evolved into a moderately affluent, sophisticated small city. Its 48,000 residents (there are 82,000 in the urban area) benefit immensely from Fredericton's status as administrative, educational and cultural capital of New Brunswick. The provincial and municipal governments, several universities and colleges and a major medical center provide good-paying jobs that have attracted a progressive, well-educated and culturally and environmentally sensitive population to the area. Collectively they appear likely to keep Fredericton the beautiful and livable place that it is today.

Landscape	Rating: 5

Fredericton is located at a lovely site astride the St. John River about 60 miles (100 kilometers) inland from the Bay of Fundy. Downtown occupies a flat surface near the south bank of the river but residential neighborhoods slope upward along the edge of the valley. The university campuses, city parks and residential streets are nicely wooded with Acadian Forest species such as maple and pine and with imported species including elm. Flower gardens are popular in residential areas June through September.

Fredericton, New Brunswick

CLIMATE

Month	High F	High C	Low F	Low C	in	mm
January	25	-4	3	-16	4.3	109
February	28	-2	7	-14	3.1	79
March	37	3	18	-8	4.1	103
April	50	10	30	-1	3.4	87
May	64	18	41	5	3.8	96
June	73	23	50	10	3.5	89
July	79	26	55	13	3.4	87
August	77	25	54	12	3.5	90
September	68	20	45	7	3.7	95
October	55	13	34	1	3.9	98
November	43	6	25	-4	4.1	103
December	30	-1	12	-11	4.3	108

Average Daily Temperature · Average Monthly Precipitation

Annual Averages

Precipitation		Snowfall	
Inches	45	Inches	109
Millimeters	1143	Centimeters	277

RATINGS

Category	poor 1	fair 2	good 3	very good 4	excellent 5
Landscape					●
Climate		●			
Quality of Life					●
Cost of Living				●	
Transportation			●		
Retail Services		●			
Health Care					●
Community Services				●	
Cultural Activities				●	
Recreational Activities				●	
Work/Volunteer Activities			●		
Crime				●	

Total Points: 45

Climate — Rating: 2

Fredericton has a fairly severe humid continental climate with four distinct seasons. Summers are sunny and warm whereas winters are cold with alternating humid and dry periods. Precipitation is ample in all seasons with heavy snow falling in winter. On average, Fredericton is sunny about 50 percent of the time, varying from about 40 percent in winter to 60 percent in summer. The frost-free period averages 120 days, just long enough for growing apples, potatoes, vegetables and flowers in summer gardens.

Quality of Life — Rating: 5

 Fredericton offers an excellent quality of life. The air is clean and although the airport is nearby, there are few flights and little aircraft noise. There are no freeways and vehicles move relatively quietly and slowly on city streets. Even so, you can drive across town in a few minutes and find parking at your destination. Public transit is good around town and is a reasonable alternative to driving. Fredericton has many attractive, tree-lined neighborhoods and boasts several beautiful parks and riverside trails. Downtown is thriving and people seem genuinely friendly and welcoming.

Cost of Living — Rating: 4

 The cost of living in Fredericton is evaluated as follows:

- *Composite.* ACCRA data are unavailable for Fredericton. I estimate that the overall cost of living is 10 percent below the Canadian average and 30 percent below the American average.

- *Housing.* Fredericton has a good supply of housing and houses are priced incredibly low by Canadian and American standards. The average price of a detached bungalow in December 2003 was $125,000 ($94,000 U.S.), nearly 50 percent below the Canadian average. Many attractive single-family residences with three bedrooms and two baths are priced between $100,000 and $200,000 ($75,000 and $150,000 U.S.). Houses north of the river are generally somewhat cheaper than those on the upscale south side.

- *Goods and Services.* Goods and services are priced a little above Canadian norms but are 10 to 20 percent below U.S. averages. Medical care is inexpensive by U.S. standards.

- *Taxes.* The overall tax burden in Fredericton is a little above the Canadian average and is about 35 percent higher than the U.S. norm for people of moderate means. Federal and provincial income taxes are modestly higher than in the U.S. but the combined federal and provincial sales tax on goods and services is twice the U.S. average. These high rates are balanced somewhat by relatively low property taxes and by the low cost of medical care provided by River Valley Health, a regional health authority operated by the province.

Transportation — Rating: 3

Fredericton offers good intracity and intercity transportation. Fredericton Transit provides service to malls and shopping centers, universities and schools, hospitals and clinics, parks and recreation sites and other destinations from its Kings Place transfer center downtown. Seniors can buy an annual pass for only $55 ($41 U.S.). Fredericton Transit also operates dial-a-ride service for the mobility impaired. Four carriers provide service from Greater Fredericton Airport to destinations in Canada and the United States. Several nonstop flights a day connect the city with Halifax, Charlottetown, Montreal, Toronto, Boston and other places. Acadian Lines furnishes intercity bus service to points throughout Atlantic Canada from downtown Fredericton.

Retail Services — Rating: 2

 Downtown Fredericton is a vital retailing center. More than 120 stores offer everything from antiques to designer fashions and jewelry, as well as essential services such as drug stores, bookstores and a grocery market. Regent Mall, on the southern periphery of town, is the largest mall. Anchored by Sears and Wal-Mart, Regent Mall features more than 115 stores and services and the Empire 10 Theatres cinema complex. An attractive skylit food court serves up pizza, fish and chips, Chinese and Japanese specialties and Tim Hortons donuts. Brookside Mall, on the less affluent north side of town, is anchored by a Zellers department store and Sobey's supermarket. The mall had several empty storefronts during our visit and needs an extensive upgrade.

Health Care — Rating: 5

 River Valley Health provides excellent medical care to west central New Brunswick from its base in Fredericton. River Valley's hospital, the Dr. Everett Chalmers Regional Hospital, is a modern acute care public hospital with a staff of 2,000 including 150 physicians. The hospital has a 24-hour emergency department and provides a full range of services including internal medicine, psychiatry, general surgery, urology, oncology, ophthalmology, orthopedics, plastic and reconstructive surgery, and speech, physical and respiratory therapies.

Community Services — Rating: 4

In addition to excellent basic public services, Fredericton has two senior centers. Fredericton Seniors Centre on the city's north side operates mainly as a meeting place for groups with special interests. These include war brides and the Retired Teachers Association, as well as various hobby groups such as quilting, nature study, carpet bowling and woodworking. The onsite Seniors Workshop is a woodworking and carpentry group for those 55 and older. Members can work in the supervised workshop on hobby crafts, small furniture repair and other projects. Stepping Stone Centre in downtown Fredericton is a meeting place and activity center for older adults. Activities there include belly and line dancing, drama, computer training and access. Travel and ski clubs organize group outings.

Cultural and Educational Activities — Rating: 4

The performing and visual arts scene is vibrant in Fredericton. The Playhouse, located downtown, is the premier venue for live performances. Home to Theatre New Brunswick, the province's leading English-language theater company, and Symphony New Brunswick, the Playhouse is also known for its "At the Playhouse" and "Onstage" series featuring music, dance and theatrical productions by touring talents. During summer you can enjoy noon-hour concerts at Christ Church Cathedral, a national historic site, outdoor concerts at several venues downtown and outdoor summer theater at Officers' Square. Fredericton is renowned for its many festivals. The Notable Arts Summer Theatre Festival in late July and early August, the New Brunswick Summer Chamber Music Festival in the second half of August, and the mid-September Harvest Jazz and Blues Festival are of particular interest.

The University of New Brunswick (UNB) and St. Thomas University (STU) also enrich the community culturally. Home to more than 10,000 full-time students between them, the federated universities are lively places. The hillside campus hosts the UNB and STU "Music on the Hill" creative arts series and four performances of the Saint John String Quartet annually. Theatre UNB produces eight plays during its October through April season. UNB's College of Extended Learning fields a large number of special interest courses for all age groups. They welcome your suggestions for potential noncredit course offerings and even invite you to write your own course proposal.

The Beaverbrook Art Gallery and several smaller galleries add much to the arts scene. The Beaverbrook Gallery, which features works of British and Canadian artists, is an absolute gem. It has extensive collections of works by Cornelius Krieghoff, expatriate Canadian impressionist James Wilson Morrice and Canada's Group of Seven. The Gallery is known for its fine collection of British paintings from the Elizabethan era to the modern period, including paintings by Gainsborough, Reynolds, Turner and Constable. Salvador Dali's Santiago el Grande is on permanent display. Gallery 78, located in historic Crocket House, has a fine selection of paintings, sculpture and crafts and is well worth a visit.

Recreational Activities	Rating: 4

 Outdoor sports are popular in all seasons in the beautiful St. John River Valley in and around Fredericton. Odell Park and Arboretum is the crown jewel of Fredericton's excellent park system. It has a duck pond, barbecue pits, picnic tables, playgrounds and a lodge. Ten miles (16 kilometers) of trails wind through the park's forested areas. In winter you can ice skate on the duck pond and ski on groomed trails. Speaking of trails, Fredericton boasts more than 40 miles (70 kilometers) of trails suitable for walkers, runners and bikers. The trails are wide, flat, safe and wheelchair accessible. If you prefer to walk the links, Fredericton has four golf courses to choose from and two more nearby.

Water sports are popular in summer in Fredericton's riverside environment but there is plenty to do when water turns to ice. Boating facilities are abundant. The Regent Street Wharf and Fredericton Yacht Club provide moorings and related services and there are several free boat-launching ramps in the city. You can rent canoes and kayaks at the Small Craft Aquatic Centre. Mataquac Provincial Park, a short distance upstream from Fredericton, is New Brunswick's largest recreation park. It is popular for camping, picnicking, swimming, sailing, power boating, golf and hiking in summer and cross-country skiing, tobogganing and ice skating in winter. Back in Fredericton, the city maintains numerous outdoor ice skating rinks and four indoor rinks and arenas.

Intercollegiate sports, movie theaters, restaurants, nightspots and festivals provide additional diversions. Fredericton's two universities offer many spectator sports including volleyball, soccer, field hockey, ice hockey and basketball. There are 10 movie screens, an adequate selection of restaurants, many nightspots with live music and occasional festivals. You may not want to miss the Annual Whiskey, Spirits and Liqueur Festival held in late October, where you can sample and learn about your favorite libations. Unbelievably, the New

Brunswick Liquor (a government monopoly) festival store gives a 10 percent discount on all show products, and the ticket price includes a cab ride home.

Work and Volunteer Activities   Rating: 3

 Fredericton has a low unemployment rate and—although there is considerable competition from college students—part-time work is generally available. The hospital, cultural venues and festivals, senior centers and various social and fraternal organizations depend heavily on volunteers.

Crime Rates and Public Safety   Rating: 4

 Fredericton has about-average crime rates for Canada but is safe by U.S. standards. The property crime rate is about 15 percent above the national average whereas the violent crime rate is about 5 percent below the national norm. There are zero homicides in Fredericton in a typical year and the community feels safe day and night.

Conclusion

Overall Rating 45 Fredericton is an undiscovered gem among Canadian retirement places. It is not perfect for everyone; some might find its winters too severe and its retail services marginal. But others would judge these faults insignificant compared to the benefits of living there.

Fredericton's strongest assets are its lovely, pollution-free landscape, excellent quality of life and high-quality, inexpensive health care. Straddling the picturesque St. John River Valley and dotted with municipal parks and gardens, the city's residential areas are modestly upscale yet remarkably affordable. The historic downtown and the university campuses are lively and aesthetically appealing places. Fredericton offers very good community services, impressive cultural and recreational choices and freedom from serious crime. Even public transit, air transport to other places and opportunities for part-time and volunteer work are unusually good for a small city. A safe and friendly place, Fredericton is a beautiful city with small-town ambiance and big-city services. For many retirees, it would be an ideal place to live.

Charlottetown, Prince Edward Island

Charlottetown, Prince Edward Island (P.E.I.) is also worth considering for retirement, especially by those hardy souls who prefer a climate with a real winter and who enjoy summer and winter outdoor activities. With a population of 33,000, Charlottetown is capital of the province, a commercial and educational center and a major tourist destination. Despite the twentieth century character of much of the city, older sections still evoke the feeling of a colonial seaport. Lovely Victorian homes are found in several neighborhoods near Charlottetown Harbour, whereas outlying neighborhoods are distinctly modern and suburban.

Charlottetown's small size offers benefits and costs. The landscape is unspoiled by pollution and the medical care system is not overwhelmed by rapid population growth. Crime rates are low and the cost of living is affordable. Quality-of-life factors, community services, cultural and educational assets and work and volunteer activities are good for a small town.

Unfortunately, there is no public transit so car ownership is a virtual necessity and congestion downtown and on streets leading there is worsening, especially during the summer tourist season. Additionally, Charlottetown's retail services are so modest that many residents take an occasional 120-mile (200-kilometer) trip to a large regional mall in Moncton, New Brunswick.

Charlottetown offers easy access to the many recreational assets of P.E.I. Sailing and power boating are popular on the waters surrounding the island and its rivers and bays are ideal places for canoeing and kayaking. P.E.I. National Park, on the island's north coast, has miles of soft sand beaches and shallow, warm water for summer swimming. There are golf courses galore, as well as many rural roads and trails suitable for biking. The island's serpentine roads through beautiful, rolling farmland provide endless opportunities for sightseeing by car. And in winter, many sites in and around Charlottetown are popular for cross-country skiing and ice skating.

All in all, Charlottetown is a desirable and highly affordable retirement refuge. It will appeal especially to those seeking a quiet life in an attractive small city set in a garden-like rural landscape.

The Northeast Retirement Region

Climate: Humid continental

Place Description	Overall Rating	Page
Burlington, Vermont	**43**	**30**
Burlington is a beautiful, amenity-rich college town overlooking Lake Champlain and backed by the Green Mountains. It will appeal for retirement especially to hardy souls who enjoy winter weather and winter sports.		
Ithaca, New York	**45**	**36**
Ithaca will appeal to those who prefer a four-season climate, enjoy summer and winter outdoor recreation and appreciate the combination of small-town virtues and big-city amenities that the best college towns provide.		
State College, Pennsylvania	**43**	**41**
State College is one of America's best places for a secure and active retirement. Penn State, the scenic mountain and valley landscape surrounding State College, and the city itself offer a rare combination of amenities appealing to retirees.		
Pittsburgh, Pennsylvania	**48**	**47**
The Pittsburgh metropolitan area has much to offer today's retirees. The Pittsburgh renaissance is a reality; the city has metamorphosed from Steel City to a corporate headquarters and service-based economy and its air is now cleaner than that of most large American cities.		
Kingston, Ontario	**47**	**52**
Kingston's strongest assets are its wonderful natural and built landscape, high quality of life, low cost of living and excellent health care. It has very good transportation and community services and a low rate of violent crime.		
Owen Sound, Ontario	**44**	**57**
Owen Sound is a near-perfect place for retirement for those seeking a relaxed, outdoors-oriented lifestyle in a safe, friendly small city.		
Stratford, Ontario	**48**	**62**
Stratford's strongest assets are its lovely landscape, world-class theater, excellent availability of community services and work/volunteer activities, very good transportation and enviably low crime rates.		
London, Ontario	**51**	**67**
London has a broad profile of strengths and few weaknesses. The city is well run and livable, with excellent ratings in culture and education, community services, health care, retailing and transportation.		
Hanover–Lebanon, New Hampshire	**not rated**	**72**
Hanover and Lebanon are lovely, small villages that offer outdoor recreation and the many cultural and educational amenities provided by Dartmouth College.		

The Northeast Retirement Region occupies part of the northeastern quadrant of the United States and extends into southern Ontario, Canada. The region, which stretches 600 miles from the White Mountains of New Hampshire and the Champlain Valley of Vermont to the rolling hills of western Pennsylvania and the flat plains of Ontario, includes some of the most pleasant rural landscapes and nine of the most appealing small cities to be found in North America. Admittedly not for the climatically faint-of-heart, Burlington, Vermont; Ithaca, New York; Hanover–Lebanon, New Hampshire; State College and Pittsburgh, Pennsylvania; and Kingston, Owen Sound, Stratford and London, Ontario will appeal primarily to those who prefer a fairly rigorous four-season climate, enjoy summer and winter outdoor recreation and appreciate the combination of small-town virtues and big-city amenities that these places provide. Others had best consider more southerly climes.

Burlington, Vermont

Explored by Samuel de Champlain in 1609 and fought over by British, French and American forces during several wars through the 1770s, the strategic and fertile Champlain Valley was first settled by Europeans in 1775. Originally an agricultural and timber processing community (Revolutionist Ethan Allen had a farm north of town), Burlington gradually emerged as a fresh-water port and commercial center for Vermont and northern New England. Founded in 1791 on a hill overlooking the town, Lake Champlain and the Adirondack Mountains, the University of Vermont now has more than 7,700 full-time students and 1,200 faculty members. The university and several other colleges give Burlington the unmistakable stamp of a college town and add immeasurably to its cultural and recreational amenities. Although Burlington itself has a population of only 40,000, nearby communities such as South Burlington, Winooski and Shelburne help bring the Chittenden County total to 160,000, making Burlington the largest metropolitan center of northern New England and the region's cultural and commercial focus. A lively town in a region of great natural beauty, Burlington and vicinity offer a plethora of winter and summer recreation. Montreal, Canada, one of the world's most sophisticated cities, is only 90 miles north.

Landscape	Rating: 5

Burlington occupies a lovely site on several natural terraces overlooking beautiful Lake Champlain and New York's Adirondack Mountains. The heavily wooded Green Mountains, cresting at more than 4,000 feet elevation 20 miles east of Burlington, and the pastoral countryside between the city and the mountains with its small farms, woodlots and streams, are highly picturesque. At lower elevations deciduous trees including sugar maple and beech are conspicuous, while at higher elevations pine is more common. The town and the college campuses are pleasantly landscaped with lawns, shade trees and shrubs and an abundance of flowers in summer. The surrounding countryside, lush and green in summer, snow white in winter, and a riot of reds and yellows in autumn, is among the most beautiful anywhere.

Burlington, Vermont

CLIMATE				
Month	Average Daily Temperature High	Low	Daily Rel. Humidity Low	Average Monthly Precipitation
	F		**%**	**Inches**
January	27	9	64	2.2
February	29	11	61	1.7
March	40	22	58	2.3
April	53	34	52	2.9
May	68	45	51	3.3
June	77	55	54	3.4
July	81	60	53	4.0
August	78	58	56	4.0
September	69	50	60	3.8
October	56	39	60	3.2
November	44	30	65	3.1
December	32	17	67	2.2

Annual Averages

Total Days		Total Inches	
Clear	58	Precipitation	36.1
Partly Cloudy	101	Snowfall	78.8
Cloudy	206		

RATINGS					
Category	poor 1	fair 2	good 3	very good 4	excellent 5
Landscape					●
Climate		●			
Quality of Life				●	
Cost of Living		●			
Transportation				●	
Retail Services			●		
Health Care				●	
Community Services				●	
Cultural Activities				●	
Recreational Activities					●
Work/Volunteer Activities		●			
Crime				●	

Total Points: 43

[Map of Burlington, Vermont area showing Lake Champlain, Adirondack State Park, and surrounding towns including Valcour, Chimney Corner, Thayer Beach, Port Kent, Keeseville, Winooski, Essex Ctr., Essex Jct., Burlington Int'l Airport, South-Burlington, BURLINGTON, Willsboro Point, Willsboro, Shelburne, St. George, Richmond, Lake Iroquois. Inset map shows location of Burlington in VERMONT. Highways shown include 87, 9, 22, 2, 89, 117, 7, 116.]

Climate	Rating: 2

 Burlington has a fairly severe humid continental climate with four distinct seasons of approximately equal length. Summers are typically pleasantly sunny and warm whereas winters are cloudy, cold and

The University of Vermont is the center of Burlington's educational and cultural life. Its Division of Continuing Education offers a wide spectrum of credit and noncredit courses to the general public. St. Michael's College hosts an Elderhostel and runs a continuing education program with some classes and programs designed specifically for seniors. Several other colleges in and around Burlington, including business and professionally oriented Champlain College, provide additional educational options. The university's Lane Series is an academic yearlong guest artist series. The recital hall at the University of Vermont is a principal venue for baroque, cello, piano and string quartet recitals and jazz concerts. Main Street's Flynn Theatre for the Performing Arts, a restored Art Deco landmark, hosts the Vermont Symphony as well as visiting national and international musical, opera and theater companies. St. Michael's Playhouse on the campus of St. Michael's College produces four professional summer theater productions annually. Other special summer events include the Jazz Festival in June at 50 venues such as City Hall Park, the Church Street Marketplace, Flynn Theatre, and numerous clubs and beaches, as well as the Mozart Festival of chamber music in July and August. The Vermont Symphony performs outdoor concerts in summer. In July and August, the Champlain Shakespeare Festival is held in the university's Royall Tyler Theatre. In October, the Vermont International Film Festival kicks off the winter cultural season.

The Fleming Museum on the university campus and the Shelburne Museum in nearby Shelburne are the area's principal visual arts venues. The Fleming displays ancient Egyptian and Middle Eastern, African, American and European art in its permanent collections and visiting exhibitions. The Shelburne Museum consists of 39 restored early New England buildings housing art and artifacts typical of the eighteenth and nineteenth centuries. The museum's Webb Galleries feature a fine collection of works by European artists including Corot, Courbet, Degas, Goya, Edouard and Claude Monet, and Rembrandt, as well as paintings by leading American artists of the past three centuries.

Burlington and its surrounding areas are a paradise for winter and summer recreation. Within 50 miles are eight downhill ski areas—including Smuggler's Notch, Stowe and Sugarbush—and upward of 20 cross-country ski areas. Ice boating, ice fishing, ice skating and snowshoeing are also popular in winter. Golf is played in summer at six courses in and around Burlington. Hiking and biking are popular in town and countryside. Seven miles of bike paths wind from park to park along the Lake Champlain shoreline. Quiet country roads between the city and the Green Mountains also provide a gorgeous billboard-free environment for biking. Seasoned hikers will enjoy the Long Trail, a segment of the famous Appalachian Trail, which extends from Maine to Georgia. It runs along the crest of the Green Mountains 20 miles east of Burlington. Burlington has 27 parks ranging from small neighborhood parks with several amenities, such as playgrounds, ball fields, and basketball or tennis courts, to large multi-purpose community parks like Leddy and Oakledge. The former boasts a beach, indoor ice rink, soccer field, playground, four tennis courts, five ball fields and trails and natural areas. The latter has a beach, picnic shelters, tennis courts, three ball fields and surfaced roads and trails. Battery Park, on a bluff overlooking downtown's waterfront park and promenade, offers spectacular views of Lake Champlain and the Adirondacks and summer evening concerts at its band shell.

For those who enjoy hunting for treasures from times past, Burlington and surrounding areas are brimming with antique shops and markets.

Like many top college towns, Burlington offers competitive intercollegiate sports and an exceptional number of movie theaters and good restaurants for its size. The University of Vermont basketball and hockey teams enjoy strong support from students and town folk, and more than 30 movie screens provide additional entertainment options. Several good restaurants downtown and at the waterfront specialize in moderately priced seafood and ethnic and American cuisine. Other restaurants are found in South Burlington and in suburban locations.

Work and Volunteer Activities   Rating: 2

 High-tech industry and the University of Vermont, neither of which generate much part-time work, dominate the local economy. Service jobs are mostly in retailing and competition with students is severe, resulting in low wages. Volunteer opportunities, though, are plentiful. RSVP and SCORE chapters help place seniors where they are most needed. The Senior Resource Directory, published by Vermont Maturity Magazine, also provides useful leads.

Crime Rates and Public Safety   Rating: 4

Burlington's crime situation has improved in recent years. The violent crime rate is among the lowest in the country and the property crime rate is now only 20 percent above the national rate in the city. Both violent and property crime rates are much lower countywide. Burglary and larceny-theft are the principal threats in both city and county.

Conclusion

Overall Rating 43 Burlington is a beautiful, amenity-rich college town overlooking Lake Champlain and backed by the Green Mountains. It will appeal for retirement especially to hardy souls who enjoy winter weather and winter sports. Others should perhaps visit Vermont in summer and autumn and reside in the subtropics.

Burlington's greatest assets are its gorgeous physical landscape and matching outdoor recreation. The Green Mountains offer some of the best skiing in the eastern United States in winter and excellent hiking and biking in summer, while Lake Champlain and rivers draining into it provide endless opportunities for canoeing, sailing, fishing and swimming. Burlington also ranks very highly in quality of life, transportation, health care, community services, cultural activities and public safety. Downtown's Church Street Marketplace and Waterfront Park are delightful pedestrian-oriented refuges from suburbia, and the city's residential areas and parklands are very pleasant. Additionally, retail services are quite good for a small town. Burlington's modest weaknesses are its long cold winters, competition for part-time work and a cost of living somewhat above the national average. Not surprisingly, Burlington residents agree that these are a small price to pay for the privilege of living in such a beautiful, socially progressive and uncrowded place.

Ithaca, New York

Home to Cornell University since 1865 and Ithaca College since 1931, Ithaca gradually evolved from a diversified commercial and industrial center to a classic college town during the twentieth century. Today, Cornell University with 19,000 students and Ithaca College with 6,500 students physically, economically and culturally dominate the community. Cornell covers 740 acres on East Hill and counts among its assets 200 major buildings, including 16 libraries. Relocated in the 1960s from its downtown campus to a new one on South Hill, Ithaca College maintains strong community ties through its outstanding cultural programs. Together, the university and college employ twice as many people as the next eight employers in the city. With a population of 29,000 (excluding students) in the city and 97,000 in Tompkins County, Ithaca is a very small place. But thanks to its institutions of higher learning and its lovely Finger Lakes Region surroundings, it boasts more culture, recreation and services than many major metropolitan centers. It is arguably New York's best small town.

Landscape	Rating: 5

Ithaca is located in the Finger Lakes Region of New York State's glaciated Allegheny Plateau. The downtown is sited on a valley floor, which opens out onto the south shore of Cayuga Lake. Residential areas climb the slopes that ring the city except on its northern (lake) side. The surrounding countryside is a rolling surface with farms, forested hillsides and spectacular waterfalls that drop into deep gorges. The region's natural vegetation is broad-leafed deciduous forest, with beech and maple predominating. The town and campuses are well landscaped with a variety of broad-leafed and coniferous trees and shrubs. The wooded, rolling terrain embracing the southern end of Cayuga Lake is extraordinarily beautiful in all seasons, especially during the autumn show of color. Distant views of the lake from the uplands are best in winter when the trees are bare of leaves.

Climate	Rating: 2

Ithaca has a fairly severe humid continental climate with four distinct seasons of about equal length. Summers are typically pleasantly sunny and warm; winters are cloudy, cold and damp. Rapid changes in weather are routine, especially in spring and autumn when warm, humid episodes alternate with cold, dry periods. Precipitation is ample in all seasons with most of winter's falling as snow. On average, Ithaca is sunny about 50 percent of the time, varying from about 30 percent in winter to 60 percent in summer. The frost-free period averages 160 days, long enough to grow grapes and other soft fruits.

Quality of Life	Rating: 5

Ithaca offers an excellent quality of life. Although a county airport is close by, little jet noise intrudes because flights are few. Air quality is excellent. There are no freeways and automobile traffic moves fairly slowly and quietly on the narrow streets. Even so, one can drive across town in a few minutes and generally find parking at destinations. Public transit is excellent around town and on the Cornell campus and is well patronized, thereby reducing the pressure of vehicles on the limited road network. Ithaca

Ithaca, New York

CLIMATE									
Month	Average Daily Temperature		Daily Rel. Humidity Low	Average Monthly Precipitation
	High	Low		
	F		**%**	**Inches**
January	30	13	71	1.8
February	32	13	67	2.0
March	42	24	62	2.3
April	54	34	56	2.9
May	66	44	56	3.3
June	75	53	58	3.7
July	80	57	58	3.5
August	78	56	60	3.4
September	71	49	63	3.5
October	59	39	62	3.3
November	47	31	69	3.1
December	35	20	73	2.6

Annual Averages

Total Days		Total Inches	
Clear	52	Precipitation	35.4
Partly Cloudy	102	Snowfall	67.3
Cloudy	212		

RATINGS

Category	poor 1	fair 2	good 3	very good 4	excellent 5
Landscape					●
Climate		●			
Quality of Life					●
Cost of Living			●		
Transportation			●		
Retail Services			●		
Health Care			●		
Community Services					●
Cultural Activities				●	
Recreational Activities				●	
Work/Volunteer Activities				●	
Crime				●	

Total Points: 45

has a good mix of modest and upscale neighborhoods and is dotted with beautiful parks, including Stewart Park on the lakefront. The refurbished historic downtown (Ithaca Commons) is a delightful automobile-free area, as are several natural areas like Cornell Plantations and Sapsucker Woods bird sanctuary on the otherwise busy Cornell campus. Ithaca residents are typically friendly, notoriously liberal and progressive and they are apparently determined to preserve the integrity and charm of their delightful little city.

Cost of Living	Rating: 3

 The cost of living in Ithaca is evaluated as follows:

- *Composite.* ACCRA data are lacking for Ithaca so those of Syracuse, 60 miles northeast, are used here. On that basis, the composite cost of living in Ithaca is estimated to approximate the national average.

- *Housing.* Housing costs have risen in recent months but remain perhaps 10 percent below the national average. Local real estate guides reveal excellent, inexpensive housing stock in Ithaca and nearby villages. Attractive older homes in the city tend to be priced between $100,000 and $150,000; even prestigious Cayuga Heights has elegant residences on large wooded lots priced between $200,000 and $250,000.

- *Goods and Services.* With the exception of utilities, which are priced perhaps 25 percent above the national average, goods and services costs are within a few percentage points of national norms.

- *Taxes.* The state and local tax burden in Ithaca is above average for most residents. State sales, excise and property taxes are well above the national average. The state income tax situation is more complex. Although working residents and retirees with large incomes from private pensions or investments pay high taxes, long-term New York residents depending largely on public pensions are more fortunate. Public pensions, social security income, and the first $20,000 from private pensions are fully exempt from New York state income tax if these payments derive from income earned in the State of New York. Migrants from other states and provinces may claim only the $20,000 exemption.

Transportation	Rating: 3

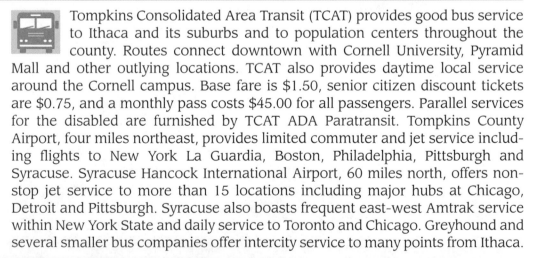 Tompkins Consolidated Area Transit (TCAT) provides good bus service to Ithaca and its suburbs and to population centers throughout the county. Routes connect downtown with Cornell University, Pyramid Mall and other outlying locations. TCAT also provides daytime local service around the Cornell campus. Base fare is $1.50, senior citizen discount tickets are $0.75, and a monthly pass costs $45.00 for all passengers. Parallel services for the disabled are furnished by TCAT ADA Paratransit. Tompkins County Airport, four miles northeast, provides limited commuter and jet service including flights to New York La Guardia, Boston, Philadelphia, Pittsburgh and Syracuse. Syracuse Hancock International Airport, 60 miles north, offers non-stop jet service to more than 15 locations including major hubs at Chicago, Detroit and Pittsburgh. Syracuse also boasts frequent east-west Amtrak service within New York State and daily service to Toronto and Chicago. Greyhound and several smaller bus companies offer intercity service to many points from Ithaca.

Retail Services	Rating: 3

 Pyramid Mall, located on the eastern outskirts of town, is Ithaca's largest indoor mall. Anchored by Best Buy, Bon-Ton, Sears and Target, the mall has more than 70 specialty stores and eating places and a

10-screen cinema complex. Historic downtown Ithaca, now dubbed Ithaca Commons, is an award-winning pedestrian promenade and marketplace with a European flair. Unique specialty shops feature apparel, arts and crafts, books, music, sporting goods and home furnishings. Center Ithaca, an attractive small shopping complex on the Commons, boasts 20 specialty shops, 2 movie theaters and several cafes in a central sky-lit area. Just southwest of downtown is the Ithaca branch of Wegman's Food Markets, perhaps the biggest and best upscale supermarket anywhere. More down to earth is the Ithaca Farmers Market at Steamboat Landing on Saturdays and Sundays in summer and autumn.

Health Care   Rating: 3

 Cayuga Medical Center, a 204-bed acute care facility, is Tompkins County's sole provider of emergency care. Its 180-member medical staff offers a full range of medical and surgical specialties as well as primary care. Excellent additional medical facilities are less than 100 miles away in Rochester and Syracuse, New York and in Sayre, Pennsylvania, renowned for its Guthrie Clinic and associated Robert Packer Hospital.

Community Services   Rating: 5

 Ithaca and Tompkins County provide excellent community services. Since Ithaca's population is predominantly young, most services are not specifically targeted toward seniors. Nonetheless, Cornell University's Public Service Center provides centralized access to most community service organizations and its Cornell Ithaca Volunteers in Training and Service (CIVITAS) program assists the elderly in a variety of ways. The local Senior Citizens' Council publishes directories, serves as a referral agency, and coordinates social programs. Ithaca College's recently established Gerontology Institute is a valuable community resource through its outreach efforts.

Cultural and Educational Activities   Rating: 4

Internationally known as an elite research-oriented university, Cornell also contributes to the performing and visual arts. The Schwartz Center for the Performing Arts stages six to twelve plays, offers the Cornell Dance Series and hosts numerous guest artists from September through May. The university's Herbert F. Johnson Museum of Art, designed by I. M. Pei, houses a collection spanning 40 centuries and six continents with particular strengths in prints and Asian and contemporary art. An outgrowth of the Ithaca Conservatory of Music founded in 1892, Ithaca College is ranked today among the nation's best small colleges for the quality and value of its educational offerings. Its Dillingham Center is home to the Hoerner and Clark Theatres where the college Department of Theatre Arts presents comedy, drama, music, opera and dance productions. So busy is the cultural calendar at Ithaca College that a concert, theatrical production, art show or public lecture, many of them free of charge, is scheduled nearly every day of the academic year.

The performing arts are also strong off campus. Professional ensembles include the 35-member Cayuga Chamber Orchestra, the Cayuga Vocal Ensemble, and the Ithaca Ballet, upstate New York's only repertory company. The Ithaca Opera Association and the New York State Baroque are also based locally. The Hanger Theatre, a professional theater since 1975, presents five mainstage productions during its summer season in Cass Park along Cayuga

Lake and reaches out to schools during the winter season. Downtown's majestic State Theater is a principal venue for concerts and plays and the nearby Kitchen Theatre produces live theatre year-round.

International, national and regional arts and crafts are exhibited at several commercial galleries. The Handwerker Gallery at Ithaca College and the John Hartell and Olive Tjaden Galleries at Cornell display primarily contemporary art by students and faculty.

Recreational Activities   Rating: 4

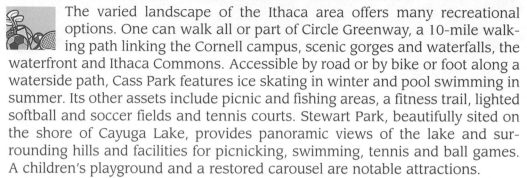 The varied landscape of the Ithaca area offers many recreational options. One can walk all or part of Circle Greenway, a 10-mile walking path linking the Cornell campus, scenic gorges and waterfalls, the waterfront and Ithaca Commons. Accessible by road or by bike or foot along a waterside path, Cass Park features ice skating in winter and pool swimming in summer. Its other assets include picnic and fishing areas, a fitness trail, lighted softball and soccer fields and tennis courts. Stewart Park, beautifully sited on the shore of Cayuga Lake, provides panoramic views of the lake and surrounding hills and facilities for picnicking, swimming, tennis and ball games. A children's playground and a restored carousel are notable attractions.

Sapsucker Woods Sanctuary and Cayuga Nature Center provide easy access to natural wonders. Sapsucker Woods, home of the Cornell Laboratory of Ornithology, has more than four miles of trails winding through the woods and over swamps and ponds. Waterfowl and other wildlife abound here. Cayuga Nature Center has five miles of trails for hiking, nature study, cross-country skiing and snowshoeing, a farm exhibit and nature programs. Four beautiful state parks with fine facilities are found within 10 miles of Ithaca. Alan H. Treman State Marine Park on the shores of Cayuga Lake is notable for picnicking, boating and fishing whereas Buttermilk Falls, Robert H. Treman and Taughannock Falls state parks boast some of the most scenic gorges and waterfalls in the eastern states. The latter three parks also have sites for camping, picnicking, hiking, swimming and fishing, among other activities. In summer, one can golf at four 18-hole and two 9-hole courses in and around Ithaca; in winter, downhill skiing is available at Greek Peak, 20 miles east of town, or at three other resorts only slightly farther afield. Cross-country skiing venues, including those at nearby state parks, are even more abundant locally.

In all seasons, wine connoisseurs can sample excellent wines at a number of family-owned wineries along the scenic Cayuga Wine Trail. Among the best of these is Cayuga Ridge Estate Winery, about 20 miles north along Highway 89. As befits a college town, Ithaca has several very good restaurants featuring mostly American, Italian and ethnic cuisine at reasonable prices. Movie theaters are found at the Commons, Fall Creek and Pyramid Mall.

Work and Volunteer Activities   Rating: 4

With nearly as many students as permanent residents in Ithaca, competition for part-time service employment is severe. Nonetheless, Ithaca has little unemployment at present and many seniors find work of some kind. Volunteerism is highly valued in the enlightened atmosphere of Ithaca. Each year thousands of student and faculty volunteers, mobilized by CIVITAS, join seniors and other residents in assisting more than 100 community agencies in the city and county.

Ithaca is one of America's safest small college towns and distinctly safer than large metropolitan areas. Although the city's property crime rate is only slightly below the national average, the rate of violent crime is extremely low. Indeed, except for larceny-theft, all subcategories of violent and property crime now exhibit below-average rates. More impressionistically, the community feels safe as one walks the sidewalks, streets and paths of downtown, residential suburbs, and the university and college campuses.

Conclusion

Overall Rating 45 If you are attracted to the excitement of a big city and dislike small towns and winter, you would not likely choose Ithaca for retirement. Ithaca is, indeed, a very small city in a region of cold, cloudy and snowy winters. As such, it will appeal primarily to those who prefer a four-season climate, enjoy summer and winter outdoor recreation and appreciate the combination of small-town virtues and big-city amenities that the best college towns provide.

Located on Cayuga Lake in the scenic hill and valley landscape of New York's Finger Lakes Region, Ithaca has a beautiful setting and offers an excellent quality of life unspoiled by congestion, pollution or unplanned growth. Downtown Ithaca Commons is a delightful pedestrian marketplace and community center, and the city's residential areas and parklands are exceptional. The small population of the Ithaca trade area somewhat limits the scope of its retail and medical services; however, transportation and community services are unusually good for a city of its size. As a result of the presence of Cornell University and Ithaca College, cultural and educational offerings are outstanding. The city and surrounding area provide abundant outdoor recreation in lovely surroundings, there are many work/volunteer options and the area is relatively free of serious crime. The cost of living is at about the national average. Ithaca is growing rather slowly so it should remain an uncrowded, civilized and environmentally attractive refuge for discerning retirees for a long time to come. It is one of America's most attractive small cities.

State College, Pennsylvania

Originally inhabited by Shawnee and Delaware Indians, the Nittany Valley of Centre County, Pennsylvania was first settled by Europeans in the 1780s. An early breadbasket for east coast cities, Centre County developed a small-scale iron industry early in the nineteenth century and, in 1855, established The Farmers' High School. Little did local residents realize that this small agriculturally oriented school would evolve into the Pennsylvania State University (Penn State), which would gradually replace farming and iron-making as the prime economic force in State College and Centre County. Penn State's campus in State College now has 41,000 students and 11,000 employees and is recognized as one of America's great public universities. Its dynamic presence has created a service-based island of economic prosperity in mountainous central Pennsylvania and has fostered State College's transition into a highly civilized and cultured community that is attracting increasing numbers of baby boomers for their retirement years. With a current population exceeding 50,000 residents

State College, Pennsylvania

CLIMATE				
Month	Average Daily Temperature		Daily Rel. Humidity	Average Monthly Precipitation
	High	Low	Low	
	F		%	Inches
January	34	19	62	2.6
February	37	20	58	2.5
March	46	27	54	3.5
April	59	38	49	3.4
May	70	48	51	3.8
June	78	57	54	3.8
July	83	61	55	3.7
August	81	59	58	3.3
September	73	52	59	3.0
October	62	41	57	2.9
November	49	33	61	3.3
December	37	23	63	2.7

Annual Averages

Total Days		Total Inches	
Clear	75	Precipitation	38.4
Partly Cloudy	102	Snowfall	46.9
Cloudy	188		

RATINGS					
Category	poor	fair	good	very good	excellent
	1	2	3	4	5
Landscape					●
Climate		●			
Quality of Life					●
Cost of Living			●		
Transportation			●		
Retail Services			●		
Health Care			●		
Community Services			●		
Cultural Activities				●	
Recreational Activities				●	
Work/Volunteer Activities			●		
Crime					●

Total Points: 43

(excluding students) in the city and about 140,000 in Centre County, State College is a lively place in a naturally beautiful and relatively unspoiled region. Its future as a highly desirable place to retire seems secure.

Landscape   Rating: 5

 State College is located in the Nittany Valley, one of countless long, narrow, steep-sided valleys in the Ridge and Valley Section of the Appalachian Mountains. The valley floor, on which Penn State and the city are built, is gently rolling and nearby mountain ridges provide a scenic backdrop to the urban landscape. The surrounding countryside is a rolling surface with farms and quaint villages in the valleys overlooked by forested hills and low mountains. The natural vegetation is broad-leafed deciduous forest with maple, oak and beech predominating. Residential neighborhoods and the sprawling Penn State campus are well wooded and nicely landscaped. Autumn colors are spectacular in town and on the wooded slopes in the countryside.

Climate   Rating: 2

 State College has a humid continental climate marked by four distinct seasons. Summers are typically sunny and warm; winters are cloudy, cold and damp. Rapid changes in weather are the norm and precipitation is adequate in all seasons, with much of winter's falling as snow. On average, State College is sunny about 55 percent of the time, varying from about 45 percent in winter to 65 percent in summer. The frost-free period averages 160 days, adequate for summer gardening.

Quality of Life   Rating: 5

 State College offers an excellent quality of life. The EPA recently designated State College as a "basic non-attainment area" for air quality. This category is assigned to areas minimally out of compliance with air quality standards. (Areas with worse air quality are classified into five categories: marginal, moderate, serious, severe, or extreme.) Although the air is clean most of the time in State College, occasional episodes of light smog occur in summer. Traffic congestion is not a problem except during major varsity sports events when much of Pennsylvania's population appears to converge on campus. Traffic noise is minimal and parking is generally adequate except on the central part of the campus where automobile access is severely constrained. The city is well planned; most neighborhoods in town and in surrounding villages are in good shape and many small parks dot the urban landscape. The traditional downtown, although no longer a center for general retailing, is a lively student-oriented entertainment complex with a good assortment of shops, restaurants and service establishments catering to students.

Cost of Living   Rating: 3

 The cost of living in State College is evaluated as follows:

- *Composite.* ACCRA data show that the overall cost of living in State College is about 4 percent below the national average.
- *Housing.* According to ACCRA, housing costs are at the national average. Our exploration of the area revealed a good variety of housing from older farmhouses in nearby villages to traditional and modern single-family residences, townhouses and condominiums in the city. Modest houses in town and in outlying communities such as Bellefonte sell for less than $150,000

whereas larger, upscale properties near the campus fetch upwards of $250,000.

- **Goods and Services.** Utility costs in State College have increased recently to about 10 percent above the national average. In contrast, health care costs have declined to 15 percent below average and transportation, groceries and miscellaneous goods and services are all priced 5 to 10 percent below national norms.

- **Taxes.** The overall state and local tax burden in State College is about 8.9 percent of income compared to the U.S. average of 9.7 percent. State income, sales and excise taxes are at or below national norms whereas property taxes are modestly above average.

Transportation   Rating: 3

Formerly somewhat isolated, State College is on the threshold of entering the freeway era. An eight-mile stretch of freeway (U.S. 220) now skirts the city on its north side. By 2007 this segment will become part of I-99, connecting the Pennsylvania Turnpike to the south of the city with I-80 to the north. Streets in town are typically two- or four-lane roads that are generally adequate for present traffic. The Centre Area Transportation Authority (CATA) provides good bus service to State College, the Penn State campus, suburban shopping centers and nearby communities. The bus fare is $1.25 but seniors ride free. The LOOP and The LINK lines serve the campus and downtown for free. For a one-way fare of $1.25, CENTRE RIDE provides curb-to-curb transportation for seniors and those whose disabilities prevent their using regular buses.

Intercity travel is possible by air, bus and rail. University Park Airport offers 18 scheduled flights a day to hubs in Pittsburgh, Philadelphia, Washington Dulles and Detroit. Fullington Trailways and Greyhound Bus Lines provide service to Pittsburgh, Harrisburg and beyond. Amtrak service west to Pittsburgh and east to Philadelphia and New York is available from Altoona and Lewistown, both less than 50 miles away.

Retail Services   Rating: 3

Nittany Mall, located on East College Avenue about five miles east of downtown, is the major regional mall. Anchored by Bon-Ton, JCPenney, Kaufmann's and Sears, the mall has more than 70 specialty stores and eating places. The mall is a fairly typical, unexceptional shopping center with few empty storefronts and relatively uncluttered aisles. Although lacking a central food court, it does have several chain and fast-food restaurants. The local Wal-Mart is located just across Benner Pike from the mall. Several smaller shopping centers and some commercial strip development along Atherton Street provide shopping alternatives. The Colonnade at State College, off North Atherton, has a Target store and an upscale Wegman's supermarket; College Avenue, just south of the Penn State campus, is lined with restaurants and watering holes catering to students and their families.

Health Care   Rating: 3

Mount Nittany Medical Center, with 200 beds and more than 180 physicians, is a nonprofit, acute care hospital providing comprehensive medical services to the State College area. It offers 24-hour emergency service, surgical and psychiatric care, cancer treatment, diagnostic imaging including CT scan and MRI, respiratory care and a neurophysiology/sleep lab, among other services.

Community Services   Rating: 3

 State College and Centre County furnish a good selection of community services to all age groups. The Centre Region Senior Center, located on Fraser Street in downtown State College, offers a wide variety of recreational activities such as classes in yoga, weight training, aquatics and safe driving. You can sing, dance, hike, enjoy special lectures or just stop in occasionally for lunch or a friendly game of cards. Legal assistance, transportation, home health care, information and referrals are provided by the Centre County Office on Aging.

Cultural and Educational Activities   Rating: 4

 Penn State predictably dominates education and culture in State College. Retirees can enroll in some Penn State courses free of charge and others can be taken at low cost. Additionally, the Community Academy for Lifelong Learning (CALL), which is a member of the Institutes for Learning in Retirement and affiliated with Elderhostel, offers academic and applied courses of great variety, special events and lectures, field trips and service projects.

The performing arts are well represented in State College. The Penn State Center for the Performing Arts presents quality music, dance, theatre and opera, often featuring national touring companies. The university's nationally recognized School of Theatre produces an assortment of mainstage events and Pennsylvania Center Stage, the professional arm of the Penn State School of Theatre, produces world-class programs during the summer season. Several community theatres including Centre Playhouse, The Next Stage, and State College Community Theatre entertain residents and visitors with musicals, comedies and drama. The musical arts are also not neglected in State College. The Penn's Woods/Penn State School of Music presents more than 200 concerts annually and the Nittany Valley Symphony, a full-size community orchestra, performs numerous concerts. Additionally, the State College Municipal Band performs band music by modern composers and the State College Choral Society presents madrigal dinners each December and other works throughout the year.

The world of art can be explored at Penn State's outstanding Palmer Museum of Art. The museum's permanent collection of more than 5,000 objects spans 35 centuries and includes American and European paintings and sculptures, contemporary and historic Asian ceramics, and art objects from ancient African, Near Eastern and European cultures. A comprehensive schedule of up to 10 special exhibitions is organized annually. Exhibitions of contemporary art by students and emerging professional artists are featured at the HUB–Robeson Center, on campus.

Recreational Activities   Rating: 4

 State College and surrounding area offer a wealth of recreational opportunities. Centre Region Parks and Recreation operates 13 parks in State College and 25 in neighboring townships. A year-round aquatics program uses two outdoor community pools in summer and an indoor high school pool during the school year. With 145,000 acres of state forest and almost 10,000 acres of state parkland in Centre County, retirees find it easy to access miles of hiking and cross-country skiing trails. Tussey Mountain Ski Area, seven miles southeast of State College, features downhill skiing December through March. During much of the year golfers can play on three public golf courses in State College and several others outside the city limits.

The university hosts exciting sports events for fans of Big Ten competition. Penn State's Nittany Lions basketball team regularly draws 16,000 enthusiastic fans to Bryce Jordan Center, and up to 107,000 people can pour into Beaver Stadium on a football Saturday. Fans also cheer on Penn State athletes engaged in wrestling, gymnastics, soccer and ice hockey. Before or after an event, be sure to sample some superb ice cream at the Creamery on the Penn State campus. Penn State has been teaching ice cream manufacture since 1892 and they have perfected the art. Ben and Jerry learned ice cream making from Penn State.

State College is also notable for its Cinema 5 Theatre downtown and Cinema 6 near Nittany Mall. You can even take in a movie at the Starlite Drive-In Theatre in summer.

Work and Volunteer Activities   Rating: 3

 Centre County regularly boasts the lowest unemployment rate in Pennsylvania and one of the lowest in the United States. Low unemployment, though, does not necessarily translate into good job prospects for seniors because of stiff competition for jobs with many of Penn State's 41,000 students. In addition to the usual volunteer assignments in libraries, museums, schools and hospitals, many seniors find rewarding roles as mentors, passing on their experiences and knowledge to students and business people through SCORE. The RSVP of Centre County connects active senior volunteers with opportunities at 120 nonprofit agencies in the area.

Crime Rates and Public Safety   Rating: 5

State College has an enviable record of public safety. The city's violent crime rate is a remarkable 80 percent below the national average. Property crime occurs at only 50 percent of the national rate. It is undeniably one of America's safest communities.

Conclusion

Overall Rating 43 State College is one of America's best places for a secure and active retirement. Penn State, the scenic mountain and valley landscape surrounding State College, and the city itself offer a rare combination of amenities appealing to retirees. The Penn State campus is beautiful and the city retains its small-town charm despite recent growth of the university and community. The quality of life and public safety in this lively town are beyond reproach and cultural, educational and recreational opportunities are very good indeed. Other advantages include good shopping, health care and transportation and a wide choice of volunteer opportunities. The local bus system provides a decent level of service and rides are free for seniors. Even the weather, although less than ideal in winter, is seldom extremely cold or hot. All in all, State College is a safe and friendly place where retirement can be lived and enjoyed at a fairly low cost. Especially for those wanting to stay close to their families and friends in the Northeast and Midwest, State College might be an ideal place for retirement.

Pittsburgh, Pennsylvania

Strategically located where the Allegheny and Monongahela Rivers join to form the Ohio, Pittsburgh has a long and checkered history. The original European settlement, named Fort Duquesne by the French, changed hands several times during the French and Indian War and was seized for good by British forces led by George Washington in 1758 and renamed Fort Pitt. After the American Revolution, Pittsburgh evolved first into a commercial city based on trade along the waterways and later into America's leading iron and steel center. But today it is hard to believe that Pittsburgh once earned its nicknames of Iron City and Smoky City. The steel industry is largely gone, replaced by corporate headquarters, commerce, higher education and health care, among other service activities. The air is now relatively clean and the city center has been revived by corporate and public sector investments. Fortunately, legacies of Pittsburgh's former industrial greatness and wealth like the Carnegie Library, Museum of Natural History and Music Hall, Museum of Art, and Carnegie-Mellon University remain to enrich the lives of residents and visitors. As a regional capital of western Pennsylvania, southeastern Ohio and northern West Virginia, and with a population of 345,000 within its city limits and around 2.4 million in the metropolitan area, Pittsburgh is one of few large American cities that can be recommended for retirement.

Landscape	Rating: 4

Pittsburgh stretches across a hill and valley landscape in the Allegheny Plateau of western Pennsylvania. The city center occupies a dramatic site on a low peninsula stretching eastward from The Point, where the Allegheny and Monongahela Rivers meet. Overlooking the rivers and downtown are steep hillsides and plateau surfaces, across which stretch the city's many neighborhoods and sundry suburban communities. The natural vegetation is broad-leafed deciduous forest and a good deal of it remains relatively intact on the steeper slopes. Elsewhere, most residential areas, parks and university campuses are well treed and nicely landscaped with trees, shrubs and flowers.

Climate	Rating: 2

Pittsburgh has a humid continental climate with warm, moderately humid summers and cold, cloudy and damp winters. Precipitation is adequate in all seasons and a good deal of winter's falls as snow. On average, Pittsburgh is sunny 45 percent of the time, varying from 32 percent in winter to 56 percent in summer. The frost-free period averages 180 days but, owing to variations in terrain, deviates from this average locally.

Quality of Life	Rating: 4

The urban geography of Pittsburgh is complex, with 90 different neighborhoods in the city and dozens of independent suburbs in outlying areas. Naturally, the quality of life varies significantly from place to place. That said, many parts of the metropolitan area including several inner city neighborhoods like Oakland, Shadyside and Highland Park offer a good to excellent quality of life, as do suburbs such as Fox Chapel, Mount Lebanon, Plum and Sewickley. Pittsburgh International Airport is about 20 miles from the city center so jet noise is a problem only on western fringes of the

Pittsburgh, Pennsylvania

CLIMATE				
Month	Average Daily Temperature High Low		Daily Rel. Humidity Low	Average Monthly Precipitation
	F		%	Inches
	1	2	3	4
January	35	20	66	2.7
February	39	22	62	2.4
March	50	30	57	3.2
April	61	39	51	3.0
May	71	49	52	3.8
June	79	58	53	4.1
July	83	62	54	4.0
August	81	61	56	3.4
September	74	54	57	3.2
October	63	43	55	2.3
November	51	34	62	3.0
December	40	25	67	2.9

Annual Averages

Total Days		Total Inches	
Clear	59	Precipitation	37.9
Partly Cloudy	103	Snowfall	43.0
Cloudy	203		

RATINGS Category	poor 1	fair 2	good 3	very good 4	excellent 5
Landscape				●	
Climate		●			
Quality of Life				●	
Cost of Living			●		
Transportation					●
Retail Services					●
Health Care					●
Community Services				●	
Cultural Activities					●
Recreational Activities					●
Work/Volunteer Activities			●		
Crime			●		

Total Points: 48

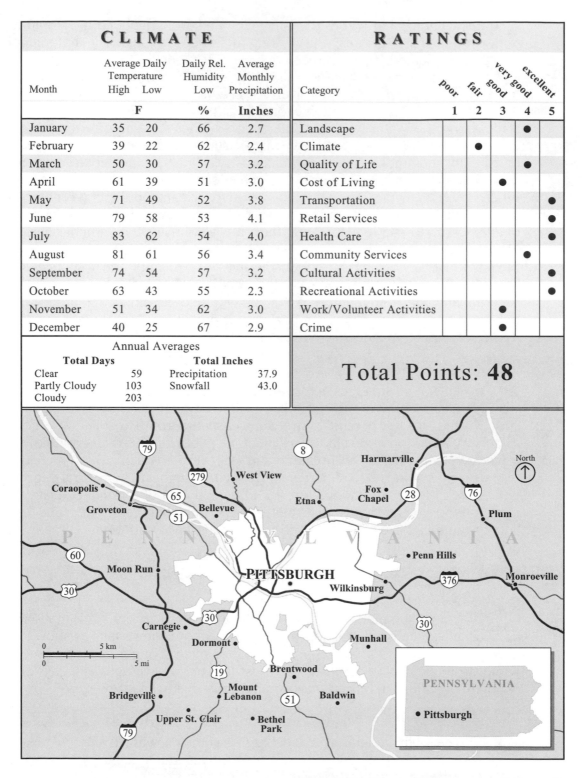

metropolitan area. Road noise is generally unobtrusive because of the limited number of freeways and the muffling of noise by terrain and woodlands. The EPA designates Pittsburgh as a "basic non-attainment area" for air quality. Minimally out of compliance with current air quality standards, Pittsburgh occasionally experiences light smog in summer. Most neighborhoods seem well maintained. The city's parks, museums and its many shopping areas and malls, including the lively and pedestrian-friendly downtown and Strip District, add to livability. The metropolitan area is tied together by a very good transit system, which includes numerous bus lines and a light rail/subway system linking southern suburbs with downtown. Pittsburgh's complex topography works against a consistent geometrical street and highway layout, so navigating the complex road network can be challenging. Rush-hour traffic is somewhat congested and parking is difficult downtown.

Cost of Living — Rating: 3

 The cost of living in Pittsburgh is evaluated as follows:

- *Composite.* ACCRA data show that the overall cost of living in Pittsburgh is about 3 percent below the national average.

- *Housing.* According to ACCRA, housing costs are about 10 percent below the national average. This makes Pittsburgh a "best buy" among large American cities for home ownership.

- *Goods and Services.* Transportation is priced about 14 percent above the national average while health care is about 16 percent below. Costs for groceries, utilities and miscellaneous goods and services are all near national norms.

- *Taxes.* The overall state and local tax burden in Pittsburgh is about 8.9 percent of income compared to the U.S. average of 9.7 percent. State income taxes are at the national average, sales and excise taxes are below average, and property taxes are above average.

Transportation — Rating: 5

 Pittsburgh has good intracity and excellent intercity transportation. The busy street and freeway system is supplemented by excellent public transit furnished by Port Authority Transit (PAT) throughout the city and suburbs. Regular fares and passes are complex and expensive; a monthly three-zone pass costs $93. The good news is that seniors (65 and older) ride free.

Intercity travel is possible by air, rail and bus. Pittsburgh International Airport (PIT) is a major hub served by 15 airlines with more than 2,000 flights weekly. Amtrak service west to Chicago and east to Philadelphia and New York is available from the Pennsylvanian station downtown. Greyhound Lines provides frequent service in all directions from its downtown terminal.

Retail Services — Rating: 5

Downtown Pittsburgh has retained its retail function even though much shopping is done in suburban malls. Major department stores downtown include Kaufmann's, Lazarus, Saks Fifth Avenue and Lord and Taylor. Across the Monongahela River are the Shops at Union Square, which consist of 68 specialty stores, eateries and nightspots in a refurbished railroad terminal. And east of downtown is the trendy Shadyside area, with its fancy stores and cozy restaurants. More remote, in the Northern Hills suburbs, are McIntyre Square, North Hills Village, Northway Mall and Ross Park Mall. All include branches of most major department stores and a host of specialty shops and restaurants. The southern suburbs boast the Century III Mall with 180 stores including Kaufmann's, JCPenney and Sears; South Hills Village consists of 120 stores anchored by Kaufmann's, Lazarus and Sears.

Health Care   Rating: 5

 With more than 20 full-service hospitals, Pittsburgh provides a full array of medical services. The University of Pittsburgh Medical Center (UPMC) is especially notable for the range and quality of its services. UPMC recently received an excellent rating from the National Committee for Quality Assurance (NCQA) and placed on the U.S. News and World Report Honor Roll as one of the "Best of the Best" hospitals in the United States. Such a high ranking requires performance at a very high level across many specialties.

Community Services   Rating: 4

 Pittsburgh and neighboring communities offer bountiful basic public services and boast an impressive number of senior centers. Forty-two senior centers are found in the City of Pittsburgh with an additional 22 in Allegheny County suburbs. Senior centers in the Pittsburgh area typically offer an excellent selection of recreational choices including games, holiday events and trips. Opportunities for volunteer work, information referral, counseling and health screening are also available. Meals are served at many centers through funding by the Allegheny County Agency on Aging.

Cultural and Educational Activities   Rating: 5

 Pittsburgh's passion for the performing arts is particularly manifest in downtown's 14-block Cultural District. At the Benedum Center for the Performing Arts, you can choose among performances by the Pittsburgh Ballet Theatre, the Pittsburgh Opera, the Pittsburgh Light Opera and the Pittsburgh Dance Council. A block away, Heinz Hall for the Performing Arts provides an acoustically outstanding setting for the Pittsburgh Symphony Orchestra, the Pittsburgh Symphony Pops and the Mellon Pittsburgh Broadway Series. Cozier venues are found at the Cultural District's Byham and O'Reilly Theatres, where you can enjoy live theatre and dance performances. Film buffs can frequent the Harris Theatre for fine independent and foreign films.

Patrons of the visual arts will be drawn a few miles east to the Oakland District and Pittsburgh's East End. The Carnegie, across Forbes Avenue from the University of Pittsburgh's Cathedral of Learning, is a cultural complex that includes the Carnegie Library, Carnegie Museum of Art, Carnegie Museum of Natural History and Carnegie Music Hall. The Carnegie Museum of Art houses an extensive collection of impressionist, post-impressionist and nineteenth and twentieth century American works, as well as a remarkable hall of architecture. Several contemporary art galleries are found downtown, and on the North Shore the Andy Warhol Museum is not to be missed.

Pittsburgh has many excellent public and private universities and colleges, only two of which are mentioned here. The University of Pittsburgh (Pitt) is a leading public research university with 32,000 students and 9,600 faculty members, research associates and staff. Pitt's Third Age Learning Community allows persons 55 and older to audit a wide assortment of undergraduate courses for $35 per course. For only slightly higher fees you can enroll in lifelong learning courses at the Community College of Allegheny County, one of the nation's largest multi-campus community colleges.

Recreational Activities   Rating: 5

 Pittsburgh and its surrounding region have much to offer outdoor enthusiasts. Frick, Highland, Riverview and Schenley Parks are the crown jewels of Pittsburgh City Parks. They offer more than 1,700 acres of lawns, wooded areas, ponds, scenic drives, trails, playgrounds and ball fields. Highland Park is home to the Pittsburgh Zoo and PPG Aquarium. You can ice skate at the Iceoplex or at PPG Place, golf on more than 100 public golf courses in the Pittsburgh region, or hike or bicycle along countless trails in city and county parks and rails-to-trails recreation corridors. And when the grand-children are in town, the young and the young at heart will want to try out the rides at Kennywood, one of America's top-rated traditional amusement parks.

Pittsburgh is a paradise for sports fans. The Mellon Arena is home to the Pittsburgh Penguins of the NHL, the new Heinz Field hosts the Pittsburgh Steelers of the NFL, and the striking new PNC Park is home of the Pittsburgh Pirates National League baseball team. These major league teams and several varsity basketball teams at local universities mean that there is always a game in town. The metropolitan area also boasts a good selection of movie theaters and restaurants of great variety.

Work and Volunteer Activities   Rating: 3

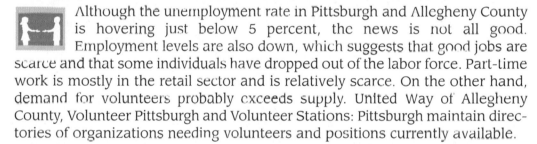 Although the unemployment rate in Pittsburgh and Allegheny County is hovering just below 5 percent, the news is not all good. Employment levels are also down, which suggests that good jobs are scarce and that some individuals have dropped out of the labor force. Part-time work is mostly in the retail sector and is relatively scarce. On the other hand, demand for volunteers probably exceeds supply. United Way of Allegheny County, Volunteer Pittsburgh and Volunteer Stations: Pittsburgh maintain direc-tories of organizations needing volunteers and positions currently available.

Crime Rates and Public Safety   Rating: 3

 As is generally true in large metropolitan areas, crime rates vary con-siderably from place to place in Pittsburgh. Violent crime occurs at twice the average rate in the City of Pittsburgh and property crime is 25 percent above the national average there. Even so, many attractive neigh-borhoods in the city are quite safe and worthy of consideration by retirees. That said, suburban jurisdictions are considerably safer, on average, than the city itself. Violent and property crime rates in the suburbs are about 30 percent below national norms.

Conclusion

Overall Rating 48 The Pittsburgh metropolitan area has much to offer today's retirees. The Pittsburgh renaissance is a reality—the city has metamorphosed from Steel City to a corporate headquarters and service-based econ-omy and its air is now cleaner than that of most large American cities. It offers residents excellent transportation, retail services, health care and a mix of cul-tural and recreational activities virtually unmatched by cities of its size. The city's three rivers, its splendidly sited and attractive downtown, its lovely rolling and wooded landscape and freedom from serious crime in most neighborhoods make for a high quality of life in much of the metropolitan area. Winter may be a little too cold and damp for some but, in most respects, Pittsburgh's physical and built environment is close to ideal. Remarkably, you can enjoy Pittsburgh and its many amenities at affordable prices. Few large American cities can make that claim.

Kingston, Ontario

Strategically located on the banks of the Cataraqui River where it flows into Lake Ontario and at that lake's outlet into the St. Lawrence River, Kingston's site has great geographic and historic interest. Count Frontenac, Governor of New France, established the first European settlement there in 1673. Fort Frontenac survived for 85 years, falling to British assault in 1758, as did all of New France two years later. After 25 years of virtual abandonment, a town plan for Kingston was laid out in 1783 in preparation for the arrival of Loyalist refugees from the rebelling American colonies. The Loyalists and settlers from Great Britain capitalized on Kingston's strategic location to build up an economy based on shipbuilding, trade and national defense during the 1800s. Kingston served as capital of Canada from 1841 to 1844, losing this honor because of its vulnerability to attack from across the American border only five miles away.

During the twentieth century Kingston grew at a moderate pace, enabling it to develop economically while protecting its architectural heritage and livability. With a population of 120,000 in the city and 150,000 in the metropolitan area, Kingston is the largest city between Toronto and Montreal, Canada's two largest cities. Its own amenities and its easy access to the immense resources of Toronto and Montreal make Kingston a very attractive place for residence.

Landscape	Rating: 5

Kingston rests on a gently rolling limestone plain where the Cataraqui River (Rideau Canal) enters Lake Ontario. Just east of town the beautiful Thousand Islands mark the outlet of Lake Ontario into the St. Lawrence River. With its many bays and inlets, Kingston is ideally situated for boating and marinas dot its shoreline. Downtown, with its many historic limestone and brick buildings, the city's tree-lined neighborhood streets and parks and the lovely Queen's University campus constitute a varied and eye-appealing landscape.

Climate	Rating: 2

Kingston experiences a fairly severe humid continental climate with four clearly defined seasons. The city receives 181 centimeters (71 inches) of snow in an average winter but accumulations at any one time seldom exceed 60 centimeters (24 inches). Winter is notable for cloudy, cold and damp weather but summer is typically sunny and warm, with hot, humid episodes often interrupted by cool, dry spells. Weather changes are frequent and abrupt in Kingston, precipitation is ample in all seasons and snow is moderately heavy December through March. Kingston is sunny about 45 percent of the time, varying from about 30 percent in winter to 60 percent in summer.

Kingston, Ontario

CLIMATE

Month	Average Daily Temperature High F	High C	Low F	Low C	Average Monthly Precipitation in	mm
January	26	-3	10	-12	2.9	74
February	27	-3	11	-12	2.4	62
March	37	3	21	-6	3.1	80
April	50	10	33	1	3.3	85
May	62	17	45	7	3.0	75
June	71	21	54	12	2.8	72
July	77	25	60	16	2.3	59
August	75	24	59	15	3.5	88
September	67	20	51	10	3.7	93
October	56	13	40	4	3.4	88
November	44	7	31	-1	3.7	95
December	33	0	17	-8	3.9	99

Annual Averages

Precipitation		Snowfall	
Inches	38.1	Inches	71.3
Millimeters	968	Centimeters	181

RATINGS

Category	poor 1	fair 2	good 3	very good 4	excellent 5
Landscape					●
Climate		●			
Quality of Life					●
Cost of Living					●
Transportation					●
Retail Services			●		
Health Care					●
Community Services				●	
Cultural Activities			●		
Recreational Activities			●		
Work/Volunteer Activities			●		
Crime				●	

Total Points: 47

Quality of Life   **Rating: 5**

Kingston provides an excellent quality of life. Noise levels are low throughout the city. The lightly used airport is near the western city limits and the only freeway, Highway 401, touches only the northern, suburban fringe. Traffic moves rather slowly and quietly on local streets and highways. The road network is adequate but parking can be tight downtown during the summer tourist season and on the periphery of Queen's University, September through April. A good bus system provides access to destinations throughout the urban area. Air quality is generally good and the city seems well planned and run. Neighborhoods, old and new, central and suburban, are typically well treed and maintained, and the city's classic Victorian downtown and its waterside parks are attractive indeed.

Cost of Living   Rating: 5

 The cost of living in Kingston is evaluated as follows:

- **Composite.** No ACCRA data are available for Kingston. I estimate that the overall cost of living in Kingston is about 10 percent below the Canadian average and about 30 percent below the U.S. average.

- **Housing.** Kingston offers a good variety of new and resale housing at reasonable prices. Houses are priced perhaps 20 percent below the Canadian average and 40 percent below the U.S. average. Many nice single-family residences in good neighborhoods are priced between $150,000 and $250,000 ($115,000 and $160,000 U.S.). Standard condominiums are priced somewhat lower but luxury units along the scenic waterfront are costlier.

- **Goods and Services.** Goods and services are priced near Canadian norms but are around 25 percent below average U.S. levels. Medical care is very inexpensive thanks to the government-financed Ontario Health Insurance Plan (OHIP).

- **Taxes.** The overall tax burden in Kingston is slightly lower than the Canadian average and approximately 30 percent higher than the U.S. average for residents of moderate means. Federal and provincial income tax rates are modestly higher than in the U.S. but the combined federal and provincial sales tax on goods and services is twice the U.S. average. These high rates are balanced somewhat by relatively low property taxes and by the low cost of medical care through OHIP.

Transportation   Rating: 5

 Kingston Transit provides excellent public transportation throughout the city and its immediate surroundings. Kingston Access Bus provides dial-a-ride service for elderly and disabled persons. Car/passenger ferry service is available hourly to nearby Wolfe Island and less frequently to Howe Island. Kingston is located halfway between Toronto and Montreal on Canada's main rail passenger corridor. Twenty trains daily link Kingston to these cities, with connections to southwestern Ontario, Western Canada, Quebec and Atlantic Canada. Coach Canada provides frequent service to Toronto and Montreal and connections to points beyond. Limousine service is available to hub airports at Toronto, Montreal, Ottawa and Syracuse, New York.

Retail Services   Rating: 3

 Cataraqui Town Center, located about 8 kilometers (5 miles) northwest of downtown Kingston, is Kingston's largest enclosed mall. Anchored by The Bay, Sears and Zellers department stores, the two-level sky-lit complex includes approximately 140 Canadian and American specialty stores, restaurants and services. The Kingston Shopping Centre has several big-box stores including Wal-Mart, Home Depot and Winners. Downtown is vibrant, architecturally interesting and popular among visitors. It boasts a number of excellent restaurants and specialty shops.

Health Care   Rating: 5

Kingston is notable among eastern Ontario locations for the quality of its medical care. Four hospitals have a total of nearly 1,300 beds. Kingston General Hospital (KGH), a 420-bed teaching facility affiliated with Queen's University, is the largest and best-equipped hospital in the city. KGH provides 24-hour emergency care, critical and trauma care and cardiac, cancer, infectious diseases and neurological care, among countless specialties. As a teaching hospital, KGH benefits from substantial investments in state-of-the-art equipment and is able to attract a cadre of exceptional medical practitioners.

Community Services   Rating: 4

Kingston provides excellent basic public services and many programs for seniors. Seniors Centre Kingston Region provides activities, information and advocacy for seniors. The Canadian Red Cross Society provides programs geared to enabling seniors to enjoy a healthy and active lifestyle.

Cultural and Educational Activities   Rating: 3

Kingston is home to four post-secondary educational institutions including the Royal Military College, Canada's West Point. Queen's University is Canada's oldest university and consistently ranks as one of the nation's top academic institutions. Queen's continuing education program, guest lecture and musical series are inexpensively or freely available to seniors. St. Lawrence College, a two-year community college, offers a multiplicity of applied courses of general interest. Kingston's 17 museums include Queen's University's Agnes Etherington Art Centre, which presents changing exhibits of contemporary and historical Canadian art as well as permanent exhibits of Inuit art, West African art and paintings by European masters. Most other museums have historic themes. Leading examples include Fort Henry, a nineteenth century fortress built to defend Kingston against a possible American invasion; Bellevue House, the home of Sir John A. Mc Donald, Canada's first prime minister; and the Marine Museum of the Great Lakes.

Kingston is known for its writers, artisans and visual and performing artists. Art blooms in galleries and cafes, along city sidewalks and in parks. On many evenings you can hear live music from blues to jazz to rock, attend a symphony concert or enjoy a play at one of four theaters showcasing local talent. The Grand Theatre, Kingston's principal performing arts facility, has a large auditorium and a smaller space, the Baby Grand on the second floor. The Kingston Symphony performs its annual series there from September through April as well as occasional concerts outdoors at Confederation Park, Fort Henry and St. Mary's Cathedral. Tickets are reasonably priced and senior discounts are given.

Recreational Activities   Rating: 3

 Recreational activities abound in Kingston. Outdoor sports such as sailing, golfing, hiking, bicycling and skiing, and indoor ones like rock climbing, tennis, swimming, dancing and fitness programs, all have their devotees. Gateway to the Thousand Islands, Kingston is a favorite port of call for Great Lakes sailors. The city's seven marinas along Lake Ontario and the Rideau Canal provide dockage for 1,700 boats. In addition to the City of Kingston's 14 public parks and recreation centers offering ice skating, swimming, fitness classes and the usual outdoor sports facilities, there are 5 major parkland areas within a 20-minute drive of town. These provide opportunities for swimming, hiking, fishing, canoeing, camping, wildlife viewing and—in winter—cross-country skiing and ice skating. Ten local area golf courses provide an interesting variety of challenges to golfers of all skill levels.

Work and Volunteer Activities   Rating: 3

 Although Kingston's unemployment rate is relatively low, part-time jobs are not abundant in an economy dominated by Queen's University and federal institutions. Part-time service jobs are mostly in retailing and tourist-related activities and competition for them with students is severe. Volunteer opportunities, though, are plentiful. Many seniors give back to the community through service to religious organizations, hospitals, schools, libraries, the visitors bureau and senior centers. Mentoring of youth through various entrepreneurship programs attracts many retired executives.

Crime Rates and Public Safety   Rating: 4

 Crime rates in Kingston are moderate by Canadian standards. The property crime rate is about 10 percent above the national average whereas the violent crime rate is nearly 30 percent below the national norm. Compared with average U.S. crime statistics, Kingston has an average rate of property crime but a violent crime rate that is fully 60 percent below the U.S. norm. More impressionistically, Kingston seems a very safe place to walk about, day or night.

Conclusion

Overall Rating 47 Several years ago the Toronto Globe and Mail rated Kingston as one of Canada's best cities in which to live and do business and went on to say, "Kingston offers a unique and enviable lifestyle" and is a good place for retirement. There is little to disagree with in this assessment. Kingston remains a jewel among small Canadian cities.

Kingston's strongest assets are its wonderful natural and built landscape, high quality of life, low cost of living and excellent health care. It has very good transportation and community services and a low rate of violent crime. Although a relatively small city, it has a good selection of retail stores of all types and sufficient cultural, educational and recreational options to satisfy nearly every taste. Winter in Kingston may be a little too long, cold and snowy for some people but the low cost of living would enable them to afford a lengthy winter vacation in Florida or the Caribbean. All in all, Kingston combines the advantages of a sophisticated city with the simple pleasures of life in an exceptional small town. Who could ask for anything more?

Owen Sound, Ontario

First settled by Europeans in the 1840s, Owen Sound flourished for several decades after 1850 as area forests were cut, sawn into lumber at local sawmills and exported to the United States via its excellent harbor. By the late 1800s, deforestation brought ruin to the forest products industry and Owen Sound became primarily a service center for the surrounding agricultural area. In the twentieth century, the city developed a diverse manufacturing base that complemented its role as a regional market town. During most of its history, though, Owen Sound's remoteness from Toronto and other fast-growing southern Ontario cities has made for relatively slow economic and population growth in the city and neighboring townships. As a consequence, the magnificent brick homes and commercial buildings of the downtown area have been preserved and, now renovated, are the heart of the city's thriving central business district. With a population of 21,000 in the city and 36,000 in the urban area, Owen Sound has recently emerged as a destination for tourists and retirees. A world apart from the hectic pace of life in the Greater Toronto Region yet only a 2.5-hour drive from Canada's largest city, Owen Sound has special appeal for those seeking a relaxed, outdoors-oriented lifestyle in a beautiful and historic small city away from crowds.

Landscape — Rating: 5

Owen Sound occupies a splendid site on the southern shore of Georgian Bay. The downtown and adjacent older residential areas are situated in a post-glacial valley, which opens up onto a magnificent natural harbor just north of the city center. Newer residential areas climb the wooded and rocky slopes of the Niagara Escarpment that ring the central city on all but its northern (bay) side. The surrounding countryside is a rolling surface with picturesque farms, forests and numerous waterfalls dropping into gorges at the foot of the escarpment. The region's natural vegetation is broad-leafed deciduous forest with beech and maple predominating. The city is well wooded with a variety of deciduous and coniferous trees supplemented by summer flowers of great variety. The wooded, rolling terrain embracing the southern arm of the bay (also called Owen Sound) is very beautiful in all seasons but especially in autumn when the sugar maple displays its brilliant red color.

Climate — Rating: 2

Owen Sound has a fairly severe humid continental climate with four clearly defined seasons. The city is famous for its abundant winter snow, which can accumulate to a depth of 10 feet. Winters are typically cloudy, cold and damp; summers are pleasantly sunny and warm. Weather changes rapidly here, especially in spring and autumn when warm, humid episodes alternate with cool, dry periods. Precipitation is ample in all seasons with most of winter's falling as snow. On average, Owen Sound is sunny about 48 percent of the time, varying from about 30 percent in winter to 60 percent in summer. The frost-free period averages 140 days, just adequate to allow productive summer gardening.

Owen Sound, Ontario

CLIMATE

Month	Average Daily Temperature High F	High C	Low F	Low C	Average Monthly Precipitation in	mm
January	28	-2	15	-9	5.3	135
February	29	-2	15	-10	3.0	78
March	37	3	22	-5	3.0	78
April	50	10	34	1	2.8	70
May	62	17	43	6	2.8	72
June	71	21	52	11	3.0	76
July	76	25	59	15	2.9	73
August	75	24	59	15	3.5	89
September	67	20	52	11	4.1	105
October	56	13	42	6	3.5	89
November	44	7	33	1	4.3	109
December	33	1	22	-5	5.0	127

Annual Averages

Precipitation		Snowfall	
Inches	43.3	Inches	137
Millimeters	1100	Centimeters	347

RATINGS

Category	poor 1	fair 2	good 3	very good 4	excellent 5
Landscape					●
Climate		●			
Quality of Life					●
Cost of Living					●
Transportation		●			
Retail Services			●		
Health Care			●		
Community Services				●	
Cultural Activities			●		
Recreational Activities				●	
Work/Volunteer Activities				●	
Crime				●	

Total Points: 44

Quality of Life Rating: 5

The quality of life is excellent in Owen Sound. With only a small, general aviation airport nearby, there is little aircraft noise. Air and water are clean and there are no noisy freeways. Automobile traffic moves relatively slowly and quietly on local streets and highways. You can drive across town in a few minutes and find parking at destinations. Public transit provides a reasonable alternative for those who prefer not to drive. Owen Sound has a good mix of well-maintained neighborhoods and several beautiful parks, most notably Harrison Park just south of downtown. The recently restored historic downtown offers good shopping in a traditional business district. Nearby are several highly scenic natural attractions including Inglis Falls, Beaver Valley and the Niagara Escarpment.

Cost of Living   Rating: 5

 The cost of living in Owen Sound is evaluated as follows:

- **Composite.** No ACCRA data are available for Owen Sound. I estimate that the overall cost of living in Owen Sound is 10 percent below the Canadian average and about 30 percent below the American average.

- **Housing.** Housing costs are about 20 percent below the Canadian average and 40 percent below the American average. Local real estate guides reveal an abundance of quality, inexpensive homes in Owen Sound and neighboring villages. Modest older single-family homes near downtown are priced around $100,000 ($75,000 U.S.) while distinctly upscale, four-bedroom houses sell for $120,000 to $240,000 ($90,000 to $180,000 U.S.). Condominiums or townhomes are typically priced between $60,000 and $100,000 ($45,000 to $75,000 U.S.).

- **Goods and Services.** Goods and services are generally priced within a few percentage points of Canadian norms but are about 25 percent below average U.S. levels. Utilities and medical care are particularly inexpensive by American standards.

- **Taxes.** The overall tax burden in Owen Sound is slightly lower than the Canadian average and perhaps 30 percent higher than the U.S. average for residents of moderate means. Federal and provincial income tax rates are modestly higher than in the U.S. but the combined federal and provincial sales tax on goods and services is twice the U.S. average. These high rates are balanced somewhat by relatively low property taxes and the very low cost of medical care through OHIP.

Transportation   Rating: 2

 Owen Sound Transit furnishes good bus service within city limits. Routes connect downtown with destinations in the urban core, areas west and east of the harbor, and the southern part of town including Harrison Park. Buses run at half-hour intervals on weekdays, less frequently on Saturdays and not at all on Sundays. Owen Sound has no commercial air or train service but Greyhound and PMCL offer intercity bus service to neighboring communities and to Toronto.

Retail Services   Rating: 3

 Heritage Place, on the eastern periphery, is the major enclosed regional mall. Anchored by Sears and Zellers department stores and a huge Food Basics supermarket, which has low prices by Canadian and U.S. standards, Heritage Place also boasts 60 specialty stores, 4 fast-food eateries and 3 restaurants. The mall is well sky-lit and fairly attractive overall. Historic downtown Owen Sound, its streets entirely rebuilt recently, is a vibrant, architecturally interesting business core. Unique specialty shops feature arts and crafts, books, apparel, hardware, home furnishings and sporting goods, among other goods and services. Several restaurants and a weekly farmers' market, open Saturdays year-round, also lure people downtown.

Health Care   Rating: 3

 Grey Bruce Health Services–Owen Sound, a 208-bed acute care facility, is the primary health care provider for the 160,000 people residing in the Grey–Bruce region. Its 85-member medical staff offers a wide range of medical and surgical specialties as well as primary care. In the annual health care report issued by MacLean's magazine, the Owen Sound facility ranked better than average in outcomes (life expectancy, heart attack and stroke survival) but near the bottom of the list for hospital resources (local services, physicians and specialists per capita).

Community Services   Rating: 4

 Owen Sound provides excellent basic public services and many targeted specifically toward seniors. The Home and Community Support Services of Grey–Bruce provides low-cost or free services including Meals on Wheels, transportation, day away programs and home maintenance referrals. The Golden Ages Seniors Center hosts an unusually rich assortment of social and recreational activities such as arts and crafts, games, movies, guest speakers, musical performances and bus trips to sundry southern Ontario attractions.

Cultural and Educational Activities   Rating: 3

Owen Sound has a remarkable repertoire of cultural events for a city of its size. Downtown's Roxy Theatre seats 400 and is the cultural center of the city and region. Home of the acclaimed Owen Sound Little Theatre, the Roxy also plays host to concert and stage productions year-round. Other major performing arts venues include the 700-seat auditorium at the Georgian Bay Collegiate Institute, where the Owen Sound Symphony performs, and the Lumley Community Centre, which doubles as an ice hockey rink and venue for four major guest artist shows each year. The annual Summerfolk Festival, Celtic Festival and Festival of Northern Lights all highlight Owen Sound's changing seasons. The Summerfolk folk music festival, held in mid-August, attracts around 12,000 people to Kelso Beach Park; September's Celtic Festival features Celtic food, music, dance and story telling; and the Festival of Northern Lights rings in the winter season with one of the best Christmas light displays in the province, several craft shows, theatrical performances and tours of historic homes.

Several art and historical museums enrich life in Owen Sound. The Tom Thomson Memorial Art Gallery is a Canadian cultural icon, housing an excellent collection of memorabilia and artwork of the celebrated Canadian painter, Tom Thomson, who grew up at Leith, just north of Owen Sound. The gallery also displays a growing collection of historical and contemporary Canadian art including a wonderful selection of the work of Thomson's colleagues, The Group of Seven. The Grey County Museum, Owen Sound Marine and Rail Museum, and Billy Bishop Heritage Museum each highlight significant aspects of the history of Owen Sound and Canada. The Grey County Museum celebrates local history through galleries, period buildings and special events. Grey County's important role as the northern terminus of the Underground Railroad is emphasized. The Owen Sound Marine and Rail Museum, located in the historic Canadian National Railway station on the waterfront, preserves the history of marine and rail transportation in the area. Housed in the boyhood home of one of Canada's greatest fighter aces of World War I, the Billy Bishop Heritage Museum includes memorabilia from both world wars.

Georgian College–Owen Sound Campus is a component of Ontario's 25 Colleges of Applied Arts and Technology system. The College's Part-time Studies courses, especially those in computer training, are of interest to seniors. Seniors 60 and older can audit courses for fees ranging from $100 to $200 (Canadian).

Recreational Activities   Rating: 4

 Owen Sound provides countless outdoor recreational opportunities. Nestled in the Niagara Escarpment, a UNESCO Biosphere Reserve, Owen Sound is a jumping-off place for excursions to the escarpment's unique wildlife habitat: home to 100 species of trees, 320 species of birds, 50 species of ferns and many of the 40 species of orchids indigenous to Ontario. Few small cities have as much green space as Owen Sound. Harrison Park is the crown jewel of the parks system. Straddling the Sydenham River just south of downtown, Harrison Park occupies a beautiful site with hiking trails and paths meandering across meadows and through wooded areas. The park features a fully-serviced campground, restaurant, picnic areas, tennis courts, swimming pools, canoeing, fishing and a bird sanctuary. If you want to take a longer hike, you can access the 740-kilometer (470-mile) long Bruce Trail along the Niagara Escarpment from several points around the city. A particularly pleasant hike will take you from Harrison Park to the Inglis Falls Conservation Area.

Boating, swimming, fishing and golf are popular summer pastimes in the Owen Sound area. Owen Sound Harbor is a well-equipped and sheltered base for boating and fishing in the Sound and Georgian Bay. Five rivers empty into the Sound and anglers can seek out Chinook salmon and rainbow, lake or brown trout in river or bay waters. A public beach is found at Kelso Beach Park on the west side of the harbor and some of Ontario's best sandy beaches are only a half hour away on the shores of Lake Huron. Three scenic and challenging 18-hole golf courses are located in or adjacent to Owen Sound and several others are nearby.

Outdoor enthusiasts will also enjoy the Owen Sound area in winter. With the province's best downhill skiing no more than 45 minutes away in the Beaver Valley and Blue Mountain areas, cross-country ski trails in Harrison Park and Inglis Falls, and ice skating at Harry Lumley Community Center, there is no reason to be inactive in winter. If you prefer more sedentary activities, you can attend top-caliber Junior A hockey games at the Lumley or take in a movie showing on one of the seven screens at Galaxy Cinemas.

Work and Volunteer Activities   Rating: 4

Owen Sound's diversified economy generates enough jobs to keep unemployment well below the average for Ontario. Part-time employment of interest to seniors is mostly in the service sector, most notably in retailing and tourism. Wages are somewhat below the Ontario average but so too are living costs. Volunteer opportunities are abundant. The Volunteer Centre promotes volunteerism and recruits, trains and refers volunteers for rewarding assignments. Volunteers are placed as drivers, counselors, leisure companions, ushers for cultural events and as volunteer workers in the library, hospital and in municipal gardening and landscaping projects, among others.

Crime Rates and Public Safety   Rating: 4

 Owen Sound has about-average crime rates for Canada but is a safe place by U.S. standards. The property crime rate is about 5 percent above the national average, whereas the violent crime rate is about 8 percent below the Canadian norm. There have been zero homicides in Owen Sound in recent years and the community feels very safe.

Conclusion

Overall Rating 44 Owen Sound is a near-perfect place for retirement for those seeking a relaxed, outdoors-oriented lifestyle in a safe, friendly small city. Buffered by distance from the frenzied pace and rampant development of the Greater Toronto Area, Owen Sound is an island of tranquility and low living costs. Its physical site, where the Niagara Escarpment skirts Georgian Bay, is gorgeous and the city's urban infrastructure and neighborhoods are in good shape. Environmental pollution, traffic congestion and urban ugliness are conspicuously absent. The revitalized downtown is the center of the community and, like Harrison Park and the city's pleasant residential areas, is a delightful place to explore on foot. Local availability of retail services, health care and cultural diversions is good and community services, recreational assets, and work and volunteer opportunities are remarkable for a small city. Owen Sound serves up a surprising assortment of leisure options. The great outdoors beckons residents and visitors alike, with plentiful diversions in all seasons, and several ongoing cultural programs and annual special events mark the entertainment calendar.

Owen Sound's principal weaknesses are the absence of fast public transportation to Toronto and other major Ontario cities (most people drive) and, for those disinterested in winter sports, the long snowy winter. All things considered, though, Owen Sound ranks as one of the best places in North America for a relaxed yet amenity-rich retirement in a beautiful and unspoiled setting.

Stratford, Ontario

Fifty years ago no one would have guessed that Stratford would be a great place to live at the beginning of the twenty-first century. Two key industries, the Canadian National Railways (CNR) locomotive shops and the furniture industry, were about to close or enter a slow, inexorable decline that would threaten the economic foundation of the city. Fortunately for Stratford, in 1953 Tom Patterson—a Stratford-born reporter for Maclean's Magazine—and a group of local supporters launched the Stratford Festival, an annual five-month cultural event that has become an enormous theatrical success and the key to making tourism a major industry for the city. Stratford's ideal location near the center of the North American automobile manufacturing industry has also spurred economic growth. With excellent rail and truck transportation to vehicle assembly plants in Ontario and the American Midwest, Stratford auto parts

Stratford, Ontario

CLIMATE						
	Average Daily Temperature				Average Monthly Precipitation	
Month	High		Low			
	F	C	F	C	in	mm
January	26	-3	14	-10	4.1	104
February	28	-2	15	-10	2.7	69
March	38	3	23	-5	3.0	75
April	51	11	34	1	3.4	85
May	65	18	44	7	3.2	83
June	74	23	53	12	3.1	77
July	78	25	57	14	3.5	90
August	76	24	56	13	3.3	83
September	68	20	49	10	4.1	104
October	56	13	40	4	3.2	81
November	42	6	31	-1	4.0	102
December	31	0	20	-7	4.4	111

Annual Averages			
Precipitation		Snowfall	
Inches	41.8	Inches	96.1
Millimeters	1064	Centimeters	244

RATINGS

Category	poor 1	fair 2	good 3	very good 4	excellent 5
Landscape				●	
Climate		●			
Quality of Life					●
Cost of Living					●
Transportation				●	
Retail Services			●		
Health Care			●		
Community Services					●
Cultural Activities				●	
Recreational Activities			●		
Work/Volunteer Activities					●
Crime					●

Total Points: 48

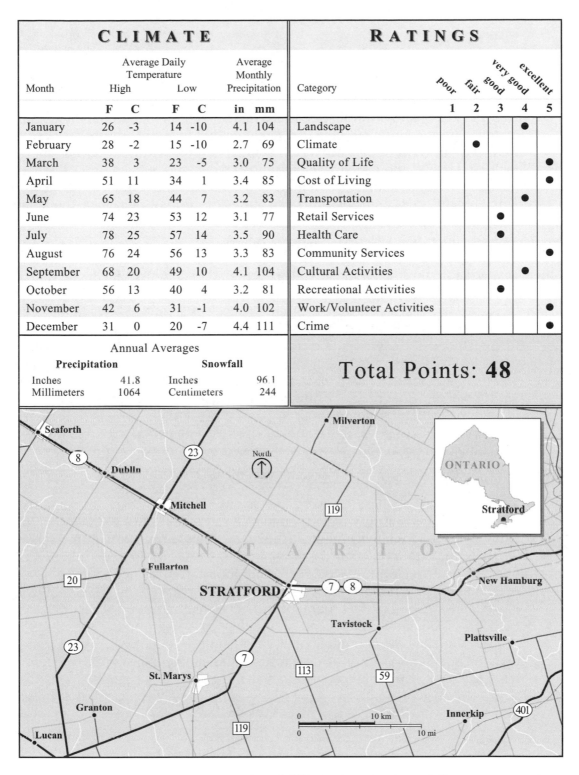

producers are well situated to fulfill the just-in-time delivery expectations of modern auto assembly plants. Today, thanks to decades of careful planning, investment and cooperation among the Stratford Festival, downtown business interests, local government and citizens, this city of 30,000 has a vibrant, pedestrian-friendly downtown, one of the best repertory theaters in the

English-speaking world, more parkland per capita than any other city in Canada and low crime rates. Not surprisingly, it ranks highly as a retirement place.

Landscape   Rating: 4

Stratford rests on a flat plain near the center of the southwestern Ontario peninsula formed by Lakes Huron, Erie, and Ontario and the rivers connecting them. The Avon River, a tributary of the Thames, bisects the city and adds interest to the gentle landscape, particularly where it widens into the small but beautiful Lake Victoria just north of the city center. Stratford neighborhoods are heavily treed with native deciduous species including maple and beech. Landscaping of public spaces and private gardens has become more sophisticated in recent years as the city and the public have emulated the good taste demonstrated by the Stratford Festival in the parklands surrounding its theaters.

Climate   Rating: 2

Stratford has a moderately severe humid continental climate marked by four clearly defined seasons. Located in the eastern fringe of the Lake Huron snowbelt, Stratford receives about 240 centimeters (96 inches) of snow in an average winter. Accumulations of a meter (about three feet) of snow on the ground are common December through February. Winters are typically cloudy, cold and damp; summers are pleasantly sunny and warm. Weather changes quickly in all seasons with warm, humid periods alternating with cooler and drier ones. Precipitation is ample in all seasons with heavy snow in winter. Stratford is sunny about 50 percent of the time, varying from 30 percent in winter to 65 percent in summer. The frost-free period averages 150 days, about average for inland areas of southwestern Ontario.

Quality of Life   Rating: 5

Stratford offers an excellent quality of life. With no major airport nearby, aircraft noise is minimal. Road noise is not obtrusive as traffic moves slowly on local streets and highways. Even at the summer height of the Stratford Festival you can drive across town in a few minutes and find a place to park. Air quality is generally good except for occasional episodes of light smog in summer. Public transit and cab service are good and relatively inexpensive. Stratford has many attractive residential neighborhoods and a number of beautiful parks and well-equipped playgrounds. The Stratford Festival enriches the community culturally and economically. Festival visitors demand quality services and their presence has enabled Stratford to redeem its historic downtown, now one of Ontario's most lively city centers.

Cost of Living   Rating: 5

 The cost of living in Stratford is evaluated as follows:

- *Composite.* No ACCRA data are available for Stratford. I estimate that the overall cost of living in Stratford is 5 percent below the Canadian average and about 25 percent below the American average.

- *Housing.* Housing costs are about 10 percent below the Canadian average and 30 percent below the American average. Prices for single-family residences throughout the city average $160,000 ($120,000 U.S.). Prime older properties in the best neighborhoods near the city center run between $200,000 and $300,000 ($150,000 and $225,000 U.S.).

- *Goods and Services.* Goods and services are priced near Canadian norms but are about 25 percent below U.S. averages. Utilities and medical care are particularly inexpensive by American standards.

- *Taxes.* The overall tax burden in Stratford is near the Canadian average and about 30 percent higher than the U.S. average for residents of moderate means. Federal and provincial income tax rates are modestly higher than in the U.S. but the combined federal and provincial sales tax on goods and services is twice the U.S. average. These high rates are balanced somewhat by low property taxes and the very low cost of medical care through OHIP.

Transportation · Rating: 4

 Stratford Transit provides good bus service to all parts of the city. Buses arrive at 20-minute intervals at rush hour and at 40-minute intervals during off-peak hours. Stratford lacks a commercial airport but the Airport Van will take you to international airports at London and Toronto. VIA Rail Canada trains and buses connect Stratford with nearby cities. Two trains a day travel eastbound to Toronto and westbound to London; buses also serve these cities and others in southwestern Ontario several times daily.

Retail Services · Rating: 3

Historic downtown Stratford is notable for its Hudson's department store and a plethora of upscale specialty shops and fine restaurants. Unlike the situation 50 years ago, local churches no longer have to feed the theater crowd. Festival Mall, on Ontario Street East, is an attractive, small sky-lit regional center. Anchored by a well-stocked Sears and a huge Canadian Tire store, which sells everything from car parts to garden plants, Festival Mall has 43 businesses in all, including 6 fast-food eateries and 35 specialty shops.

Health Care · Rating: 3

Stratford General Hospital, a modern 134-bed facility, provides general and specialized short-term care, diagnostic imaging, long-term treatment and emergency and outpatient services. The hospital is adequate for routine needs and more specialized care is only 65 kilometers (40 miles) away in London, site of some of the finest medical facilities in Canada.

Community Services · Rating: 5

 Stratford boasts excellent basic public services, with many oriented specifically toward seniors. Stratford Lakeside Seniors Association meets in Kiwanis Community Centre in Victoria Park. Activities there include shuffleboard, billiards, tai chi and cards. Seniors can also use the library, participate in arts, crafts and fitness programs and take field trips. The Department of Parks runs a Seniors Skating Club and sets aside early morning hours at their pools for adult lap swimming. Stratford Meals on Wheels and Neighborly Services delivers meals, hosts a group-dining program, provides a variety of transportation options and runs an exercise program for seniors. It also helps out with home maintenance and repair and is a valued information source for seniors.

Cultural and Educational Activities   Rating: 4

 Stratford offers residents and visitors an awesome array of cultural events. Overlooking Lake Victoria is the magnificent Festival Theatre, the Stratford Festival's major venue since 1957. With 1,824 seats, the Festival Theatre fields major performances of classic Shakespeare, classic and contemporary drama, comedies and musicals. Smaller productions are staged in the nearby Tom Patterson and Avon/Studio Theatres. The Stratford Festival runs May through October. At the height of the Festival season at the end of July and beginning of August, Stratford Summer Music presents a veritable barrage of top-flight musical performances ranging from classical to jazz at several venues including Knox Church, City Hall Auditorium, the Church Restaurant, Lower Queen's Park and on a barge in Lake Victoria. Stratford's heavy arts emphasis is also seen in visual arts displays at Gallery Stratford and at many commercial studios in the downtown area including the first rate Gallery Indigina, which features Inuit art and art of the Pacific Northwest.

Higher education assets are thin in Stratford but abundant 65 kilometers (40 miles) to the east and southwest in Waterloo and London. Waterloo is home to the University of Waterloo, Wilfrid Laurier University and Conestoga College; London is home to the University of Western Ontario and Fanshawe College. Conestoga College and Fanshawe College are both components of Ontario's 25 College of Applied Arts and Technology System. Conestoga College operates a small branch campus in Stratford and Fanshawe College fields occasional Saturday courses there.

Recreational Activities   Rating: 3

 With more than 1,000 acres of groomed parkland, Stratford has plenty of space to play. Upper and Lower Queen's Park, along the Avon River and Lake Victoria, have areas devoted to tennis, lawn bowling, playgrounds, picnicking and sports fields as well as trails for walking or jogging. The adventurous can also rent canoes and paddle boats to navigate the waters of Lake Victoria or go ice skating at the arena upslope from the lake. You can cross-country ski around the lake in winter and ride your bike safely on designated bicycle-friendly streets during the warmer seasons. Elsewhere in Stratford you can golf at a 9-hole municipal course in the city or challenge the links at 11 other public or private courses in the Stratford region. Other municipal recreational facilities include two additional indoor ice rinks, courts for volleyball and badminton and an outdoor pool. The newly upgraded YMCA offers indoor swimming, a well-equipped fitness center, exercise classes and gymnastics.

Less strenuous activities include taking in a movie at 5-Screen Cinema, attending a Junior B hockey game, enjoying the varied books and digital resources of the Stratford Public Library or indulging in fine food and drink at one of downtown's many excellent restaurants.

Work and Volunteer Activities   Rating: 5

 Thanks to the Festival, Stratford's status as the market center of Perth County, and the city's diverse industrial base, unemployment is low and jobs are plentiful. Part-time employment is mainly in tourism-related activities, general services and retailing. Volunteer work is also plentiful. The Stratford Area Association for Community Living organizes volunteers to help the disabled participate in community and religious events and to attend movies and other events. The Festival, schools, Stratford General Hospital, St. John Ambulance, the public library and the YMCA are among the most popular agencies depending on volunteers.

Crime Rates and Public Safety   Rating: 5

 Stratford is unusually safe by Canadian standards and even safer relative to U.S. averages. The property crime rate is 20 percent below the national average and the violent crime rate is fully 40 percent below the Canadian norm. In an average year there are zero homicides in Stratford and the city feels very safe to residents and visitors alike.

Conclusion

Overall Rating 48 Few places offer the combination of virtues that make Stratford one of North America's best places to live. The vibrant city center filled with sumptuous restaurants and intriguing specialty shops is only a short walk from Stratford Festival theaters and the parkland bordering the Avon River and Lake Victoria. Festival-related tourism adds immeasurably to the city's quality of life because it attracts and sustains upscale services not generally available in small cities. Although the Stratford Festival naturally dominates the city's cultural calendar, many other cultural and recreational opportunities also keep boredom at bay. Shoppers enjoy a wealth of options in the beautifully restored, historic downtown and restaurants there cater to every taste and style.

Stratford's strongest assets are its lovely landscape, world-class theater, excellent availability of community services and work/volunteer activities, very good transportation, and enviably low crime rates. Retail services, recreational activities and health care are good, especially for a small place. Although Stratford's cold, snowy winters are a liability for many people, they would not be for those who enjoy winter sports like cross-country skiing and ice skating. All things considered, Stratford promises retirees the joys of small-town life together with amenities typically found only in large cities. Almost unbelievably, this high quality of life is very affordable; Stratford has among the lowest living costs of North American cities suitable for upscale retirement.

London, Ontario

In 1793 Governor Simcoe chose the site of present-day downtown London as the future capital of Upper Canada (Ontario). Toronto later got the nod as provincial capital but this only temporarily set back London's development. By the 1830s, southwestern Ontario had become a popular destination for British and American immigrants and London soon emerged as the regional center for the rich farmlands around it. The coming of the Great Western Railway in 1854 strengthened the city's competitiveness in commerce and manufacturing, thereby fostering further economic and population growth. With a current population of around 340,000 in the city and 440,000 in the metropolitan area, London ranks as Ontario's fourth-largest city. Its diverse economy—strong in manufacturing, commerce, medical care and higher education—supports a good standard of living for residents and enables the city to maintain its strong

London, Ontario

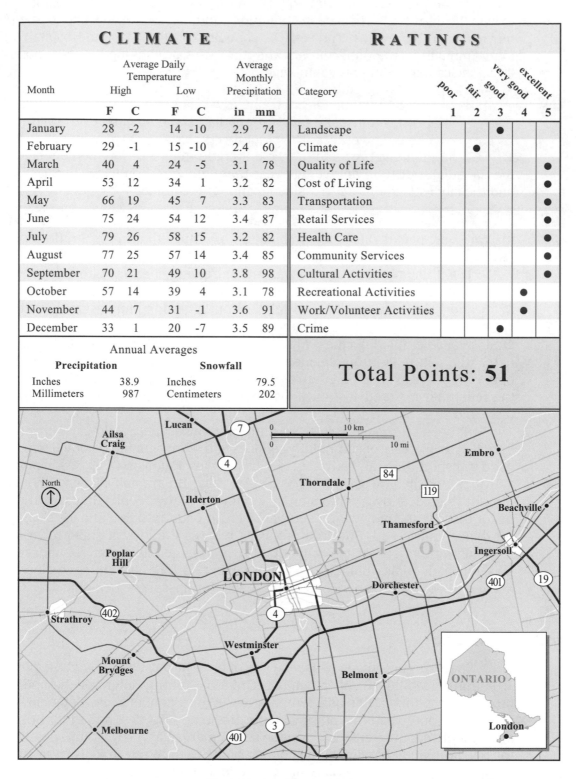

CLIMATE						
Month	Average Daily Temperature High F	High C	Low F	Low C	Average Monthly Precipitation in	mm
January	28	-2	14	-10	2.9	74
February	29	-1	15	-10	2.4	60
March	40	4	24	-5	3.1	78
April	53	12	34	1	3.2	82
May	66	19	45	7	3.3	83
June	75	24	54	12	3.4	87
July	79	26	58	15	3.2	82
August	77	25	57	14	3.4	85
September	70	21	49	10	3.8	98
October	57	14	39	4	3.1	78
November	44	7	31	-1	3.6	91
December	33	1	20	-7	3.5	89

Annual Averages

Precipitation		Snowfall	
Inches	38.9	Inches	79.5
Millimeters	987	Centimeters	202

RATINGS Category	poor 1	fair 2	good 3	very good 4	excellent 5
Landscape			●		
Climate		●			
Quality of Life					●
Cost of Living					●
Transportation					●
Retail Services					●
Health Care					●
Community Services					●
Cultural Activities					●
Recreational Activities				●	
Work/Volunteer Activities				●	
Crime			●		

Total Points: 51

infrastructure and excellent municipal services. London has recently invested heavily in redevelopment of its central core even as suburban residential, retail and commercial expansion proceeds apace. A pleasant and amenity-rich community halfway between Detroit and Toronto and less than an hour's drive from the sandy beaches of Lakes Erie and Huron, London has much to offer residents of all ages. It is one of Canada's most livable cities.

Landscape   Rating: 3

London is located at the forks of the Thames River not far from the center of the southwestern Ontario peninsula formed by Lakes Huron, Erie and Ontario and the rivers connecting them. The Thames and the several parks bordering it add interest to the nearly flat plain on which the city is built. The self-styled "Forest City" has more than 160,000 trees lining its streets and dotting its parks. Deciduous species, including sugar maple, are at their best during the autumn show of color and are a deep green during the balmy summer.

Climate   Rating: 2

London has a moderately severe humid continental climate characterized by four clearly defined seasons. Located on the southeastern fringe of the Lake Huron snowbelt, London receives about 200 centimeters (80 inches) of snow in an average winter. Accumulations of half a meter (17 inches) of snow on the ground are normal December through February, but thaws are common. Winters are typically cloudy, cold and damp; summers are generally sunny and warm although occasional hot and humid episodes bring discomfort in July and August. Precipitation is adequate throughout the year. London is sunny about 50 percent of the time, varying from 30 percent in winter to 65 percent in summer.

Quality of Life   Rating: 5

The quality of life is excellent. Although London International Airport is only 7 kilometers (4.5 miles) from downtown, jet noise is minimal because approach and departure flight paths do not usually cross the city. Road noise is not obtrusive in most residential areas as traffic moves relatively slowly on local streets and the busy freeway 401 skirts only the southern industrial fringe of the city. Even at rush hour you can drive across town in 30 minutes and expect to find parking. Air quality is generally good except for occasional episodes of light smog in summer. Public transit is excellent and is a viable alternative to driving. The city has many diverse and attractive neighborhoods and countless beautiful and well-equipped parks and recreation centers. Downtown, with its new Covent Garden Market, arena, convention center, public library and numerous shops and restaurants, is enjoying a modest revival.

Cost of Living   Rating: 5

 The cost of living in London is evaluated as follows:

- *Composite.* No ACCRA data are available for London. I estimate that the overall cost of living in London is 5 percent below the Canadian average and about 25 percent below the American average.

- *Housing.* Housing costs about 10 percent below the Canadian average and 30 percent below the American average. Prices for single-family residences throughout the city average $150,000 ($112,000 U.S.). Condominiums average around $100,000 ($75,000 U.S.). Housing in prime locations in northern London near the University of Western Ontario (UWO) commands considerably higher prices.

- *Goods and Services.* Goods and services are priced near Canadian norms but are about 25 percent below U.S. averages. Utilities and medical care are particularly inexpensive by American standards.

- *Taxes.* The overall tax burden in London is near the Canadian average and about 30 percent higher than the U.S. average for people of moderate means. Federal and provincial income tax rates are modestly higher than in the U.S. but the combined federal and provincial sales tax on goods and services is twice the U.S. average. These high rates are somewhat offset by low property taxes and the low cost of medical care through OHIP.

Transportation	Rating: 5

London provides excellent intracity and intercity transportation. The good local street system is seldom overburdened and public transit is excellent. London Transit (LT) operates an all-bus system reaching all parts of the city. Service levels are good; most bus routes operate at 15- to 30-minute intervals on weekdays and a little less frequently on weekends. London ParaTransit provides the physically disabled with pre-booked, curb-to-curb service. You can travel to cities near and far by air, rail and bus. London International Airport provides direct flights to Pittsburgh, Toronto, Windsor/Detroit, Ottawa and Montreal. VIA Rail Canada provides frequent passenger service west to Windsor and east to Toronto. Good motor coach service links London with cities throughout Ontario.

Retail Services	Rating: 5

London has three major shopping malls, each with two or three anchor stores and nearly 200 specialty stores and service establishments. Westmont Mall, anchored by Sears and Zellers department stores, and White Oaks Mall, anchored by the Bay and Wal-Mart, are typical, large regional malls. Slightly upscale from these is Masonville Place, located not far from the University of Western Ontario (UWO) on the northern fringe of town. Masonville Place is anchored by the Bay, Sears and Zellers. It has a large cinema complex and three full-service restaurants, as well as a plethora of fast-food stands at its large food court. Downtown London, after years of decline, is now rebounding nicely. Funky Richmond Row has many restaurants and boutiques featuring clothing and gift items, local crafts and antiques. The Galleria, in the heart of downtown, is a rather eclectic indoor mall with specialty shops, movie theaters, restaurants and a UWO Centre for Continuing Studies, whereas Kingsmills is a delightful, old-fashioned upscale department store on Dundas Street.

Health Care	Rating: 5

London is one of Canada's premier centers for medical care. London Health Sciences Centre (LHSC), Victoria Campus is associated with the UWO medical school and is London's largest hospital. It offers virtually every medical specialty available in Ontario. Other hospitals include LHSC, University Campus, St. Joseph's Health Center, London Psychiatric Hospital and Thames Valley Children's Center. Parkwood Hospital specializes in holistic medicine.

Community Services

 Like most Canadian cities, London provides excellent basic public services and others oriented especially toward seniors. Five senior centers, including downtown's Horton Street Senior Centre, offer their patrons a wealth of activities and special events. Daily programs typically include exercise, tai chi, line and square dancing, arts and crafts, bowling, cards, bingo, darts, mini-golf and indoor swimming, among other activities. Special events include October-fest, Christmas dinner, a New Year's dance and day trips to Port Stanley on Lake Erie, Toronto and other nearby attractions.

Cultural and Educational Activities
Rating: 5

 The University of Western Ontario (UWO), with upwards of 30,000 students, is an important focus of culture and education in London and southwestern Ontario. The university's Continuing Studies Program fields a large selection of personal development courses on campus and at its handy downtown location in Galleria London. Courses of interest to seniors are not expensive and many offer senior discounts. The Faculty of Music at UWO presents a concert series from October through April, with programs ranging from symphonic works, chamber music and opera to jazz and band music. Concerts take place at several locations on campus at noon and evening and many are free. The UWO's Talbot Theatre serves as a venue for music, dance and drama. Live theater is also performed at the Grand, Old Factory and Palace Theatres downtown. Several venues in central London, including Centennial Hall and the new Central Library's Wolfe Auditorium, host a wide variety of musical choices by Orchestra London and other resident and visiting ensembles. Museum London is notable for its eclectic artistic and historic shows and for its London International Movie Series, which offers the best of foreign, Canadian and independent cinema, September through May.

Recreational Activities
Rating: 4

 Summer or winter, the London area provides plenty of diversions for participants and spectators alike. Three municipal golf courses with 18, 27 and 45 holes offer fine golf inexpensively. City parks, most notably Gibbons Park, Fanshawe Conservation Area, Greenway Park and Springbank Park, boast multiple opportunities for picnicking. London Parks and Recreation will even rent you picnic kits including equipment for baseball, soccer, volleyball and other recreational activities. The city's excellent network of pathways, especially the Thames Valley Parkway along the banks of the Thames River, provides perfect conditions—in season—for walking, jogging, cycling and inline skating. Year-round indoor swimming is possible daily at three community pools. In winter, you can ice skate at several municipal rinks and cross-country ski on trails blazed in several parks. Two small ski areas are close to town but better skiing can be found on the slopes of the Niagara Escarpment in the Georgian Bay region about 160 kilometers (100 miles) north. Popular spectator sports include minor league baseball and hockey, and varsity football and hockey played by the UWO Mustangs. Major league baseball, basketball, and hockey and CFL football, as well as a bounty of other cultural and recreational activities, are only two hours away in Toronto, Canada's entertainment capital.

London's dynamic economy provides many opportunities for paid and volunteer work. Part-time work is mostly in the service sector, especially in retailing. Volunteer work is readily available in schools, libraries, hospitals, museums, parks and in various public and private social service organizations.

Crime Rates and Public Safety   **Rating: 3**

 Crime rates are low to moderate in London. The property crime rate is 20 percent above Canadian and American norms but the city is comparatively safe from violent crime. The violent crime rate is 20 percent below the national average and approximately 50 percent below the average for the United States.

Conclusion

Overall Rating 51   Located on the Thames River and on major road and rail routes 200 kilometers (120 miles) southwest of Toronto, London is highly accessible to Canada's metropolis yet spared its congestion, air pollution and high cost of living. London has a broad profile of strengths and few weaknesses. The city is well run and livable, with excellent ratings in culture and education, community services, health care, retailing and transportation. Its cost of living is moderate by Canadian standards, low by American. Recreational choices are very good and Toronto's cultural and recreational bounty is nearby. Violent crime is low and the overall quality of life is outstanding. London's weaknesses are minor and are related to its physical geography and style. Although the built environment is well planned and maintained, there is no denying that London is built across an almost featureless plain. Winters there are cold and snowy and a few weeks every summer are hot and humid. And it lacks the excitement of some larger cities and college towns. On balance, though, London is a desirable place where you can afford to live well and in peace. For many people it would be an ideal choice.

Hanover–Lebanon, New Hampshire

Hanover–Lebanon, New Hampshire is also worth considering for retirement. Hanover is a beautiful little college town located on the eastern bank of the Connecticut River. Lebanon, just five miles south of Hanover, also offers an excellent quality of life but at a lower cost. The Green Mountains of Vermont lie a few miles to the west; the White Mountains of New Hampshire are a few miles to the east.

Hanover–Lebanon's strongest assets are its lovely physical landscape, outdoor recreation and the many cultural and educational amenities provided by Dartmouth College. The Green and White Mountains offer some of the best skiing in the eastern United States. Ten ski resorts lie within an hour's drive. In summer, one can canoe or kayak on the Connecticut River or hike the Appalachian Trail, which runs through Hanover. Classes at Dartmouth's Institute for Lifelong Education are inexpensive and the campus hosts several hundred concerts, films and plays each year. Other pluses include first-rate medical care at Dartmouth-Hitchcock Medical Center, excellent air quality, good public transit and low crime rates. The overall tax burden is low. New Hampshire does not tax sales or most income.

Hanover and Lebanon's principal weaknesses are their long, cold, cloudy winters, limited employment opportunities and, at least in Hanover, high housing costs. Some may be put off by the towns' small size-they are little more than villages. But don't be deceived; they have a lot to offer.

The Midwest Retirement Region

Climate: Humid continental

Place Description	Overall Rating	Page
Madison, Wisconsin	**48**	**75**
Madison's strongest assets are probably its gorgeous physical landscape, excellent quality of life and superb health care and community services.		
Bloomington, Indiana	**43**	**81**
Indiana University, the scenic hill country surrounding Bloomington, and the city itself offer an unbeatable combination of culture and recreation to suit every taste from grand opera and ballet to basketball and fishing.		

The Midwest Retirement Region occupies only a small part of the central states area sometimes described as America's Heartland or Middle West. Stretching roughly 400 miles from southeastern Wisconsin to southern Indiana, this small region belies the popular image of the Middle West as an uninteresting landscape of industrial cities and uniform farmland. Though farming and industry are important here (northern Illinois and Indiana are part of the rich Corn Belt agricultural region and Chicago is one of America's largest manufacturing centers) the choicest retirement spots are neither heavily industrial nor located in monotonous landscapes.

Madison, Wisconsin, capital of the state and home of the University of Wisconsin, and Bloomington, Indiana, site of the main campus of Indiana University, are the twin jewels of the Midwest Retirement Region. Occupying a rolling glaciated surface and embraced by four beautiful lakes, Madison experiences a fairly rigorous four-season climate and will appeal especially to those who enjoy both winter and summer recreation. Bloomington is located on a gently rolling plain surrounded by southern Indiana's scenic hill country. Warmer in all seasons than Madison, Bloomington is a little too mild for winter sports on natural snow and ice. Both cities offer the cultural and recreational amenities, services and high quality of life characteristic of the best Big Ten college towns.

Madison, Wisconsin

Little more than a place on a map when it was selected as territorial capital in 1838, Madison struggled along as a remote frontier village until Wisconsin attained statehood and established the University of Wisconsin in 1848. State government and higher education have been the twin pillars of the city's economy ever since. Even today the public sector is preeminent in Madison's economy. About one-quarter of Greater Madison's labor force, or more than 74,000 people, are employed in local, state or federal government jobs. The University of Wisconsin, ranked consistently as one of the nation's best public universities, has 40,000 students and more than 28,000 employees

Madison, Wisconsin

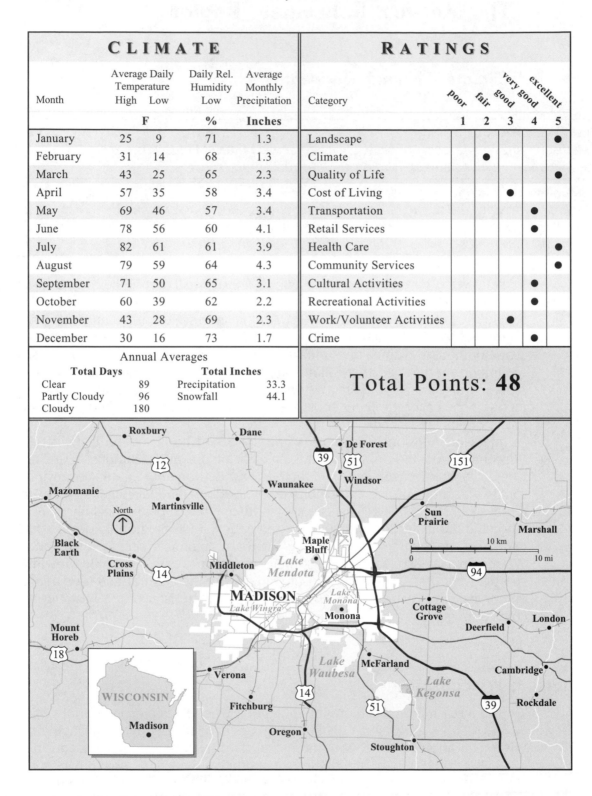

CLIMATE

Month	Average Daily Temperature High	Low	Daily Rel. Humidity Low	Average Monthly Precipitation
	F		%	Inches
January	25	9	71	1.3
February	31	14	68	1.3
March	43	25	65	2.3
April	57	35	58	3.4
May	69	46	57	3.4
June	78	56	60	4.1
July	82	61	61	3.9
August	79	59	64	4.3
September	71	50	65	3.1
October	60	39	62	2.2
November	43	28	69	2.3
December	30	16	73	1.7

Annual Averages

Total Days		Total Inches	
Clear	89	Precipitation	33.3
Partly Cloudy	96	Snowfall	44.1
Cloudy	180		

RATINGS

Category	poor 1	fair 2	good 3	very good 4	excellent 5
Landscape					●
Climate		●			
Quality of Life					●
Cost of Living			●		
Transportation				●	
Retail Services				●	
Health Care					●
Community Services					●
Cultural Activities				●	
Recreational Activities				●	
Work/Volunteer Activities			●		
Crime				●	

Total Points: 48

counting student workers at the university and its hospitals and clinics. Wisconsin's 1,000-acre campus, overlooking Lake Mendota, is one of the most beautiful in the country and nicely complements the impressive state capitol, one mile away. With a population of 215,000 in the city and 440,000 in the metropolitan area (Dane County), Madison is a lively and progressive town offering outstanding cultural and recreational amenities in an unspoiled environment.

Landscape — Rating: 5

 Centered on a natural isthmus between Lake Mendota and Lake Monona and extending around these and other smaller lakes, Madison occupies a magnificent site. The land, part of America's glaciated interior plains region, is gently rolling and well wooded with a mixture of broad-leafed deciduous trees—oak, maple and hickory—predominating. The lakes, with much of their shorelines occupied by upscale residences and parks, offer a scenic backdrop to the urban area. Proximity to Lake Mendota is one of the many charms of the University of Wisconsin. The lake is visible from most places on the campus, the union terrace overlooks it and the lovely lakeshore path traversed by students on their way to class parallels it. With its eclectic blend of neoclassical and modern architecture and its carefully landscaped grounds and plazas, the campus is a delight to eye and mind.

Climate — Rating: 2

 Madison's climate is a fairly severe variant of the humid continental climate found in the Middle West. Winters are long and cold; summers are relatively short but delightfully warm and sunny. Lying west of the Great Lakes, Madison is not as cloudy or snowy in winter as snowbelt cities like Cleveland and Buffalo but it is somewhat colder. Average annual snowfall is upwards of 40 inches and the ground is snow covered 60 percent of the time from mid-December through March. Rapid changes in weather are routine in all seasons, and precipitation is adequate with maximum amounts occurring in summer when it is most needed. On average, Madison is sunny 55 percent of the time, varying from 45 percent in winter to 66 percent in summer. The frost-free period averages 170 days, extending from late April through mid-October.

Quality of Life — Rating: 5

 Madison offers an excellent quality of life. Although there is some noise pollution from freeways and highways, the city's many trees buffer residential neighborhoods from much of it. Rush-hour traffic is moderately heavy in the city center where governmental and educational facilities are concentrated, and parking is tight downtown and on the university campus. Generally though, Madison's excellent road system and fine public transit allow easy access to area attractions. Air quality is excellent and the city is a model of good planning and progressive government. Most neighborhoods are architecturally interesting, well landscaped and maintained. Downtown's tree-lined State Street Mall, with its shops, restaurants, galleries and theaters, is a gem. An abundance of city parks and miles of bikeways and walking paths add to the city's peaceful ambiance.

Cost of Living — Rating: 3

The cost of living in Madison is evaluated as follows:

- *Composite.* ACCRA data show that the overall cost of living in Madison approximates the national average.

- *Housing.* According to ACCRA, housing costs are about 10 percent above the national average. Local sources and our exploration of the area suggest that Madison offers a good variety of resale housing at moderate prices. In Greater Madison, many attractive single-family residences with three bedrooms and two baths are priced between $150,000 and $225,000. Condominiums and smaller homes are available at lower prices. In general, Madison's slightly higher-than-average housing costs appear to reflect the area's better-than-average housing stock rather than a shortage of housing or any undue inflation of prices.

- *Goods and Services.* Goods and services are priced near national norms. Health care, utilities and miscellaneous goods and services are priced about 4 percent below their national averages whereas groceries and transportation are slightly above.

- *Taxes.* In a state known for the excellence of its public services, it is not surprising that the overall state and local tax burden is about 11.7 percent of income compared to the U.S. average of 9.7 percent. Property and income taxes are above national norms whereas sales and excise taxes are lower than average.

Transportation   Rating: 4

I-90 and I-94 skirt Madison on the east so most trips within the city are on two-lane and multi-lane surface streets. The excellent street and highway network is seldom overburdened. Although more auto trips than bicycle trips are made per day, the approximately 100,000 daily bicycle trips in summer significantly reduce traffic congestion and air pollution. Madison Metro Transit, with 140 buses, provides excellent local bus service focused on downtown and the University of Wisconsin. Metro Plus offers dial-a-ride service for the elderly and handicapped. Discounts are available to students and seniors. Dane County Airport, five miles northeast, is served by Northwest Airlines and six commuter carriers. Nonstop destinations include Chicago, Cincinnati, Cleveland, Dallas/Fort Worth, Denver, Detroit, Milwaukee, Minneapolis, New York, Pittsburgh and St. Louis. Bus service to many points is offered by Badger Coaches, Greyhound Bus Lines and Val Galder Bus Company. Daily Amtrak service east to Chicago and west to Seattle and Portland is available from Columbus, 25 miles east.

Retail Services   Rating: 4

Downtown Madison is in excellent shape with many attractive shops and restaurants, including a Land's End outlet store near the capitol. State Street Mall, a revitalized, pedestrian-friendly shopping street stretching from Capitol Square to the university campus, is a favorite of residents and visitors. Typical suburban shopping is available at Madison's twin malls: East Towne Mall, just west of I-40, and West Towne Mall, off Belt Line Highway near the western fringe of Madison. Each is anchored by Boston, JCPenney and Sears department stores and includes more than 100 specialty stores and services and a food court. Several Wal-Mart and Target discount stores are also found in outlying parts of the city.

Health Care   Rating: 5

Madison offers unusually excellent medical care, particularly for a relatively small city. The University of Wisconsin Hospital and Clinics, a research and teaching hospital of the University of Wisconsin Medical School, is a state-of-the-art facility providing the widest range of specialties and services. With 471 beds, it is the largest general hospital in Madison. Meriter Capital Hospital and St. Mary's Hospital Medical Center are only slightly smaller. Both also have a wide variety of specialties and services. William S. Middleton Memorial Hospital, a 99-bed facility, provides medical care for veterans.

Community Services   Rating: 5

Taxes are high in Madison but they do pay for excellent basic public services as well as those oriented toward seniors. The Madison Senior Center, located downtown, provides an unusual variety of services and activities free or at nominal cost. Classes in arts and crafts, computers and dancing are scheduled regularly, lectures are presented on topics such as travel and nutrition, a tai chi program occurs twice weekly and movies are shown twice monthly. The Senior Center cooperates with RSVP to recruit seniors for volunteer service and with AARP to provide tax assistance. Health screenings are provided periodically and noontime meals are hosted weekdays. Similar programs are offered at the Northside and Westside Senior Centers in suburban Madison.

Cultural and Educational Activities   Rating: 4

The University of Wisconsin, with more than 40,000 students from all over the world, is a vital center of education and culture. Its comprehensive continuing education program offers an enormous variety of credit and noncredit courses to the general public. Edgewood College, a small liberal arts institution, and Madison Area Technical College provide additional educational choices. All three institutions host a variety of theatrical performances, music and lectures.

The performing and visual arts are flourishing in Madison. The Civic Center with its Madison Art Center, the elegant 2,200-seat Oscar Mayer Theatre and the more intimate Isthmus Playhouse, home of Madison Repertory Theatre, are principal venues. A dozen other local live theater production companies are currently active including Broom Street Theater, one of the country's oldest and best experimental theaters. Additionally, several dance companies produce musical theater ranging from classical dance to jazz and tap dancing. Only 35 miles west in the village of Spring Green—site of Frank Lloyd Wright's home—Taliesin and his school of architecture, the American Players Theatre Company, performs Shakespeare and other classics outdoors in summer.

Madison is alive with the sound of music in countless informal and formal settings. You can stroll down State Street and listen to street musicians, walk up Bascom Hill to hear the ringing of the Carillon Tower bells, enjoy a summer evening on the capital lawn listening to the Wisconsin Chamber Orchestra's Concerts on the Square. At the Civic Center you can attend performances by the Madison Civic Opera, the Madison Symphony Orchestra, the Wisconsin Chamber Orchestra and Ballet Colbert. Various nightspots provide popular music and dancing nearly every night of the week.

The visual arts are showcased at several galleries and museums. The Madison Art Center contains three floors of changing exhibits of modern and contemporary art. The Elvehjem Museum of Art at the University of Wisconsin houses more than 15,000 works of art including American and European drawings, paintings, prints and sculpture, as well as ancient and Asian art.

Recreational Activities   Rating: 4

 Madison's changing seasons allow for all kinds of outdoor recreation. More than 21,000 acres of lakes and 150 parks and recreation areas in Greater Madison provide water recreation and dry-land activities. Boating, canoeing, sailing, water-skiing, fishing and swimming are popular in summer. Golf—which is played on more than 20 courses in Dane County, including 5 that are municipally operated—and biking, racquetball, roller skating and tennis have longer spring through autumn seasons. Biking is a major mode of transportation as well as a recreational activity in Madison. More than 150 miles of bike trails and routes encircle Lake Monona and crisscross the city. Winter activities are also understandably popular in this land of snow and ice. The lakes are normally frozen over from late December through late March, with ice fishing occurring in January and February. Ice skaters have 40 outdoor rinks to choose from, as well as the Hartmeyer Ice Arena. There are more than 100 miles of cross-country ski trails in Greater Madison, while several modest downhill ski areas are located within 50 miles of the city. The University of Wisconsin, a member of the Big Ten Conference, competes energetically in a variety of varsity sports. Madison's fans are typically enthusiastic and loyal, especially when supporting their football and hockey "Badgers." Like other top college towns, Madison boasts an unusually good selection of movie theaters and restaurants for its size. More than 20 kinds of ethnic restaurants are scattered throughout this increasingly diverse city. Those who prefer to do their own cooking throng to Saturday's massive but orderly farmers' market, May through October. One of the biggest and best farmers' markets in the country, Madison's sells everything from fresh produce to bratwurst, smoked trout and local cheese.

Work and Volunteer Activities   Rating: 3

 Madison's moderate economic and population growth in the 1990s, its preponderance of service sector jobs and an unemployment rate hovering around three percent annually all imply a favorable job market for seniors. However, the presence of 80,000 students, many of whom need to work while pursuing their education in a county of 440,000 people, does not. Competition for part-time jobs on campus and in retailing is especially acute. Plenty of opportunities, though, are available for volunteers in area schools, hospitals, libraries, museums and social service organizations. The local chapter of the RSVP is helpful in securing placements.

Crime Rates and Public Safety   Rating: 4

 Madison is one of the safest cities of its size. Crime rates are declining and the countywide property crime rate is now about 10 percent below the national average. The violent crime rate is only about 50 percent of the national rate and homicides are rare indeed.

Overall Rating 48

Greater Madison (Dane County) has several times been rated among the best places to live in America. Like every other place, though, Madison is not perfect for everyone. Some would find its winters too harsh, its taxes too high and its housing a bit expensive. But others would argue that these faults, if they are faults, are a small price to pay to live in such a wonderful place.

Madison's strongest assets are probably its gorgeous physical landscape, excellent quality of life and superb health care and community services. Embraced by four beautiful lakes and dotted with municipal parks, the city's residential areas are among the most attractive in North America. Attractive too are Capitol Square, the historic State Street pedestrian mall, and the University of Wisconsin campus. Madison also offers very good intercity and intracity transportation, good shopping, and a plethora of cultural and recreational choices commonly found only in much larger cities. Perhaps best of all, Madison is a safe, friendly and progressive community with a healthy mix of people and diversions. You will not be bored here.

Bloomington, Indiana

The home of Indiana University since 1820, Bloomington remains a classic Big Ten college town despite significant diversification of its economy over the years. The university physically and culturally dominates the community. Even though enrollment has grown to 38,000 students, much of the beautiful 1,850-acre campus retains the charm of an earlier age with historic and modern buildings secluded amidst gardens and woods. With a population of 70,000 (excluding students) in the city and 122,000 in Monroe County, Bloomington is a small place. But thanks to the university, it has more culture and recreation than most metropolitan areas and at bargain prices. Additional big-city assets are readily available in nearby Indianapolis, 50 miles north, and Cincinnati, 120 miles east.

Landscape   **Rating: 4**

Bloomington is situated at an elevation of 800 feet on the gently rolling Mitchell Plain, a porous limestone formation notable for its architectural-grade building stone, in south central Indiana. The rugged and forested hills and valleys of Brown County, with their several state and federal parks and forests, are a few miles east. A number of small lakes, including Lake Monroe and Lake Lemon, are within 10 miles of town. The area's natural vegetation is broad-leafed deciduous forest, with beech, maple, oak and ash predominating. The town and campus are attractively planted with these and other ornamental trees and shrubs.

Climate   **Rating: 3**

Bloomington has a humid continental climate with four distinct seasons including a long, warm to hot summer and a short, relatively mild winter. Although marked day-to-day weather changes are routine, Bloomington weather is, on average, a little sunnier and much less snowy in winter than that experienced in cities 200 miles north near the Great Lakes. Summers are typically sunny and warm, with episodes of hot, sultry weather

Bloomington, Indiana

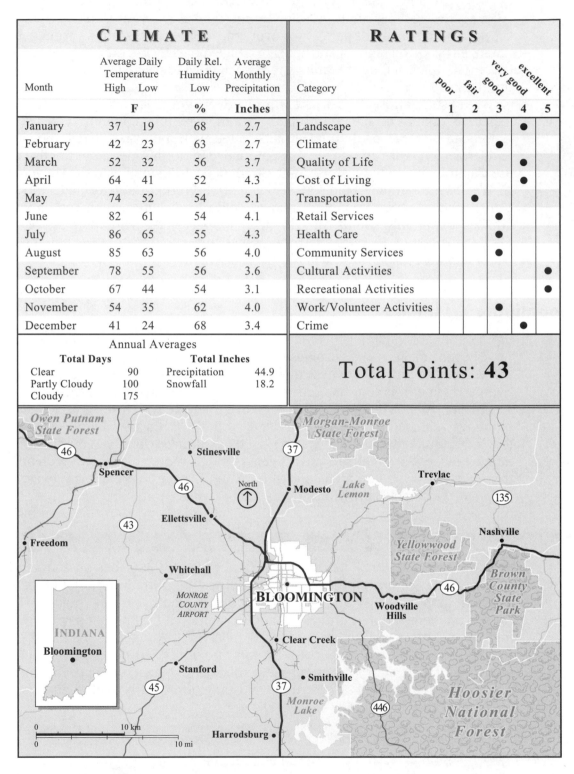

CLIMATE				
	Average Daily Temperature		Daily Rel. Humidity	Average Monthly
Month	High	Low	Low	Precipitation
	F		**%**	**Inches**
January	37	19	68	2.7
February	42	23	63	2.7
March	52	32	56	3.7
April	64	41	52	4.3
May	74	52	54	5.1
June	82	61	54	4.1
July	86	65	55	4.3
August	85	63	56	4.0
September	78	55	56	3.6
October	67	44	54	3.1
November	54	35	62	4.0
December	41	24	68	3.4

Annual Averages

Total Days		Total Inches	
Clear	90	Precipitation	44.9
Partly Cloudy	100	Snowfall	18.2
Cloudy	175		

RATINGS					
Category	poor	fair	good / very good	very good / excellent	excellent
	1	2	3	4	5
Landscape				●	
Climate			●		
Quality of Life				●	
Cost of Living				●	
Transportation		●			
Retail Services			●		
Health Care			●		
Community Services			●		
Cultural Activities					●
Recreational Activities					●
Work/Volunteer Activities			●		
Crime				●	

Total Points: 43

broken by the arrival of cooler and drier air from Canada. Spring and autumn weather is perhaps the most pleasant of the year with warm days balanced by cool nights. Bloomington is sunny about 55 percent of the time, varying from about 40 percent in winter to 70 percent in summer. The frost-free season lasts about 180 days and precipitation is well distributed throughout the year.

The quality of life is very good in Bloomington. There is no major airport nearby and no freeway so noise pollution is minimal except adjacent to the Highway 46 bypass. Air quality is excellent even though high humidity reduces visibility in summer. Parking is adequate in most places but is heavily restricted and tight on the central campus; here public transit and walking are recommended. Local manufacturing is dominated by relatively clean electrical goods and elevator production, and noxious industries are absent. Although Bloomington is not uniformly affluent, most neighborhoods are wooded, show pride of ownership and are served by an excellent network of city parks. Downtown's revitalized Courthouse Square and Kirkwood Avenue, which links it to the university, provide lively venues for walking, shopping and dining. The campus, ranked recently as one of the most beautiful in the nation, is a delight to the senses as one walks its meandering paths along the Jordan River, up and down hills and through the woods. Unfortunately, the university also generates heavy traffic at rush hour and during major sports events. This overwhelms the city's marginal road system creating transient but nightmarish knots of congestion.

Cost of Living   **Rating: 4**

 The cost of living in Bloomington is evaluated as follows:

- *Composite.* ACCRA data for Bloomington show a composite cost of living about 5 percent below the national average.

- *Housing.* According to ACCRA, housing costs are about 12 percent below the national average. Housing costs are kept down by low wage levels prevailing in Bloomington rather than by an abundance of new housing. Even Indiana University professors' salaries are lower than at many comparable flagship state universities. Service sector and industrial wages are also relatively low. Only a small proportion of housing in Bloomington itself is new although new subdivisions are being built beyond the city limits in Monroe and Brown counties. Resale homes of varied size, type and price are available but the market seems tight. Smaller houses are typically priced between $100,000 and $150,000 while luxury homes are priced upwards of $200,000. Condominiums are considerably cheaper.

- *Goods and Services.* Goods and services are generally priced near national norms. Groceries, transportation and miscellaneous goods and services are priced within 2 percent of their national averages whereas utilities and health care are about 10 percent below their national norms.

- *Taxes.* The overall state and local tax burden in Bloomington approximates the national average. Income taxes are above the national norm but sales, excise and property taxes are lower than average.

Transportation   **Rating: 2**

Transportation is perhaps Bloomington's weakest attribute. As yet no freeway connects it to Indianapolis and the local street network is marginal in the context of increasing traffic. Bloomington Transit provides good bus service to the campus community and to most parts of town via its nine routes. Nonetheless, most people drive everywhere except on the central campus where walking and public transit work better. Bloomington has a small commuter airport but Indianapolis International Airport, 50 miles north, is a better choice. It offers nonstop jet service to more than 35 destinations including major hubs at Atlanta, Chicago and St. Louis. Indianapolis also provides Amtrak service six times a week to Chicago and three times a week to Washington, D.C. Greyhound intercity bus service is available from Bloomington and Indianapolis, and the Bloomington Shuttle links Bloomington with Indianapolis International Airport.

Retail Services   Rating: 3

College Mall, located east of the university on 3rd Street, is the major regional mall. Anchored by L.S. Ayres, Sears and Target stores, College Mall also boasts more than 90 specialty shops and eateries. A health foods-oriented grocery store is nearby and a farmers' market is held Saturday mornings in the mall parking lot. Adjacent to College Mall are several additional shopping centers featuring grocery stores, specialty shops and restaurants. Scattered about the city are several smaller shopping centers typically anchored by supermarkets. A Wal-Mart is located in the southwest corner of town at the junction of Highways 37 and 45. Most interesting of all are the beautifully restored specialty stores and restaurants of the four blocks facing Courthouse Square downtown. Less than half a mile from the Sample Gates entrance to the Indiana University campus, this area has become popular with students and Bloomington residents in recent years.

Health Care   Rating: 3

Bloomington Hospital serves nine counties and is the largest health care facility in south central Indiana. With 355 beds in the hospital and more than 300 physicians on staff, Bloomington Hospital provides good medical care in a wide range of specialties. Cancer care and heart care including angioplasty, open-heart surgery and cardiac rehabilitation are particular emphases. A much greater variety of medical services is found only an hour away in Indianapolis. Its 19 accredited medical centers include 7 teaching hospitals, among which the Indiana University Medical Center is perhaps most renowned.

Community Services   Rating: 3

Basic community services are very good in Bloomington but most are not targeted specifically toward seniors. That said, the Bloomington Area Agency on Aging publishes several directories of special interest to seniors and provides referrals for legal, medical and personal assistance services. AARP and RSVP are also active in Bloomington, providing information and volunteer employment leads to seniors. A dozen or so social and fraternal organizations host socials, dances and other entertainment.

Cultural and Educational Activities   Rating: 5

Indiana University, with more than 38,000 students and 1,500 faculty members on the Bloomington campus, is the state's top liberal arts institution of higher learning. With more than 130 undergraduate majors and upwards of 320 other degree programs organized in 13 schools and colleges, the university is an enormous educational, cultural and recreational asset. Noncredit courses offered by the School of Continuing Education are open to Indiana residents at nominal cost and do not require formal admission to the university. Classes in arts and sciences, business, computer science, horticulture and other fields are typically offered. The university's internationally acclaimed School of Music fields a year-round program of ballet, opera and music at the Musical Art Center, a state-of-the-art concert hall completed in 1971. Additionally, concerts or recitals are presented nearly every day by various student and faculty ensembles of the School of Music. The Indiana University Auditorium, which seats up to 3,760 patrons, hosts a variety of touring Broadway shows, ballet and dance companies, international celebrities and other entertainment. Productions ranging from the classics to original plays by Indiana University students are presented each year in two campus theaters by the Department of Theater and Drama. Fortunately, all this culture is priced so reasonably that one can afford to partake of it several times a week all year long.

The visual arts are not neglected at Indiana University. Just across Fine Arts Plaza from the Auditorium is the university's stunning glass and concrete art museum, designed by I. M. Pei. Its permanent collection includes works by Matisse, Monet, Picasso, Rodin and Warhol. The museum also boasts an ancient and Asian gallery, as well as collections from Africa, the Americas and Oceania. Also located on Fine Arts Plaza is the Lilly Library, home of some of the world's rarest books and manuscripts. The collection includes a Gutenberg Bible and George Washington's letter accepting the Presidency. Nearby is Indiana University's Main Library, one of the finest university libraries in the United States.

Culture is not confined to the campus. The Waldron Art Center in downtown Bloomington is a focus of the visual arts. The Bloomington Playwright's Project produces new plays by playwrights from all over the country, Windfall Dancers perform a repertoire of modern and jazz dance and the Bloomington Symphony presents classical concerts. Several arts and crafts fairs are held annually, including the Fourth Street Festival on Labor Day weekend. Also in summer, plays are performed by the Indiana University Department of Theater and Drama to full houses at the historic Brown County Playhouse in the charming village and art colony of Nashville, 20 miles east of Bloomington.

Recreational Activities   Rating: 5

 Bloomington and surrounding area offer an excellent variety of recreational opportunities. The Bloomington Parks and Recreation Department operates 21 parks, 8 recreational facilities, a golf course and the Lake Griffy Natural Area. Parks and recreation facilities include baseball diamonds, basketball and tennis courts, sports fields, an indoor ice skating rink and two swimming pools. Upwards of 3,000 acres of woodland provide hiking and nature observation. Golfers can choose among three additional golf courses including Indiana University's championship course. The university also provides high-caliber sports events for fans of Big Ten competitions. Hoosiers basketball and football teams draw huge, enthusiastic crowds to their games at Assembly Hall and Memorial Stadium. Interest in soccer, swimming and diving, cross country and tennis competitions runs high, and the whole campus turns out for the Little 500, a 200-lap bicycle race made famous in the movie Breaking Away. Bloomington also offers 20 movie screens at 5 movie theater chains and several good restaurants serving inexpensive conventional and nouvelle American cuisine.

Within 20 miles of Bloomington, two lakes, two state parks, two state forests and Hoosier National Forest provide lovely scenery and many activities. Lake Lemon, a 1,650-acre lake nestled in the hills northeast of Bloomington and owned by the city, provides boat launching, canoeing, fishing, swimming and camping, as does the much larger Lake Monroe just southeast of town. Brown County State Park, 15 miles east of Bloomington, and McCormick's Creek State Park, 14 miles northwest, are good places for picnicking, camping, swimming and hiking, as are Morgan–Monroe and Yellowwood State Forests and Hoosier National Forest. Sightseeing by car or bike along the country roads of Monroe and Brown counties is delightful in all seasons but especially when the hillsides explode in autumn's colors.

Work and Volunteer Activities   Rating: 3

Competition for jobs in Bloomington's service-based economy is severe owing to the large student population. Even though unemployment remains relatively low, wages are likewise below average. Fortunately, low wages are balanced by a relatively low cost of living, so even low-paying part-time openings in retailing and service industries are snapped up. Volunteers serve in schools, in museums on and off campus, at Bloomington Hospital and Monroe County Library and in other public service areas. RSVP is helpful in finding the right niche.

Crime Rates and Public Safety   Rating: 4

Bloomington is one of America's safest mid-sized college towns and much safer than large metropolitan areas. Although the city's property crime rate approximates the national norm, the rate of violent crime is fully 70 percent below the national average. Residents perceive the community to be safe and it certainly feels that way as one walks downtown sidewalks or campus paths, daytime or evening.

Conclusion

Overall Rating 43 Often overlooked as a retirement town, perhaps because of its Midwest location and continental climate, Bloomington deserves better. In reality this small southern Indiana college town is one of America's best places for an active retirement. Indiana University, the scenic hill country surrounding Bloomington, and the city itself offer an unbeatable combination of culture and recreation to suit every taste from grand opera and ballet to basketball and fishing. The Indiana University campus is among the most beautiful in the land, while the town, with its mature, wooded residential areas and historic Courthouse Square, retains its small-town charm despite recent growth and downtown renovation. Shopping, health care, community services and work and volunteer opportunities are more than adequate.

Bloomington's modest transportation infrastructure results in considerable traffic congestion at rush hour and during special events at the university, but distances are short in town so the inconvenience is not too great. The bus system provides adequate service, crime is under control and the weather—although less than ideal in summer and winter—is rarely extremely hot or cold. All in all, Bloomington is a safe and friendly place that offers a plethora of cultural and recreational amenities at low cost. For many it would be an ideal place for retirement.

5   The Upper South Retirement Region

Climate: Humid subtropical

Place Description	Overall Rating	Page
Charlottesville, Virginia	**46**	**88**
Charlottesville is a beautiful college town offering many advantages for retirement. Its greatest strengths are its lovely landscape, high quality of life, excellent health care and plentiful recreational choices.		
Lexington, Virginia	**42**	**93**
Lexington is a perfect little college town. Its physical and human environment is nearly ideal. Its site in Virginia's beautiful Shenandoah Valley, within view of the Blue Ridge Mountains, is beautiful and its historic colleges and downtown are idyllic.		
Chapel Hill, North Carolina	**48**	**98**
Chapel Hill may not be the idyllic small college town that it was 30 years ago but it remains an exquisite city offering many advantages for retirement.		
Pinehurst–Southern Pines, North Carolina	**42**	**103**
The Sandhills region centered on Pinehurst and Southern Pines is an ideal retirement place for golfers and a very good one for devotees of outdoor recreation wishing to live in a fairly cosmopolitan small town.		
Asheville, North Carolina	**49**	**109**
Asheville ranks highly on most indicators of suitability for retirement; its principal weaknesses are moderate crime rates and a rather weak downtown.		
Hendersonville, North Carolina	**47**	**114**
Like its neighbor Brevard, Hendersonville is a highly desirable place for retirement for those wishing to live in a safe and friendly small city offering many amenities typical of much larger places		
Brevard, North Carolina	**46**	**119**
Brevard is a near-perfect place for retirement for those wishing to live in a charming, friendly and safe small town offering an abundance of amenities typically found only in much larger cities.		

The Upper South Retirement Region extends 400 miles inland from the Atlantic Coast of Virginia and North Carolina to the Blue Ridge Mountains. The heavily wooded mountains, fertile valleys and swift-flowing streams of the Blue Ridge provide lovely settings for the college town of Lexington, Virginia and the resort and retirement communities of Asheville, Hendersonville and Brevard, North Carolina. Between the Tidewater and Blue Ridge regions lies the gently rolling surface of the Piedmont Plateau and Inner Coastal Plain where Charlottesville, Virginia and Chapel Hill and Pinehurst–Southern Pines, North Carolina are sheltered from urban sprawl by surrounding farms and forests. Charlottesville and Chapel Hill are defined and dominated by the University of Virginia and the University of North Carolina, each the premier public university of their states. Both towns offer natural beauty, a high quality of life, excellent health care and plentiful service and leisure options. Pinehurst–Southern Pines is an ideal retirement spot for golfers.

Charlottesville, Virginia

Founded in 1762 by an Act of the Virginia General Assembly and named for Queen Charlotte, wife of King George III, Charlottesville has been steeped in history from colonial times. Its most famous son, Thomas Jefferson, founded and designed the University of Virginia, which remains to this day among the most beautiful of American college campuses and the center of life in Charlottesville. History also lives on at Monticello, Jefferson's home, just south of town, and at Court Square and the historic downtown area, which still constitute the legal and retail center for the city and Albemarle County. With a population of about 46,000 in the city and 81,000 in the county, the urban area is relatively small. But thanks to the university and its many resources, Charlottesville is able to offer residents an upscale and cosmopolitan way of life. Additional amenities typical of larger cities can be found in Richmond, 70 miles southeast, and Washington D.C., 120 miles northeast.

Landscape	Rating: 5

Charlottesville is located in central Virginia where the Piedmont Plateau meets the foothills of the Blue Ridge Mountains. Spread across a gently rolling surface with an average elevation of 600 feet, the city's landscape is very attractive with higher vantage points like Monticello providing gorgeous vistas of the Blue Ridge off to the west. A lush southern deciduous forest featuring oak, maple, elm and hickory trees envelops the city and its picturesque agricultural surroundings, which now include hundreds of acres of grape vines and numerous wineries. Residential areas in town exhibit many large magnolias as well as flowering shrubs such as azalea, camellia and rhododendron.

Climate	Rating: 3

Charlottesville has a temperate version of the Southeast's humid subtropical climate. Winters are mild for the latitude but summers are hot and humid. Precipitation averages 49 inches annually and is well distributed seasonally. About 24 inches of snow accumulates in the city in a normal winter, but much more falls in the Blue Ridge. Snow typically persists on the ground in town for only a few days at a time as cold waves are soon followed by warm spells. Average high temperatures vary from 48 degrees in winter to 86 degrees in summer; overnight lows are about 20 degrees lower. On average, Charlottesville is sunny about 60 percent of the time and enjoys a frost-free period of 210 days. Its principal climatic negative is summer's combination of heat and humidity. This results in discomfort and a hazy atmosphere that can hide the Blue Ridge from view. Weather conditions are much more pleasant in spring and autumn when temperature and relative humidity readings are lower.

Quality of Life	Rating: 5

Charlottesville provides an excellent quality of life. There is little noise from automobile traffic or airplanes and air quality is excellent. The city is uncrowded and there is little traffic congestion. Parking is

Charlottesville, Virginia

CLIMATE

Month	Average Daily Temperature High	Low	Daily Rel. Humidity Low	Average Monthly Precipitation
	F		%	Inches
January	45	26	53	3.7
February	49	29	50	3.3
March	58	36	48	4.1
April	69	45	45	3.3
May	76	54	51	4.9
June	84	62	53	4.5
July	88	66	53	4.9
August	86	64	56	4.1
September	80	58	57	4.9
October	70	47	52	4.2
November	59	39	52	3.7
December	49	30	54	3.3

Annual Averages

Total Days		Total Inches	
Clear	112	Precipitation	48.9
Partly Cloudy	107	Snowfall	24.2
Cloudy	147		

RATINGS

Category	poor 1	fair 2	good 3	very good 4	excellent 5
Landscape					●
Climate			●		
Quality of Life					●
Cost of Living		●			
Transportation			●		
Retail Services				●	
Health Care					●
Community Services				●	
Cultural Activities				●	
Recreational Activities					●
Work/Volunteer Activities			●		
Crime			●		

Total Points: 46

adequate downtown and at other major destinations; public transit use, especially by students, reduces pressure on the transportation infrastructure. The city seems well planned. Heavy industry is absent and the city is generally free of unsightly industrial areas. Most neighborhoods are well maintained and attractively landscaped, featuring a good variety of contemporary and historic homes. Commercial development is largely confined to downtown and the Highway 29 strip with its several malls. Downtown's historic Main Street business district, now a charming and vibrant pedestrian mall, is a triumph of good planning over three decades by the Charlottesville Downtown Foundation. It is a wonderful center for community life and, along with the University of Virginia, lends a unique character to the city.

Cost of Living   Rating: 2

 The cost of living in Charlottesville is evaluated as follows:

- **Composite.** ACCRA data show that the overall cost of living in Charlottesville is about 10 percent above the national average.

- **Housing.** Housing costs are about 16 percent above the national average but housing is not expensive considering its quality. The city has a good stock of houses of various styles in attractively landscaped neighborhoods.

- **Goods and Services.** ACCRA data suggest that the costs of most goods and services are above the national average. Groceries, transportation, utilities and miscellaneous goods and services are all priced 4 to 11 percent above national norms. In contrast, health care costs are now about 4 percent below the national average.

- **Taxes.** The state and local tax burden in Charlottesville is about 8.5 percent of income compared to the U.S. average of 9.7 percent. Property, sales and excise taxes are below national norms whereas income taxes are above average.

Transportation   Rating: 3

 Local travel is easy by car but public transit provides a viable alternative, especially to destinations downtown and at the University of Virginia. Charlottesville Transit System (CTS) and University Transit System (UTS) serve the wider community and the university community, respectively, but riders can transfer from one system to the other. CTS service is thin; buses operate 6:00 a.m. to midnight, six days a week, at hourly intervals. UTS operates seven days a week during the academic year but only on weekdays during summer and student holiday periods. Intercity rail service is exceptional, as Charlottesville is located on north–south and east–west lines. About 40 trains per week connect the city to destinations like Washington, New York, New Orleans and Chicago. Charlottesville–Albemarle Regional Airport offers commuter service to Charlotte, Cincinnati, New York La Guardia and Washington Dulles, among other locations.

Retail Services   Rating: 4

Charlottesville's historic downtown pedestrian mall, with its red brick promenade and historic Georgian-style buildings, is a wonderful place to shop. There you will find more than 150 stores, restaurants and galleries—mostly independently owned—and 2 movie theater complexes. Charlottesville Fashion Square, an indoor mall on Highway 29, is the city's largest mall. Anchored by Belk, JCPenney and Sears department stores, the mall also features about 70 specialty shops including many national chain stores, services and casual eateries. Also on Highway 29 are the upscale Barracks Road Shopping Center and freestanding Wal-Mart and Kmart discount stores.

Charlottesville is notable for the excellence of its medical care. The University of Virginia Health Sciences Center is one of the best academic medical centers in the nation. Its Health System, closely associated with the University of Virginia School of Medicine, is an integrated network of primary and secondary care offering services from wellness programs and routine checkups to the most technologically advanced care. Health System's more than 500-bed hospital and clinics throughout Charlottesville and neighboring counties attract patients from the local area, Virginia and the Southeast. Services provided include primary and emergency care, comprehensive cancer and cardiac care, women's health concerns and gastrointestinal care and neurology, among others. Also in Charlottesville is Martha Jefferson Hospital, a nonprofit community facility furnishing state-of-the-art health care services to central Virginia. Martha Jefferson's more than 200 physicians represent more than 30 specialties. Key services include cancer and cardiac care, critical care, diagnostics, endoscopy and rehabilitation.

Community Services   **Rating: 4**

Charlottesville and Albemarle County provide a good selection of community services to all age groups from children to seniors. Facilities and services of the Senior Center are available to anyone 55 or older. The center offers recreational and educational programs such as games, book reviews, music, travelogues, arts and crafts classes, and parties, picnics and out-of-town trips.

Cultural and Educational Activities   **Rating: 4**

The University of Virginia (UVA) and downtown Charlottesville are dual centers of culture and the arts. UVA's Cabell Hall Auditorium is the home of the Charlottesville and University Symphony Orchestra while Old Cabell Hall hosts a Tuesday Evening Concert Series. Plays produced by the university's Drama Department are performed on campus at the Culbreth Theatre. A thriving arts scene invigorates the downtown area with a wide range of theatrical and musical events. Lane Auditorium in the County Office Building and the Downtown Mall Amphitheater are major venues. The Charlottesville Municipal Band presents free winter and spring concerts in Lane Auditorium before moving to the Downtown Mall Amphitheater for its summer evening concert series. The Amphitheater is also home to summer's Fridays After Five concerts by various ensembles.

Charlottesville plays host to two major cultural events each year. The Virginia Festival of the Book and the Virginia Film Festival attract visitors from all over the state. Nearby Ashlawn–Highland, home of President James Monroe, hosts a Summer Festival of Opera and Musical Theatre in June, July and August, as well as other musical, dance and drama programs.

The University of Virginia and Piedmont Virginia Community College (PVCC) both offer comprehensive adult education programs. The university's School of Continuing Education fields a wide variety of credit and noncredit courses on topics ranging from computers to foreign languages and literature. PVCC also offers a wide variety of courses from art to technology. Seniors can audit PVCC courses at no charge or take them for credit for nominal fees.

Diverse recreational options exist in and near Charlottesville. Spectator sports and participatory activities are popular here. The Virginia Cavaliers regularly host nationally ranked intercollegiate teams in football and basketball. Both city and county have excellent park systems and recreational programs. Charlottesville's 25 parks cover 890 acres and boast 6 recreation centers. Amenities include playgrounds, picnic shelters, sports fields, gymnasiums, pools and a golf course. Albemarle County's 7 parks and 3 recreation centers cover approximately 2,000 acres. Their amenities include picnic shelters, nature trails and swimming and boating facilities. Golf can be played at UVA's Birdwood Golf Course, at Charlottesville's Meadow Creek Golf Course and at several other public, semi-private and private golf courses within a 30-mile radius of the city.

For a small city, Charlottesville has an excellent selection of movie theaters and restaurants. Quite a variety of cuisine, ranging from Brazilian and Indian to Colonial American, are available in settings as varied as the Historic Mitchie Tavern, the Downtown Mall and suburban shopping centers.

Within an hour's drive of town are numerous wineries, Shenandoah National Park and the Blue Ridge Parkway. The Monticello viticulture area, centered on Charlottesville, is now producing fine wines from European grape varieties formerly thought ill suited to the central Virginia environment. Many area wineries welcome visitors and offer facility tours and wine tasting. You can follow the Skyline Drive in Shenandoah National Park and the Blue Ridge Parkway southward along the crest of the Blue Ridge Mountains all the way to Great Smoky Mountains National Park in North Carolina. Scenic overlooks on both roads provide beautiful vistas of the mountains, the Shenandoah Valley and the upper Piedmont and easy access to many sites offering camping, hiking and picnicking in Shenandoah National Park and George Washington National Forest.

| Work and Volunteer Activities | Rating: 3 |

 Although local unemployment rates have been below the national average in recent years, seniors continue to face tough competition from college students for paid work. Volunteer work, though, is plentiful. Hospitals, libraries, schools, colleges and historic sites such as Monticello and Ashlawn–Highland depend heavily on volunteers.

| Crime Rates and Public Safety | Rating: 3 |

 Charlottesville's crime statistics are somewhat mixed. The metropolitan area has lower-than-average rates for violent and property crime but the situation in the City of Charlottesville is less satisfactory. In Charlottesville proper, the rate of violent crime is twice the national average while the property crime rate is at the national average. Upscale neighborhoods in the city and its surrounding areas appear quite safe.

| Conclusion |

 Overall Rating 46 Charlottesville is a beautiful college town offering many advantages for retirement. Its greatest strengths are its lovely landscape, high quality of life, excellent health care and plentiful recreational choices. Its temperate subtropical climate will appeal to those who appreciate experiencing four distinct seasons but wish to avoid winter's worst rigors. There is little traffic congestion. Residential neighborhoods and the downtown are appealing and air quality is excellent. The threat of earthquakes and hurricanes is very low, and tornadoes are infrequent in central Virginia. For a small city, Charlottesville provides an exceptional array of community and retail services, which are easily supplemented by the vast resources of nearby Richmond and Washington. Leisure activities to suit every taste are available in Charlottesville and nearby in the upper Piedmont and Blue Ridge Mountains, supplemented by big-city attractions only two hours away in Washington. Charlottesville's principal weaknesses are middling crime rates, limited work and air transportation choices, and a cost of living somewhat above the national average. Charlottesville rates as one of America's best small towns for a physically and mentally stimulating retirement.

Lexington, Virginia

The historic town of Lexington, with its beautifully restored and revitalized nineteenth century downtown, lovely residential neighborhoods and picturesque campuses, is an exquisite southern college town and an excellent site for retirement. Founded in 1777 as the county seat of Rockbridge County, the town owes much of its character and success to heroic figures like George Washington, Stonewall Jackson, Robert E. Lee and George Marshall, who once walked its streets. George Washington rescued Liberty Hall Academy (later to become Washington College) from financial oblivion in 1796 with a bequest of $50,000 and Robert E. Lee, as president of Washington College, revitalized the college during his 1865–1870 tenure. After his death in 1870, the institution was renamed Washington and Lee University. It has subsequently developed into one of America's outstanding small liberal arts colleges and is a vital center of cultural life in Lexington. Virginia Military Institute (VMI) is also significant in the history and intellectual life of Lexington. Thomas J. (Stonewall) Jackson was a professor at VMI prior to the Civil War, and that institution has educated thousands of citizen–soldiers over the years including George C. Marshall and George S. Patton.

With a population of just 7,000 in town and 34,000 in Rockbridge County, Lexington is a small town. But thanks to its colleges, it is able to offer residents an upscale and interesting lifestyle. Additional amenities are available in Charlottesville, 75 miles northeast, and in Washington, 190 miles away.

Landscape	Rating: 5

Lexington is located in west central Virginia on the gently rolling surface of the Shenandoah Valley. Bracketed by the Blue Ridge Mountains to the southeast and the Allegheny Mountains to the northwest, the Shenandoah Valley is a lovely, largely rural region offering easy access to some of the most scenic terrain in the eastern states. Lexington's site at an elevation of 1,100 feet is extraordinarily beautiful. The town is skirted by the Maury River and enveloped by woodlands and small farms. Its residential areas and the college campuses are nicely landscaped in a collage of lawns, flowers and seasonally flowering dogwood and redbud under a canopy of large trees such as oak, maple, magnolia and pine.

Lexington, Virginia

CLIMATE

Month	Average Daily Temperature High	Average Daily Temperature Low	Daily Rel. Humidity Low	Average Monthly Precipitation
	F		%	Inches
January	44	21	53	3.0
February	48	22	50	2.8
March	58	31	48	3.5
April	68	38	45	3.2
May	76	49	50	4.0
June	83	58	52	4.1
July	87	62	53	3.9
August	85	61	56	3.1
September	79	54	57	3.5
October	69	41	52	3.1
November	58	31	52	3.0
December	48	24	54	2.9

Annual Averages

Total Days		Total Inches	
Clear	105	Precipitation	40.0
Partly Cloudy	112	Snowfall	22.0
Cloudy	148		

RATINGS

Category	poor 1	fair 2	good 3	very good 4	excellent 5
Landscape					●
Climate			●		
Quality of Life					●
Cost of Living				●	
Transportation		●			
Retail Services		●			
Health Care		●			
Community Services			●		
Cultural Activities			●		
Recreational Activities					●
Work/Volunteer Activities			●		
Crime					●

Total Points: 42

Climate · **Rating: 3**

Lexington experiences an upland version of the Southeast's humid subtropical climate. Weather changes are frequent and sometimes dramatic in autumn, winter and spring, with steadier weather characterized by hot and humid conditions prevailing in summer. Spring and autumn are delightful with milder temperatures and somewhat lower humidity. On average, winter days are cool rather than severely cold. The annual precipitation of 40 inches is well distributed throughout the year. About 22 inches of snow falls in a typical winter but it seldom lasts more than a few days at a time on the ground. Lexington enjoys an average frost-free season of 180 days and is sunny about 60 percent of the time.

Quality of Life   Rating: 5

 Lexington is a delightful community noted for its excellent quality of life. There is little noise from aircraft or motor vehicles. I-64 and I-81 come within three miles of town and provide convenient access to points east, west, north and south, yet are far enough away so as not to disturb the tranquility. The town and Rockbridge County comply fully with all national air quality standards. Lexington is clean and uncrowded and there are no noxious industries. Parking appears adequate downtown and on the college campuses. The community is well planned and maintained. In the mid-1970s, the downtown streets were completely rebuilt, utility wires were put underground and brick sidewalks were installed in place of concrete. Meanwhile the Lexington Downtown Development Association restored and revitalized the retailing core. Currently, the entire downtown, Washington and Lee University, and VMI are listed in the National Register of Historic Places. And, thanks to the patronage of visitors and local residents, the charming downtown is economically thriving. Residents are particularly friendly and helpful even by the standards of other small college towns, and the uniformly polite greeting from VMI cadets is refreshing indeed.

Cost of Living   Rating: 4

 The cost of living in Lexington is evaluated as follows:

- *Composite.* ACCRA data show that the overall cost of living in Lexington is modestly below the national average.

- *Housing.* Housing costs are about 6 percent above the national average. Many attractive homes with three or four bedrooms and two baths are priced between $150,000 and $255,000. Prices are somewhat lower in nearby Buena Vista and in the surrounding countryside.

- *Goods and Services.* ACCRA data suggest that in Lexington most categories of goods and services are priced modestly below national norms. Costs of miscellaneous goods and services are just below the national average, whereas groceries, transportation and health care are priced 5 to 12 percent below their national norms. Costs of utilities are about 6 percent above the national average.

- *Taxes.* The state and local tax burden in Lexington is about 8.5 percent of income compared to the U.S. average of 9.7 percent. Property, sales and excise taxes are below national norms whereas income taxes are above average.

Transportation | Rating: 2

Although the private automobile dominates local transportation, the town is small enough that walking and bicycling are viable alternatives for many trips. There is no local bus service. I-64 and I-81 intersect about three miles east of town, providing convenient access to Roanoke, Charlottesville and Washington, among other locations. Greyhound bus service is available in Buena Vista. Amtrak trains stop in Clifton Forge, 30 miles west, and in Staunton, 40 miles north. Three trains per week travel west to Chicago and three east to Charlottesville and Washington. Additional northbound and southbound trains serve Charlottesville. Roanoke Woodrum Regional Airport, 50 miles south, provides nonstop jet service to four destinations including major hubs in Atlanta, Charlotte and Pittsburgh. Nonstop commuter destinations include Detroit and Washington.

Retail Services | Rating: 2

Lexington's charming downtown features a wide variety of unique shops, restaurants and services, many housed in magnificently restored historic buildings. Several bookstores, antique shops and specialty food stores grace the downtown. Other shops stock gifts, original art, prints and posters, college merchandise, sporting goods, and men and women's clothing. Typical mass merchandise may be bought at the local Wal-Mart on Highway 11, two miles north of town.

Health Care | Rating: 2

Stonewall Jackson Hospital, a community nonprofit facility with 38 beds and about 30 physicians on staff, provides primary health care services. Specialties provided include emergency services, family medicine, internal medicine, general surgery, ophthalmology, orthopedics, radiology and obstetrics/gynecology. Substantially greater medical care assets are available in Charlottesville, 75 miles northeast, and Roanoke, 55 miles south.

Community Services | Rating: 3

Basic public services are more than adequate. The Rockbridge Regional Library, headquartered in Lexington, is complemented by the college libraries, which are also open to the public. The colleges and various clubs and social organizations including the Jaycees, Lions Club, Rotary, Kiwanis, art and history clubs, and garden and social clubs offer members and guests a good mix of services.

Cultural and Educational Activities | Rating: 3

Life in Lexington is significantly enhanced by the presence of two excellent colleges. Washington and Lee University is the ninth oldest institution of higher learning in the country and one of the strongest liberal arts colleges. Adjacent to its picturesque white colonnaded, red brick buildings and grounds is the expansive campus and parade ground of the Virginia Military Institute, the nation's oldest state-supported military college and fourth oldest technical college. Senior residents of Lexington may audit classes at Washington and Lee and attend summer session at VMI.

Concerts and plays are performed regularly by students, faculty and local and visiting artists at Washington and Lee's splendid Lenfest Center. Both colleges also sponsor numerous lectures free to the public. All summer long much of Lexington's culture moves outdoors. On the western edge of town, the professional Theater at Lime Kiln presents regional theater and music under the stars, May through October, and moves productions indoors to the Troubadour Theater downtown between November and April. Lexington's Davidson Park is the scene of Friday evening "Lexington Alive" concerts, while every two or three weeks in summer "Fridays in the Park" concerts are held in Glen Maury Park in nearby Buena Vista.

Recreational Activities   Rating: 5

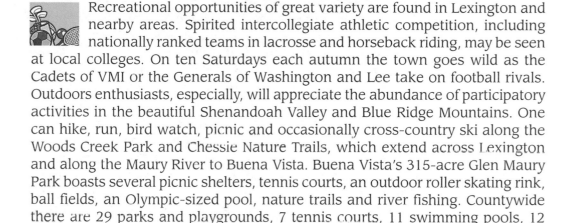 Recreational opportunities of great variety are found in Lexington and nearby areas. Spirited intercollegiate athletic competition, including nationally ranked teams in lacrosse and horseback riding, may be seen at local colleges. On ten Saturdays each autumn the town goes wild as the Cadets of VMI or the Generals of Washington and Lee take on football rivals. Outdoors enthusiasts, especially, will appreciate the abundance of participatory activities in the beautiful Shenandoah Valley and Blue Ridge Mountains. One can hike, run, bird watch, picnic and occasionally cross-country ski along the Woods Creek Park and Chessie Nature Trails, which extend across Lexington and along the Maury River to Buena Vista. Buena Vista's 315-acre Glen Maury Park boasts several picnic shelters, tennis courts, an outdoor roller skating rink, ball fields, an Olympic-sized pool, nature trails and river fishing. Countywide there are 29 parks and playgrounds, 7 tennis courts, 11 swimming pools, 12 campgrounds and 18 picnicking sites. Golf can be played at the Lexington Golf and Country Club. The Virginia Horse Center, a nationally renowned equestrian facility, lies just north of town. You can canoe on the Maury River and ten miles east drive the Blue Ridge Parkway, which offers spectacular vistas of the Shenandoah Valley and the Piedmont Plateau and easy access to the hiking, swimming, camping and other recreational resources of George Washington and Jefferson National Forests.

Historically significant attractions are also plentiful in Lexington and Rockbridge County. Within a 20-mile radius are Natural Bridge, once owned by Thomas Jefferson, and the Cyrus McCormick Farm, with its restored blacksmith shop, gristmill and museum.

The best-known sites in Lexington itself include Lee Chapel and Museum on the Washington and Lee University campus, the VMI and George Marshall museums at VMI, and the Rockbridge Historical Society and Stonewall Jackson House, downtown. Indeed, the college campuses and downtown Lexington are themselves historically and architecturally notable. Downtown also features a variety of dining experiences from informal sandwich and pub fare to full-course restaurant meals in gracious pre-Civil War buildings.

Work and Volunteer Activities   Rating: 3

In recent years, unemployment rates in Lexington and Rockbridge County have been well below the national average. Even so, paid employment opportunities are limited by the small size of the local economy. Retailers, especially Wal-Mart and Lowes, employ some seniors. Many others find satisfaction in volunteer activities. Stonewall Jackson Hospital depends heavily on its 200 volunteers, as do the community's several educational institutions, cultural organizations, museums and libraries. Lexington's excellent visitor center is also staffed largely by energetic and helpful retirees.

Lexington and Rockbridge County are too small to be listed in the FBI's annual report *Crime in the United States*. Crime data from the local police department confirm that the incidence of property and violent crime in the town and the county are well below nation norms. Lexington, particularly, feels safe and secure, night or day.

Conclusion

Overall Rating 42 Lexington is a perfect little college town. Its physical and human environment is nearly ideal. Its site in Virginia's beautiful Shenandoah Valley, within view of the Blue Ridge Mountains, is beautiful and its historic colleges and downtown are idyllic. The valley's upland variant of the humid subtropical climate, with four distinct seasons and few severely hot or cold days, will appeal to many. Lexington's quality of life is excellent; it is clean, uncrowded and peaceful and its residents are unusually friendly and well educated. For a small town, the availability of community services, culture, recreation, work and volunteer activities is quite good. The community is relatively free of crime, and living costs are low. Only the town's modest endowment of retail and health care services and the absence of public transit and a commercial airport detract from its otherwise high rating. If you are open to retirement in a special college town amidst the natural beauty and recreational assets of the Shenandoah Valley and Blue Ridge Mountains, give Lexington a careful look.

Chapel Hill, North Carolina

Described beautifully in Thomas Wolfe's classic autobiographical novel *Look Homeward Angel,* Chapel Hill remains one of America's exquisite smaller cities and an excellent place for an active retirement. Founded in 1795 as the home of the University of North Carolina (UNC), the nation's first state university, Chapel Hill's civic life is very much intertwined with that of the academic community. The square-mile campus, with its Georgian-style red brick buildings linked by brick paths and surrounded by wooded and grassy landscapes, dominates the town. The university provides educational, cultural and recreational opportunities galore and some of the best medical facilities in the United States. Downtown Chapel Hill, which stretches along Franklin Street where it parallels the campus, is one of the most vibrant downtowns in America and a delightful place to shop, dine or be entertained. With a population of about 50,000 in Chapel Hill itself, about 17,000 in adjacent Carrboro and 121,000 in Orange County, the city and its surrounding areas are much busier than they were 30 years ago. Even so, Chapel Hill residents would argue that their community continues to offer the best of small-town life in a highly cosmopolitan environment.

| Landscape | Rating: 4 |

Chapel Hill is located toward the eastern edge of the Piedmont Plateau in the central part of North Carolina. Spread across a gently to steeply rolling surface with an average elevation of 500 feet, the city is so heavily wooded that in some neighborhoods little sunlight reaches the ground when the trees are in leaf. Much of the city is sheltered by a canopy of large

Chapel Hill, North Carolina

CLIMATE

Month	Average Daily Temperature High	Average Daily Temperature Low	Daily Rel. Humidity Low	Average Monthly Precipitation
	F		%	Inches
January	49	27	55	4.4
February	53	29	52	3.6
March	62	37	49	4.5
April	71	45	45	3.2
May	78	54	54	4.4
June	85	62	56	4.0
July	89	66	58	4.0
August	87	65	60	4.5
September	81	58	59	4.5
October	71	45	53	3.7
November	62	37	52	3.6
December	53	30	55	3.2

Annual Averages

Total Days		Total Inches	
Clear	111	Precipitation	47.6
Partly Cloudy	106	Snowfall	5.2
Cloudy	148		

RATINGS

Category	poor 1	fair 2	good 3	very good 4	excellent 5
Landscape				●	
Climate			●		
Quality of Life					●
Cost of Living		●			
Transportation					●
Retail Services			●		
Health Care					●
Community Services					●
Cultural Activities					●
Recreational Activities					●
Work/Volunteer Activities			●		
Crime			●		

Total Points: 48

deciduous trees including oak, maple and hickory, while suburban areas are enveloped in a pine forest. Flowering shrubs such as dogwood and azalea are characteristic understory plantings.

Climate Rating: 3

 Chapel Hill experiences a fairly mild variant of the Southeast's humid subtropical climate. Winter weather is cool and quite variable from day to day, whereas summer weather is relatively steady with average highs in the upper-80s and average lows in the mid-60s. Spring and autumn are the most pleasant seasons, with mild to warm days and cool nights. Annual precipitation averages 48 inches and is well distributed throughout the year. Only five inches of snow accumulates in a normal winter and snow seldom persists on the ground for more than a few days. On average, Chapel Hill is sunny approximately 60 percent of the time and enjoys a frost-free period of about 200 days. The city's principal climatic negative is summer's fatiguing combination of heat and humidity. In contrast, weather conditions are nearly ideal in spring and autumn when temperature and relative humidity readings are lower.

Quality of Life Rating: 5

 Chapel Hill is notable for its excellent quality of life. Although there is some aircraft noise from the local airport and automotive noise from the traffic along the U.S. 15–501 bypass, noise levels are not excessive. Traffic congestion is increasing downtown and on the Carolina campus, and parking is tight. Fortunately, Chapel Hill's excellent public transit allows bus riders to escape driving and parking hassles. The city and campus are well planned and maintained and no heavy industry blights the landscape. Even so, the EPA designates Chapel Hill as a "basic non-attainment area" for air quality. The city is minimally out of compliance with air quality standards and frequently experiences light smog, especially in summer. Local shopping malls are wisely located on the periphery of town so as not to disrupt the village atmosphere of the traditional downtown, yet are easily accessed by car or public transportation. Residential neighborhoods are distinctly upscale and feature a good variety of housing from historic brick or frame dwellings near the city center to sprawling, brick ranch-style houses on the edge of town, all on wooded or carefully landscaped lots. Although Chapel Hill is not as quiet or peaceful as it was 20 or 30 years ago, its residents seem as friendly and well educated as ever, and they are very content with their lifestyle.

Cost of Living Rating: 2

 The cost of living in Chapel Hill is evaluated as follows:

- *Composite.* ACCRA data show that the overall cost of living in Chapel Hill is about 15 percent above the national average and about 18 percent above that of nearby Raleigh and Durham.

- *Housing.* Housing costs have risen sharply in Chapel Hill in recent years and are now about 25 percent above the national average. Most middle-class housing is priced between $250,000 and $400,000. Such high prices reflect the high quality of Chapel Hill houses and the prestige value of the community. Comparable housing is available in the Raleigh-Durham area for perhaps 30 percent less.

- *Goods and Services.* ACCRA data indicate that most goods and services are rather expensive in Chapel Hill. Although transportation is priced at the national average, groceries, health care and miscellaneous goods and services are all priced 5 to 12 percent above the national average. Utilities costs have risen sharply during the past few years and are now 20 percent above the national average.

- *Taxes.* The state and local tax burden in Chapel Hill is about 10.1 percent of income compared to the U.S. average of 9.7 percent. Property, sales and excise taxes are somewhat below national norms whereas income taxes are well above average.

Transportation   Rating: 5

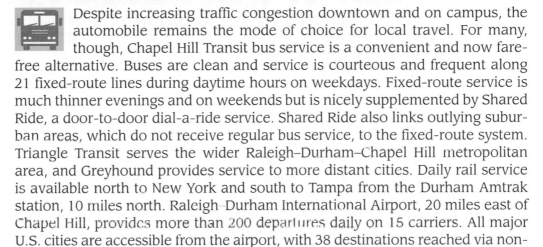

Despite increasing traffic congestion downtown and on campus, the automobile remains the mode of choice for local travel. For many, though, Chapel Hill Transit bus service is a convenient and now fare-free alternative. Buses are clean and service is courteous and frequent along 21 fixed-route lines during daytime hours on weekdays. Fixed-route service is much thinner evenings and on weekends but is nicely supplemented by Shared Ride, a door-to-door dial-a-ride service. Shared Ride also links outlying suburban areas, which do not receive regular bus service, to the fixed-route system. Triangle Transit serves the wider Raleigh–Durham–Chapel Hill metropolitan area, and Greyhound provides service to more distant cities. Daily rail service is available north to New York and south to Tampa from the Durham Amtrak station, 10 miles north. Raleigh–Durham International Airport, 20 miles east of Chapel Hill, provides more than 200 departures daily on 15 carriers. All major U.S. cities are accessible from the airport, with 38 destinations reached via non-stop flights.

Retail Services   Rating: 3

The downtown areas of Chapel Hill and neighboring Carrboro are busy and exciting places despite competition from suburban malls and shopping centers. At all hours Franklin Street is alive with people strolling, shopping, dining and enjoying popular entertainment. Carr Mill Mall and Weaver Street Market, notable for its specialty shops and large upscale grocery, is also popular. University Mall, on South Estes Drive, is Chapel Hill's largest shopping center. Anchored by A Southern Season, an exquisite 59,000-square-foot gourmet specialty store, and Dillard's, the mall includes art galleries, national chain stores, specialty stores and other unique shops. A farmers' market operates on Saturdays, from March through December, and on Wednesdays, from April through October, in downtown Carrboro.

Health Care   Rating: 5

Chapel Hill is justifiably renowned for the excellence of its medical care. The University of North Carolina (UNC) Hospitals include North Carolina Children's Hospital, North Carolina Memorial Hospital, North Carolina Neurosciences Hospital and North Carolina Women's Hospital. With 668 beds, 550 resident physicians and 983 attending physicians, UNC Hospitals make up an outstanding teaching facility offering comprehensive health care services. Only 10 miles away in Durham is the outstanding Duke University Medical Center, noted especially for cardiac care and surgery. A large VA hospital is also located in Durham.

Community Services   Rating: 5

 Chapel Hill, Carrboro and Orange County provide an excellent array of community services. Organizations such as RSVP, Welcome Wagon and Newcomers Club help new residents feel at home. Senior centers operate in Chapel Hill, Carrboro and Hillsborough in Orange County, and at numerous locations in the Raleigh–Durham area. Their programs include athletic and recreational activities, arts and crafts classes and workshops, and travel.

Cultural and Educational Activities   Rating: 5

 The University of North Carolina, with 24,000 students and 2,400 faculty members, is the focus of culture and education in Chapel Hill. Its 1,600-seat Memorial Hall is home to the Carolina Union Performing Arts Series, which features musical concerts, musical theater and dance. The Carolina Union also hosts concerts, lectures and art exhibits in smaller performance venues at its campus facility. The UNC Departments of Music and Dramatic Art contribute much to community cultural life. The Music Department, one of the best in the country, sponsors a series of concerts showcasing classical music at Hill Hall and Person Hall. PlayMakers Repertory Company, a nationally recognized program of the Dramatic Art Department, presents six productions each academic year at the Paul Green Theatre on campus. Additional theatrical and musical events are offered in the intimate setting of the 300-seat Arts Center Theater in Carrboro, and the North Carolina Symphony pays frequent visits to Chapel Hill. Nearby venues in Raleigh and Durham, most notably those at Duke University, also schedule major performing arts series.

The visual arts are not neglected. The University's Ackland Art Museum's permanent collection exhibits Western art from the classical to contemporary eras, as well as the art of Africa and Asia. The Morehead Planetarium and Science Center offers indoor astronomy, scientific exhibits and lectures, and an art gallery. Art exhibits may also be seen at the historic Horace Williams House downtown and at many privately owned galleries in Chapel Hill and Carrboro.

The university has much to offer educationally whether attendees enroll in a course or program. Its exceptional five million-volume library system is open to retirees, as are public lectures and symposia. In addition to regular academic programs, which are not expensive for state residents, seniors have access to classes on a wide variety of subjects at bargain prices through the Carolina College for Lifelong Learning.

Recreational Activities   Rating: 5

 Whether your sports and recreational interests are passive or active, Chapel Hill and its surrounding areas have opportunities for everyone. UNC is a member of the NCAA's Atlantic Coast Conference, fielding 28 varsity teams in women's and men's intercollegiate sports. The Carolina Tar Heels football and basketball teams regularly pack the house at Kenan Stadium and Dean E. Smith Center. Chapel Hill and Carrboro have excellent parks and recreation facilities; neighboring communities provide additional resources. Chapel Hill's 14 parks contain picnic areas, play equipment, nature trails, athletic fields, lighted tennis courts, recreation centers, indoor and outdoor pools, and volleyball courts. The Parks and Recreation Department sponsors a summer outdoor concert and movie series and two big street fairs—Apple Chill in April and Festifall in October. Carrboro's eight parks and recreation facilities provide picnic shelters and playgrounds, athletic fields, and basketball and tennis courts. The Chapel Hill–Carrboro YMCA boasts an Olympic-sized indoor pool and numerous other athletic facilities. Just outside of town you can boat and fish at beautiful University Lake or enjoy a wider range of water sports at B. Everett Jordan Reservoir. Golf is played at the university's Finley Golf Course or at several other public courses within a 20-mile radius of Chapel Hill. Ice skating is available all year at the Triangle SportsPlex in Hillsborough.

Chapel Hill is remarkable for its fine selection of excellent restaurants and movie houses. Several are clustered downtown on or just off Franklin Street; others are located at several of the city's smaller shopping centers. Restaurants offer a good variety of cuisines, from regional American to North Italian and Chinese.

Work and Volunteer Activities   Rating: 3

Although the local economy is strong and unemployment is low, retirees face severe competition from thousands of college students for paid work. Consequently, many older adults join local senior centers or get involved by volunteering. The YMCA, SCORE, local libraries, North Carolina Botanical Gardens, UNC Hospitals and RSVP are among the many organizations dependent on volunteers.

Crime Rates and Public Safety   Rating: 3

Crime rates are moderate in Chapel Hill. The city's violent crime is about 5 percent below the national average while the property crime rate exceeds the national average by 25 percent. A high rate of larceny-theft largely accounts for the high property crime rate; rates for burglary and auto theft are near or below national norms.

Conclusion

Overall Rating 48 Chapel Hill may not be the idyllic small college town that it was 30 years ago but it remains an exquisite city offering many advantages for retirement. Its wooded landscape is pleasing to the eye and the community earns excellent ratings in quality of life, transportation, health care, community services and leisure activities. Residential neighborhoods, the downtown commercial core and the UNC campus are attractive. Although some may find summer's heat, humidity and occasional light smog oppressive, most appreciate the mildness of the other seasons. The city's principal weaknesses are its middling crime rates, modest endowments of retail services and part-time work opportunities for seniors, and a rather high cost of living. Assuming you can afford to live here, though, Chapel Hill is one of America's best choices for an active and rewarding retirement.

Pinehurst–Southern Pines, North Carolina

Referred to as the Pine Barrens by Scottish settlers who managed to eke out a meager living farming its poor, sandy soils during the eighteenth century, the Sandhills region centered on Pinehurst and Southern Pines has developed into a major resort and retirement center during the last 100 years. Attracted by the mild winter weather and good rail service, John Patrick founded Southern Pines as a health resort in 1887. Pinehurst was established as a winter

Pinehurst-Southern Pines, North Carolina

CLIMATE

Month	Average Daily Temperature High	Low	Daily Rel. Humidity Low	Average Monthly Precipitation
	F		%	Inches
January	52	32	51	4.5
February	59	35	50	4.0
March	67	41	48	5.2
April	75	47	45	3.6
May	81	55	50	5.3
June	87	62	48	4.6
July	89	66	56	5.0
August	88	66	58	4.6
September	83	60	55	4.1
October	74	49	51	3.7
November	61	38	52	3.0
December	56	34	51	4.5

Annual Averages

Total Days		Total Inches	
Clear	112	Precipitation	51.8
Partly Cloudy	106	Snowfall	5.6
Cloudy	147		

RATINGS

Category	poor 1	fair 2	good 3	very good 4	excellent 5
Landscape				●	
Climate			●		
Quality of Life					●
Cost of Living			●		
Transportation		●			
Retail Services		●			
Health Care				●	
Community Services				●	
Cultural Activities			●		
Recreational Activities				●	
Work/Volunteer Activities				●	
Crime				●	

Total Points: 42

resort in 1895 by Boston philanthropist James Tufts, who hired famed landscape architect Frederick Law Olmsted to design the village's New England-style layout, and a young Scot, Donald Ross, to design Pinehurst's first golf course. Their inspired designs helped define Pinehurst particularly, and the Sandhills area generally, as one of America's classic resort and retirement communities.

With a population of about 10,500 in Pinehurst, 11,500 in Southern Pines and 79,000 in Moore County, Pinehurst–Southern Pines today boasts more than 40 golf courses, many of championship caliber, and a plethora of other recreational attractions including tennis, horseback riding, polo, hiking and biking. Shopping in the villages' charming downtowns and at the local mall is adequate for day-to-day needs, and the amenities of the Raleigh–Durham–Chapel Hill metropolitan area are only 70 miles away.

Landscape · Rating: 4

Pinehurst–Southern Pines is located in the Sandhills toward the western edge of North Carolina's Coastal Plain. Named for their deep sandy soils and gently rolling landscape, the Sandhills region is higher and better drained than most parts of the Coastal Plain. Rain disappears quickly into the sands so the environment seems relatively dry even though annual precipitation totals nearly 50 inches. Much of the landscape is mantled in a longleaf pine forest that also includes seasonally colorful magnolia, azalea, camellia, dogwood, holly, and other flowering trees and shrubs.

Climate · Rating: 3

Good air and water drainage modify the humid subtropical climate, making it somewhat milder and drier than in surrounding areas. Winter weather is quite variable from day to day but is usually mild enough for golf. Summer's combination of heat and humidity, though, discourages afternoon play. Spring and autumn are nearly perfect, with warm days followed by cool nights. Annual precipitation averages 52 inches and is fairly evenly distributed throughout the year. Less than six inches of snow accumulates in a typical winter and generally melts within a day or so. On average, the Sandhills area is sunny about 60 percent of the time and has a frost-free period of about 215 days. The region's principal climatic negative is summer's fatiguing, hot humid weather. On the other hand, weather conditions are very pleasant in spring and autumn when moderate temperatures and humidity prevail.

Quality of Life · Rating: 5

The quality of life in the Sandhills region is excellent. Pinehurst and Southern Pines are both quiet with little noise from road or air traffic. Air quality is excellent and the low population density, good urban design and absence of heavy industry contribute to uncrowded streets except during major golf tournaments. The park-like atmosphere of the towns is pronounced, especially in the uniformly affluent Pinehurst, which reminds one of much more expensive Carmel, California. In both communities, a good variety of historic and contemporary housing lines well-wooded streets surrounding the village centers. Pinehurst's central core, with Olmsted's complex of looping tree-lined streets converging on the village shopping district, is uniquely charming, but the traditional downtown and grid pattern residential area of Southern Pines are also attractive. Residents and visitors tend to be affluent, well mannered and friendly. Both communities are enviably peaceful and free of the stresses commonly associated with urban areas.

The cost of living in Pinehurst–Southern Pines is evaluated as follows:

- *Composite.* No ACCRA data are available for the Sandhills region but inferences can be drawn from ACCRA data for nearby cities such as Raleigh and Durham. Additional data were gathered from field observations and local sources. On these bases, I estimate that the overall cost of living in Pinehurst–Southern Pines approximates the national average.

- *Housing.* Exploration of the area reveals a moderate supply of housing of varied age and style for sale at reasonable prices. Many single-family residences, with three bedrooms and two baths and located alongside or near golf courses, sell for between $150,000 and $275,000. Condominiums are less expensive—some adjacent to fairways are priced between $100,000 and $150,000. A good selection of senior housing from apartments to long-term care facilities is also available.

- *Goods and Services.* Groceries, utilities, transportation, health care and miscellaneous goods and services are all priced within 5 percent of their national norms.

- *Taxes.* The state and local tax burden in Pinehurst–Southern Pines is about 10.1 percent of income compared to the U.S. average of 9.7 percent. Property, sales and excise taxes are somewhat below national norms whereas income taxes are well above average.

| Transportation | Rating: 2 |

 Local travel is primarily by private automobile; there is no fixed-route public transit in Moore County. Several transportation companies provide taxi and limousine service locally and to Raleigh–Durham International Airport. Greyhound furnishes intercity bus service. Daily rail service north to Washington and New York, and south to Tampa and Miami, is available from the Southern Pines Amtrak station. Raleigh–Durham International Airport, 65 miles north, provides comprehensive air service to all major American cities.

| Retail Services | Rating: 2 |

 Although the historic downtown areas of Southern Pines and nearby Aberdeen, with their antique and specialty shops, galleries and restaurants, are pleasant enough, the Pinehurst Village shopping district, laid out by Frederick Law Olmsted, is nothing short of idyllic. Essentially a replica of a late nineteenth century New England town center, Pinehurst Village is a perfect place to stroll from boutiques to galleries to restaurants. Goods and services sold here are typically of excellent quality.

A variety of specialty stores and a gourmet grocery are found along the U.S. 15–501 retail strip between Pinehurst and Southern Pines. Pinecrest Plaza is a modern shopping center that features a Belk department store, numerous clothing stores, specialty shops and restaurants. The local Wal-Mart is located a little farther south in Aberdeen.

Health Care   Rating: 4

Pinehurst–Southern Pines is notable among smaller places for the high quality of its medical care. FirstHealth Moore Regional Hospital in Pinehurst is an acute care, nonprofit, 400-bed facility serving as regional referral center for a 16-county area. With a medical staff of more than 160 physicians representing most major medical specialties, the hospital has capabilities usually found only in larger metropolitan areas.

Community Services   Rating: 4

Pinehurst, Southern Pines and Moore County collectively provide an excellent array of community services. Moore County Transportation Services transports older adults to shopping, work and medical facilities. The County Department of Aging provides arts and crafts, educational, exercise, and social and recreational programs. It also operates four nutritional sites that provide hot lunches, runs a Meals on Wheels program, and hosts popular annual special events such as Senior Games in the Pines and the Senior Citizens Handicraft and Hobby Fair.

Cultural and Educational Activities   Rating: 3

Sandhills Community College in Pinehurst is a focus for education and culture. The college's continuing education division provides a variety of academic and practical courses of general interest; its Owens Auditorium is the site of the Sandhills Little Theater, which offers five community theater productions each year. Owens Auditorium also hosts band, orchestral, choral, jazz and visiting artists concerts. The Arts Council of Moore County provides a variety of programs for its members. It owns the Performing Arts Center in downtown Southern Pines, which hosts Jazz in January concerts, visits by the North Carolina Symphony Orchestra, plays and a travelogue series. Sunrise Theater in Southern Pines also hosts theatrical productions and cinema.

Recreational Activities   Rating: 4

Golf is played year-round on courses suited to all skill levels. Pinehurst # 2, the jewel of the golfing crown and one of eight courses at the Pinehurst Resort, was the site of the 1999 U.S. Open Championship and will be again in 2005. Forty-two additional courses, most of which operate on a daily fee basis, are found within a 25-mile radius of Pinehurst # 2. The whole area—Pinehurst, Southern Pines and neighboring communities—is truly a golfers' heaven.

As befits a major year-round resort area, many recreational choices tempt golfers and non-golfers alike. Horseback riding, tennis, archery, trap and skeet shooting and hunting are popular sports. Area streams and small lakes offer many attractive sites for sailing, canoeing and fishing, while more than 10 fitness trails circling lakes and reservoirs and traversing scenic woodlands provide countless opportunities for hiking, jogging and bicycling. Municipal parks in Aberdeen, Pinehurst, Southern Pines and neighboring communities boast a good variety of facilities including tennis and volleyball courts, ball fields, playgrounds, and picnic areas and shelters. Indoor fitness facilities are open to the public on a daily fee basis at Moore Regional Health and Fitness Center. Its assets include an eight-lane lap pool, sauna and steam room, indoor track, racquetball, weight and workout equipment and aerobics classes. Alternately, you can bowl or play pool at the large Sandhills Bowling Center in Aberdeen, enjoy croquet and lawn bowling at the Pinehurst Resort and Country Club, take in a movie at a local movie house or dine at one of the excellent restaurants in Pinehurst or Southern Pines. American cuisine is the norm here, with several dining rooms offering a health-conscious menu in addition to their regular fare.

For spectator sports, you must travel 100 miles to Charlotte or 70 miles to the Raleigh–Durham–Chapel Hill area. Charlotte has NFL football whereas the latter cities offer outstanding NCAA basketball and football at North Carolina State, Duke and the University of North Carolina. Raleigh also boasts an NHL hockey franchise.

Work and Volunteer Activities   Rating: 4

 The Sandhills economy, based mainly on tourism and retailing, has generated a number of jobs in recent years and seniors compete effectively for many of these positions. Volunteer work is also abundant. FirstHealth Moore Regional Hospital, the Pinehurst, Southern Pines, Aberdeen Convention and Visitors Bureau, the Sandhills Chamber of Commerce, Southern Pines Library, the County Department of Transportation Services, the County Department of Aging and area schools provide many volunteer openings.

Crime Rates and Public Safety   Rating: 4

Although Moore County as a whole has crime rates lower than the national average, great variations occur from place to place. Pinehurst and most rural and golf course communities have among the lowest crime rates in the nation. On the other hand, a very high incidence of violent and property crime in one minority neighborhood in the western part of Southern Pines skews that city's overall crime rate to levels not experienced in most parts of town. As elsewhere, if you pick your neighborhood carefully, there is little to fear from crime in Pinehurst or Southern Pines.

Conclusion

Overall Rating 42 The Sandhills region centered on Pinehurst and Southern Pines is an ideal retirement place for golfers and a very good one for devotees of outdoor recreation wishing to live in a fairly cosmopolitan small town. The heavily wooded, gently rolling Sandhills landscape is beautiful, and the region's climate is mild enough for outdoor activities in all four seasons. The quality of life is excellent throughout the region and especially so in the charming Village of Pinehurst and the historic center of Southern Pines. Residential areas, parks and village retail centers are delightful places to walk about in an environment unspoiled by pollution, traffic congestion, architectural ugliness or crime. Local availability of health care, community services, recreation and work and volunteer opportunities is exceptional for such small towns. Even the area's more modest assets in retail services, transportation and culture meet most peoples' day-to-day needs, and much greater resources are only an hour or two away in Raleigh–Durham–Chapel Hill and Charlotte. Finally, all the advantages of living in Pinehurst–Southern Pines are available at a cost of living near the national average. On that basis, the Sandhills region is surely a best buy among America's upscale retirement places.

Asheville, North Carolina

Founded in 1793 as a small crossroads village in the wilderness of western North Carolina, Asheville has blossomed in the twentieth century into one of the major mountain resorts in the eastern United States. With a population nearing 70,000 in the city and 212,000 in Buncombe County, Asheville is the regional center for manufacturing, transportation, health care, retailing, and banking and professional services. Virtually surrounded by the unspoiled grandeur of the Blue Ridge Mountains, Asheville is small enough to retain much of the intimacy and gentle pace of a small city while offering urban services and amenities usually found only in much larger places. Although the majority of recent residential development has occurred in nearby retirement oriented communities like Hendersonville and Brevard, Asheville remains a choice retirement locale for those desiring a busy, productive lifestyle in an environment of great natural beauty.

Landscape   Rating: 5

Asheville is located at an elevation of 2,200 feet on the rolling surface of the Asheville Plateau. The French Broad River flows across the western part of the city, adding interest to the landscape and posing an occasional threat of flooding to low-lying areas. The older part of town is built on the fairly gentle plateau surface but newer neighborhoods extend into the densely wooded foothills of the Blue Ridge. From almost any vantage point, Asheville's site is spectacular. The Blue Ridge Mountains, traversed by the scenic Blue Ridge Parkway, arc around the city from northeast to southwest and extend off to the west where they meld with the peaks of the Great Smokies. Several peaks visible from town, including Mount Pisgah, are more than a mile high. They provide a lush green backdrop to Asheville in summer and a snowy white one in winter. The lower slopes of the mountains and much of the city are clothed in a luxuriant southern forest of deciduous and coniferous trees grading into hardy northern conifers such as spruce at higher elevations.

Climate   Rating: 4

Asheville enjoys an upland variant of the humid subtropical climate; the city's moderate elevation causes temperatures to be a little cooler in all seasons than those recorded nearer sea level at the same latitude. Precipitation averages 37 inches annually and is well distributed throughout the year. About 14 inches of snow falls in the city in a normal winter, but considerably more accumulates in the mountains. Snow seldom persists on the ground for more than a few days at a time in Asheville because winter days are fairly mild, with temperatures rising well above freezing most afternoons. Spring and autumn weather varies from day to day but is generally pleasant. Summer has the steadiest weather of the year, with warm to hot days and cool nights. On average, the city is sunny about 60 percent of the time and has an average frost-free season of 195 days.

All in all, Asheville's climate is quite pleasant. It offers four distinct seasons, the stimulation of frequent weather changes during much of the year, and ample precipitation. Its principal negative is high relative humidity, especially in summer. This results in discomfort and a hazy atmosphere that impedes views of the Blue Ridge. Conditions are more pleasant in spring and autumn when relative humidity reaches its annual minimum.

Asheville, North Carolina

CLIMATE

Month	Average Daily Temperature High	Average Daily Temperature Low	Daily Rel. Humidity Low	Average Monthly Precipitation
	F		%	Inches
January	46	27	59	3.1
February	50	29	56	3.2
March	58	36	53	3.9
April	67	44	50	3.2
May	74	52	57	3.5
June	81	60	59	3.2
July	84	64	63	3.0
August	83	62	63	3.3
September	77	56	64	3.0
October	68	45	57	2.4
November	58	37	56	2.9
December	50	30	59	2.6

Annual Averages

Total Days		Total Inches	
Clear	101	Precipitation	37.3
Partly Cloudy	113	Snowfall	14.2
Cloudy	151		

RATINGS

Category	poor 1	fair 2	good 3	very good 4	excellent 5
Landscape					●
Climate				●	
Quality of Life				●	
Cost of Living			●		
Transportation			●		
Retail Services					●
Health Care					●
Community Services				●	
Cultural Activities				●	
Recreational Activities					●
Work/Volunteer Activities				●	
Crime			●		

Total Points: 49

Quality of Life — Rating: 4

The quality of life in Asheville varies from good to excellent depending on proximity to annoyances like the airport and freeways. Some jet noise is encountered on the southern edge of town near the airport, and the I-40 and I-240 loop around central Asheville impacts nearby areas with traffic noise, although not severely. Air quality is good and most parts of town are free of unsightly industrial areas. There is little evidence of crowding or traffic congestion. Plenty of parking is available at the malls and downtown. Unfortunately, the large downtown parking ramps are among the ugliest seen anywhere and quite out of character with the central business district's many delightful art deco buildings that date from the 1920s and 1930s. The downtown is undergoing something of a revival with an eclectic mix of antique and specialty shops, apparel stores, arts and crafts galleries, bookstores and restaurants. Nonetheless, some storefronts downtown remain empty, and the area's New Age flavor may not appeal to all. Most residential neighborhoods—whether in the older core of the city, in the hills overlooking downtown, or in the suburban fringe—are pleasant and show considerable pride of ownership.

Cost of Living   Rating: 3

 The cost of living in Asheville is evaluated as follows:

- *Composite.* ACCRA data for Asheville reveal an overall cost of living approximating the national average.

- *Housing.* Housing costs are about 10 percent above the national average but the housing stock is excellent. Many attractive older homes with three bedrooms and two baths, located in leafy settings in the city, were recently priced between $200,000 and $300,000. The lower slopes of the mountains just north and east of downtown are dotted with lovely homes on heavily wooded lots, many offering spectacular views of the Asheville Plateau and the Blue Ridge Mountains.

- *Goods and Services.* ACCRA data show that groceries, utilities, transportation, health care and miscellaneous goods and services are all priced slightly below their national averages.

- *Taxes.* The state and local tax burden in Asheville is about 10.1 percent of income compared to the U.S. average of 9.7 percent. Property, sales and excise taxes are somewhat below national norms whereas income taxes are well above average.

Transportation   Rating: 3

 Travel by automobile is the norm in Asheville but Asheville Transit is a reasonable alternative. Operated by the City of Asheville, this agency provides bus service to all parts of the city including downtown, residential areas, hospitals, schools, universities and shopping malls. Bus service is free downtown; elsewhere fares are nominal. Seniors pay only $15 for a monthly pass. Unfortunately, there is no Sunday service and service is infrequent Monday through Saturday, with hourly or half-hourly service being typical. Greyhound provides intercity bus travel. Air travel is possible from Asheville Regional Airport, 12 miles south. Nonstop jet service connects Asheville Airport to major hubs at Atlanta and Charlotte. A greater variety of flights is provided at Greenville–Spartanburg Airport, 68 miles south. Daily Amtrak service north to New York and south to New Orleans is also available in Greenville.

Retail Services   Rating: 5

Most shopping occurs at two major malls and several smaller shopping centers. The downtown business district, although somewhat revitalized in recent years in a rather funky New Age style, is not yet a competitive threat to the rather antiseptic mainstream retailers at the malls. Asheville Mall, in the eastern part of town, is by far the largest retailing complex. Anchored by Belk, Dillard's, Sears and JCPenney department stores, the mall also includes 100 specialty stores and restaurants and a multi-screen cinema complex. Biltmore Square, on the southwestern fringe of the city, has Belk, Dillard's, Goody's and Proffitt's stores as anchors, plus 50 specialty shops and a six-screen theater. Two Wal-Mart and four Kmart discount stores are located in smaller shopping centers around the city. Considerably upscale from these is historic Biltmore Village, located near the entrance to the Biltmore Estate in south Asheville. It markets a variety of arts and crafts, gifts, antiques and apparel in charming turn-of-the-century buildings.

Health Care   Rating: 5

Asheville is justifiably renowned for the quality and sophistication of its medical care. Mission Hospitals offer almost every medical specialty from neonatology to gerontology. Cardiac care, women's health, oncology, orthopedics, urology and emergency and trauma services are among their special strengths. With about 800 beds, Mission is by far the largest hospital complex in western North Carolina and the medical referral center for the region. Veterans can use the facilities of the Asheville VA Medical Center. This 232-bed hospital offers a wide range of medical services and functions as a major VA system referral center.

Community Services   Rating: 4

State and local government and private organizations make available a fine assortment of programs and services. Especially notable is the North Carolina Center for Creative Retirement, which is affiliated with the University of North Carolina at Asheville. At the Center's College for Seniors, anyone age 55 or older may take as many courses as they can schedule during a semester for a nominal tuition of around $100. The Buncombe County Council on Aging, the Land-of-Sky Regional Council, Meals on Wheels of Asheville–Buncombe and Transportation Assistance for the Elderly also furnish valuable resources and opportunities to seniors.

Cultural and Educational Activities   Rating: 4

Cultural and educational opportunities are abundant and varied in Asheville. The Asheville Symphony and visiting ballet and operatic companies perform at the Thomas Wolfe Auditorium downtown. Asheville Community Theater provides a series of professional theatrical productions annually, and a foreign film series offers feature films not generally shown in mainstream movie houses. Music and dance are featured at the annual Mountain Dance and Folk Festival, and the nearby Brevard Music Festival hosts a staggering list of classical and popular music events during a six-week summer season.

The visual arts are also prominent locally. The Asheville Art Museum, the Folk Art Center, the Asheville Art League, the Arts Alliance and Pack Place showcase native American and contemporary artistic works and handicrafts. Biltmore Estate is the pride of Asheville. This 255-room French Renaissance chateau built by George Vanderbilt in 1895 is America's largest private residence. The house, which is surrounded by magnificent gardens, contains Mr. Vanderbilt's collection of 50,000 art objects, antiques and furnishings. It merits repeated visits.

Finally, the University of North Carolina at Asheville (UNCA) deserves favorable mention. Rated as one of the country's best public arts universities, UNCA offers undergraduate and graduate degrees in the liberal arts. In affiliation with the North Carolina Center for Creative Retirement, it also offers a great variety of low-cost short courses of interest to seniors.

Recreational Activities   Rating: 5

 Recreational options are also plentiful in Asheville and vicinity. The city has an excellent system of public parks, well equipped with sports and recreation facilities. Golf is played year-round on 14 area courses open to the public, and some of America's most prestigious golf club retirement communities are found nearby. Tennis is also popular at 23 tennis facilities.

Outdoor enthusiasts appreciate Asheville for its proximity to national parks and forests. The Blue Ridge Parkway, best thought of as a long, narrow national park, skirts Asheville and provides access to some of the highest and most scenic mountain regions of the eastern United States. Great Smokey Mountains National Park, only 60 miles west of town, may be reached via the parkway or alternate routes. The national park is notable for gorgeous vistas of heavily wooded mountains and valleys from roadside overlooks or from points along the park's more than 850 miles of trails. Picnicking, sightseeing, camping, hiking, swimming and fishing are popular activities. Outside the park, numerous lakes and rivers provide opportunities for boating, sailing, rafting, canoeing and fishing. The mountains are also valued for hunting, and in winter skiing is possible at several resorts within 100 miles of the city.

The Asheville area is also known for the variety and excellence of its restaurants, some of which are clustered downtown while others are widely scattered throughout the urban area. Movie theaters, bowling centers, and the excellent Asheville–Buncombe Library System offer additional diversions.

Work and Volunteer Activities   Rating: 4

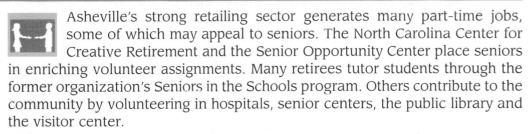 Asheville's strong retailing sector generates many part-time jobs, some of which may appeal to seniors. The North Carolina Center for Creative Retirement and the Senior Opportunity Center place seniors in enriching volunteer assignments. Many retirees tutor students through the former organization's Seniors in the Schools program. Others contribute to the community by volunteering in hospitals, senior centers, the public library and the visitor center.

Crime Rates and Public Safety   Rating: 3

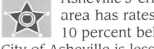 Asheville's crime statistics are somewhat mixed. The metropolitan area has rates of violent and property crime that are 35 percent and 10 percent below national norms. Unfortunately, the situation in the City of Asheville is less satisfactory. There rates of violent and property crime are about 35 percent and 70 percent above national averages. These latter data

largely reflect fairly high rates of aggravated assault, burglary and larceny–theft in poorer neighborhoods of the city. Affluent areas in the city and suburbs are quite safe.

Overall Rating 49 Asheville ranks highly on most indicators of suitability for retirement; its principal weaknesses are moderate crime rates and a rather weak downtown. The city's greatest strengths are its lovely natural setting, high-quality health care, strong retail sector and plentiful recreation. Its subtropical climate, moderated by elevation, appeals to those who desire four seasons but do not want to be snowbound for days at a time. Although suburban areas and nearby towns like Hendersonville and Brevard have attracted an increasing percentage of the Asheville region's retirees in recent years, Asheville still rates highly in quality of life factors. There is little traffic congestion and air quality is good. The city provides very good community services and ample opportunities in culture, education, part-time work and volunteerism. Happily, all these positives are available at a cost of living at the national average. What more could one ask of a retirement town?

Hendersonville, North Carolina

Once a hunting ground for the Cherokee, Hendersonville received its first town charter in the 1840s when it had a population of several hundred residents living a basic farming existence. As transportation improved, Hendersonville became a popular summer resort for lowland Carolinians who came to the mountains to escape that season's intense heat. In the twentieth century its long-standing reputation as a health and summer resort has contributed to its becoming the leading retirement center of North Carolina's mountainous west. Although only 25 miles south of Asheville and 22 miles east of Brevard, Hendersonville is separated by open space from these neighboring centers and retains its own unique identity. Yet it is close enough to them for its residents to easily access their many attractions. With a population approximating 11,500 in the city and 92,000 in Henderson County, the urban area is small enough to possess small-town charm while large enough to offer the many amenities crucial to upscale retirement. Notable for abundant cultural opportunities, an attractively refurbished pedestrian-friendly downtown and lovely residential areas, Hendersonville also offers convenient access to the Blue Ridge and Great Smokey Mountains. Not surprisingly, local residents tend to congratulate themselves on their good fortune to live here.

Hendersonville rests at an elevation of 2,200 feet on the gently rolling surface of the valley of the French Broad River. Virtually surrounded by the foothills of the Blue Ridge, with major peaks along the Blue Ridge Parkway only 20 or 30 miles to the north and northwest, Hendersonville has a beautiful setting. Much of the county is forested with oaks and pines on the lower hillsides and hardier coniferous trees at higher elevations. Gentle slopes in the valley typically offer a visually appealing mixture of land uses featuring farmland, golf courses and suburban housing interspersed with wooded areas.

Hendersonville, North Carolina

CLIMATE

Month	Average Daily Temperature High	Average Daily Temperature Low	Daily Rel. Humidity Low	Average Monthly Precipitation
	F		**%**	**Inches**
January	47	25	59	5.2
February	51	27	56	4.6
March	59	34	53	5.9
April	67	41	50	4.2
May	74	51	57	4.9
June	81	59	59	4.8
July	84	64	63	4.5
August	83	62	63	5.4
September	77	56	64	4.3
October	68	43	57	4.0
November	58	35	56	4.6
December	50	28	59	4.3

Annual Averages

Total Days		Total Inches	
Clear	110	Precipitation	56.6
Partly Cloudy	103	Snowfall	9.2
Cloudy	152		

RATINGS

Category	poor 1	fair 2	good 3	very good 4	excellent 5
Landscape					●
Climate				●	
Quality of Life					●
Cost of Living			●		
Transportation		●			
Retail Services			●		
Health Care				●	
Community Services				●	
Cultural Activities				●	
Recreational Activities					●
Work/Volunteer Activities			●		
Crime					●

Total Points: 47

Climate **Rating: 4**

 The local climate is broadly similar to that of Asheville and Brevard, although somewhat rainier than Asheville and less rainy than Brevard. The upland variant of the humid subtropical climate is pleasantly mild compared to that experienced at lower elevations in the Carolinas. The annual average of 57 inches of precipitation is evenly distributed seasonally. About nine inches of snow falls in the city in a typical winter but considerably more accumulates in the mountains. Snow tends to persist on the ground in town for only a few days at a time because winters are fairly mild, with average highs near 50 degrees. Spring and autumn weather varies considerably from day to day but most days are warm and nights are cool. Summer weather is steadier with average highs in the low 80s and lows near 60 degrees. The frost-free period averages 180 days, allowing outdoor gardening from mid-April through early October. In summary, Hendersonville's climate is mild yet variable enough to be stimulating. It features four clearly defined seasons, frequent changes in weather and moderate levels of sunshine. Its major negatives are high relative humidity and moderately heavy precipitation throughout the year.

Quality of Life   Rating: 5

 Hendersonville offers residents an excellent quality of life. It is quiet, although not as quiet as Brevard, and its air quality is excellent. The city is peaceful, clean and uncrowded, and parking is adequate downtown and at the mall. There are no noxious industries and population densities are low. Traffic is fairly light, though major streets can be moderately busy at rush hour. The city itself seems well planned; its nicely landscaped, revitalized downtown is delightful and its residential areas are attractive. These days, though, most new homes are found outside the corporate limits in county territory where attractive single-family residences are rather widely scattered across the landscape. Residents are friendly and helpful and seem anxious to welcome visitors and potential residents alike to their delightful city and region.

Cost of Living   Rating: 3

 The cost of living in Hendersonville is evaluated as follows:

- *Composite.* ACCRA data are unavailable for Hendersonville but costs there likely do not differ greatly from those of nearby Asheville. The overall cost of living approximates the national average.

- *Housing.* Data from local sources suggest that the median price of a home with three bedrooms and two baths is about $200,000. A great variety of housing is available, ranging from factory-built houses on their own land for $80,000 to condominiums priced between $80,000 and $120,000 to suburban estate homes on huge lots for prices exceeding $300,000. A drive through the many desirable neighborhoods reveals attractive homes in wooded settings or perched on hillsides offering breathtaking views.

- *Goods and Services.* ACCRA data for Asheville and local sources of information suggest that in Hendersonville groceries, utilities, transportation, health care and miscellaneous goods and services are all priced slightly below their national averages.

- *Taxes.* The state and local tax burden is about 10.1 percent of income compared to the U.S. average of 9.7 percent. Property, sales and excise taxes are somewhat below national norms whereas income taxes are well above average.

Transportation   Rating: 2

Travel in Hendersonville is overwhelmingly by private automobile but limited, hourly public transit is now available. Three bus routes connect downtown with destinations such as Pardee Hospital, Blue Ridge Mall and Asheville Airport. From there you can transfer to Asheville Transit and reach many destinations in the Greater Asheville area. Greyhound also provides bus service to Asheville and, from there, to all parts of the country. Commercial air transportation is available from Asheville Regional Airport, 11 miles north; Greenville–Spartanburg Airport, 50 miles southeast, provides a greater variety of flights. Daily Amtrak service north to New York and south to New Orleans is also available in Greenville.

Retail Services   Rating: 3

Historic downtown Hendersonville—centered on the distinctively serpentine Main Street, lined with trees, shrubbery, and flower planters and featuring bright green benches placed strategically along wide sidewalks—is the heart and soul of the city. Added to the National Register of Historic Places in 1988, downtown is home to 150 businesses making up an ideal mix of specialty shops, antiques stores and service and eating establishments. Unlike many older downtowns, Historic Hendersonville is thriving, being extremely popular with residents and visitors alike. In contrast, Blue Ridge Mall, located two miles east of the city center near I-26, is less successful. Although anchored by Belk, JCPenney and Kmart stores, many empty stores were observed there during a recent visit.

Health Care   Rating: 4

Pardee Hospital is a county-owned, nonprofit community hospital. With 222 beds and more than 180 physicians representing 31 specialties on staff, Pardee Hospital provides very good medical care. Services include 24-hour emergency care, intensive care, medical, surgical, orthopedic, cancer and coronary care, radiation therapy and advanced diagnostics, and psychiatric services, among others. Nearby Asheville offers excellent additional medical resources.

Community Services   Rating: 4

The city and county provide high-quality services. Opportunity House, a nonprofit organization located at 1411 Asheville Highway in Hendersonville, houses classrooms, woodworking and woodcarving rooms, facilities for lapidaries and potters, two auditoriums and a large kitchen. Opportunity House is the area's largest organizer of activities for newcomers, hobbyists and seniors. It provides lectures, arts and crafts courses, exercise classes, bridge, sports, trips, dinners and dances. College courses are fielded in cooperation with Blue Ridge Community College. Also notable is the Henderson County Public Library, located in downtown Hendersonville. With more than 200,000 books, extensive reference and audio and videotape collections, and varied program offerings, the library is a valuable resource for people of all ages.

The performing arts are well represented in Hendersonville and the surrounding area. Flat Rock Playhouse, designated as the State Theater of North Carolina and recognized as one of the top summer-stock theaters in America, is only three miles south of town. From late May through mid-October it produces comedies, musicals and dramas having wide audience appeal. Theatrical entertainment is also offered by the Hendersonville Little Theater and the Belfry Players, while musical performances suiting all tastes are provided by the Hendersonville Community Concert Band, the Carolina Chamber Singers, Henderson Chorale and the 70-piece Hendersonville Symphony Orchestra. Additionally, the Hendersonville Friends of Chamber Music annually hosts five concerts featuring outstanding guest artists from around the country. Within a 30-minute drive of Hendersonville, top-quality musical talent is also featured in summer at the nearby Brevard Music Center, and Asheville hosts a multitude of cultural and artistic offerings throughout the year.

The visual arts and education are also significant in Hendersonville. The Arts Center, located in the historic Skyland Hotel on Main Street, includes classrooms, studio space and a gallery for local and visiting art shows. The Singleton Center in Flat Rock features bimonthly exhibitions of the works of local, regional and national artists in its main gallery. Also in Flat Rock is state-supported Blue Ridge Community College, which offers academic and applied courses of interest to students of all ages, as well as lectures and concerts for the general public.

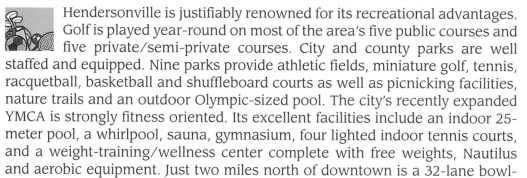 Hendersonville is justifiably renowned for its recreational advantages. Golf is played year-round on most of the area's five public courses and five private/semi-private courses. City and county parks are well staffed and equipped. Nine parks provide athletic fields, miniature golf, tennis, racquetball, basketball and shuffleboard courts as well as picnicking facilities, nature trails and an outdoor Olympic-sized pool. The city's recently expanded YMCA is strongly fitness oriented. Its excellent facilities include an indoor 25-meter pool, a whirlpool, sauna, gymnasium, four lighted indoor tennis courts, and a weight-training/wellness center complete with free weights, Nautilus and aerobic equipment. Just two miles north of downtown is a 32-lane bowling center, the largest in western North Carolina.

Movie buffs can choose among three unique venues. The most conventional of these is the five-screen 4-Seasons Cinema located near Blue Ridge Mall. Skyland Arts Cinema is located downtown in the former ballroom of the Skyland Hotel. This theater seats 70 in comfortable chairs at small tables. Catering to sophisticated audiences, this unique theater serves food, coffee, wine and beer and screens independent, art-house and foreign films. Devotees of high-quality foreign and alternative films are welcome to join the Henderson Film Society, which screens films at the Smoky Mountain Theater at Lake Point Landing in Hendersonville.

Outdoors enthusiasts benefit from Hendersonville's proximity to national parks and forests. The Blue Ridge Parkway, which passes within 12 miles of the city, provides convenient access to Pisgah National Forest and is the most scenic route to Great Smokey Mountains National Park, 70 miles west of town.

A limited number of part-time jobs of interest to seniors are typically available in local retail and service industries. Larger numbers of Hendersonville's active senior population do important volunteer work at the local hospital, library, visitors bureau and various cultural and educational venues. Opportunity House makes extensive use of volunteers from its membership of 2,000 in carrying out its many senior and community programs.

Crime Rates and Public Safety   Rating: 5

Hendersonville and Henderson County are among America's most crime-free places. The countywide violent crime and property crime rates are currently 80 percent and 67 percent below national norms. Such an excellent public safety record doubtless derives in part from the favorable demographics of the county population but it also reflects a highly visible and effective police presence in the community.

Conclusion

Overall Rating 47
Like its neighbor Brevard, Hendersonville is a highly desirable place for retirement for those wishing to live in a safe and friendly small city offering many amenities typical of much larger places. Its gently rolling landscape in the foothills of the Blue Ridge Mountains is beautiful and its mild, upland variant of the humid subtropical climate will appeal to many. The local quality of life is excellent. The delightfully refurbished yet traditional downtown is a joy whether one is shopping, seeking entertainment, food or drink or simply walking about. Air quality is excellent and there is little noise, visual pollution or traffic congestion. Most services and amenities essential for upscale retirement are well represented in Hendersonville and are easily augmented in nearby Asheville. Health care, community services, culture and recreation are strong pluses here, while retail services and work and volunteer opportunities are good for a small city. Finally, all these blessings are available at a moderate cost of living in a virtually crime-free environment. This makes Hendersonville very appealing indeed.

Brevard, North Carolina

Although only 35 miles southwest of Asheville and 22 miles west of Hendersonville, Brevard is a world apart from these larger western North Carolina cities. It is a picture postcard-perfect place reminiscent of the mythical town of Mayberry in the classic Andy Griffith television show. But Brevard is no Disneyesque movie set; it is a real community of lovely but unpretentious frame and brick homes on sloping tree-lined streets surrounding a thriving, traditional downtown business district. With a population of about 7,200 within the corporate limits and 30,000 in Transylvania County, Brevard preserves the look and feel of a small town while offering many amenities not generally available in places of its size. Thanks to Brevard College and the Brevard Music Festival, higher culture is as abundant in town as outdoor recreation is in the nearby Blue Ridge Mountains. The town's friendly residents congratulate themselves on their good fortune to live in Brevard and agree that it is an ideal place in which to retire.

Brevard, North Carolina

CLIMATE

Month	Average Daily Temperature High	Average Daily Temperature Low	Daily Rel. Humidity Low	Average Monthly Precipitation
	F		%	Inches
January	47	24	59	5.9
February	52	25	56	5.2
March	59	32	53	6.5
April	67	39	50	4.7
May	74	49	57	5.9
June	79	57	59	5.8
July	82	61	63	5.1
August	80	60	63	5.4
September	75	54	64	5.1
October	68	41	57	4.9
November	58	33	56	5.7
December	50	26	59	6.0

Annual Averages

Total Days		Total Inches	
Clear	110	Precipitation	66.2
Partly Cloudy	103	Snowfall	8.4
Cloudy	152		

RATINGS

Category	poor 1	fair 2	good 3	very good 4	excellent 5
Landscape					●
Climate				●	
Quality of Life					●
Cost of Living			●		
Transportation		●			
Retail Services			●		
Health Care			●		
Community Services			●		
Cultural Activities					●
Recreational Activities					●
Work/Volunteer Activities			●		
Crime					●

Total Points: 46

Landscape   **Rating: 5**

Brevard lies in a fertile southwest to northeast-trending valley drained by the French Broad River. With rolling hills to the southeast of town and Pisgah National Forest and the Blue Ridge Mountains forming its northwestern boundary, Brevard's setting is unusually beautiful. Fully 85 percent of the county, known locally as the Land of Waterfalls, is wooded and 35 percent is included in national forest. Although Brevard itself is located at an elevation of 2,230 feet, elevations as high as 6,000 feet above sea level are found only 10 or 12 miles to the northwest in the Blue Ridge Mountains. Except for patches of farmland on the rolling valley floor, much of the valley, the town and the lower slopes of the mountains are wooded with oaks and pines, grading into hardier conifers like spruce at the highest elevations.

Climate   Rating: 4

 Brevard's climate is similar to that of Asheville but considerably rainier. The upland humid subtropical climate, moderated by elevation, is a little cooler and wetter all year than the climate at places at the same latitude but nearer sea level. The town's annual average of 66 inches of precipitation is evenly distributed seasonally. About 8 inches of snow falls in the valley in a normal winter but much more accumulates in the higher mountains. Snow seldom persists for long in Brevard because winter days are typically mild. Spring and autumn weather is generally pleasant, with warm days and cool nights. Summer weather is relatively steady with average highs in the low 80s, average lows around 60 degrees and abundant rainfall. The frost-free period averages 170 days. In summary, Brevard's climate is mild yet stimulating. It features four clearly defined seasons, frequent changes in weather and moderate levels of sunshine. Its principal negatives are high relative humidity and rather heavy precipitation.

Quality of Life   Rating: 5

 Brevard provides an excellent quality of life. There is little noise from automobiles or aircraft. Air quality is excellent. The town is peaceful, clean and uncrowded. Parking is adequate downtown, at local shopping centers and on the grounds of the Brevard Music Festival. There are no heavy industries and population densities are low. Traffic is light, except on festival evenings in summer. The town is well planned and its nicely landscaped neighborhoods reflect a pleasing combination of moderate affluence, good taste and a desire to preserve the community's unique character.

Brevard is growing more slowly than Asheville or Hendersonville and thus has been spared the rough edges of these and other Sunbelt cities. Historic downtown Brevard is charming and economically healthy, thanks to the hard work of members of the Heart of Brevard Downtown District and the patronage of local shoppers and visitors. Residents are extremely friendly and welcoming; they evidently dearly love their little town and seek to keep it the perfect place it is.

Cost of Living   Rating: 3

The cost of living in Brevard is evaluated as follows:

- *Composite.* ACCRA data are unavailable for Brevard but costs there probably do not differ greatly from those of nearby Asheville. The overall cost of living is slightly below the national average.

- *Housing.* Data from local real estate sources indicate that the median price of a single-family residence with three bedrooms and two baths in the City of Brevard is between $140,000 and $180,000, with condominiums being perhaps half as expensive. Just outside the city limits, many new homes priced between $120,000 and $200,000 are on the market.

- *Goods and Services.* ACCRA data for Asheville and local sources suggest that in Brevard groceries, utilities, transportation, health care and miscellaneous goods and services are priced at or slightly below national norms. Day-to-day purchases are available locally at reasonable prices. Competition between local Wal-Mart and Kmart stores and a popular seasonal farmers' market helps keep costs down.

- *Taxes.* The state and local tax burden in Brevard is about 10.1 percent of income compared to the U.S. average of 9.7 percent. Property, sales and excise taxes are below national norms whereas income taxes are well above average.

Transportation — Rating: 2

Travel in the Brevard area is largely by private automobile but most destinations are so close that walking or bicycling are reasonable alternatives to driving. Transylvania County Transportation System provides dial-a-ride service on weekdays, 6:30 a.m. to 6:00 p.m., at nominal cost. Commercial air travel is possible from Asheville Regional Airport, 22 miles north, but Greenville–Spartanburg Airport, 70 miles southeast, provides a greater variety of flights. Daily Amtrak service north to New York and south to New Orleans is also available in Greenville.

Retail Services — Rating: 3

The Heart of Brevard Downtown District, centered on Broad and Main Streets, is thriving. It boasts more than 150 businesses in a compact 16-block area studded with historic buildings. A genuine working business district, rather than a glitzy or pretentious shopping area targeting tourists, the downtown offers a full range of goods and services. A hardware store, a charming toy store, and several jewelry and music stores as well as numerous restaurants and specialty food stores are among the highlights here. Three days a week, July through October, the Transylvania County Farmers Market sets up downtown. On the outskirts of town, discount shopping is available at Kmart and Wal-Mart.

Health Care — Rating: 3

Transylvania Community Hospital, with 94 beds and more than 40 physicians and surgeons on staff, provides good, routine medical care including coronary and cancer care, acute and intensive care and 24-hour emergency service. Nearby Asheville offers excellent and comprehensive medical resources.

Community Services — Rating: 3

Brevard, Transylvania County, Brevard College and several fraternal organizations furnish high-quality services to residents. Especially notable is the Transylvania County Library. With more than 80,000 books and periodicals, this facility is exceptionally well funded and stocked for a small-town library. The library at Brevard College, just north of downtown, nicely supplements its resources. Local branches of social and fraternal organizations such as AARP, Elks, Eastern Star, Jaycees, Kiwanis, Lions, Masons,

Rotary and Shrine provide many services to members and the community. Transylvania Community Hospital operates the local Meals on Wheels program.

Cultural and Educational Activities   Rating: 5

 Although strong cultural and educational programs are ongoing throughout the year, summer is a special time in Brevard. From late June through early August, the Brevard Music Festival hosts a seemingly endless series of more than 40 consecutive chamber music, pops and symphonic concerts, as well as musical theater and opera at its covered open-air auditorium. Indefatigable music lovers can take in the entire summer program for a season ticket price of only $325. Brevard College hosts the Brevard Chamber Orchestra and Brevard Little Theater as well as faculty and student musical recitals in its outstanding new Porter Center for the Performing Arts. The college's continuing education program is of particular interest to seniors. Each year more than 250 noncredit courses in academic subjects, health and fitness activities, cultural experiences, local interest topics and field courses, hobbies and self-improvement courses are offered. Courses are also available for audit by seniors at the Brevard campus of Blue Ridge Community College, which also hosts a series of lectures, plays and concerts. Additional cultural and educational resources are found in Asheville and Hendersonville. The May through October program of plays and musicals at the Flat Rock Playhouse, home of the State Theatre of North Carolina, is especially noteworthy.

Recreational Activities   Rating: 5

 Brevard and nearby areas offer many and varied recreational choices. Golf is played year-round on 4 local courses, with more than 20 additional golf courses being found within an hour's drive in the Asheville–Hendersonville area. Tennis is played locally on 18 tennis courts, 10 public and 8 at the Racquet Club. Swimming is popular at the municipal swimming pool and in the lakes and rivers of Pisgah National Forest. Main Street, downtown, is the site of the recently renovated one-screen Falls Theatre. Several excellent restaurants and a wonderful 1950s-atmosphere soda shop offer additional diversions downtown. An 18-lane bowling facility is located on U.S. 64 West.

Pisgah National Forest, which borders Brevard on the northwest, provides residents and visitors with unlimited outdoor recreation. Popular pursuits there include sightseeing by car, picnicking, camping and hiking; canoeing, swimming and fishing in countless lakes and streams; and hunting for deer, turkey, waterfowl and small game. In winter, cross-country skiing is possible on numerous trails at higher elevations. The Blue Ridge Parkway is only 20 miles away at its closest approach to Brevard. It provides a wonderfully scenic route to Great Smokey Mountains National Park through some of the eastern United States' most dramatic valley and mountain landscapes.

Work and Volunteer Activities   Rating: 3

 Brevard's strength as a center for culture, education, recreation and retailing generates a number of part-time jobs of interest to seniors. Many retirees find fulfilling volunteer work at the Music Center, county library, Transylvania Community Hospital, and at the local chamber of commerce and visitor center.

Brevard consistently rates as one of America's safest towns. According to FBI statistics, the city and county rank far below national norms in all crime categories. Local lore has it that "crime is almost nonexistent" and that many people don't bother locking their doors at night. Such personal security doubtless derives in part from Brevard's small size and from the favorable demographics of its population. But it probably also is a result of the good work of the city's excellent police force, which is much in evidence and clearly in touch with the community and its needs.

Conclusion

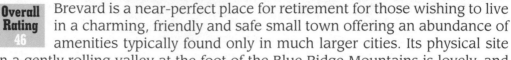

Overall Rating 46

Brevard is a near-perfect place for retirement for those wishing to live in a charming, friendly and safe small town offering an abundance of amenities typically found only in much larger cities. Its physical site in a gently rolling valley at the foot of the Blue Ridge Mountains is lovely, and its mild, upland humid subtropical climate is seldom severely hot or cold. It offers residents an excellent quality of life. Environmental pollution, traffic congestion and urban ugliness are entirely lacking. The strong downtown district is the center of the community and, like the city's lovely residential neighborhoods, is a delightful place to enjoy on foot. Local availability of retail and community services, health care and part-time and volunteer work is good, and the cultural and educational assets of Brevard and vicinity are remarkable for a small town and easily augmented in nearby Asheville.

Brevard's major weakness is the absence of a fixed-route public transit system, so access to a car is almost essential. On the other hand, its many benefits are available at a cost of living slightly below the national average. All things considered, Brevard ranks as one of the best places in America for sophisticated small-town retirement in an exceptionally beautiful and unspoiled setting.

The Southeast Coast Retirement Region

Climate:
Humid subtropical–Sarasota, Gainesville, Tallahassee, Thomasville, Covington, Savannah, Fairhope

Tropical savanna–Boca Raton, Naples

Place Description	Overall Rating	Page
Boca Raton, Florida *Boca Raton is exceptional in Florida for the strength and breadth of its upscale amenities.*	49	126
Naples, Florida *Despite rampant growth of golf course communities and tract housing on its periphery, Naples has managed so far to retain its essential character as a charming resort and retirement town.*	42	132
Sarasota, Florida *Sarasota city and county are unique in Florida for the enormous variety and high quality of services, culture and recreation offered residents and visitors.*	47	137
Gainesville, Florida *Gainesville remains one of America's choice locations for retirement. Not too big, not too small, this north central Florida college town provides everything essential for upscale retirement at reasonable prices.*	47	143
Tallahassee, Florida *Tallahassee is seldom ranked among North America's best retirement places. It deserves better!*	44	148
Thomasville, Georgia *Rated as "one of the best retirement towns in the South" by Consumer Guide in 1988, Thomasville persists as one of America's best small towns for retirement.*	41	154
Covington, Louisiana *Part of the New Orleans Metropolitan Area, yet physically and psychologically separated from the Crescent City by 24 miles of Lake Pontchartrain, Covington and neighboring north shore communities are in many ways a world apart from New Orleans.*	43	159
Savannah, Georgia *Although Savannah is a busy port and industrial center located a few miles upstream from the mouth of the Savannah River, its chief claim to fame is its lovely historic district.*	**not rated**	164
Fairhope, Alabama *Perched atop a high bluff overlooking Mobile Bay, the lovely little city of Fairhope is the most attractive of several towns along the bay's subtropical Eastern Shore.*	**not rated**	165

The Southeast Coast Retirement Region stretches 800 miles from Boca Raton, on Florida's fabled Gold Coast, to Covington, just across Lake Pontchartrain from New Orleans. Long the favorite state for retiree relocation, Florida has experienced runaway growth over several decades that has destroyed the natural beauty of large areas, pushed public services to the limit and overwhelmed the state's infrastructure. As a result, few Florida cities are now able to provide the high quality of life and the amenities crucial to retire in style. Nonetheless, Boca Raton, Naples and Sarasota, three affluent resort and retirement towns in South Florida, Gainesville in north central Florida, and Tallahassee in the Florida Panhandle, although not entirely free of growing pains caused by rapid urban expansion, remain among the most livable places in Florida. Also highly desirable are Thomasville, Georgia and Covington, Louisiana. Both offer gracious living at modest cost in a tranquil subtropical environment. Savannah, Georgia and Fairhope, Alabama are also worth considering for retirement.

Boca Raton, Florida

Boca Raton has a short history. Seminole Indians hunted, gardened and camped in the Boca Raton area from 1825 to 1925 but European settlement was delayed until Henry Flagler's railroad opened South Florida to development in 1895. As recently as 1903, only five families had settled in the area and fruit and vegetable farming persisted as the major industry into the 1920s. The next 75 years, though, changed everything in Boca Raton. Now engulfed in urban sprawl stretching 100 miles from south of Miami to north of Palm Beach, the city of Boca Raton has managed to retain its identity as an oasis of good living, with miles of white sand beaches, cultural, educational and recreational amenities, excellent shopping and safe, attractive neighborhoods. With a population of 76,000 in the city and 200,000 in Greater Boca Raton, the urban area will undoubtedly continue to grow yet should be able to retain its status as one of Florida's top locales for truly upscale retirement for some time to come.

Landscape	Rating: 4

Boca Raton occupies a flat plain between the Atlantic Ocean on the east and the Everglades on the west. On the east side of town, separated from the mainland by the Intracoastal Waterway, is a long, narrow barrier island with miles of white sand beaches. Since the Gulf Stream is just off shore, water temperatures hover in the 70s and 80s all year. Elevations in Boca Raton range from sea level to about 20 feet above sea level, so the entire city is susceptible to sea-water flooding from hurricanes. Although the natural vegetation of coastal southeast Florida consists of grasses, pines and bald cypress, these have been almost entirely replaced in the urban area by exotic ornamentals such as royal and coconut palms, which do well only in tropical conditions. Boca Raton's attractive landscape also includes many kinds of flowering plants including bougainvillea and subtropical tree species such as magnolia, oak and Australian pine.

Boca Raton, Florida

CLIMATE

Month	Average Daily Temperature High	Average Daily Temperature Low	Daily Rel. Humidity Low	Average Monthly Precipitation
	F		%	Inches
January	76	58	59	2.8
February	77	58	57	2.8
March	80	62	56	3.0
April	83	66	55	3.4
May	87	71	59	5.7
June	90	74	66	7.3
July	92	75	64	6.0
August	92	75	64	6.9
September	91	74	66	7.0
October	87	71	63	5.7
November	82	66	61	4.2
December	78	61	56	2.5

Annual Averages

Total Days		Total Inches	
Clear	75	Precipitation	57.3
Partly Cloudy	159	Snowfall	0.0
Cloudy	131		

RATINGS

Category	poor 1	fair 2	good 3	very good 4	excellent 5
Landscape				●	
Climate			●		
Quality of Life				●	
Cost of Living		●			
Transportation				●	
Retail Services					●
Health Care					●
Community Services				●	
Cultural Activities					●
Recreational Activities					●
Work/Volunteer Activities				●	
Crime				●	

Total Points: 49

The climate of Boca Raton, like that of the rest of southernmost Florida, is tropical savanna. This climate is virtually frost-free and features only two seasons. The winter half of the year—November through April—is warm, sunny and relatively dry, whereas the summer half of the year—May through October—is hot and humid with frequent afternoon thundershowers. Annual precipitation averages 57 inches, nearly half of which falls between June and September. Boca Raton is sunny about 70 percent of the time and has a frost-free period of 365 days. The principal climatic negative is the long, hot humid summer. In contrast, winter conditions are nearly ideal.

Quality of Life   Rating: 4

 The quality of life is very good in Boca Raton. Noise pollution is mainly a problem adjacent to I-95, Florida's Turnpike, U.S. 1 and Boca Raton Airport. Residential areas are generally quiet and air quality is excellent despite rapid urbanization inland and increasing traffic in the area. Boca Raton and neighboring municipalities in Palm Beach and Broward Counties depend heavily on the automobile for local transportation and have provided adequate parking wherever needed. There are no really poor neighborhoods in Boca Raton proper, although the same cannot be said for all of Palm Beach County.

Boca Raton's long public beach is protected by a system of beachfront parks unequalled in southeast Florida. Although the city lacks a strong, traditional downtown, centrally located Mizner Park—with its upscale apartments and townhomes, pedestrian-friendly courtyard and a variety of boutiques, galleries and restaurants—serves as a focal point for the community. The city appears well planned and managed and has been able to retain, at least in its older sections, a small-town character unique in southeast Florida.

Cost of Living   Rating: 2

 The cost of living in Boca Raton is evaluated as follows:

- *Composite.* ACCRA data are unavailable for Boca Raton but inferences can be drawn from ACCRA data for nearby West Palm Beach and from local sources. The overall cost of living is estimated to be 10 percent above the national average.

- *Housing.* Boca Raton has an excellent variety of new and resale housing at prices ranging from moderate to expensive. Average house prices are about 10 percent above the national average, with three-bedroom single-family homes averaging around $260,000. Condominiums are a little cheaper. Generally, properties between U.S. 1 and the beach are relatively expensive, especially those with access to the Intracoastal Waterway. In contrast, housing in traditional neighborhoods five to ten miles inland, and in gated golf course communities remote from the ocean, are more reasonably priced.

- *Goods and Services.* Utilities and health care are priced near national norms in Boca Raton. Groceries, transportation and miscellaneous goods and services are all priced nearly 10 percent above their national averages.

- *Taxes.* The state and local tax burden in Boca Raton is about 9.1 percent of income compared to the U.S. average of 9.7 percent. Florida has no state income tax but property taxes are near the national average and sales and excise taxes are rather high.

Transportation   Rating: 4

Boca Raton is strongly automobile oriented and has a good street and highway network. Palm Tran provides fixed-route bus service seven days a week throughout Palm Beach County. Buses serve downtown Boca Raton, major malls, the airport, Tri-Rail (commuter) stations, hospitals and other major destinations. Service is marginal at best, with trip intervals deteriorating to hourly on weekends. Discounts are available to several categories of users including seniors. Tri-Rail connects Boca Raton with major cities in Palm Beach, Broward and Dade counties and with international airports at West Palm Beach, Fort Lauderdale and Miami. These airports provide frequent nonstop jet service to major airports throughout the United States. Greyhound Lines provides service to points north and south of Boca Raton and Amtrak offers service three times a day from nearby Deerfield Beach to points north and south, including New York and Miami.

Retail Services   Rating: 5

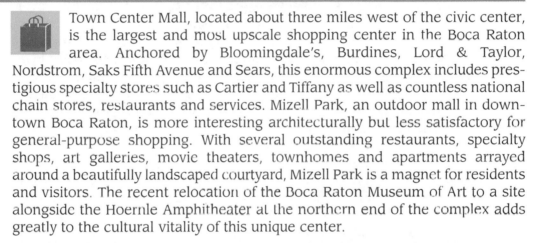
Town Center Mall, located about three miles west of the civic center, is the largest and most upscale shopping center in the Boca Raton area. Anchored by Bloomingdale's, Burdines, Lord & Taylor, Nordstrom, Saks Fifth Avenue and Sears, this enormous complex includes prestigious specialty stores such as Cartier and Tiffany as well as countless national chain stores, restaurants and services. Mizell Park, an outdoor mall in downtown Boca Raton, is more interesting architecturally but less satisfactory for general-purpose shopping. With several outstanding restaurants, specialty shops, art galleries, movie theaters, townhomes and apartments arrayed around a beautifully landscaped courtyard, Mizell Park is a magnet for residents and visitors. The recent relocation of the Boca Raton Museum of Art to a site alongside the Hoernle Amphitheater at the northern end of the complex adds greatly to the cultural vitality of this unique center.

Health Care   Rating: 5

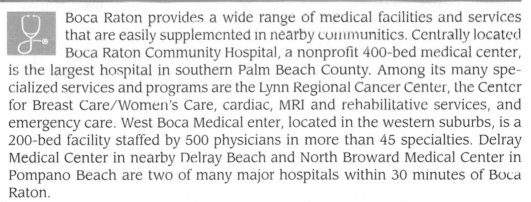
Boca Raton provides a wide range of medical facilities and services that are easily supplemented in nearby communities. Centrally located Boca Raton Community Hospital, a nonprofit 400-bed medical center, is the largest hospital in southern Palm Beach County. Among its many specialized services and programs are the Lynn Regional Cancer Center, the Center for Breast Care/Women's Care, cardiac, MRI and rehabilitative services, and emergency care. West Boca Medical enter, located in the western suburbs, is a 200-bed facility staffed by 500 physicians in more than 45 specialties. Delray Medical Center in nearby Delray Beach and North Broward Medical Center in Pompano Beach are two of many major hospitals within 30 minutes of Boca Raton.

Community Services   Rating: 4

Basic public services, as well as those targeted toward seniors, are better in Boca Raton than in most Florida cities. Boca Raton Senior Services is an information and referral service for seniors 60 and older. Mae Volen Senior Center is a nonprofit organization that provides diverse services for senior citizens. Weekday activities range from health screenings and lectures to a host of recreational activities. Hot lunches are furnished, and numerous homebound services such as transportation to medical appointments and the supermarket are offered. The Boca Raton Recreation Services Department publishes the Recreator three times annually. This useful publication documents the location of recreation sites and classes offered by or at city facilities. Concerts, dances and holiday celebrations are some of the fun events that you can enjoy free of charge.

Cultural and Educational Activities   Rating: 5

 Florida Atlantic University (FAU), with more than 20,000 degree-seeking undergraduate and graduate students, is the premier institution of higher learning in Boca Raton and Palm Beach County. A state-supported university, FAU allows retirees to enroll in courses at nominal cost through its Lifelong Learning Society. Courses are also available at the Boca Raton campus of Palm Beach Community College at low cost.

Being located roughly halfway between, and within a 40-minute drive of, the large metropolitan centers of West Palm Beach and Fort Lauderdale poses both disadvantages and advantages for Boca Raton. The city is overshadowed by the richer cultural offerings of its neighbors, yet their offerings are easily accessible by local residents. The Boca Raton Museum of Art, now located in a new 44,000-square-foot building in Mizner Park, and the Caldwell Theatre Company, South Florida's acclaimed regional professional theater, are the twin jewels of the local arts scene. The museum's permanent collection consists of more than 3,000 works of nineteenth and twentieth century European and American art, contemporary art, graphics, photography, sculpture and ceramics. Resident and visiting theatrical companies perform in the intimate 305-seat Caldwell Theatre. Additionally, the Florida Philharmonic Orchestra performs at FAU, at the top notch Broward Center for the Performing Arts in Fort Lauderdale, and at the Raymond F. Kravis Center for the Performing Arts in West Palm Beach. The latter two major venues host a wide variety of excellent shows and performances every year.

Recreational Activities   Rating: 5

 Nature's blessings and human efforts to protect and enhance the natural environment make Boca Raton a perfect place for recreation outdoors. Tropical weather, with water temperatures in the 70s and 80s throughout the year, and five miles of city-owned beachfront parks offer countless opportunities for sunbathing, swimming, diving and snorkeling. At Red Reef Park you can see coral reefs, tropical fish and even a few barracuda in safe, shallow waters. Lifeguards protect the white, sandy beach. The park has picnic areas, grills, observation gazebos and a boardwalk. Other oceanfront parks provide additional amenities including tennis, volleyball and basketball courts, softball fields and nature and fitness trails.

In 1991 Boca Raton launched the Environmentally Sensitive Lands Program in order to acquire, preserve and manage endangered habitat in inland areas of the city. The first five nature preserves—Serenoe Preserve, Cypress Knee Slough Preserve, Blazing Star Preserve, Yamato Scrub Preserve and Sugar Sand Park—are now open. In addition to protecting threatened habitat, these areas provide the public with hiking and nature trails, picnic areas and nature information centers. All in all, Boca Raton operates 1,000 acres of parks and recreation facilities making it among the top cities in Florida in parkland acreage per capita.

Locals claim that it is never too cold to play golf in Boca Raton and Palm Beach County and they are probably right. Palm Beach County has nearly 150 courses, including the historic Boca Raton Resort and Club course. Mere mortals might prefer to save a few dollars by playing at several other public and semi-private courses in the Boca Raton area. A complete list of area courses is available from the Boca Raton Chamber of Commerce.

If your preference is spectator sports, with few exceptions you need to travel an hour or so to Miami. There you can cheer on the Florida Marlins (major league baseball), Miami Dolphins (NFL football), Miami Heat (NBA basketball) and, improbable as it may seem, the Florida Panthers (NHL hockey). In Boca Raton you can support the FAU Owls football team or luxuriate at the Boca Raton Royal Palm Polo Club, where the world's best polo players and their horses compete January through April.

Like its Gulf Coast rival Naples, Boca Raton boasts an exceptional list of restaurants, including several four- and five-star establishments. American, seafood, Continental, Italian, Chinese, Mexican and Indian are among the varied cuisines available.

Work and Volunteer Activities   Rating: 4

Boca Raton likes to style itself as part of southeast Florida's Internet Coast but the reality is that most jobs open to seniors lie in the service sector, where more service jobs are becoming available as retailing continues to grow along with population in Palm Beach County. Openings for volunteers are many and varied, especially in health care. Fifteen thousand volunteers serve in one way or another at Boca Raton Community Hospital. Schools, libraries, museums and parks also depend heavily on volunteers.

Crime Rates and Public Safety   Rating: 4

Although Palm Beach County crime rates are about 50 percent above the national average, those in the city of Boca Raton are much lower. The property crime rate there is only slightly below the national norm but overall violent crime is nearly 50 percent below average. Most areas of the city seem very safe.

Conclusion

Overall Rating 49 Boca Raton is exceptional in Florida for the strength and breadth of its upscale amenities. Its strengths in retailing, health care, culture and recreation are unsurpassed by cities of its size and it remains an oasis of calm and civility amidst the chaotic urban sprawl of Florida's Gold Coast. Washed by warm Gulf Stream waters, Boca Raton's miles of public beaches are an enormous asset, as are its more than 1,000 acres of parkland, recreation areas and wilderness preserves. Community services and work/volunteer opportunities are very good. Crime rates are low in the city, although not countywide. Boca Raton is not quite perfect. There is some noise pollution near the airport and busy highways and some might find its summers too long, hot and humid and its cost of living a little high. On balance, though, Boca Raton offers a rare combination of amenities and a high quality of life in a beautiful tropical environment.

Naples, Florida

First settled in the 1880s when it was accessible only by water, Naples remained a remote outpost in coastal southwest Florida until its isolation was broken by the arrival of the railroad in 1927. Although the Great Depression and World War II slowed growth, improvements in road and air transportation beginning in the 1950s led to accelerating population growth and economic development in Naples and Collier County over the next five decades. After Hurricane Donna devastated much of Naples in 1960, the city was rebuilt according to a master plan that has produced a townscape with distinctive architecture and a manicured look in residential areas and public spaces. Like Palm Beach on Florida's east coast, Naples is a relatively small, affluent city rapidly becoming engulfed in countywide urban sprawl beyond its city limits. With a population of only 21,000, the city of Naples now constitutes only eight percent of the Naples metropolitan area (Collier County) and its percentage of the county total will doubtless continue to decline in coming years. Nonetheless, with its lovely white sand beaches, cultural and recreational amenities, excellent shopping and uniquely attractive historic neighborhoods, Naples can be expected to remain the premier community of Collier County and one of Florida's top locales for a truly upscale retirement.

Landscape   Rating: 4

Naples is the southernmost city on Florida's west (Gulf) coast. With an average elevation of six feet above sea level, Naples is flat and unusually susceptible to flooding from hurricane storm surges, yet it continues to attract new residents drawn by its tropical ambiance. Although the natural vegetation of coastal southwest Florida consists largely of grasses, pines and bald cypress, these have been replaced in the urban area by exotic tropical ornamentals such as royal and coconut palms, which thrive only in tropical or near-tropical conditions. Naples' beautiful landscape also includes a plethora of flowering plants including several varieties of bougainvillea and magnificent stands of magnolia, laurel oak and Australian pines, which provide shade that is badly needed during the long, hot summer.

Climate   Rating: 3

Although most retirement guidebooks describe the climate as subtropical, the correct term is tropical savanna. In the mainland United States, this virtually frost-free climate is found only in southernmost Florida; the rest of the state has a humid subtropical climate with somewhat cooler winters and occasional frosts. Naples' climate features two seasons. The winter half of the year— November through April—is warm, sunny and relatively dry, while the summer half—May through October—is hot and humid with frequent afternoon thundershowers. Annual precipitation averages 52 inches, with more than 60 percent of the annual total falling between June and September. Naples is sunny about 70 percent of the time and has an average frost-free season of 365 days. The area's principal climatic negative is the long, hot humid summer. In contrast, weather conditions are generally pleasant from November through April.

Naples, Florida

CLIMATE

Month	Average Daily Temperature High	Average Daily Temperature Low	Daily Rel. Humidity Low	Average Monthly Precipitation
	F		**%**	**Inches**
January	75	53	59	2.0
February	76	54	57	2.2
March	79	58	56	2.1
April	83	62	54	2.0
May	87	67	57	4.2
June	90	72	63	8.2
July	91	73	65	8.0
August	91	73	67	8.1
September	90	73	67	8.1
October	87	68	63	3.6
November	82	62	61	2.0
December	77	56	61	1.5

Annual Averages

Total Days		Total Inches	
Clear	98	Precipitation	51.9
Partly Cloudy	168	Snowfall	0.0
Cloudy	99		

RATINGS

Category	poor 1	fair 2	good 3	very good 4	excellent 5
Landscape				●	
Climate			●		
Quality of Life					●
Cost of Living	●				
Transportation		●			
Retail Services					●
Health Care			●		
Community Services			●		
Cultural Activities			●		
Recreational Activities					●
Work/Volunteer Activities			●		
Crime			●		

Total Points: 42

Gulf of Mexico

Palm River

Naples Park

North Naples

The Moorings

NAPLES

NAPLES MUNICIPAL AIRPORT

East Naples

Golden Gate

Port Royal

Lely

Naples Manor

Belle Meade

Old Marco Jct.

Royal Palm Hammock

Collier-Seminole State Park

FLORIDA

Marco

North

0 10 km
0 10 mi

FLORIDA

Naples

Quality of Life   **Rating: 5**

The quality of life is excellent in Naples proper but is a little less satisfactory in outlying suburbs. There is little noise pollution in Naples itself except along major boulevards and adjacent to the municipal airport. Residential areas in town are typically quiet but suburban areas adjacent to I-75 suffer additional noise. Air quality is excellent throughout Collier County, but the rapid urbanization of areas north and east of the city contributes to increased traffic congestion along the Tamiami Trail (U.S. 41) especially during the busy winter tourist season. Both city and county cater to automobile use, so parking is satisfactory. There are no poor neighborhoods in Naples proper, but Collier County has pockets of poverty in its rural inland area.

Naples' long public beach is a wonderful asset, its historic shopping districts are charming and much of the city has a park-like ambiance with nicely treed and flowered neighborhoods. Although the city's park acreage is relatively modest, Naples' parks are well equipped, landscaped and maintained, and additional county and state parks are just outside the city limits. Naples is a well-planned and well-managed city whose notable flaw is the absence of an adequate public transit system.

Cost of Living   Rating: 1

 The cost of living in Naples is evaluated as follows:

- *Composite.* No ACCRA data are available for Naples or Collier County but inferences can be drawn from ACCRA data for the affluent south Florida city of Fort Lauderdale. Additional data were gathered from local sources and field observations. On these bases, I estimate that the overall cost of living in Naples is 10 to 30 percent above the national average, depending on location.

- *Housing.* Exploration of the area indicates that Naples and Collier County have a good variety of new and resale housing available over a wide price range. The most expensive properties are single-family residences along the beach in Naples proper; prices of $500,000 to $1,000,000 are not unusual here. Inland a few blocks, attractive older single-family homes can be found in the $300,000 to $500,000 price range. Outside the city limits and east of the Tamiami Trail prices are considerably lower; the newest developments inland 10 or 15 miles feature single-family residences and condominiums

- *Goods and Services.* Aside from housing, living costs in Naples are only moderately above the national average but they are considerably higher than in less attractive Florida cities. Groceries, utilities, health care, transportation and miscellaneous goods and services are priced 5 to 20 percent above national norms.

- *Taxes.* The state and local tax burden in Naples is about 9.1 percent of income compared to the U.S. average of 9.7 percent. Florida has no state income tax. Property taxes, reflecting high property values, exceed the national average in the city of Naples but are lower on less expensive properties in inland areas of the county. Sales and excise taxes are also rather high.

Transportation   Rating: 2

 Naples has virtually no public transit, a serious omission in a resort and retirement town. Five Collier Area Transit (CAT) bus lines provide modest levels of service, mostly to suburban areas outside the city limits. Not surprisingly, Naples residents are almost entirely dependent on the automobile for local travel, and traffic congestion is gradually worsening. Intercity travel is mostly by car or air. Limited commuter and jet service is available at Naples Municipal Airport, just east of downtown, but better service is offered at Southwest Florida Regional Airport, 37 miles north via I-75. It provides nonstop jet service to more than 30 destinations.

Retail Services — Rating: 5

You can shop till you drop at any number of upscale retailing sites in Naples. Especially charming are the older downtown shopping districts along Fifth Avenue and Third Street. Fifth Avenue South, with its flower boxes, pocket parks and quaint storefronts, provides an ambiance conducive to strolling, shopping and dining. Third Street South and the Avenues, in historic Old Naples, have more than 100 distinctive galleries, boutiques and restaurants. The Waterside Shops at Pelican Bay, just north of the Naples city limits, is a unique assemblage of distinguished shops including Saks Fifth Avenue and restaurants nestled within an oasis of waterfalls, lagoons and luxuriant tropical vegetation. More ordinary is Coastland Center, the major regional mall. Anchored by Burdines, Dillard's, JCPenney and Sears department stores, this large enclosed mall features an abundance of specialty shops and national chain stores. Smaller shopping centers are widely scattered about the metropolitan area. Larger stores found in these centers include Beall's, Kmart, Target and Wal-Mart.

Health Care — Rating: 4

For a small city, Naples provides unusually good medical care. Naples Community Hospital, a branch of NCH Healthcare System, is the primary medical provider for the county. A 500-bed acute care facility, it provides a wide range of services including medical, surgical, and emergency care, cancer care, and cardiac surgery and rehabilitation. North Collier Hospital, also a unit of NCH Healthcare, is an 88-bed medical, surgical and rehabilitation unit serving the north county area beyond the city limits. In addition, the metropolitan area boasts a large number of community-oriented clinics providing routine care and referrals.

Community Services — Rating: 3

Municipal, county and private organizations provide a good array of community services. The Collier Council on Aging for Active Seniors publishes a free directory listing services available to seniors. The Naples Senior Citizens Club meets weekly at Norris Community Center in Cambier Park, downtown. In East Naples, the Senior Citizens Club meets regularly at the East Naples Community Center.

Cultural and Educational Activities — Rating: 3

Formerly a rather sleepy place, Naples has emerged as a lively cultural center in recent years. The Philharmonic Center for the Arts is the home of the Naples Symphony Orchestra and Chorus and the Miami City Ballet. It also hosts concerts, chamber music and Broadway plays. Plays are also produced by the Naples Players at the strikingly attractive Sugden Community Theatre on Fifth Avenue South. During the winter season, residents and visitors gather on Sunday afternoons in Cambier Park for free concerts by the Naples Concert Band. In summer, attention shifts to the free Friday evening popular music series at Waterside Shops at Pelican Bay.

Growth in southwest Florida prompted the state to establish Florida Gulf Coast University at a site just north of the Collier County line in 1997. Over time it should become a major educational asset for Fort Myers and Naples. Meanwhile, the Naples campus of Edison Community College offers lifelong learning courses on a wide variety of practical subjects for nominal fees, as do Naples and Collier County public schools.

Recreational Activities   Rating: 5

A unique combination of recreational assets in a tropical environment provides year-round opportunities for outdoor recreation. Miles of sugary, white sand beaches with warm, shallow water are among America's best. Even in winter the Gulf water temperature is around 66 degrees, just warm enough for swimming, while in summer it exceeds 80 degrees. Fishing is popular from the beach, Naples Pier and boats.

Much of the open space in Naples and Collier County is devoted to golf courses but land is also allocated to parks, biking and jogging paths, nature preserves and wildlife sanctuaries. With more than 50 golf courses, 70 percent of which are private, Collier County is a haven for golfers and spectators. Ladies PGA and Senior PGA tournaments are held in Naples each January and February. Among Collier County communities, Naples has especially well-equipped and maintained parks. Cambier Park, downtown, is notable for its lighted tennis courts, horseshoe, shuffleboard and basketball courts, playground, community theater and auditorium. Fleishmann Park, located next to Coastland Center Mall, features lighted racquetball, volleyball and basketball courts, lighted football/soccer and softball/baseball fields and a community game room. Bicycling, jogging, in-line skating, and walking are popular along several biking and jogging paths. Biking is also popular on lightly traveled residential streets west of U.S. 41. Nature lovers appreciate the Naples area for its state, federal, and privately protected wild areas. Especially notable are the Audubon Society's Corkscrew Swamp Sanctuary, 30 miles north of town, Collier-Seminole State Park, 15 miles southeast, and Everglades National Park, whose northern (Shark Valley) entrance is off U.S. 41, 75 miles east of Naples.

Reflecting its status as a prime winter resort, Naples boasts an exceptional list of restaurants offering menus of excellent quality and great variety. Seafood, Continental, Italian and American cuisines are especially favored locally. Three large multiplex theater complexes provide good choices for moviegoers.

Work and Volunteer Activities   Rating: 4

The booming Collier County economy, based heavily on tourism, retailing, financial and real estate services and construction, continues to generate large numbers of jobs. Minimal competition from college students allows seniors to compete effectively for part-time work, especially in the service sector. Openings for volunteers are also abundant. Hospitals, schools, libraries, museums, nature preserves and visitor centers are particularly dependent on volunteer staff. The Volunteer Center of Collier County is helpful in placing people where they are most needed.

The Naples metropolitan area (Collier County) crime rate is moderate overall, with rates of violent and property crime close to national norms. In the city of Naples, the violent crime rate is about 30 percent below the national average while the property crime rate is 30 percent above the national norm. Residential neighborhoods, recreation areas and commercial districts in the city of Naples all appear quite safe.

Conclusion

Overall Rating 42 Despite rampant growth of golf course communities and tract housing on its periphery, Naples has managed so far to retain its essential character as a charming resort and retirement town dedicated to leisure pursuits and gracious living. Beautifully landscaped with royal and coconut palms, magnolia, flowering vines and shrubs and other exotic species, the town exudes affluence and good taste in a tropical setting. Perhaps unique amid the urban sprawl of south Florida, Naples offers an excellent quality of life. Fifth Avenue downtown and Old Naples are delightful places to shop. Outdoor recreation—from year-round swimming at Naples Beach, to golf at countless area courses, to walking the elevated boardwalks through local wildlife sanctuaries—is unparalleled elsewhere. The community offers very good health care and opportunities for work and volunteer activities, a good range of community services and cultural activities, and moderate crime rates. Other than the long, hot humid summer, which many find fatiguing, the principal obstacles to the good life in Naples are the virtual absence of public transportation and the rather high cost of living. For those who can afford it, though, Naples may well be the mainland USA's best example of a tropical paradise.

Sarasota, Florida

Although a few Europeans settled the shores of Sarasota Bay as early as the 1700s, the area first became popular as a winter resort early in the twentieth century when the railroad connected the formerly isolated community with the northern states. Much credit for subsequent growth and cultural development of Sarasota and its offshore island beach communities of Longboat Key, Lido Key, St. Armands Key and Siesta Key belongs to John Ringling, who selected the town as the home base for his Ringling Brothers and Barnum and Bailey Circus in 1927. Ringling effectively promoted Sarasota and his circus and heavily invested in local real estate and the arts. His Italian Renaissance-style art museum and terra-cotta mansion on the shores of Sarasota Bay are legacies of his 1920s investments. Today appropriately nicknamed the Cultural Coast, Sarasota is unique among Florida retirement towns in the diversity and quality of its cultural offerings. In addition, it has much to offer in outdoor recreation, excellent shopping, and varied and attractive residential neighborhoods in a beautiful, subtropical environment. With a population exceeding 55,000 in the city and 350,000 in Sarasota County, the metropolitan area is a busy and exciting place. Although not without problems, Sarasota should persist as one of America's best retirement places for some time to come.

Sarasota, Florida

CLIMATE				
Month	Average Daily Temperature High / Low **F**	Daily Rel. Humidity Low **%**	Average Monthly Precipitation **Inches**	
January	73 / 52	59	2.7	
February	74 / 53	55	2.2	
March	78 / 58	55	3.4	
April	82 / 61	51	2.0	
May	87 / 67	52	2.2	
June	90 / 72	60	6.7	
July	91 / 74	63	6.7	
August	91 / 74	64	8.1	
September	90 / 72	62	7.4	
October	85 / 66	58	3.1	
November	80 / 60	56	2.1	
December	74 / 54	58	2.3	

Annual Averages

Total Days		Total Inches	
Clear	103	Precipitation	48.8
Partly Cloudy	142	Snowfall	0.0
Cloudy	120		

RATINGS

Category	poor 1	fair 2	good 3	very good 4	excellent 5
Landscape				●	
Climate			●		
Quality of Life			●		
Cost of Living			●		
Transportation			●		
Retail Services					●
Health Care					●
Community Services				●	
Cultural Activities					●
Recreational Activities					●
Work/Volunteer Activities					●
Crime	●				

Total Points: 47

Landscape	**Rating: 4**

Sarasota occupies a virtually flat plain halfway down Florida's west (Gulf) coast. Somewhat sheltered by barrier islands with miles of white sand beaches, the city proper is nonetheless susceptible to sea-water flooding from hurricanes as elevations range from sea level along the bay to only 20 feet above sea level inland. Natural vegetation varies from marsh grass to pine and oak but much has been replaced by exotic species including flowering plants and palms that thrive in the near tropical climate.

Climate   Rating: 3

 Like most of Florida, Sarasota has a humid subtropical climate featuring hot, humid summers and warm, relatively dry winters. About 60 percent of annual precipitation falls during the rainy season (June through September), mostly in the form of afternoon thundershowers, and the combination of heat and humidity can be fatiguing. In contrast, the dry season (November through April) is delightful with warm days, cool nights and abundant sunshine. On average, Sarasota is sunny 66 percent of the time and experiences only one or two frosts per winter.

Quality of Life   Rating: 3

 The quality of life is generally good in Sarasota. Air quality is excellent but noise pollution is annoying alongside major highways, especially U.S. 41 (the Tamiami Trail) and I-75 and adjacent to Sarasota–Bradenton International Airport. Although the city is uncrowded, rush-hour traffic congestion is worsening on the Tamiami Trail during the winter tourist season. Sarasota city and county are relatively young and automobile oriented so parking is widely available and free. The urban area includes a wide variety of neighborhoods, with less desirable tracts confined to inland areas north of downtown. Mainland developments near the bay and on the offshore keys are especially attractive. The Sarasota County Parks and Recreation Department operates 14 public beaches and a fine array of parks and playgrounds throughout the county. For the most part, city and county appear well planned and tastefully landscaped. In particular, the revived historic downtown shopping district, St. Armands Circle and its unique shops and restaurants, and several bayside parks offer a pedestrian-friendly ambiance not often found in Florida's bustling cities.

Cost of Living   Rating: 3

 The cost of living in Sarasota is evaluated as follows:

- *Composite.* ACCRA data for Sarasota show a composite cost of living approximately 5 percent above the national average.

- *Housing.* According to ACCRA, housing costs are about 13 percent above the national average. Exploration of the area indicates that an enormous variety of housing is available ranging from luxury single-family residences and condominiums in beachfront locations to modest homes inland. Generally, properties on barrier islands like Siesta Key and St. Armands Key are expensive, with some residences fetching upwards of $500,000. In contrast, plenty of two- and three-bedroom, two-bath homes are available on large, well-treed lots in attractive neighborhoods a few miles inland for $100,000 to $200,000.

- *Goods and Services.* Aside from housing, living costs in Sarasota approximate the national average. Groceries, utilities, transportation, health care and miscellaneous goods and services are all priced within 6 percent of national norms.

- *Taxes.* The state and local tax burden in Sarasota is about 9.1 percent of income compared to the U.S. average of 9.7 percent. Florida has no state income tax but property taxes are near the national average and sales and excise taxes are rather high.

Transportation — Rating: 3

Sarasota is strongly automobile oriented and has adequate roads for current demand. Sarasota County Transportation Authority provides fixed route bus service throughout the county's urbanized area six days a week. Buses serve downtown, major malls, beaches, the airport, residential areas and neighboring communities. Service levels are marginal at best; service on most lines is hourly and confined to daytime hours, so you need to plan your travel carefully. Fares are reasonable and senior discounts are offered. Sarasota-Bradenton International Airport, five miles north, provides adequate commercial air service. Nonstop jet service is available to 15 destinations including major hubs at Atlanta, Charlotte, Detroit and St. Louis, among others. Greyhound Lines provides intercity bus service from Sarasota but no rail passenger service is available.

Retail Services — Rating: 5

Sarasota has the usual large enclosed malls plus numerous quaint downtown and village shopping areas. Sarasota Square Mall, located alongside the Tamiami Trail on the southern periphery of town, is Sarasota's largest mall. Anchored by Burdines, Dillard's, JCPenney and Sears, it has more than 140 specialty shops—mostly branches of national and regional chains—a large food court, 12 AMC theaters and a cafeteria. Closer to downtown along the Tamiami Trail is Southgate Plaza, an upscale mall with an atypical and rather interesting layout. Anchored by Burdines, Dillard's and Saks Fifth Avenue, Southgate Plaza has the usual chain stores plus some upscale stores—for example, Talbots and Williams–Sonoma—not commonly found in malls. Even more interesting are St. Armands Circle and streets spoking off it, which boast more than 100 distinctly upscale shops and restaurants in a charming and beautifully landscaped setting; downtown Venice with its quaintly restored shops and restaurants; and the nicely revitalized Main Street in downtown Sarasota.

Health Care — Rating: 5

Sarasota provides excellent health care. Six fully accredited hospitals with a total of 1,600 beds offer more than 25 medical specialties. Sarasota Memorial Hospital, Doctors Hospital of Sarasota and Bon Secours Venice Hospital are the largest regional facilities with the widest array of services. An additional 50 general surgical hospitals provide an enormous range of medical services 50 miles north in the Tampa Bay Region.

Community Services — Rating: 4

A very good supply of community services of interest to seniors is available in Sarasota. Nonprofit Senior Friendship Centers exist in Sarasota and Venice; they also host activities at several other sites. No membership dues are charged but nominal donations are suggested for meals at special events. Center activities include dancing and dancing lessons, jazz concerts, cards, bingo, arts and crafts classes and activities, and health and exercise programs. Sarasota city and county parks and recreation facilities, social clubs and public libraries provide additional services.

Cultural and Educational Activities   Rating: 5

 Ever since John and Mabel Ringling settled here in the 1920s, Sarasota has been a haven for visual and performing artists and for patrons of the arts. Today the Ringling Museum houses more than 1,000 paintings, largely from the Renaissance and Baroque periods. Highlights of the collection include five large oil paintings by Peter Paul Rubens. Regular and rotating exhibitions may also be seen at the Sarasota Visual Art Center, the Selby Gallery at the Ringling School of Art and Design and the Venice Art Center. More than 30 commercial art galleries are clustered near downtown's theater district or at St. Armands Circle.

Sarasota's performing arts calendar is so full that its richness can only be hinted at here. The Van Wezel Performing Arts Hall, designed by Frank Lloyd Wright and renowned for its outstanding acoustics, presents performances by distinguished touring musical, dance and theatrical companies. It is home to the Sarasota Ballet of Florida, the Florida West Coast Symphony Orchestra and Gloria Musicae, a professional chorale ensemble. The beautifully restored downtown Sarasota Opera House hosts four operas by the critically acclaimed Sarasota Opera Company each February and March. The FSU Center for the Arts, located on the Ringling property, is home to the Asolo Theater Company, one of the state of Florida's four official theatrical troupes, and to the outstanding Asolo Theatre Festival, which runs from November through May. Performances are staged at the 500-seat Mertz Theatre and the more intimate 161-seat Cook Theatre.

Sarasota is also home to several institutions of higher learning. The University of Florida at Sarasota/New College, part of the University of Florida system, offers junior-, senior- and graduate-level courses in business administration, education, social and behavioral sciences and engineering. For casual students, though, Manatee Community College, with campuses in Bradenton and Venice, might be a better choice. Its continuing education program provides a great variety of non-degree courses of interest to seniors for nominal fees. The winter lecture series presented by Sarasota's Institute of Lifelong Learning on topics like the arts, foreign affairs and cultural and social issues, is also of interest.

Recreational Activities   Rating: 5

 With wide, white sand beaches stretching for 35 miles along warm Gulf waters, it is no wonder that Sarasota is famous for beach-going activities. Even so, sunning and swimming are only the beginning of the area's outdoor recreational possibilities. Bays, bayous and the Gulf of Mexico boast some of the best fishing in the state, while the Intracoastal Waterway, bays and inshore waters provide opportunities for all kinds of boating. Local waters are also ideal for snorkeling and scuba diving.

Although many retirees live in luxurious golf course communities or are members of private country clubs, competing public and semi-private courses where one can play on a pay-for-play basis offer a variety of challenges. About two-thirds of Sarasota County golf courses, including several of championship caliber, are open to the general public. The county is also notable for its excellent network of public parks and recreational facilities operated by city, county and state authorities. Sarasota County alone operates 117 parks and recreation facilities. These range from beach access trails and small neighborhood parks, playgrounds and picnic areas to community and metropolitan parks that typically include sports fields, lighted tennis courts, swimming facilities, gymnasium and recreation buildings, trails and nature centers. Oscar Scherer State Recreation Area, just north of Venice, and Myakka River State Park, 20 miles southeast of Sarasota, offer camping, picnicking, hiking, boating, fishing and nature appreciation, among other activities.

Consistent with its role as a major resort area, Sarasota has a good assortment of high-quality restaurants downtown, at St. Armands Circle, and at various shopping centers. Seafood, Continental, Italian and American cuisines are widely available. Mainstream movies may be seen at several large multiplex theater complexes while international and American films by independent filmmakers are exhibited by the Sarasota Film Society at its Burns Court Cinema.

Work and Volunteer Activities   Rating: 5

The Sarasota County economy has grown fast in recent years and steadily generates jobs in tourist related services, retailing and financial and real estate services. Seniors are quite competitive for part-time work owing to the absence of severe competition from college students. Many seniors are able to find volunteer work in schools, hospitals, libraries, museums and parks.

Crime Rates and Public Safety   Rating: 2

Crime rates are high in the city of Sarasota but considerably lower countywide. In Sarasota itself, violent crime occurs at a rate more than twice the national average, and the rate of property crime is little better. In contrast, countywide rates of violent and property crime are only slightly above their national norms. Clearly, where you live in the Sarasota area largely determines your potential exposure to crime. Suburban areas in general, and upscale neighborhoods in particular, are much safer than areas adjacent to poor neighborhoods just northeast of downtown.

Conclusion

Overall Rating 47 Sarasota city and county are unique in Florida for the enormous variety and high quality of services, culture and recreation offered residents and visitors. Renowned as Florida's Cultural Coast for its repertoire of first-rate ballet, chorale, dance, opera, symphony, theater and visual arts programs and venues, Sarasota is also notable for remarkable outdoor recreational assets. An abundance of golf courses and more than 120 parks and recreational areas strategically located in town, astride bays, bayous and inshore waters, and along the county's 35 miles of white sandy beaches, offer recreational options to suit every taste. Shopping and health care are excellent, work and volunteer opportunities are outstanding and community services are better than in most Florida cities. Although Sarasota and its offshore keys are only a few feet above sea level, the local landscape with its luxurious subtropical vegetation, waterside vistas and charming residential and retailing areas, is most attractive. Sarasota is not quite perfect. Its summers may be too hot and humid for some, a few neighborhoods are blighted and provide a less-than-ideal quality of life, public transit is marginal and crime rates are sobering. All in all, though, Sarasota offers a combination of amenities seldom found in medium-sized retirement towns and at a cost of living scarcely above the national average. It merits a serious look by those seeking a coastal Florida lifestyle with culture.

Gainesville, Florida

Although founded in 1854 and named for Revolutionary War General Edmund Gaines, Gainesville remained a quiet agricultural community until the twentieth century. Two events—the great freeze of February 1895, which killed more than 90 percent of the orange trees of northern Florida, and the establishment in Gainesville of the University of Florida in 1906—pointed the town and surrounding Alachua County in new directions. Area agriculture diversified, with cattle ranching replacing citrus growing, and Gainesville gradually evolved into a leafy college town offering a rare combination of small-town charm, natural beauty and bountiful cultural and educational amenities. With a population of 100,000 in the city and 230,000 in the metropolitan area (Alachua County), Gainesville remains a small town that has avoided being swept up in the frenzied growth typical of central and south Florida. Nonetheless, assets typical of major metropolitan areas are nearby. Jacksonville is 70 miles northeast, Orlando is 115 miles southeast and Tampa is 125 miles south of Gainesville.

Landscape   Rating: 4

Gainesville occupies a gently rolling plain about midway across the northern extremity of the Florida peninsula. Elevations in town vary between 100 and 200 feet and numerous sinkholes, some filled with water forming small lakes and ponds, give variety to the landscape. The prevailing natural vegetation is pine forest in drier areas and prairie grasses in wetlands. Residential neighborhoods and the huge University of Florida campus are planted with a variety of ornamental species including pine, live oak, magnolia and palmetto, which lend a distinctly subtropical ambiance to the community.

Climate   Rating: 3

Gainesville has a humid subtropical climate characterized by long, hot, humid and rainy summers and mild and somewhat drier winters. More than half of annual precipitation falls during the rainy season (June through September), largely in the form of afternoon thundershowers that provide temporary relief from the wilting summer heat. Winter weather is quite variable with cold fronts bringing occasional frosts and limiting the frost-free period to 290 days. Spring and autumn are pleasant with warm days, cool nights and the seasonal maxima of sunshine. Gainesville is sunny about 70 percent of the time in spring and autumn, 66 percent in summer and 60 percent in winter.

Quality of Life   Rating: 5

The quality of life is typically excellent in Gainesville. Air quality is excellent and noise pollution is an annoyance only along I-75 on the western fringe of town and alongside a few major boulevards such as Archer and Williston Roads. The city's small size and low population density

Gainesville, Florida

CLIMATE

Month	Average Daily Temperature High (F)	Average Daily Temperature Low (F)	Daily Rel. Humidity Low (%)	Average Monthly Precipitation (Inches)
January	66	43	62	3.4
February	69	45	57	3.6
March	75	50	55	4.0
April	81	55	52	2.2
May	87	63	51	2.8
June	89	69	55	7.1
July	91	71	58	6.9
August	90	71	60	7.2
September	87	69	64	5.3
October	81	60	63	2.7
November	74	51	62	2.1
December	68	44	63	2.7

Annual Averages

Total Days		Total Inches	
Clear	94	Precipitation	50.0
Partly Cloudy	145	Snowfall	0.0
Cloudy	126		

RATINGS

Category	poor (1)	fair (2)	good (3)	very good (4)	excellent (5)
Landscape				●	
Climate			●		
Quality of Life					●
Cost of Living			●		
Transportation					●
Retail Services			●		
Health Care					●
Community Services				●	
Cultural Activities				●	
Recreational Activities					●
Work/Volunteer Activities				●	
Crime		●			

Total Points: 47

give it an uncrowded feeling with little traffic congestion, even at rush hour. Adequate parking is available in most areas and the University of Florida encourages public transit use by providing free bus privileges to students. Gainesville's service-based economy lacks noxious industries and the city appears well planned, especially when compared with the sprawling urban complexes of South Florida. Most residential neighborhoods are attractive with housing of various styles sited on large wooded lots. The revitalized historic downtown area, with its unique combination of shops, restaurants, nightclubs, theaters and housing, offers a lively pedestrian-friendly alternative to suburban malls and shopping centers. Excellent park systems in the city and county also contribute to Gainesville's high quality of life.

Cost of Living   Rating: 3

 The cost of living in Gainesville is evaluated as follows:

- *Composite.* ACCRA data for Gainesville show a composite cost of living approximately at the national average.

- *Housing.* According to ACCRA, housing costs are about 8 percent above the national average. However, exploration of the area indicates that Gainesville housing offers good value when you take into account the low cost of land and the high quality of the housing stock. You will pay less, on average, for the lot on which your house sits in Gainesville than in many American cities; therefore, more of your housing dollar is available to pay for the house itself. Many three-bedroom, two-bath houses on large wooded lots in beautiful neighborhoods are available for prices between $150,000 and $250,000.

- *Goods and Services.* Goods and services are typically priced near national norms in Gainesville. Groceries, utilities and miscellaneous goods and services are all priced within 3 percent of their national averages, whereas health care and transportation exceed their national norms by 10 percent.

- *Taxes.* The state and local tax burden in Gainesville is about 9.1 percent of income compared to the U.S. average of 9.7 percent. Florida has no state income tax but property taxes are near the national average and sales and excise taxes are rather high.

Transportation   Rating: 5

 I-75 skirts the western side of Gainesville so most travel in town is on local streets. The road infrastructure seems adequate for current demand. Gainesville Regional Transit System (RTS) provides excellent bus service on a network of routes focused on the Downtown Plaza and the University of Florida campus. Santa Fe Community College, Oaks Mall, area hospitals and most other destinations can be reached by bus. On weekdays most buses run at 20- to 30-minute intervals from early morning until 9:00 p.m. Less frequent service is available on weekends. Fares are reasonable.

Intercity travel is possible by air, bus and rail. Gainesville Regional Airport provides limited nonstop jet service to hub airports at Atlanta and Charlotte. Jacksonville International Airport, 60 miles away, offers nonstop flights to more than 20 destinations. Greyhound Lines provides intercity bus service to points north and south, while Amtrak furnishes twice daily bus/rail connections to major points north and south including New York and Miami.

Retail Services   Rating: 3

 The Oaks Mall, located on Newberry Road (State Road 26) just east of I-75, is Gainesville's major mall. Anchored by Belk, Burdines, Dillard's, JCPenney and Sears, this large enclosed shopping center has more than 140 specialty shops (many run by national chains), restaurants and services. Also in suburban locations are a Target store near the junction of Archer Road and I-75 and a Wal-Mart and Sam's Club adjacent to Gainesville Mall, in the northern part of town. Perhaps most interesting is the revitalized historic downtown core of Gainesville, where you can stroll along brick sidewalks lined with unique shops, lively restaurants and nightclubs, a beautifully restored theater and bed and breakfast inns.

Health Care   Rating: 5

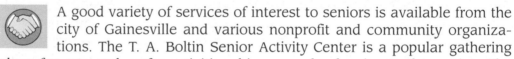

Gainesville offers outstanding medical care by virtue of the presence of the University of Florida Health Science Center. The university medical system includes three units of Shands Hospital. Shands Hospital at the University of Florida is a 570-bed facility with centers specializing in cardiovascular, neurological, cancer and transplantation services. Shands at AGH (formerly Alachua General Hospital) is a full-service hospital with 367 beds and more than 200 physicians on staff. It specializes in cardiac and cancer care, neuroscience, women's health and emergency care. Shands at Vista is an 81-bed behavioral health facility. North Florida Regional Medical Center, with 278 beds, and a large Veterans Administration hospital are the city's other major medical facilities. Both provide diverse inpatient and outpatient services.

Community Services   Rating: 4

A good variety of services of interest to seniors is available from the city of Gainesville and various nonprofit and community organizations. The T. A. Boltin Senior Activity Center is a popular gathering place for arts and crafts activities, bingo, cards, dancing and exercise. The center also organizes day and overnight field trips to the casinos of Biloxi, Mississippi and other places. The Gainesville Department of Recreation and Parks operates a Wellness Center at its Martin Luther King, Jr. Multi-purpose Center. Seniors can use fitness equipment there for a nominal annual fee. AARP and RSVP are also active in Gainesville, providing access to paid and volunteer employment and information useful to seniors. Social clubs and organizations and the public library offer additional services.

Cultural and Educational Activities   Rating: 4

The University of Florida, with more than 45,000 students and 4,000 faculty, is the state's flagship institution of higher learning. With more than 100 undergraduate majors, 200 graduate programs and 5 major professional schools, the university is a wonderful educational and cultural asset. Senior Florida residents may audit courses on a "space available" basis. The university's state-of-the-art 1,800-seat Center for the Performing Arts regularly hosts quality theater, dance and symphonic and orchestral concerts. Adjacent to the Center are the Samuel P. Harn Museum of Art and the Florida Museum of Natural History. The Harn Museum displays a wide selection of art from around the world; the Florida Museum is the largest natural history museum in the southeastern United States.

Housed in a beautiful, neoclassical building in the heart of historic downtown Gainesville is the Hippodrome State Theatre, one of four state-supported theaters in Florida. The Hippodrome produces eight shows annually, each cast with actors from throughout the country and from the Hippodrome's own professional company. The Hippodrome's theatrical events are presented in a uniquely intimate space; no seat is more than seven rows from the stage, so there is not a bad seat in the house. Even so, prices are remarkably low. Season tickets are priced around $125. In addition to the theater, the building houses an 80-seat cinema featuring avant-garde, limited release, and foreign films, as well as an art gallery displaying the works of North Florida artists.

Recreational Activities   Rating: 5

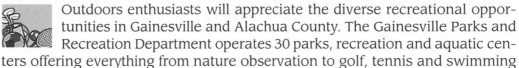 Outdoors enthusiasts will appreciate the diverse recreational opportunities in Gainesville and Alachua County. The Gainesville Parks and Recreation Department operates 30 parks, recreation and aquatic centers offering everything from nature observation to golf, tennis and swimming lessons and play. Bivens Arm Nature Park, a 57-acre preserve of oak hammock and marsh that is accessed in part by an elevated boardwalk, provides solitude and excellent bird watching only two miles from downtown. Golf is a bargain at the city's Ironwood Golf Course; greens fees are around $20. Golf is also played on six other local private and public courses including the University of Florida Golf Club.

Gainesville is virtually surrounded by natural beauty that can be easily reached by car or bicycle. The city is in the heart of Florida's natural springs region, which has the world's largest number of high-flow freshwater springs. With 60 miles of on-street bike lanes and a 15-mile paved State Trail connecting Gainesville with Hawthorne along an old railroad right-of-way, the city is distinctly friendly to bicyclists. You can ride north to visit Devil's Millhopper State Geologic Site, a spectacular sinkhole 120 feet deep and 500 feet wide, or go southwest to Kanahapa Botanical Gardens with its 62 acres of gardens, meadows and woodlands. Just south of town is Paynes Prairie Preserve, a wildlife sanctuary encompassing 20,000 acres of marsh and swamp, sinkhole lakes and pine woods. The northern part of the Preserve is traversed by the Gainesville–Hawthorne State Trail, with overlooks providing good vantage points for viewing wildlife. And just east of town is Newnans Lake, a 10-square mile freshwater lake popular for boating and fishing.

Consistent with its college town role, Gainesville boasts first-rate intercollegiate sports and a good selection of movie theaters and restaurants. The town really comes alive when fans of the Florida Gators turn out for NCAA basketball and football games at the university's Stephen C. O'Connell Center and Ben Griffin Stadium. Several fine restaurants clustered in the historic downtown area provide American, Continental and Italian specialties at reasonable prices. Also downtown is the Hippodrome Theatre art movie house. Six cinema chains show mainstream movies on 27 screens at other locations around town.

Work and Volunteer Activities   Rating: 4

Gainesville's booming service-based economy continues to generate jobs, especially at the university, in health care and in retailing. Competition with college students is acute, though, particularly for part-time jobs on campus and in retailing. RSVP offers an excellent free guide to retirement living in Alachua County and assists seniors in finding volunteer work. Volunteers serve in local schools, hospitals, parks, museums and libraries, or serve as advocates for the aging and other groups. In a recent year more than 500 Alachua County RSVP volunteers provided in excess of 100,000 hours of service at more than 75 volunteer sites in the community. Those seeking paid work may obtain assistance through the AARP Senior Community Employment Program.

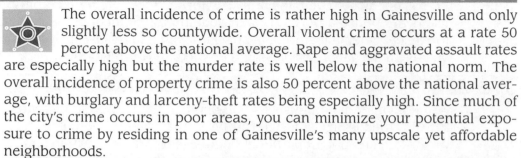

The overall incidence of crime is rather high in Gainesville and only slightly less so countywide. Overall violent crime occurs at a rate 50 percent above the national average. Rape and aggravated assault rates are especially high but the murder rate is well below the national norm. The overall incidence of property crime is also 50 percent above the national average, with burglary and larceny-theft rates being especially high. Since much of the city's crime occurs in poor areas, you can minimize your potential exposure to crime by residing in one of Gainesville's many upscale yet affordable neighborhoods.

Conclusion

Overall Rating 47 Gainesville remains one of America's choice locations for retirement. Not too big, not too small, this north central Florida college town provides everything essential for upscale retirement at reasonable prices. The University of Florida, around which Gainesville is built, is the key element in the town's prosperity and a major supplier of its amenities. The community's fine quality of life, health care, cultural and recreational amenities and transportation all reflect facilities and services provided by the university and the needs of its faculty, staff and students. Gainesville also provides above-average community services and work and volunteer opportunities. As a regional capital, Gainesville is also able to provide a range of retail services unusual for a city of its size.

Thanks to its inland location and moderate elevation, Gainesville is spared the worst danger from hurricanes: storm surge flooding of low-lying areas. The natural landscape, a gently rolling surface mantled in forest and dotted with marshes and lakes, is beautiful and unspoiled and the town's wooded residential neighborhoods and historic downtown are unusually attractive. Only Gainesville's long, hot and humid summers and elevated crime rates detract significantly from the community's overall high rating. If you are seeking college town amenities at low prices in an inland subtropical environment, give Gainesville a careful look.

Tallahassee, Florida

The site of present-day Tallahassee was once the home of Apalachee Indians, many of whom were Christianized by Spanish missionaries by the 1670s. Subsequently, wars involving Britain, France and Spain so depleted the Apalachee population that when Andrew Jackson's raiders reached Tallahassee in 1818 they found the Indian village abandoned and only a few survivors in the surrounding area.

Tallahassee became Florida's capital almost by default. Between 1818 and 1823, Pensacola and St. Augustine, then Florida's largest towns, refused to concede capital status to the other. As a result, Governor Duval forced a compromise whereby Tallahassee, halfway between the rival communities, became capital of Florida. Tallahassee's role as state capital and later also as the site of Florida State University (FSU) and Florida A&M University (FAMU), has led to steady economic and population growth. With nearly 160,000 people in the city and 300,000 in the metropolitan area (Gadsden and Leon Counties), Tallahassee is no longer the sleepy state capital of half a century ago.

Tallahassee, Florida

CLIMATE				
Month	Average Daily Temperature High	Low	Daily Rel. Humidity Low	Average Monthly Precipitation
	F		%	Inches
January	64	40	58	5.4
February	67	42	54	4.6
March	74	48	51	6.5
April	80	53	47	3.6
May	87	62	50	5.0
June	91	70	56	6.9
July	92	73	61	8.0
August	92	73	61	7.0
September	89	69	58	5.0
October	81	57	53	3.3
November	73	48	55	3.9
December	66	42	58	4.1

Annual Averages

Total Days		Total Inches	
Clear	102	Precipitation	63.2
Partly Cloudy	129	Snowfall	0.0
Cloudy	134		

RATINGS					
Category	poor 1	fair 2	good 3	very good 4	excellent 5
Landscape				●	
Climate			●		
Quality of Life				●	
Cost of Living			●		
Transportation				●	
Retail Services			●		
Health Care				●	
Community Services					●
Cultural Activities					●
Recreational Activities					●
Work/Volunteer Activities			●		
Crime	●				

Total Points: 44

Nonetheless, it retains a pleasant, small-town atmosphere, charming and friendly neighborhoods, a sense of history and place and unspoiled natural beauty, all characteristics in short supply in the urban chaos of central and south Florida.

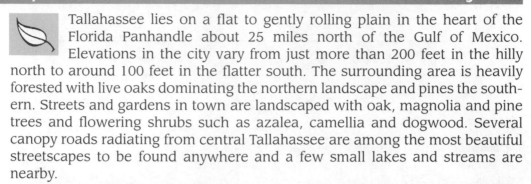

Tallahassee lies on a flat to gently rolling plain in the heart of the Florida Panhandle about 25 miles north of the Gulf of Mexico. Elevations in the city vary from just more than 200 feet in the hilly north to around 100 feet in the flatter south. The surrounding area is heavily forested with live oaks dominating the northern landscape and pines the southern. Streets and gardens in town are landscaped with oak, magnolia and pine trees and flowering shrubs such as azalea, camellia and dogwood. Several canopy roads radiating from central Tallahassee are among the most beautiful streetscapes to be found anywhere and a few small lakes and streams are nearby.

| Climate | Rating: 3 |

Like the rest of northern Florida, Tallahassee has a humid subtropical climate featuring hot, humid summers and mild winters. Precipitation is ample and well distributed throughout the year. Snow is virtually unknown and the weather is typically sunny. It is sunny more than half the time every month, with spring and early summer being the sunniest period. Relative humidity is moderate but the combination of 90-degree temperatures and relative humidity exceeding 60 percent on summer afternoons is stifling. In contrast, most days between October and early May are pleasant. Occasional winter frosts limit the frost-free period to about 270 days.

| Quality of Life | Rating: 4 |

The quality of life is very good in Tallahassee. Air quality is excellent and noise pollution is annoying mainly along I-10 in the northern part of town and near Tallahassee Regional Airport on the southern periphery. The city's modest size and low population density give it a small-town feeling. There is little traffic congestion and parking is adequate and cheap or free in most areas except near the capitol and immediately adjacent to the most heavily developed parts of the two university campuses. Tallahassee's service-based economy lacks noxious industries and the city appears well planned. Most residential areas are exceptionally attractive with houses sited on large, wooded lots. The revitalizing historic downtown, with its museums, upscale shops, hotels, restaurants and watering holes, is a vast improvement over the deteriorating downtown scene only a decade ago. Tallahassee's excellent park system and numerous nearby county and state parks also contribute to the city's high quality of life.

| Cost of Living | Rating: 3 |

The cost of living in Tallahassee is evaluated as follows:

- *Composite.* ACCRA data for Tallahassee show that the composite cost of living is at the national average.

- *Housing.* According to ACCRA, housing costs are about 4 percent below the national average. Tallahassee housing offers excellent value when you take into account the low cost of land, the large wooded lots and the quality of the housing stock. Many three-bedroom, two-bath houses on large wooded lots in lovely neighborhoods are available for prices between $150,000 and

$250,000. Two-bedroom, two-bath condominiums are priced around $100,000.

- *Goods and Services.* Goods and services are priced near national norms in Tallahassee. Groceries, utilities, health care and miscellaneous goods and services are all priced within 2 percent of their national averages, whereas transportation exceeds the national norm by about 7 percent.

- *Taxes.* The state and local tax burden in Tallahassee is about 9.1 percent of income compared to the U.S. average of 9.7 percent. Florida has no state income tax, but property taxes are near the national average and sales and excise taxes are rather high.

Transportation   Rating: 4

 I-10 crosses the north side of Tallahassee on an east–west trajectory that has little utility for most suburb-to-center travel. Most trips in town are on local streets that appear adequate for current demand. Taltran, the municipal bus company, provides fairly good bus service on a network of routes focused on downtown and the FSU campus. Major destinations including the capitol complex, the universities, hospitals and malls can be reached by bus. Intercity travel is possible by air, bus and rail. Tallahassee Regional Airport provides nonstop service to hub airports at Atlanta, Charlotte and Miami. Greyhound offers bus service to many points and Amtrak provides rail passenger service three times a week to points east and west including Jacksonville, Orlando, New Orleans and Los Angeles.

Retail Services   Rating: 3

Governor's Square Mall, located on Apalachee Parkway less than two miles east of the state capitol, is Tallahassee's major mall. Anchored by Burdines, Dillard's, JCPenney and Sears, this sky-lit and architecturally interesting indoor mall has more than 150 specialty shops, restaurants and services. Ficus trees lining its major corridors are a nice touch and the mall's large food court is unusually attractive. A smaller mall and large cinema complex are adjacent to Governor's Square. Tallahassee Mall, located a little less than three miles north of downtown, is anchored by Dillard's, Goody's and Parisian department stores and Burlington Coat Factory. Somewhat downscale from Governor's Square, Tallahassee Mall boasts more than 100 specialty shops, restaurants and services and a 20-screen cinema complex. Tallahassee's revitalizing downtown is not yet a significant retailing area. Its Adams Street Commons features shops, restaurants and bars catering mainly to daytime customers from the adjacent state capitol complex. Antique stores and art galleries line Main Street in downtown Havana, 16 miles north of Tallahassee.

Health Care   Rating: 4

Tallahassee Memorial HealthCare (TMHC) and Capital Regional Medical Center (CRMC) together provide the most comprehensive medical care available in northwestern Florida. TMHC operates Tallahassee Memorial Hospital, a 770-bed, nonprofit teaching hospital staffed by 330 physicians in 35 specialties, and 11 satellite clinics in 5 counties. The hospital's specialties include behavioral health, cancer and diabetes treatment, family practice, heart and vascular care, neuroscience, women's health and comprehensive critical care. CRMC, formerly Tallahassee Community Hospital, is now located in a new building with 180 beds and the latest medical technology. Hospital services include emergency and intensive care, radiology, respiratory care, physical therapy, heart surgery, orthopedic and urological services and neurosurgery. Excellent medical care is also available at Archbold Memorial Hospital in Thomasville, Georgia, 35 miles north.

Community Services   Rating: 5

 Excellent community services of interest to seniors are provided by the city, the universities and various nonprofit and community organizations. The Tallahassee Parks and Recreation Department sponsors fitness programs at six community centers and arts and crafts at a seventh. The Tallahassee Senior Center, located in a large and impressive building on North Main Street, is a popular activity center. More than 90 different programs, groups, activities and services offer something for everyone. Social clubs, religious organizations, the public library and the YMCA offer additional services.

Cultural and Educational Activities   Rating: 5

 Florida State University (FSU), with more than 36,000 students and 4,000 faculty members, is a wonderful educational and cultural asset. Senior Florida residents may audit courses for free on a "space available" basis and enjoy the university's cultural offerings at nominal cost. The FSU School of Music is one of the best in the land, enrolling more than 1,000 students and staging performances in facilities ranging from 100-seat Lindsay Recital Hall to the 1500-seat Ruby Diamond Auditorium. The School of Music hosts more than 400 faculty and student solo, chamber music, opera, choral, orchestral, band, jazz and guest artist concerts each year. Most concerts are free, while about 20 are ticketed at moderate prices. The FSU School of Theater runs a top-rated theatrical training program and annually produces three series of plays and musicals at the Fallon Mainstage, Lab Theatre and Augusta Conrad Studio Theatre, on campus. FSU's several musical and theatrical venues also host the Tallahassee Ballet, the Tallahassee Symphony and countless visiting professional ensembles.

Cultural attractions are also abundant off campus. Downtown Tallahassee is being reborn as a center for the performing and visual arts. The Civic Center hosts concerts by top musical artists and the new Mary Brogan Museum features visual art exhibitions and hands-on science experiences. Nearby Florida A&M University and Tallahassee Community College produce popular musicals and drama.

Recreational Activities   Rating: 5

 Outdoor recreation abounds in Tallahassee and vicinity. The city Parks and Recreation Department manages 3,100 acres of parks and recreation facilities offering everything from nature observation and rose gardens to golf, tennis, equestrian activities and swimming. Golf is bargain priced at the city's two 9-hole and two 18-hole public courses and fairly inexpensive at several semi-private and private courses.

Tallahassee is surrounded by natural beauty easily reached by car or bicycle. Nine off-road bike paths, including the paved 16-mile St. Marks Trail, reach outward from central and suburban Tallahassee to woodlands, lakes and rivers. Bike lanes on several city streets provide additional opportunities for biking in town. Alfred B. Maclay State Gardens, located only six miles north of the city center, features more than 40 varieties of camellias, azaleas, exotic flowers, trees and shrubs. The grounds also include facilities for boating, canoeing, fishing, swimming, picnicking and hiking. Within a two-hour drive of the city are several of Florida's best beaches. One of these, the beach at St. Joseph Peninsula State Park, was rated number one in the nation in the 2002 Best Beaches Report.

Thanks to its role as a major college town, Tallahassee boasts top-quality intercollegiate sports and a good selection of movie theaters and restaurants. Basketball and football games played by the Florida A&M University Rattlers and the Florida State University Seminoles really make the town jump.

Work and Volunteer Activities   Rating: 3

Tallahassee has enviably low unemployment in good times and bad. Part-time employment in service sector jobs such as retailing is plentiful. That said, competition for jobs with college students is acute, especially for part-time work on campus and in retailing. Volunteers serve the community in many ways. Hospitals, parks, museums, libraries and the visitors bureau are among the major employers.

Crime Rates and Public Safety   Rating: 1

Crime rates are rather high in Tallahassee. Violent crime occurs at a rate twice the national average. The aggravated assault rate is particularly high but the homicide rate is near the national norm. The overall rate of property crime is about 50 percent above the national average; burglary and larceny–theft rates are especially high, while the auto theft rate is rather low.

Local authorities argue that most violent crime and much of the property crime occur in several poor, economically depressed neighborhoods and that most parts of Tallahassee are attractive and safe. Our travels in Tallahassee tend to confirm that such is the case. Here, as elsewhere, you can minimize your potential exposure to crime by picking your home site carefully. Fortunately, homes in exceptional neighborhoods are plentiful and affordable in Tallahassee.

Conclusion

Overall Rating 44 Tallahassee is seldom ranked among North America's best retirement places. It deserves better! Tallahassee is not located alongside a tropical beach and has not gained fame as a theme park or golf resort site. But it does have much to offer those seeking retirement in an environmentally unspoiled, amenity-rich, subtropical city where costs are low. Unlike many Florida cities, which are suffering from an excess of growth and a deficit of good taste and sound planning, Tallahassee retains much of its historic southern charm. Its wooded, hilly landscape and attractive, well-maintained neighborhoods help earn it very good ratings in landscape and quality of life. Likewise, its varied transportation choices and medical facilities are very good, especially for a small, livable city. You will not be bored in Tallahassee. The faculty, staff and students of Florida State and Florida A&M Universities generate much of the demand supporting quality community services and they produce and support excellent cultural, educational and recreational activities. Additionally, retail services and work and volunteer opportunities are good, and the climate is agreeable except perhaps during the hot, humid summer.

Tallahassee's major drawback is its high rates of violent and property crime. Luckily, you can choose among many excellent, affordable and relatively crime-free neighborhoods in this friendly and welcoming city. If you want to move to Florida and live well at a reasonable price while avoiding the crowds, Tallahassee is surely worth a careful look.

Thomasville, Georgia

Benefiting from its status as the southern terminus of a railroad connecting with the north, Thomasville blossomed into a major winter resort in the 1880s and 1890s. Northerners first came for their health, believing that the warm pine-scented air was a remedy for pulmonary ailments. Others soon joined them to escape winter's rigors and to enjoy the area's hunting, fishing and genteel social life.

Although Thomasville's "grand hotel era" came to a close when improved transportation opened Florida to tourism after 1900, a substantial legacy of landmark mansions and plantation homes has survived to the present. Together with Thomasville's colorful and vital Victorian downtown, natural beauty and cultural advantages, these lovingly restored homes make Thomasville a special place. With its population essentially stable at about 18,000, Thomasville is peaceful and friendly and has avoided the unfortunate side effects of rampant growth. Fortunately, metropolitan amenities including a regional airport and a wider choice of retail services are only 35 miles away in Tallahassee, Florida.

Landscape   Rating: 4

Thomasville is located on a gently rolling plain in scenic southwest Georgia approximately 17 miles north of the Florida state line. Elevations in town vary from about 200 to 300 feet. The town's surrounding area is agricultural with much of the land forested with pine and live oak. In town, streets and gardens are planted with oak, magnolia and pine, along with dogwood, camellia, azalea and roses. Several small lakes and rivers are found nearby.

Climate   Rating: 3

Like adjacent northern Florida, Thomasville has a humid subtropical climate with hot, humid summers and mild winters. Annual precipitation is ample and well distributed in all seasons; snow is almost unknown. It is sunny more than half the time every month and up to 70 percent of the time in spring and early summer. Although relative humidity is moderate overall, the combination of 90-degree temperatures and relative humidity exceeding 60 percent on summer afternoons can be stifling. On the other hand, most days between October and April are very pleasant. Occasional winter frosts result in a frost-free period of about 260 days.

Quality of Life   Rating: 5

The quality of life in Thomasville is excellent. Lacking noxious industries, busy streets and freeways, the town is spared noise, traffic congestion and air pollution. Free parking is abundant. Most residential neighborhoods, old and new, are attractive with houses characteristically sited on large lots graced with lawns, trees and ornamental shrubs. The city is well endowed with parkland and seems intelligently planned and zoned. Fortunately, no large mall potentially damaging to Thomasville's beautifully

Thomasville, Georgia

CLIMATE

Month	Average Daily Temperature High	Low	Daily Rel. Humidity Low	Average Monthly Precipitation
	F		%	Inches
January	63	40	58	5.6
February	67	43	54	4.6
March	73	48	51	5.5
April	79	53	47	3.4
May	85	62	50	3.6
June	90	68	55	5.7
July	91	71	61	6.0
August	91	70	61	5.3
September	88	66	58	4.5
October	81	56	53	3.0
November	74	48	55	3.3
December	66	42	58	3.6

Annual Averages

Total Days		Total Inches	
Clear	102	Precipitation	54.1
Partly Cloudy	129	Snowfall	0.4
Cloudy	134		

RATINGS

Category	poor 1	fair 2	good 3	very good 4	excellent 5
Landscape				●	
Climate			●		
Quality of Life					●
Cost of Living				●	
Transportation		●			
Retail Services		●			
Health Care					●
Community Services			●		
Cultural Activities			●		
Recreational Activities				●	
Work/Volunteer Activities			●		
Crime			●		

Total Points: 41

restored historic downtown retailing district, with its brick-paved streets, wide sidewalks and one-of-a-kind businesses, exists in the county. People are welcoming, justifiably proud of their community and determined to preserve its unique character.

The cost of living in Thomasville is evaluated as follows:

- *Composite.* ACCRA data are unavailable for Thomasville so statistics for Valdosta, a nearby small Georgia town, are used. On that basis the composite cost of living in Thomasville is estimated to be about 7 percent below the national average.

- *Housing.* Housing costs are perhaps 15 percent below the national average even though the quality of the local housing stock is unusually high. Many attractive houses with three bedrooms and two bathrooms in good neighborhoods are priced between $70,000 and $120,000. Luxurious, large brick homes on wooded lots in gorgeous neighborhoods are priced between $150,000 and $250,000. Elegantly restored Victorian mansions are occasionally available at higher prices, while several condominium complexes typically have units selling for less than $100,000.

- *Goods and Services.* Goods and services, except for utilities, are priced at or slightly below national norms. Utility bills are about 15 percent below the national average.

- *Taxes.* The state and local tax burden in Thomasville is about 10.3 percent of income compared to the U.S. average of 9.7 percent. State income and sales and excise taxes exceed national norms whereas property taxes are lower than the national average.

Transportation   **Rating: 2**

The private automobile dominates local transportation. There is no fixed-route bus system but Thomas County Area Transit provides limited dial-a-ride service. Thomasville's road infrastructure is more than adequate to handle the limited demands put upon it. Tallahassee Regional Airport, about 40 miles southwest, provides nonstop jet service to hub airports at Atlanta, Charlotte and Miami. Greyhound bus service to many points is available from Thomasville and Tallahassee, and Amtrak service westbound to Los Angeles and eastbound to Jacksonville and Miami is provided three times a week from Tallahassee.

Retail Services   **Rating: 2**

Thomasville's award winning "Main Street" program has, over the past 25 years, spurred the rehabilitation of hundreds of buildings and businesses along brick-paved Broad Street and neighboring streets in the city center. The charming Victorian downtown is a wonderful place to walk and shop and attracts thousands of visitors as well as Thomasville residents. With its art galleries, service establishments, antique and specialty shops, restaurants and two small department stores, downtown is far and away the best place to shop in Thomas County. Plenty of free parking is available in two municipal lots located on Crawford Street behind the stores facing Broad, so there is no need to go to the mall. In fact, there is no major mall to go to except for Governor's Square Mall, 35 miles away in Tallahassee. Ordinary shopping is possible, though, at the local Wal-Mart on the edge of town.

Health Care Rating: 5

 Thomasville offers exceptional medical care. John D. Archbold Memorial Hospital is the leading medical center of southwest Georgia. With 264 beds and more than 120 physicians on staff representing upwards of 30 specialties, Archbold anchors a regional nonprofit health care system. It is especially noted for its cancer treatment, cardiac care, neurosurgery and rehabilitation services. Additional excellent, comprehensive medical services are only 35 miles away in Tallahassee.

Community Services Rating: 3

 The city provides excellent basic public services including police, fire protection/emergency service and utilities. The Thomas County Public Library headquartered in downtown Thomasville, the Thomasville Parks and Recreation Department and numerous civic and service clubs provide a variety of informational, fitness, recreational and social services to seniors.

Cultural and Educational Activities Rating: 3

 Among small cities, Thomasville is a cultural standout. The Thomasville Cultural Center Auditorium, located in a former public school, is the primary venue for top-flight musical and theatrical productions hosted by the Thomasville Entertainment Foundation. The Foundation presents four programs a year, featuring symphony orchestras, chamber music ensembles, jazz groups and world-renowned soloists. Exhibits and classes are also offered through the Center. On Stage and Company, a community theater group, produces four plays each year at its downtown theater.

Thomas University, a fully accredited private four year institution, enrolls upwards of 600 students on its historic and picturesque campus. Its sports, musical and theatrical events are of interest to the community. Continuing education is offered by Thomas Technical Institute, a unit of the Georgia Department of Technical and Adult Education. Courses of special interest to seniors include computer science, Spanish, auto repair, defensive driving and floral design. Flower and nature lovers can also enjoy the community's eight active garden clubs and several nature preserves including the Birdsong Nature Center.

Recreational Activities Rating: 4

Thomasville's lovely landscape and warm climate encourage outdoor activities year-round. The city operates 22 parks and recreation sites covering more than 400 acres. Well equipped and well maintained, Thomasville parks provide everything one could want in an urban park system. Typical facilities include picnic areas and shelters, nature areas, playgrounds and sports fields and courts. Remington Park is a large multi-purpose park with picnic tables, shelters and grills, playground areas, tennis, handball and basketball courts, and soccer and ball fields. In contrast, Paradise Park, a lovely oasis near downtown, is oriented toward picnicking, children's play and nature appreciation in a woodland setting. The city also operates a swimming pool, two running tracks and the 18-hole Country Oaks Golf Course, which is open for play all year. Golf is also played at Glen Arven Country Club, a classic course founded in 1896 and a favorite of presidents including Dwight D. Eisenhower and other dignitaries. Area lakes and ponds and the nearby Ochlockonee River provide good freshwater fishing, while the Gulf of Mexico, less than an hour away, offers opportunities for pier and deep-sea fishing. Abundant wildlife in the woods of plantations south of town allows for hunting of deer, wild hog, dove, duck and quail. Sport shooting of clay pigeons is also popular. Two YMCAs offer a variety of adult fitness and sports activities including lap swimming. Their facilities include a Nautilus center with whirlpool and sauna, basketball, racquetball and volleyball courts and a fitness track. An eight-screen cinema, bowling complex, skating rink, and several interesting restaurants round out the local entertainment scene. Additional leisure choices are found in nearby Tallahassee. Assets there include resident ballet, symphony and theater companies, performances by touring artists, more than 30 movie screens, 8 golf courses, a diversity of good restaurants and NCAA basketball and football featuring the Seminoles of Florida State University and the Rattlers of Florida A&M.

Work and Volunteer Activities   Rating: 3

Employment opportunities are limited by the small size of the city. Nonetheless, some retirees find jobs in Thomasville's many small factories, at hospitals and in retailing, albeit at low wages. Volunteers serve in local religious organizations, schools, social organizations, and in the active Chamber of Commerce and Visitor Bureau. Various events, including the April Thomasville Rose Festival, depend heavily on volunteers, as does the Thomas County Library.

Crime Rates and Public Safety   Rating: 3

The overall rate of property crime is 80 percent above the national average, with burglary and larceny-theft rates being especially high. On the other hand, the city's violent crime rate is 30 percent below the national average. Within this broad category, murder, rape and aggravated assault rates are low and robbery rates are high. Although Thomasville has a fairly high incidence of relatively minor crimes against property, its low violent crime rates indicate that it is not a dangerous place to live. The historic downtown, public areas and parks, and neighborhoods where retirees are apt to live all appear pleasant and safe.

Conclusion

Overall Rating 41

Rated as "one of the best retirement towns in the South" by Consumer Guide in 1988, Thomasville persists as one of America's best small towns for retirement. It will appeal especially to those seeking gracious living at modest cost in a tranquil subtropical environment. It would not satisfy those requiring good public transportation or the excitement and diversity of activities found in larger cities. The community's quality of life is near perfect; almost 20 years ago, it was labeled "a storybook town near the Florida border" and that description is still apt. The natural landscape of gently rolling hills clad with oak and pine and the town's exquisite residential neighborhoods and colorful, historic downtown are appealing. Health care and recreational opportunities are exceptional for a small town and are even better if the assets of nearby Tallahassee are considered. Community services, culture, and work and volunteer activities are all quite good and the city's crime rate is not particularly threatening. If you are seeking a laid- back retirement in a lovely little town offering better than average amenities, Thomasville merits serious examination.

Covington, Louisiana

Founded in 1813 as the seat of government for St. Tammany Parish, Covington and neighboring communities on the north shore of Lake Pontchartrain soon gained fame as health resorts offering fresh air and "healing" artesian waters in pleasant surroundings. Visitors from New Orleans first came by excursion boat across the lake and later by circuitous rail and road routes. Completion of the Lake Pontchartrain Causeway in 1956 improved accessibility by directly connecting New Orleans with the north shore via a 24-mile, 30-minute commute. As a result, thousands of New Orleanians have relocated to the western half of St. Tammany, making it the fastest growing parish in Louisiana.

Covington, Mandeville, Abita Springs and other western St. Tammany towns have a combined population exceeding 100,000 and rank highly for retirement. Covington and Mandeville, especially, have many attractive tree-shaded residential areas and clearly defined historic downtown areas. They offer a delightful, laid-back lifestyle in an area of great natural beauty close, but not too close, to the bright lights and unique cultural amenities of the Crescent City of New Orleans.

Landscape   Rating: 4

Covington is located on the banks of the Bogue Falaya River about seven miles north of Lake Pontchartrain. Like other places in western St. Tammany, Covington lies on a nearly flat plain but unlike New Orleans, just across the lake, it is not below sea level. Typical elevations in the Covington area are 20 to 40 feet above sea level, probably high enough to escape the worst flooding should a hurricane strike the community head on. The parish is fertile, with farmed areas alternating with lush green forest. Residential areas are heavily planted with live oak, magnolia, pine and azalea.

Climate   Rating: 3

Like the nearby Gulf Coast, Covington has a humid subtropical climate with long, hot humid summers and short, mild winters. Winter's typical mildness is interrupted by occasional cold waves that can drop temperatures below 20 degrees for short periods. Even so, daytime highs are nearly always above freezing, even during polar outbreaks. Annual precipitation is ample and well distributed throughout the year. Snowfall is insignificant. Sunshine levels vary from about 50 percent in winter to about 60 percent in other seasons. Summer days are generally unpleasantly muggy owing to the combination of 90-degree temperatures and over 60 percent relative humidity. In contrast, spring and autumn weather is often delightful with warm days, cool nights and slightly lower humidity. Occasional frosts in winter limit the frost-free period to about 250 days.

Quality of Life   Rating: 5

The quality of life in Covington is excellent. The air is clean and most locations away from I-12 and several major boulevards are free of serious noise pollution. As a result of the area's small-town character, crowding and traffic congestion are minimal except on the approaches to the Lake Pontchartrain Causeway at rush hour. Plenty of free parking is available but there is no public transit. Taxis are the only alternative to the private

Covington, Louisiana

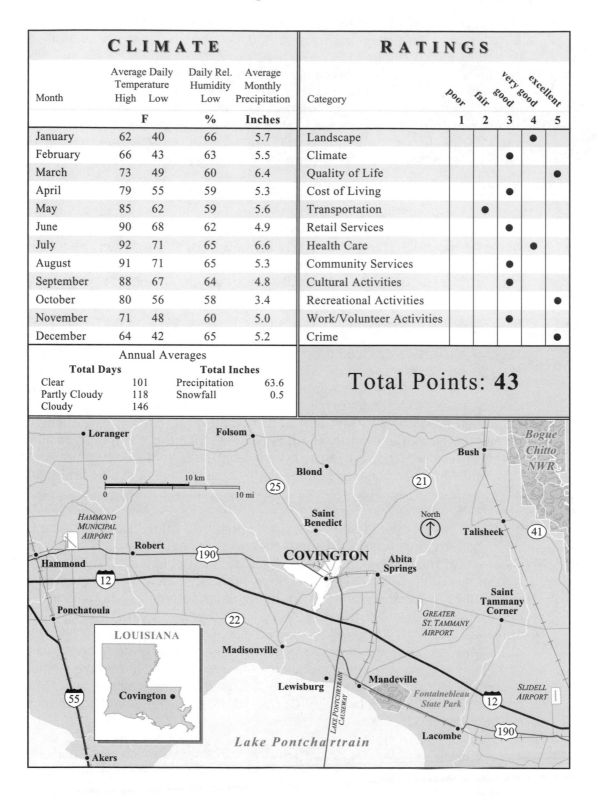

CLIMATE				
Month	Average Daily Temperature High Low		Daily Rel. Humidity Low	Average Monthly Precipitation
	F		%	Inches
January	62	40	66	5.7
February	66	43	63	5.5
March	73	49	60	6.4
April	79	55	59	5.3
May	85	62	59	5.6
June	90	68	62	4.9
July	92	71	65	6.6
August	91	71	65	5.3
September	88	67	64	4.8
October	80	56	58	3.4
November	71	48	60	5.0
December	64	42	65	5.2

Annual Averages

Total Days		Total Inches	
Clear	101	Precipitation	63.6
Partly Cloudy	118	Snowfall	0.5
Cloudy	146		

RATINGS					
Category	poor 1	fair 2	good 3	very good 4	excellent 5
Landscape				●	
Climate			●		
Quality of Life					●
Cost of Living			●		
Transportation		●			
Retail Services			●		
Health Care				●	
Community Services			●		
Cultural Activities			●		
Recreational Activities					●
Work/Volunteer Activities			●		
Crime					●

Total Points: 43

car. Covington itself is a lovely, heavily treed community of older homes on large lots. Parts of Mandeville are similar but newer residential developments between the two towns, while attractive enough, manifest a more suburban character with large houses on somewhat smaller lots. Several large city and state parks add to the area's livability. Covington's restored downtown is a gem among historic districts. People seem content with their community and determined to keep it a safe and secure place sheltered by distance from crime-ridden New Orleans.

Cost of Living   Rating: 3

 The cost of living in Covington is evaluated as follows:

- *Composite.* ACCRA data for metropolitan New Orleans, of which St. Tammany Parish is a part, are utilized in the absence of separate data for Covington. On that basis the composite cost of living in Covington approximates the national average.

- *Housing.* Housing costs are slightly above average in Covington and considerably higher than in the city of New Orleans. Local sources suggest an average home price above $200,000 in western St. Tammany, but this reflects an abundance of upscale housing rather than high prices per se. Your housing dollar goes far in Covington.

- *Goods and Services.* ACCRA data suggest that transportation and miscellaneous goods and services are priced near the national average. Summer air conditioning and winter heating cause utility bills to be about 10 percent above the national average, whereas grocery and health care costs are 5 to 10 percent below national norms.

- *Taxes.* The state and local tax burden in Covington and neighboring communities is 9.1 percent of income compared to the U.S. average of 9.7 percent. Louisiana sales and excise taxes substantially exceed the national average but property and income taxes are very low. Income from public pensions and social security is entirely exempt from Louisiana income tax.

Transportation   Rating: 2

Local transportation is almost entirely by car; the western St. Tammany area lacks a fixed-route public transit system. This situation appears unlikely to change as many residents oppose public transit out of fear that "outsiders" would come in and pose a threat to the community. Limited dial-a-ride service is available to the elderly and disabled. A van service connects Covington with New Orleans. New Orleans International Airport, 40 miles south, is a medium hub with 50 nonstop jet destinations including Atlanta, Dallas and Los Angeles. Amtrak provides daily service from New Orleans north to Chicago and New York and service three times a week west to Los Angeles and east to Miami. Greyhound bus service to many points is also available in New Orleans.

Retail Services   Rating: 3

Very much in the economic shadow of New Orleans but growing rapidly, Covington provides a steadily improving range of services. These are easily supplemented by a 30-minute drive to New Orleans. Downtown Covington is charming with many boutiques, specialty shops, galleries and restaurants located in historic buildings. In March 2004, the first phase of Stirling 21/12 Centre, Western St. Tammany's first regional mall, opened near the junction of I-12 and Louisiana Highway 21 in Covington.

Anchored by Belk, JCPenney, Marshalls and Target department stores, the mall also boasts a Cost Plus World Market and numerous specialty stores. A Wal-Mart beside Highway 190 provides basic shopping.

Health Care — Rating: 4

With two full-service hospitals and several physical therapy and rehabilitation centers, Covington provides very good medical care that is easily supplemented by medical centers in Lacombe and New Orleans. Lakeview Regional Medical Center, with 185 beds, and St. Tammany Parish Hospital, a 200-bed nonprofit facility that recently added two wings, are highly-rated hospitals. Both offer nearly 40 specialties including emergency and intensive care, cancer and cardiac care, rehabilitation, wellness programs and classes in stress reduction and relaxation. Louisiana Heart Hospital in nearby Lacombe is a 58-bed specialty care facility for the diagnosis and treatment of coronary disease. New Orleans boasts 26 fully accredited hospitals including six American Medical Association-certified teaching facilities.

Community Services — Rating: 3

St. Tammany Parish and numerous community service organizations provide an assortment of services for all age groups. The St. Tammany Parish Library operates branches in all major communities including Covington, Mandeville, Abita Springs and Madisonville. The New Image Seniors Club, AARP, SCORE, the Council on Aging, and the YMCA are very active locally.

Cultural and Educational Activities — Rating: 3

The visual and performing arts are well represented in Covington and vicinity. The St. Tammany Art Association coordinates artistic events and area galleries display a surprising variety of art. An annual highlight is November's Three Rivers Art Festival, a juried arts show accompanied by food, music and entertainment in the galleries and streets of downtown Covington. Music and theater are also well represented locally. Choral concerts are presented by the Northshore Performing Arts Society, bluegrass music by the Piney Woods Opry and band music by several West Tammany groups. Playmaker's Inc., one of America's oldest little theaters, presents several productions per year as do the new North Star Theater in Mandeville and SkyFire Theater in downtown Covington.

The performing arts calendar of New Orleans is filled with symphonic and chamber music concerts, recitals, ballet, opera and theater from September through May. Resident ensembles including the Louisiana Philharmonic Orchestra, the New Orleans Ballet and the New Orleans Opera present a seemingly endless series of first-rate events often featuring internationally known guest artists. Jazz at Preservation Hall in the French Quarter is a New Orleans institution and an annual jazz festival is held in early spring. The Saenger Performing Arts Center, on Canal Street, presents Broadway musicals and concerts, and several other good theatrical companies provide additional entertainment choices.

Recreational Activities — Rating: 5

 A long-time playground for residents of New Orleans, the north shore of Lake Pontchartrain remains a focus of outdoor recreation and small-town living. Nearby New Orleans offers an array of sophisticated cultural and recreational attractions the envy of many larger cities. Covington's beautiful subtropical landscape, laced with rivers and bayous and fronting on Lake Pontchartrain, is highly conducive to outdoor recreation. Water sports are big here. Lake Pontchartrain sports flotillas of sailboats and other pleasure craft, the Tchefuncte and Bogue Falaya Rivers provide ideal spots for power boating and water-skiing, and scenic bayous offer quiet havens for fishing, canoeing and kayaking. Mandeville's North Shore Nature Center features elevated boardwalks through pristine cypress swamps for close-up bird watching and wildlife observation. Walkers, joggers, cyclists and skaters enjoy the 31-mile long Tammany Trace linear park, a rails-to-trails conversion with miles of paved trail crossing some of the most scenic areas of St. Tammany Parish. Western St. Tammany also claims four country clubs and two public golf courses, six athletic clubs, a bowling complex, eleven municipal parks and playgrounds, Fontainebleau State Park on Lake Pontchartrain, and Fairview Riverside State Park on the Tchefuncte River. Elements of the movie "Eve's Bayou" were filmed in the latter park a few years ago. Both parks are notable for camping, picnicking, hiking, boating and fishing; Fontainebleau also has lake swimming and bicycle trails. Western St. Tammany also boasts four multiplex cinemas and several good restaurants and cafes.

The "Big Easy" across the lake, New Orleans, is justifiably famous for its Mardi Gras festivities but the Covington area too is prone to partying. Mardi Gras parades, balls and parties are followed each spring by Chef Soiree, held in Bogue Falaya Park and featuring samplings from more than 100 of the north shore's finest restaurants and watering holes, as well as live entertainment. In April, bird watchers from all over the country attend the Great Louisiana Bird Fest. In June and July, seafood fanciers converge on the Bayou Lacombe Crab Festival and Mandeville Seafood Festival. In September, the parties go afloat as upwards of 100 classic antique and contemporary wooden boats gather along the Tchefuncte River in Madisonville for a weekend of food and entertainment.

Unlimited additional recreational options are available just across the lake. New Orleans assets include NFL football, NCAA basketball and football at Tulane University, basketball at the University of New Orleans, the multiple attractions of City Park—which covers 1,500 acres and is the fifth largest urban park in the United States—and the Audubon Zoo. Last but not least, the architectural and historic sites, antique shops, night spots and fine restaurants of the French Quarter engender frequent visits to the Crescent City.

Work and Volunteer Activities   Rating: 3

Although the Covington area is growing rapidly in population, job growth is mostly confined to the service sector—especially retailing and real estate—and wages are low. Many retirees find fulfillment in volunteer work for local hospitals, schools, libraries, the Chamber of Commerce and various other volunteer-based nonprofit organizations. AARP and SCORE help seniors secure placements.

Crime Rates and Public Safety   Rating: 5

Crime rates continue to decline in the Covington area and St. Tammany Parish now ranks as one of America's safest retirement locales. The property crime and violent crime rates there are now a remarkable 60 to 70 percent below national norms. Residents need to be wary, though, when visiting New Orleans. Violent crime rates there are among the highest in the nation.

Overall Rating 43 Part of the New Orleans Metropolitan Area, yet physically and psychologically separated from the Crescent City by 24 miles of Lake Pontchartrain, Covington and neighboring north shore communities are in many ways a world apart from New Orleans. A blend of small town, suburban and rural elements, the Covington area offers a high quality of life and outstanding outdoor recreation in a beautiful, quiet and safe environment. Viewed in isolation from New Orleans, as it is in the ratings, it has only modest transportation assets. But local retail, health care and cultural resources are good and the enormous assets of the metropolitan center are routinely utilized by north shore residents, who value their separate identity yet enjoy the city's resources. Although some might find Covington's long, hot humid summers disagreeable, few would object to the weather in winter, spring or autumn. A more serious concern is the absence of public transit; a car is a virtual necessity here. That said, Covington might well suit those seeking retirement in a lovely, subtropical, small-town setting yet within easy reach of the bright lights and metropolitan amenities of one of America's most interesting cities.

Savannah, Georgia

Although Savannah is a busy port and industrial center located a few miles upstream from the mouth of the Savannah River, its chief claim to fame is its lovely historic district. With more than 2,400 architecturally and historically significant buildings in a 2.5-square mile area, the Savannah Historic District is a national treasure. Just to the east, the Intracoastal Waterway separates the city and its mainland suburbs from Tybee, Little Tybee, Wilmington and Skidaway Islands, which form the northern echelon of Georgia's famous Golden Isles.

With a population of 140,000 in the city and 235,000 in Chatham County, Savannah suffers from some typical urban ills including high crime rates in inner city areas. Although the city meets federal air quality standards, sulfurous emissions from a riverfront pulp and paper mill occasionally taint the air. Savannah's long, hot humid summer may also be disagreeable to some people. On balance, though, Savannah has much to offer. It is big enough to provide the services and amenities needed to retire well. Local bus service is satisfactory and Amtrak runs 14 trains weekly northbound to New York and 14 southbound to Florida. Nonstop jet service to major hub airports is available from Savannah International Airport. The city provides very good health care and services for seniors, shopping is good at two regional malls and at trendy shops in the historic district, and the cultural scene is lively. The Savannah Civic Center Theater and Arena host the Savannah Symphony Orchestra and nationally known touring artists and the City Lights Theater Company offers its playbill in the newly renovated Avon Theater. Coastal waters, island beaches and warm, subtropical weather provide endless opportunities for boating, sailing, fishing and swimming. Living costs are slightly below the national average and the state/local tax burden is moderate, making Savannah not only attractive but also affordable.

Fairhope, Alabama

Perched atop a high bluff overlooking Mobile Bay, the lovely little city of Fairhope is the most attractive of several towns along the bay's subtropical Eastern Shore. Canopied with large live oaks, magnolias and pines, this well-planned community boasts outstanding residential neighborhoods and a charming, architecturally interesting and commercially viable downtown. Below the bluff is a city park with picnicking and playground facilities, a sandy beach and a municipal fishing pier extending far into the bay.

Fairhope's population of 13,000 makes for modest transportation and retail assets and limited part-time work opportunities. Baldwin County Transit provides service throughout the county but buses run infrequently. Intercity bus, rail and air transportation is available from Mobile, 25 miles west. More than 100 clubs and service organizations offer many opportunities to contribute to the community.

Fairhope provides an excellent quality of life at low cost. The town was founded in 1894 by followers of Henry George, who advocated taxing only land. Much of the city is still owned by the Single Tax Corporation, which rents land to homeowners on renewable 99-year leases. This keeps housing prices low by curtailing land speculation. Other advantages of Fairhope include low taxes (Alabama does not tax most retirement income), low crime rates, clean air, very good community services and health care, and surprisingly strong cultural and recreational assets. The town has long attracted creative people; the number of writers and artists living here is remarkable. The Eastern Shore Art Center is the focus of the visual arts, while the professional Jubilee Fish Theater and several little theater associations produce plays. Faulkner Junior College and a branch campus of the University of South Alabama offer courses of interest to seniors. Local resources for golf, tennis, horseback riding, boating, sailing and fishing are almost endless. Few small towns offer as much.

The Interior South Retirement Region

Climate: Humid subtropical

Place Description	Overall Rating	Page
Oxford, Mississippi	**47**	**167**
Oxford is an idyllic little college town. In many ways it reminds me of Chapel Hill, North Carolina as it was 30 or 40 years ago: charming, friendly, safe and uncrowded.		
Hot Springs, Arkansas	**41**	**173**
It is easy to understand why Hot Springs has become a favorite location for retirement. The city's physical site is scenic with low mountains and a national park in town and three large lakes nearby.		
Fayetteville, Arkansas	**46**	**178**
Fayetteville is one of America's most pleasant and affordable college towns and is an excellent place for an active retirement.		

The Interior South Retirement Region, stretching from the rolling hills of northern Mississippi to the Ouachita Mountains and Ozark Plateaus of Arkansas, has long evoked an image of subsistence farming, moonshining, poverty and isolation. For decades the region lost population as jobs and better living conditions in cities such as St. Louis, Kansas City, Dallas and Tulsa lured young people away. However, the long-term trend of out-migration has reversed in the last 30 years as utility companies and the government built dams and highways that created a large number of scenic artificial lakes and eliminated rural isolation. Increasing numbers of people are relocating for retirement to rural counties in the uplands and to several attractive small cities.

Fayetteville and Hot Springs, Arkansas and Oxford, Mississippi, stand out as centers suitable for upscale retirement. Oxford and Fayetteville owe much of their success and character to the University of Mississippi and the University of Arkansas, respectively, while Hot Springs has long been famous for its "healing waters" and beautiful lake and mountain areas. The many amenities of these towns are available at a cost of living below the national average.

Oxford, Mississippi

With its picturesque courthouse square, magnolia-studded University of Mississippi campus and street and neighborhood scenes seemingly lifted from the novels of native son William Faulkner, Oxford is the quintessential southern college town. Founded in 1835 on land purchased from a Chickasaw Indian woman, the town was named Oxford after the English university town in hopes that its famous name would help the community attract its own university. The plan worked; state officials chose Oxford and the University of Mississippi opened its doors in 1848. Since that date the fate of Oxford has been inextricably linked to the fortunes of the university, affectionately known locally

Oxford, Mississippi

CLIMATE				
Month	Average Daily Temperature High Low		Daily Rel. Humidity Low	Average Monthly Precipitation
	F		**%**	**Inches**
January	50	28	62	5.3
February	55	31	62	4.6
March	64	39	54	5.9
April	73	47	50	5.2
May	80	57	57	5.7
June	88	65	54	4.6
July	91	69	56	4.1
August	90	67	55	3.5
September	85	60	55	3.7
October	75	47	53	3.8
November	63	39	58	5.4
December	54	31	62	6.0

Annual Averages

Total Days		Total Inches	
Clear	120	Precipitation	57.7
Partly Cloudy	97	Snowfall	3.0
Cloudy	148		

RATINGS

Category	poor 1	fair 2	good 3	very good 4	excellent 5
Landscape				●	
Climate			●		
Quality of Life					●
Cost of Living			●		
Transportation			●		
Retail Services				●	
Health Care				●	
Community Services				●	
Cultural Activities				●	
Recreational Activities				●	
Work/Volunteer Activities				●	
Crime					●

Total Points: 47

and throughout the state as Ole Miss. With a population just exceeding 12,000 in the city and 40,000 in Lafayette County, Oxford is a small town. But thanks to the university, it is able to offer residents an upscale and fairly cosmopolitan existence. Amenities typically available in larger cities can be found 75 miles northwest in Memphis, Tennessee and 165 miles south in Jackson, Mississippi.

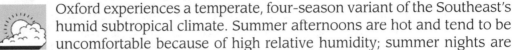

Landscape   **Rating: 4**

Oxford is located in north central Mississippi about 50 miles south of the Tennessee state line. Nestled among rolling hills at an elevation of 450 feet, the town has an extraordinarily beautiful natural landscape. A luxuriant southern mixed forest of oak and pine envelops the community. In town, large magnolias are conspicuous on campus and along many residential streets. Flowering shrubs and vines such as redbud and wisteria add seasonal color, especially in spring.

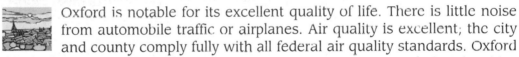

Climate   **Rating: 3**

Oxford experiences a temperate, four-season variant of the Southeast's humid subtropical climate. Summer afternoons are hot and tend to be uncomfortable because of high relative humidity; summer nights are warm. Spring and autumn weather is generally pleasant, with warm days and cool nights. Winters are mild with average daily highs in the 50s and lows in the 30s. The normal annual precipitation of 58 inches is well distributed throughout the year and only about three inches of snow accumulates on the ground in a typical winter. The town enjoys an average frost-free season of 210 days and is sunny about 63 percent of the time.

Quality of Life   **Rating: 5**

Oxford is notable for its excellent quality of life. There is little noise from automobile traffic or airplanes. Air quality is excellent; the city and county comply fully with all federal air quality standards. Oxford is clean and uncrowded. There are no noxious industries, population densities are low and traffic congestion is unknown. Parking is adequate downtown, at the mall and on campus. The town is well planned and its pleasant, wooded residential neighborhoods reflect the community's moderate affluence, good taste and concern for historic preservation. The town is growing relatively slowly so it has been spared the rampant residential subdivision and commercial development characteristic of the periphery of many Sunbelt cities. Historic downtown Oxford is charming and economically thriving, thanks to the hard work of the Downtown Council and the loyalty of local shoppers. Residents are unusually friendly and congenial, even in comparison with those of other small college towns. They clearly appreciate the exceptional quality of life in their idyllic corner of the world and are determined to preserve it.

Cost of Living   **Rating: 3**

 The cost of living in Oxford is evaluated as follows:

- *Composite.* ACCRA data are currently unavailable for Oxford so statistics for Vicksburg, which were similar to those of Oxford in the recent past, are utilized here. On that basis, the composite cost of living in Oxford is estimated to be slightly below the national average.

- *Housing.* Housing costs approximate the national average. One local source recently gave $135,000 as the median price of a single-family residence and noted proudly that Oxford housing is the most expensive in the state. Be that as it may, this quaint garden town offers a variety of housing styles from grand pre-Civil War and smaller historic homes to modern bungalows. Most new construction occurs in the countryside around Oxford and prices range from $175,000 to $300,000. Although few resale houses are on the market at any one time, a nice 1,800-square-foot house with three bedrooms, two baths, den and study, near the Ole Miss campus, was recently listed for $95,000.

- *Goods and Services.* ACCRA data suggest that goods and services in Oxford are priced at or slightly below their national averages. Costs of miscellaneous goods and services approximate the national average, whereas groceries, utilities, transportation and health care are priced 5 to 10 percent below national norms.

- *Taxes.* The state and local tax burden for the general public is 9.3 percent of income compared to the U.S. average of 9.7 percent. State income and property taxes are low but sales and excise taxes are rather high. The news is better for retirees. All income from federal, state, and private pensions and social security is totally exempt from state income tax and those 65 and older also receive a break on property taxes.

Transportation   Rating: 3

The private automobile dominates local transportation; the town is too small to support a fixed-route transit system. The needs of the transit dependent are not ignored, though. The State of Mississippi Elderly and Handicapped Transit Service provides dial-a-ride shuttle service to local facilities, and the city offers taxi service to the general public. Greyhound provides intercity bus service. Oxford–University Airport offers general aviation service but Memphis International Airport, 65 miles away, is the major regional airline hub. Memphis International is served by most major carriers and provides non-stop jet service to about 50 destinations. Amtrak service northbound to Chicago and southbound to New Orleans is available from Memphis.

Retail Services   Rating: 4

Oxford's charming Downtown Square offers unique and distinctly upscale shopping. The freshly painted and beautifully decorated J. E. Neilson Company, the oldest department store in the South and the first business established in Oxford, is the pride of the community. Nearby is Square Books, an award-winning bookstore and a great place to browse. Additional specialty shops and several restaurants line the rest of the blocks facing the square.

Oxonians love their little downtown; one local resident said that people prefer shopping there and that the mall is less successful. Even so, Oxford Mall is conveniently located just 1.5 miles west of downtown. Anchored by JCPenney, it includes a number of small specialty shops and a movie theater complex. Many Oxford residents occasionally travel 50 miles east to The Mall at Barnes Crossing, in Tupelo. This regional mall, anchored by JCPenney, McRae's, Parisian and Sears, boasts the largest assemblage of stores in northern Mississippi.

Health Care   Rating: 4

 Baptist Memorial Hospital–North Mississippi is a major regional medical center serving Oxford and much of northern Mississippi. With more than 210 beds and 80 physicians representing upwards of 30 specialties on staff, Baptist Memorial meets most medical care needs of Oxford residents. It recently added Baptist Memorial Cancer Institute, a new acute care rehabilitation unit and a surgical outpatient facility to its campus. Larger facilities and a wider range of medical services are only an hour away in Memphis, Tennessee.

Community Services   Rating: 4

Oxford, Lafayette County, the University of Mississippi and religious and community organizations offer a fine variety of services to residents. The Oxford Public Library is unusually good for a small-town facility, and its assets are easily supplemented by those of the University of Mississippi libraries. RSVP, AARP, and several fraternal associations of retirees provide social and recreational opportunities for seniors. Local religious organizations sponsor, among other social services, a Meals on Wheels program and The Pantry, which provides food free of charge to those in need.

Cultural and Educational Activities   Rating: 4

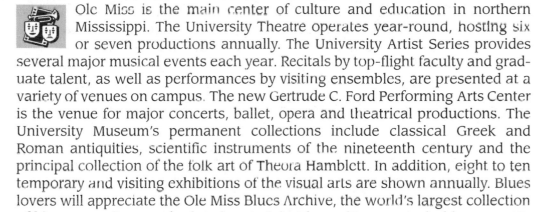 Ole Miss is the main center of culture and education in northern Mississippi. The University Theatre operates year-round, hosting six or seven productions annually. The University Artist Series provides several major musical events each year. Recitals by top-flight faculty and graduate talent, as well as performances by visiting ensembles, are presented at a variety of venues on campus. The new Gertrude C. Ford Performing Arts Center is the venue for major concerts, ballet, opera and theatrical productions. The University Museum's permanent collections include classical Greek and Roman antiquities, scientific instruments of the nineteenth century and the principal collection of the folk art of Theora Hamblett. In addition, eight to ten temporary and visiting exhibitions of the visual arts are shown annually. Blues lovers will appreciate the Ole Miss Blues Archive, the world's largest collection of blues recordings and related materials. Those 65 years and older are entitled to enroll in regular Ole Miss courses free of charge, and the university's Institute for Continuing Studies offers additional courses of interest to the general public for nominal fees. Free public lectures are frequent occurrences on campus, and each year the university hosts the Faulkner Conference and the Oxford Conference for the Book, which attracts people from all over the world.

Recreational Activities   Rating: 4

 Recreational opportunities appealing to most tastes are found in and around Oxford. Spectator sports are enjoyed by students and town folk alike. The Rebels of Ole Miss regularly host nationally ranked intercollegiate teams in football, basketball, baseball, tennis, track and golf. If your interests are participatory, the Oxford area also has much to offer. Golf is available at 2 challenging 18-hole public courses, while tennis can be played at 37 outdoor public courts and at 2 private country club courts. Swimming is popular at the 50-meter municipal pool and at the university's indoor pool. The city maintains four local parks with picnic, playground and sporting facilities.

Organized programs for football, baseball, softball, volleyball, soccer and tennis exist for all age groups. Other recreational assets in Oxford include a skating rink, an 18-lane bowling center and 12 movie theaters. At nearby Sardis Lake, you can picnic, hike, camp, swim, boat and fish for bass and crappie. Within a 50-mile radius of town are Wall Doxey State Park, Holly Springs National Forest and Lakes Enid, Grenada and Arkabutla, each offering recreational opportunities similar to those of Sardis Lake. Back in Oxford, you can sample the fare at one of the city's fine restaurants, a number of which occupy attractive sites on the Downtown Square. Quite a variety of menu styles, ranging from traditional southern fried chicken and fresh fish to exotic ethnic cuisine, are found locally.

Work and Volunteer Activities   Rating: 4

Oxford's economy has done well in recent years. Unemployment is insignificant and work and volunteer opportunities are available. Unfortunately, most part-time jobs are in the service sector and competition for work from the large college student population keeps wages low. Volunteer service is a way of life for many in the community and is coordinated effectively by the United Way, which publicizes the personnel needs of 29 agencies and recruits volunteers to fill them.

Crime Rates and Public Safety   Rating: 5

Oxford is one of the safest communities in the country. Remarkably, in several recent years there were zero homicides and zero forcible rapes in Oxford. The overall violent crime rate is now about 70 percent below the national average and the property crime rate is 30 percent below the national norm. The town has a very secure feel to it and residents do not hesitate to walk its streets at any time of day or night.

Conclusion

Overall Rating 47 Oxford is an idyllic little college town. In many ways it reminds me of Chapel Hill, North Carolina as it was 30 or 40 years ago: charming, friendly, safe and uncrowded. Its physical and human environment is close to ideal. Its site on a rolling, wooded plain is pleasant, and its temperate subtropical climate provides four distinct seasons with few severely cold or hot days. Oxford's quality of life is excellent. Environmental pollution, traffic congestion and visual ugliness, the bane of many fast-growing Sunbelt cities, are almost entirely lacking here. The state's dial-a-ride shuttle service for the elderly and handicapped and the city taxi service for the general public compensate for the lack of a fixed-route public transit system. The availability of retail and community services, culture and recreation and work/volunteer activities, is very good. Even health care, typically a weak point in smaller towns, is very good locally. Remarkably, all the benefits of the good life in Oxford come at an overall cost of living slightly below the national average. All things considered, Oxford ranks as one of America's best places for sophisticated retirement in an exceptionally beautiful and unspoiled setting.

Hot Springs, Arkansas

The famous thermal springs that issue from the lower slopes of Hot Springs Mountain have long attracted visitors and settlers to the area. First discovered by Native Americans perhaps 10,000 years ago, the springs were visited by Hernando de Soto and his Spanish troops in 1541 and by French trappers and traders during the seventeenth century. Shortly after the United States acquired the area from France in the 1803 Louisiana Purchase, American settlers attracted in part by the "healing waters" began to move into the area. In 1832 the federal government established the Hot Springs National Reservation, which became Hot Springs National Park in 1921. Today, Hot Springs has much to offer retirees. Surrounded by mountains and lakes, it offers abundant outdoor recreational opportunities in a beautiful environment where living costs are low. With a population near 36,000 in the city and 89,000 in surrounding Garland County, the urban area is large enough to offer the amenities most people want yet small enough to avoid congestion and environmental pollution.

Landscape	Rating: 4

Hot Springs is nestled in several valleys amidst the gently rolling Ouachita Mountains in south central Arkansas. Elevations in the city range from 300 to 800 feet with summit levels in the adjacent national park rising several hundred feet higher. Dense forests of oak, hickory and short-leaf pine cover the mountains and much of the lowlands. Flowering trees are common and successive seasons feature changing displays of flowers and brightly colored foliage. Redbud and dogwood bloom in the woods in early spring, while flowering southern magnolias lend a special beauty to historic Bathhouse Row in early summer. Most residential areas, whether in town next to the national park or on the periphery adjacent to Lake Hamilton, are well wooded with large shade trees that provide shelter from summer's sun.

Climate	Rating: 3

Hot Springs has a humid subtropical climate characterized by four distinct seasons, heavy precipitation, moderate amounts of sunshine and pronounced day-to-day and seasonal weather changes. Rainfall is well distributed seasonally with 58 inches falling in an average year. Snowfall is insignificant with an average annual total of only 5 inches. Winter, spring and autumn weather tends to be changeable from day to day whereas summer weather is pretty consistently hot and humid. Winter days are mild; winter nights are cold. Spring and autumn weather is the most pleasant of the year, with generally warm days and cool nights. The city enjoys a frost-free period of 230 days so gardening is possible from late March through mid-November. On average, Hot Springs is sunny 62 percent of the time, but winter is cloudier than the other seasons.

Quality of Life	Rating: 4

Hot Springs offers a very good quality of life. The city is rather quiet in the off season but busier in summer due to heavy tourist traffic. Noise pollution is not severe as vehicles move relatively slowly on most area streets and highways and there is little aircraft noise. Air quality is

Hot Springs, Arkansas

CLIMATE

Month	Average Daily Temperature High	Average Daily Temperature Low	Daily Rel. Humidity Low	Average Monthly Precipitation
	F		**%**	**Inches**
January	51	30	60	3.7
February	57	33	58	3.9
March	66	41	55	5.3
April	74	49	55	5.3
May	81	58	57	6.4
June	89	66	57	5.0
July	94	70	54	4.2
August	94	68	53	3.1
September	87	62	55	4.1
October	76	50	52	5.2
November	63	40	57	6.3
December	53	32	60	5.2

Annual Averages

Total Days		Total Inches	
Clear	119	Precipitation	57.7
Partly Cloudy	100	Snowfall	5.0
Cloudy	147		

RATINGS

Category	poor 1	fair 2	good 3	very good 4	excellent 5
Landscape				●	
Climate			●		
Quality of Life				●	
Cost of Living				●	
Transportation			●		
Retail Services			●		
Health Care			●		
Community Services			●		
Cultural Activities			●		
Recreational Activities				●	
Work/Volunteer Activities				●	
Crime			●		

Total Points: 41

excellent owing to the community's low population, an absence of heavy industry and the typical turbulence of the local atmosphere. The city is uncrowded and-for the most part-free of serious traffic congestion except along a narrow stretch of Central Avenue at Bathhouse Row. There, traffic can be heavy, making parking difficult during the summer tourist season. Most residential neighborhoods are well maintained and nicely treed. Those adjacent to the wooded slopes of the national park in the northern part of town or alongside Lake Hamilton on the southern edge are especially scenic. Unfortunately, much of the landscape between these areas is uninspiring. The city sprawls outward along Central Avenue toward Lake Hamilton. Much of the strip and shopping center development along the road is distinctly unappealing and offers a startling contrast to the charming and historic Bathhouse Row commercial area.

Cost of Living   Rating: 4

 The cost of living in Hot Springs is evaluated as follows:

- *Composite.* Recent ACCRA data show the overall cost of living in Hot Springs to be about 12 percent below the national average.

- *Housing.* According to ACCRA, housing costs are fully 25 percent below the national average. Local sources and exploration of the Hot Springs area confirm an abundance of inexpensive housing, especially on the periphery toward Lake Hamilton. Relatively new and luxurious condominiums on the lake sell for less than $150,000. A good supply of single-family homes priced between $100,000 and $250,000 is found in several parts of the city.

- *Goods and Services.* Goods and services are priced below national norms. Utilities, groceries and miscellaneous goods and services costs are about 6 percent below the national average, while transportation and health care are bargains at prices 10 and 12 percent, respectively, below average.

- *Taxes.* The state and local tax burden in Hot Springs is 10 percent of income compared to the U.S. average of 9.7 percent. State income taxes approximate the national average, property taxes are lower than average and sales and excise taxes are higher.

Transportation   Rating: 3

Although most people who can drive do so in Hot Springs, Hot Springs Intracity Transit (IT) provides a useful alternative. Operated by the city of Hot Springs, IT provides inexpensive bus service from a downtown transit center to major destinations including Garland County Community College, St. Joseph's Mercy Medical Center, National Park Medical Center, Hot Springs Mall and Lake Hamilton. Most suburban residential areas are not served. Hot Springs Trolley Company provides excellent service in the downtown historic district including Bathhouse Row and to the observation tower on Hot Springs Mountain, for nominal fares. Limited commuter airline service is available out of Hot Springs Airport, but Little Rock International Airport is a better choice for commercial air travel. Located about 50 miles northeast and accessible from Hot Springs by shuttle bus, Little Rock International offers nonstop jet service to more than 15 destinations including major hubs at Dallas and St. Louis. Amtrak provides daily service from Little Rock and Malvern to points between Chicago and San Antonio via the Texas Eagle train. Hot Springs Shuttle connects the city and train stations.

Retail Services   Rating: 3

Retail services sufficient to meet the needs of most people are available locally. Hot Springs Mall, located on the southern edge of the city near Lake Hamilton, is the major regional shopping complex. Anchored by Dillard's, JCPenney and Sears department stores, the mall houses many of the usual national and regional chain specialty stores and restaurants. A smaller shopping center, also on Central Avenue but closer to downtown, features Wal-Mart and Kroger stores. The city's historic downtown is no longer a major shopping area for local residents but remains commercially viable thanks to the popularity of its quaint shops among tourists frequenting Bathhouse Row on the other side of Central Avenue.

Health Care   Rating: 3

Two general hospitals provide good health care locally, and the greater medical resources of Little Rock are only an hour away. St. Joseph's Mercy Health Center, a nonprofit hospital operated by the St. Louis-based Sisters of Mercy Health Care System, has 257 private suites and offers a wide range of services. In addition to the usual clinical services like cardiac, cancer and diabetic care, the hospital reaches out to the community with its senior centers and Meals on Wheels, home health and mobile health programs. National Park Medical Center, a 166-bed for-profit hospital, also provides wide-ranging services including open-heart surgery and cardiac rehabilitation. The hospital's home health agency provides an array of in-home services including personal care.

Community Services   Rating: 3

Services of interest to seniors are well developed in this retirement-oriented city. The Senior Citizens Center, located just west of the city center, is a focus of social and recreational activities for retirees, while the Community Adult Center offers similar opportunities for the general adult population. Several retiree clubs and social organizations including the local AARP chapter provide additional support for active seniors.

Cultural and Educational Activities   Rating: 3

Although Hot Springs is too small to support classic resident ensembles like symphony orchestras and opera companies, its arts culture has broadened greatly during the past 15 years. Each year the Hot Springs Documentary Film Festival showcases more than 50 classical and experimental American and foreign documentaries at the historic Malco Theatre, downtown. During the first two weeks in June, the city hosts the Hot Springs Music Festival. This musical extravaganza brings together more than 200 musicians who perform in 30 orchestral and chamber music concerts and open rehearsals. The Hot Springs Jazz and Blues Festival, which features nationally known modern and traditional jazz artists, rounds out the summer season each September. The visual arts are also well represented. Artists and gallery owners have renovated many Victorian buildings in the historic district into attractive studios and galleries, while the Hot Springs Arts Center spotlights the work of resident artists in its monthly exhibits. Continuing education courses of interest to seniors are offered at the Shepherds Center and at the Senior Citizen Center of Hot Springs.

Recreational Activities   Rating: 4

 Surrounded by mountains and lakes, Hot Springs and its immediate surroundings offer excellent opportunities for recreation in a setting of great natural beauty. Nearby Lakes Catherine, Hamilton and Ouachita are excellent sites for boating, fishing, water-skiing and swimming. Parks adjacent to the lakes feature picnicking, hiking and camping, while Hot Springs National Park is especially notable for bathing, picnicking, walking and sightseeing along Bathhouse Row and hiking on the trails of its forested, mountainous areas. The city's nine neighborhood parks provide additional recreational facilities. Golf, tennis and bowling facilities are more than adequate locally. Three area 18-hole public golf courses and one 9-hole public course are supplemented by eight additional courses at local country clubs and in nearby planned communities. Movie theaters and good, inexpensive restaurants featuring a surprising variety of cuisines are well represented in Hot Springs. Finally, fans of thoroughbred racing can try their luck at centrally located Oaklawn Park all year. Live racing extends from late January to mid-April and simulcast racing from other tracks may be viewed there the rest of the year.

Work and Volunteer Activities   Rating: 4

 Wages are low in Hot Springs but so too are living costs. Many seniors find work in service industries and especially in tourist related activities. Offering volunteer services through more than 150 volunteer organizations is a big part in the lives of many senior citizens not ready for total retirement. Volunteers in Parks (VIPs) lead guided tours, greet and assist visitors at the information desk, staff the bookstore, serve as campground aides and maintain trails in Hot Springs National Park, while Friends of the Fordyce (Bathhouse) and Hot Springs National Park Inc. raise funds to upgrade park facilities. Hot Springs hospitals also depend heavily on volunteer help.

Crime Rates and Public Safety   Rating: 3

 Countywide, the violent crime rate approximates the national average while the property crime rate is about 20 percent above the national norm. More importantly, potential exposure to crime varies drastically over relatively short distances in Hot Springs. Although rates of violent and property crime are well above national norms in the city of Hot Springs, outlying suburban districts are much safer. This goes a long way toward explaining the apparently reckless comment of a local woman who said that she doesn't lock her doors in daytime at Lake Hamilton. In fairness to the city and its residents, it should be noted that many lovely, older inner city neighborhoods bordering the national park appear safe and peaceful. On the other hand, you can encounter sub-marginal living conditions in poor, inner city areas only a mile or two away.

Conclusion

Overall Rating 41 It is easy to understand why Hot Springs has become a favorite location for retirement. The city's physical site is scenic with low mountains and a national park in town and three large lakes nearby. Its sunny, warm climate with four clearly defined seasons appeals to many, and its quality of life is good. The city is small and uncrowded and suffers from none of the problems of pollution and congestion characteristic of large cities. Its rankings in retail and community services and volunteer activities are good, and its health care and transportation assets are more than adequate. Together, the city, the national park and the surrounding lake and mountain countryside offer residents many cultural and recreational options. The major drawbacks to retirement in Hot Springs are probably its hot, humid summers and an above-average incidence of crime. Not much can be done about the weather, but housing costs are so low in Hot Springs that you can more easily afford a very nice house in an upscale and relatively safe neighborhood here than in most other desirable communities. On that basis, Hot Springs is worthy of careful examination.

Fayetteville, Arkansas

Founded in 1828 when northwestern Arkansas was opened to American settlement and described 12 years later by a disgruntled resident as a lawless and uncivilized place, Fayetteville has matured since World War II into the region's most sophisticated and attractive city. To a large extent, the present success of Fayetteville has its roots in the efforts of local citizens in the immediate post-Civil War era to have their community chosen as the site for the Arkansas land grant college. Their efforts were rewarded with the 1872 opening of Arkansas Industrial College, which evolved ultimately into the University of Arkansas, the flagship institution of the state's higher education system. The university is justifiably the pride of Fayetteville, the center of its cultural and social life and its principal employer. With a population exceeding 60,000 in the city and 170,000 in Washington County, Fayetteville is large enough to offer the amenities most people seek, in a relaxed yet vibrant college town.

Landscape	Rating: 5

Fayetteville is situated at an elevation of 1,300 feet amidst the gently rolling hills of the Ozark Plateau in the northwestern corner of Arkansas. Although the city's setting is not as spectacular as that of Boulder, Colorado, the surrounding hills, mantled in a dense growth of broadleafed deciduous trees, provide a lovely backdrop to the community's well-treed and landscaped neighborhoods.

Climate	Rating: 4

Fayetteville experiences a temperate variant of the humid subtropical climate found throughout the southeastern United States. The town's moderate elevation causes the four distinct seasons to be a little cooler than at lower elevations. Even so, summer afternoons can be uncomfortable because of high temperatures and humidity. Spring and autumn weather is quite changeable from day to day but, on average, is the most pleasant of the year. Winters are not severe, although occasional cold waves can temporarily drop temperatures well below seasonal norms. Annual precipitation averages 46 inches and is well distributed throughout the year; only 10 inches of snow accumulates on the ground in a typical winter and it melts within a few days. The city enjoys a frost-free season of 180 days and is sunny about 60 percent of the time.

Fayetteville, Arkansas

CLIMATE

Month	Average Daily Temperature High	Average Daily Temperature Low	Daily Rel. Humidity Low	Average Monthly Precipitation
	F		**%**	**Inches**
January	44	24	61	2.1
February	51	29	60	2.4
March	59	38	56	4.2
April	69	46	55	4.3
May	76	55	59	5.1
June	84	64	59	5.3
July	89	69	56	3.1
August	89	67	54	3.0
September	81	59	58	4.8
October	70	47	54	3.7
November	57	37	59	4.7
December	48	28	63	3.2

Annual Averages

Total Days		Total Inches	
Clear	116	Precipitation	46.0
Partly Cloudy	96	Snowfall	10.0
Cloudy	153		

RATINGS

Category	poor 1	fair 2	good 3	very good 4	excellent 5
Landscape					●
Climate				●	
Quality of Life					●
Cost of Living			●		
Transportation			●		
Retail Services				●	
Health Care				●	
Community Services			●		
Cultural Activities				●	
Recreational Activities				●	
Work/Volunteer Activities				●	
Crime			●		

Total Points: 46

(Map of Fayetteville, Arkansas area showing Tontitown, Springdale, Spring Valley, Ozark National Forest, Johnson, Goshen, Fayetteville, Farmington, Baldwin, Wesley, Rhea, Greenland, Elkins, Prairie Grove, Beaver Lake, Springdale Municipal Airport, Drake Field; highways 412, 71, 540, 16, 15, 62. Inset map of Arkansas showing Fayetteville.)

Quality of Life   Rating: 5

The quality of life is excellent in Fayetteville. There is little noise pollution as the I-540 freeway skirts the city's western side and the new Northwest Arkansas Regional Airport is 20 miles away toward the northwest. Air quality is excellent; the city and county comply fully with all federal air quality standards. Some residents complain, though, that air-borne chicken dander causes allergic reactions. This would not be surprising since millions of broiler chickens are raised annually in northwest Arkansas. Traffic congestion is unknown and parking is more than adequate at the local mall and downtown, although it is tight adjacent to the old core of the university campus. Residential neighborhoods are quite varied but all are well treed, landscaped and maintained. Residents seem friendly, well educated and proud of their community.

Cost of Living   Rating: 3

 The cost of living in Fayetteville is evaluated as follows:

- *Composite.* ACCRA data for Fayetteville reveal a composite cost of living about 5 percent below the national average.

- *Housing.* Housing is inexpensive. ACCRA data show housing costs to be about 5 percent below the national average. Exploration of the local area revealed a good variety of desirable housing. Attractive modern suburban houses on large wooded lots on the edge of town were priced between $150,000 and $250,000; those in slightly more remote locations were priced lower. Several historic districts close to downtown and the University of Arkansas campus offer additional choices. The Washington–Willow historic district has some of Fayetteville's finest homes. Many large houses there, some newly renovated, are priced between $150,000 and $350,000. The nearby Wilson Park neighborhood has many mid-sized houses, built in the 1950s and 1960s, priced between $120,000 and $200,000.

- *Goods and Services.* Except for utilities, which are priced about 10 percent above the national average, goods and services costs are below national norms. Transportation and miscellaneous goods and services costs are 2 percent; health care costs are about 5 percent; and groceries costs are 11 percent below their national averages.

- *Taxes.* The state and local tax burden in Fayetteville is 10 percent of income compared to the U.S. average of 9.7 percent. State income taxes approximate the national average, property taxes are lower than average and sales and excise taxes are higher than average.

Transportation   Rating: 3

 Although Fayetteville residents typically drive to most destinations, public transit alternatives are available. Ozark Regional Transit operates 39 buses and trolleys that offer service on fixed routes. Razorback Transit, operated by the university, serves the campus community. Northwest Arkansas Regional Airport, 20 miles northwest of town, is served by five airlines that provide direct service to 12 major cities including Chicago, Dallas, Los Angeles, New York and St. Louis. Drake Field, the local Fayetteville airport, is now a general aviation facility.

Northwest Arkansas Mall, located on College Avenue at the northern edge of the city, is the major regional mall. Its more than 90 stores are anchored by Dillard's, JCPenney and Sears department stores. A large food court and twin movie theaters are other assets of this mall, which has abundant parking and is accessible by public transit. Evelyn Hills Shopping Center and Fiesta Square, both on College Avenue, offer additional shopping. The Square is the historic center of downtown Fayetteville; it provides a refreshing change from the sameness of malls. Items at the unique, interesting and typically upscale stores here are supplemented several days a week by the wares and fresh produce of a casual farmers' market in the Square.

Health Care   Rating: 4

Washington Regional Medical Center (WRMC) is the only nonprofit, community-owned health care system in northwestern Arkansas. The 233-bed acute care hospital moved into new quarters on an 80-acre tract near North Hills Medical Center and I-540 in 2003. WRMC offers a wide variety of medical services including emergency and intensive care, cardiac surgery and care, diabetic and pulmonary rehabilitation, diagnostic radiology and special imaging. The local VA Medical Center, located on College Avenue, provides specialty clinics for urology, orthopedics, diabetes, mental health and substance abuse, as well as dental, cardiopulmonary and imaging services to veterans. Additional medical facilities and services are found in neighboring Springdale and Rogers.

Community Services   Rating: 3

Fayetteville, Washington County and the University of Arkansas offer a fine array of services to the public. Fayetteville Senior Activity Center hosts activities such as dances, cards, billiards, bingo and quilting. Classes in arts and crafts, exercise and computing are available to seniors as are hot lunches and transportation for those unable to drive.

Cultural and Educational Activities   Rating: 4

Thanks to the University of Arkansas and the philanthropy of the Walton family, Fayetteville is an oasis of higher education and culture. In addition to regular university courses, available for audit by seniors on a "space available" basis, the university's Continuing Education Center schedules a great variety of courses of interest to the general public and hosts an Elderhostel program of short courses, which attracts locals and visitors alike. Additionally, Fayetteville public schools offer a variety of personal enrichment and applied arts courses through their adult and community education program.

The performing arts are well represented on campus and off. The university Music Department at the Campus Fine Arts Concert Hall hosts a Fine Arts Concert Series, often featuring internationally acclaimed musicians. In addition, the university offers quality drama at the University Theater, art exhibits at a gallery in the Fine Arts Building and miscellaneous musical events ranging from open-air band concerts on the lawn in front of Old Main to rock concerts at Barnhill Arena. Just off campus in the heart of town is Fayetteville's magnificent Walton Arts Center with its three auditoriums, art gallery and outdoor amphitheater. The Arts Center presents about 50 performances annually, varying from classical music by the North Arkansas Symphony and North Arkansas Symphonic Band to plays by Ozark Stageworks. Touring artist bookings at the Center have recently included the New York City Opera and professional productions of *Cats, Miss Saigon* and *Cabaret*.

Recreational Activities   Rating: 4

Varied recreational opportunities are found in Fayetteville and the nearby Ozarks. The city's 58 parks, consisting of more than 3,300 acres in all, are mostly in a relatively natural state. Only three percent of their total acreage is devoted to sports facilities. Fishing and hiking are popular at Lake Fayetteville, Lake Sequoyah and Lake Wilson parks. The latter facility also has an outdoor swimming pool. Walker Park has tennis, volleyball, racquetball and handball courts, while the Fayetteville Youth Center has an indoor swimming pool plus youth and adult sports programs. The university has a variety of sports facilities including the Health, Physical Education and Recreation (HPER) fitness complex available to the university community. It might be worth signing up for a course to gain access to them if you are not otherwise associated with the university. Alumnus or not, you are always welcome at Razorback Stadium and Bud Walton Arena for intercollegiate football and basketball. Golfers can choose among six local golf courses plus four more in the Greater Fayetteville–Springdale–Rogers area. A little farther afield, Ozark National Forest lakes, rivers and mountains provide countless sites for fishing, swimming, boating, sightseeing, picnicking, camping, hiking and hunting. Back in town, the city continues to expand its network of bike lanes along streets and off-road bike and hiking paths, some along abandoned railroad rights-of-way. These make recreational bicycling safer and more attractive than it was previously. Finally, almost everyone can enjoy an occasional movie at one of the many cinema complexes or a meal at one of several excellent restaurants. Restaurant meals are a bargain in Fayetteville.

Work and Volunteer Activities   Rating: 4

The economy of northwestern Arkansas has been booming in recent years, fueled especially by growth of the University of Arkansas and corporate giants Wal-Mart and Tyson. Jobs, especially part-time jobs, are plentiful although competition with students and an absence of unionization keep wages low. Wal-Mart and other retailers are among the principal employers of seniors. The local RSVP can be helpful in placing you in a suitable niche in one of the community's many public facilities or service organizations.

Crime Rates and Public Safety   Rating: 3

The Fayetteville–Springdale–Rogers metropolitan area is one of the safer urban/suburban areas. Unfortunately, the situation in Fayetteville itself is a little less positive. This anomaly is, in part, the result of Fayetteville having a large nonresident (student) population, which contributes somewhat to the incidence of crime but not to the population base on which crime rates are computed. That said, the property crime rate in the city of Fayetteville is about 33 percent above the national average, largely because of a high incidence of larceny–theft. Local burglary and auto theft rates are well below national norms. Significantly, the violent crime rate is 35 percent below the national average and the community feels safe. Indeed, I saw many vehicles with their windows left open, and several residents told me that Fayetteville is a safe college town with a good police department.

Conclusion

Overall Rating 46 Fayetteville is one of America's most pleasant and affordable college towns and is an excellent place for an active retirement. Its physical setting among the forested hills of the Ozark Plateau is scenic and its urban character is quite attractive. Its four-season humid subtropical climate is tempered by elevation and is moderately sunny with little snow. Although some may deem its winters a little too cold or its summers a little too hot, few would criticize its excellent quality of life. There is little environmental pollution or traffic congestion. The city has good transportation facilities, including satisfactory public transit, and is expanding its network of bike paths and lanes. Infrastructure development is keeping up with demand and residential neighborhoods are typically attractive. Retail, health care, cultural, community service and recreation assets are substantial, as are opportunities for work and volunteerism. Fortunately, the many amenities of Fayetteville are available at a cost of living about five percent below the national average.

8 The Heart of Texas Retirement Region

Climate: Humid subtropical

Place Description	Overall Rating	Page
Austin, Texas	**49**	**186**
Economically thriving Austin, Texas offers a wealth of resources for active retirement. Often characterized as the live music capital of the world, Austin is one of only 14 American cities with its own ballet, opera and symphony.		
San Antonio, Texas	**50**	**191**
San Antonio is not perfect but it has much to offer retirees. Rush-hour traffic congestion getting in and out of downtown, high property crime rates and hot summers are all less than ideal.		
Kerrville, Texas and Fredericksburg, Texas	**not rated**	**197**
Kerrville and Fredericksburg, two delightful Texas Hill Country towns, are also worth considering for retirement. Situated in ruggedly beautiful terrain 65 miles northwest of San Antonio and 90 miles west of Austin, both places are a world apart from the traffic, crime and urban sprawl of these fast-growing south central Texas metropolitan areas.		

Texas is America's second largest state in land area (after Alaska) and in population (after California). Yet much of the state is not especially attractive for retirement. Its largest cities, Dallas–Fort Worth and Houston, suffer heavy air pollution and traffic congestion, high crime rates and out-of-control urban sprawl. On the other hand, most small Texas cities suffer from inadequate public services and a dearth of amenities important to seniors.

The Heart of Texas Retirement Region, located in south central Texas where the coastal plain meets the Texas Hill Country, is different. Its two major cities, Austin and San Antonio, are large enough to provide the services and amenities retirees demand but are not so large as to suffer the environmental degradation and declining quality of life characteristic of larger Texas cities. Austin, state capital of Texas and home of its flagship public university, is attracting retired alumni of the University of Texas from all over the country as well as retired Texas state employees and retirees from other states. San Antonio has long lured back Air Force and Army veterans once based at its five military bases, and in recent years it has attracted many former visitors who came to the city as tourists or conferees and liked what they saw. On a smaller scale, people are moving into small Texas Hill Country towns like Fredericksburg and Kerrville, which offer a peaceful and high-quality life in a lovely, clean environment only an hour or so from the many attractions of Austin and San Antonio.

Austin, Texas

Chosen as capital of the Republic of Texas in 1840 and named for Stephen F. Austin, pioneer American colonizer of Texas, Austin struggled along as a remote frontier capital until its physical and cultural isolation was broken after the Civil War by the arrival of the railroad and the establishment of the University of Texas. Now the flagship institution of the statewide University of Texas system, the University of Texas at Austin—with 52,000 students—is the largest university in the nation and a major center of scientific research. It has attracted remarkable academic talent to Austin, served as a catalyst for high-tech industrial development and helped transform a formerly provincial and conservative city into a cosmopolitan, environmentally aware and progressive one.

For decades now, Austin has been rated as one of America's most pleasant mid-sized cities. Despite rapid population growth to more than 680,000 in the city, 830,000 in Travis County, and 1.3 million in the metropolitan area, Austin remains relatively unspoiled. Its beautiful site, warm sunny climate, good urban design and abundant amenities should keep it for some time one of the nation's choice locales for an active retirement.

Landscape — Rating: 4

 Austin occupies a gently rolling plain in south central Texas. Toward the western edge of the city the land rises dramatically at the Balcones Escarpment, which marks the eastern edge of the Edwards Plateau (Texas Hill Country). The Colorado River, which traverses the city from northwest to southeast, has been impounded into a series of picturesque lakes including Lake Austin and Town Lake. A park-like landscape of oak and hickory groves separated by tall grass prairie is the predominant natural vegetation but a wide selection of broad-leafed and coniferous trees has been planted in the city. Most neighborhoods are well treed and landscaped.

Climate — Rating: 3

 Austin lies toward the western margin of the humid subtropical climatic region and is considerably drier than Houston or other Gulf Coast locations. Summers are consistently very hot and moderately humid, whereas winter conditions alternate between warm and humid and cool and dry. Spring and autumn are nearly ideal with warm days and cool nights. Austin is sunny about 50 percent of the time in winter and more than 70 percent of the time in summer. Occasional winter frosts result in a frost-free season averaging 270 days, and snowfall averages less than one inch annually.

Quality of Life — Rating: 4

Overall, Austin provides a very good quality of life. Noise pollution is a problem chiefly near the airport and adjacent to I-35, Loop 360 and several major boulevards. Lacking heavy industry and chronic traffic congestion, Austin meets all federal air quality standards. Parking is generally not a problem except on campus, near the capitol and downtown but traffic is steadily increasing, especially downtown and on freeways and streets connecting it to the suburbs. Downtown Austin has seen considerable construction in recent years including hotels, office buildings, retail stores and residential lofts and condos. Residential neighborhoods, including several older

Austin, Texas

CLIMATE				
Month	Average Daily Temperature High Low		Daily Rel. Humidity Low	Average Monthly Precipitation
	F		**%**	**Inches**
January	60	40	60	1.9
February	65	44	59	2.0
March	73	51	56	2.1
April	79	58	57	2.5
May	85	65	61	5.0
June	91	71	57	3.8
July	95	73	51	2.0
August	96	73	50	2.3
September	90	69	56	2.9
October	81	60	55	4.0
November	70	49	58	2.7
December	62	42	60	2.4

Annual Averages

Total Days		Total Inches	
Clear	115	Precipitation	33.7
Partly Cloudy	114	Snowfall	0.9
Cloudy	136		

RATINGS					
Category	poor 1	fair 2	good 3	very good 4	excellent 5
Landscape				●	
Climate			●		
Quality of Life			●		
Cost of Living		●			
Transportation					●
Retail Services					●
Health Care				●	
Community Services				●	
Cultural Activities					●
Recreational Activities					●
Work/Volunteer Activities					●
Crime		●			

Total Points: 49

ones north of the University of Texas, are nicely landscaped and maintained. The university is an enormous asset to the community, and the city's outstanding network of parks, recreation centers and natural areas adds greatly to its livability. Austin residents are strong environmentalists, ensuring that planning and zoning are geared to preserve their high quality of life in the face of inevitable population growth.

Cost of Living — Rating: 3

 The cost of living in Austin is evaluated as follows:

- *Composite.* ACCRA data indicate that the composite cost of living in Austin approximates the national average.

- *Housing.* According to ACCRA, housing costs are 8 percent below the national average. Exploration of the area indicates that Austin housing offers good value. Attractive inner city neighborhoods a mile or two north of the university campus feature an eclectic variety of housing styles priced between $150,000 and $350,000. Suburban areas offer new and near-new tract homes over a wide price range.

- *Goods and Services.* Most goods and services are priced within 10 percent of national norms. Groceries and transportation are bargains at prices 7 to 10 percent below average, whereas miscellaneous goods and services and health care costs are 4 to 9 percent above average. Utility costs are 25 percent above the national average because of the high cost of summer air conditioning.

- *Taxes.* The state and local tax burden is 7.8 percent of income compared to the U.S. average of 9.7 percent. Texas does not tax income and property taxes approximate the national average. Conversely, sales and excise taxes are higher than average.

Transportation — Rating: 5

 Although not as elaborate as San Antonio's, Austin's street and freeway network is quite adequate and most people get around by car. Capital Metro's more than 250 clean and relatively new buses provide excellent transit service. Buses provide access to major malls and shopping centers, the central business district, major parks and recreation areas, the university and the airport. Fares are low and seniors 65 and older ride free. Bicycling is a popular transportation mode especially in central Austin in and around the University of Texas. Austin Bergstrom International Airport provides nonstop jet service to more than 31 destinations including major hubs at Dallas and Houston. Amtrak offers daily trips northbound to Chicago and three trips weekly westbound to Los Angeles. Kerrville Bus Company and Greyhound provide frequent motor coach service to locations in Texas and beyond.

Retail Services — Rating: 5

The central business district located between the capitol and Town Lake no longer dominates retailing, but unique shopping areas have grown up along Lamar Boulevard and South Congress Avenue. West Sixth Street downtown boasts an eclectic variety of unique stores, art galleries and restaurants. More conventional shopping is available in several major malls mostly located adjacent to loop highways. Highland Mall is the oldest of Austin's indoor shopping centers and perhaps the most attractive. Anchored by Dillard's, Foley's and JCPenney department stores, the mall has 130 specialty stores and restaurants. Barton Creek Square, with 180 stores and restaurants and a 14-screen cinema complex, is the largest Austin mall. Its department stores include Dillard's, Foley's, JCPenney, Nordstrom and Sears. Lakeline Mall is anchored by Dillard's, Foley's, JCPenney and Sears department stores and features 140 specialty retailers and restaurants and a nine-screen movie theater complex. On the northern periphery of the city is the well-named Arboretum with more than 40 upscale specialty shops and eateries in a greenbelt setting. Many small shopping centers and neighborhood shopping streets scattered about the city provide shopping experiences ranging from upscale boutique to 1960s funky.

Health Care   Rating: 4

 Medical care is very good in Austin. Five major medical centers together furnish virtually every conceivable medical specialty and service. Largest of these, with about 600 beds, is Seton Medical Center, part of the nonprofit Seton Healthcare Network, which also runs Brackenridge Hospital. The latter facility is a teaching hospital and regional referral center especially notable for cancer and cardiac care. Other major facilities include the associated St. David's Hospital, North Austin Medical Center and South Austin Hospital, which are typical general hospitals providing a broad repertoire of services.

Community Services   Rating: 4

 Basic public services as well as those catering to seniors are very good in Austin. Four senior centers host a variety of classes, social and recreational activities and wellness programs. Community centers offer additional social and recreation programs for all age groups. Austin's Capital Area Agency on Aging is an important source for information and counseling.

Cultural and Educational Activities   Rating: 5

The University of Texas is an exceptional educational and cultural asset. Seniors may audit regular courses on a "space available" basis or participate for nominal fees in courses offered through the university's Learning Activities for Mature People Program. The Community Schools Program of Austin City Schools offers an enormous list of adult education courses and the Parks and Recreation Department targets seniors with arts and crafts and sports and fitness classes, among others. Austin Community College also fields courses in the liberal arts, communications, photography and other subjects of interest to seniors. Bass Concert Hall, Bates Recital Hall and Hogg Auditorium on the University of Texas campus book everything from Broadway shows to classical and popular music performances by imported and local talent. Productions by the Austin Lyric Opera, Austin Symphony Orchestra and Ballet Austin are performed in the larger Bass Concert Hall; those by individual guest artists and smaller ensembles are typically staged in Bates Hall or Hogg Auditorium. Among Austin's other excellent musical groups are the Austin Civic Orchestra, which performs classical and popular works, the Austin Vocal Arts Ensemble, which presents quality choral music both a cappella and with orchestra, and La Follia, Austin's baroque period instrumental ensemble. Some of Austin's best classical musicians may be heard for free at the Thursday Noon Concert Series at Central Presbyterian Church.

Popular music and theater are also vibrant in Austin. The city is famous for its country, blues and rock music, which can be heard live at more than 100 nightspots. Free tickets are available for taping sessions of the PBS show Austin City Limits, which features performances of country, blues and rock by stars such as Willie Nelson, Lyle Lovett and B. B. King. The city also boasts more than 10 legitimate theaters that stage everything from comedy to tragedy and from classical to cutting-edge productions. In season, you can enjoy theater under the stars at Zilker Hillside Theatre in Zilker Park. Among Austin's more than 20 museums are the Austin Museum of Art, the Huntington Gallery, the George Washington Carver Museum and the Lyndon Baines Johnson (LBJ) Presidential Library and Museum. The Austin Museum of Art, housed in part in a 1916 Mediterranean villa overlooking Lake Austin, emphasizes twentieth century American art in its changing programs. The Huntington Gallery, housed in two locations on the University of Texas campus, includes more than 12,000 works and is generally regarded as one of the top 10 university art museums in the country. The George Washington Carver Museum is the first African-American neighborhood history museum in Texas; it features artifacts, photographs, oral histories and archival materials. On a different scale is the monumental LBJ Presidential Library and Museum. Housing more than 36 million official and personal documents and exhibits, the complex depicts President Johnson's life from his boyhood to his retirement at his Texas Hill Country ranch.

Recreational Activities   Rating: 5

 Austin and the adjacent Texas Hill Country are a mecca for the outdoors oriented. With 12,000 acres of undeveloped greenbelt around the city there is plenty of room for recreation and nature protection. Austin's excellent network of urban parks has nearly 30 swimming pools, 200 tennis courts and all kinds of sports fields. Zilker Park, Austin's largest and most popular park, offers year-round swimming in the 68-degree water of Barton Springs pool, the most famous of several natural spring-fed swimming holes in and around Austin. The park also features a 10.1-mile hike and bike trail around Town Lake, playgrounds, picnicking facilities, a botanical garden and the Austin Nature Center. Upstream on the Colorado River are Lakes Austin and Travis where boating, fishing and swimming are popular. The nearby Texas Hill Country, with its many lakes and wild areas, provides plenty of opportunities for hiking, biking, horseback riding, swimming, fishing and hunting. Golfers can enjoy a round of golf on more than 20 municipal or daily fee courses in the metropolitan area.

Spectator sports are largely courtesy of the University of Texas. Its NCAA Longhorns basketball and football teams attract a loyal following and the Round Rock Express provides Texas League baseball at a state-of-the-art, family-oriented baseball stadium. The city also boasts more than 100 movie screens and a good selection of restaurants specializing in regional American, Southwest, Mexican and ethnic cuisines, and, of course, steak.

Work and Volunteer Activities   Rating: 5

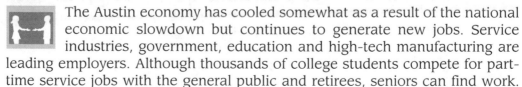 The Austin economy has cooled somewhat as a result of the national economic slowdown but continues to generate new jobs. Service industries, government, education and high-tech manufacturing are leading employers. Although thousands of college students compete for part-time service jobs with the general public and retirees, seniors can find work.

The city of Austin's Experience Unlimited job referral system does a good job of putting them in touch with potential employers. Demand for volunteer help probably exceeds supply. Placements are readily available in Austin area schools, hospitals, libraries, social and recreational organizations and places of worship.

Crime Rates and Public Safety   Rating: 2

 Crime rates are somewhat mixed in Austin. In the city itself, the violent crime rate is slightly below the national average but the property crime rate is 60 percent above the national norm. Metropolitan area-wide crime rates are somewhat lower. The violent crime rate there is about 25 percent below the national average whereas the property crime rate is 25 percent above the national norm. As elsewhere, you must choose your neighborhood carefully in order to minimize potential exposure to crime.

Conclusion

Overall Rating 49 Economically thriving Austin, Texas offers a wealth of resources for active retirement. Often characterized as the live music capital of the world, Austin is one of only 14 American cities with its own ballet, opera and symphony. The University of Texas lends a cosmopolitan air to the community, hosting visiting performing artists and fielding competitive intercollegiate basketball and football teams. Environmentalists and the outdoors oriented will appreciate the city's abundance of greenbelt, parkland and recreation facilities. The city is also notable for the excellence of its transportation, retail services and work and volunteer opportunities. Health care and community services are very good, the urban landscape is well planned and attractive, and the quality of life is high. Long, hot summers and higher-than-average property crime rates are the principal drawbacks in Austin. Nonetheless, the city remains a premier choice for stimulating retirement at a reasonable cost.

San Antonio, Texas

With a population of 1.2 million in the city and upwards of 1.7 million in the metropolitan area, San Antonio is a unique place and one of few large American cities recommended for retirement. Despite rapid growth in recent decades, the city retains much of its old Spanish–Mexican flavor with its five missions, including the Alamo, numerous parks and plazas, and historic neighborhoods. Nearly 60 percent of the population is Hispanic, about 35 percent Anglo. The downtown, much of which dates from before 1930, has been revitalized in concert with construction of the 2.5-mile long Riverwalk, a tree-lined park and footpath beside the diminutive San Antonio River. Formerly a run-down residential area, the Riverwalk, with its lovely landscaping and adjacent shops and restaurants, now symbolizes the beauty and romance of San Antonio and serves as a magnet drawing tourists, residents and investment back into the city center. Beyond downtown, residential neighborhoods and commercial areas sprawl outward, enveloping the military bases that have long lent stability to the local economy. Although not without problems, San Antonio's unusual combination of urban character and amenities, climate and low cost of living makes it appealing for retirement.

San Antonio, Texas

CLIMATE				
Month	Average Daily Temperature High Low		Daily Rel. Humidity Low	Average Monthly Precipitation
	F		**%**	**Inches**
January	62	39	59	1.7
February	67	42	57	1.8
March	74	50	54	1.9
April	80	57	56	2.6
May	86	66	60	4.7
June	91	72	57	4.3
July	95	74	52	2.0
August	95	74	51	2.6
September	90	69	55	3.0
October	82	59	54	3.9
November	71	49	56	2.6
December	64	41	58	2.0

Annual Averages

Total Days		Total Inches	
Clear	105	Precipitation	33.1
Partly Cloudy	119	Snowfall	0.7
Cloudy	141		

RATINGS					
Category	poor 1	fair 2	good 3	very good 4	excellent 5
Landscape				●	
Climate			●		
Quality of Life				●	
Cost of Living				●	
Transportation					●
Retail Services					●
Health Care					●
Community Services				●	
Cultural Activities					●
Recreational Activities					●
Work/Volunteer Activities				●	
Crime		●			

Total Points: 50

[Map of San Antonio, Texas area showing highways 16, 1604, 35, 10, 410, 90, 37, 87, 281, 35 and surrounding towns including Grey Forest, Helotes, Shavano Park, Hill Country Village, Hollywood Park, Bracken, Live Oak, Selma, Cibolo, Schertz, Castle Hills, Windcrest, Converse, Leon Valley, Balcones Heights, Olmos Park, Alamo Heights, Terrell Hills, Kirby, China Grove, Saint Hedwig, Kelly AFB, Lackland AFB, Brooks AFB, Fort Sam Houston, Randolph Air Force Base, Macdona, La Coste, Southton, Earle, Elmendorf. Inset shows Texas state with San Antonio location. San Antonio Intl. Airport, Stinson Municipal Airport, Castroville Municipal Airport, Mitchell Lake, Calaveras Lake, Camp Bullis.]

Landscape   **Rating: 4**

San Antonio is located in south central Texas just east of the Balcones Escarpment, which marks the eastern edge of the Texas Hill Country. The southern part of town is fairly flat at an elevation of about 600

feet. Northward from downtown the land gradually rises to a gently rolling surface about 200 feet higher. The city is underlain by limestone so drainage is good. The San Antonio River flows southward through downtown where it has been channeled and dammed to enhance the picturesque Riverwalk area. An oak and hickory woodland is the predominant natural vegetation but many exotic trees and shrubs add botanic variety.

Climate	Rating: 3

 San Antonio lies toward the western margin of the humid subtropical climatic region and is considerably drier than Houston or other Gulf Coast locations. Summers are consistently very hot and moderately humid, while winter weather conditions alternate between warm and humid and cool and dry. Spring and autumn are nearly ideal with warm days and cool nights. San Antonio is sunny about 50 percent of the time in winter and more than 70 percent of the time in summer. Occasional winter frosts result in a frost-free period averaging 280 days and snowfall is insignificant.

Quality of Life	Rating: 4

 There are two very different San Antonios. The southern half of the city, on the flat plains near the military bases, is relatively poor, lacks amenities, experiences considerable crime and is clearly unsuitable for upscale retirement. In contrast, slightly hilly northern San Antonio, with most of the city's cultural attractions, parks, other amenities and better residential areas, is where most middle-class retirees prefer to live. The latter area is emphasized in the following discussion.

The quality of life is generally very good. Noise pollution is principally a problem near the airport and adjacent to the freeways, of which there are many. Despite the large number of vehicles on the roads, parking is adequate in most areas. Traffic congestion is worsening as the population grows but is not yet a serious problem except on the central part of the freeway network in and around downtown at rush hour. There are few heavy industries to foul air or water, but heavy automobile use contributes to air pollution. The EPA recently designated San Antonio as a "basic non attainment area" for air quality, which means that the city is minimally out of compliance with current air quality standards. Although the air is relatively clean much of the year, San Antonio experiences light smog on many summer days. Many excellent, well-treed and maintained neighborhoods, old and new, grace the landscape. The city's parks, recreation centers, museums and zoo add to its livability, and the lively central business district, embracing Hemisfair Plaza, Market Square, the Alamo, the Riverwalk and Rivercenter Mall, is among the best small downtowns in the nation. The city is tied together by an excellent road network and good public transit. The people seem laid back and friendly, especially for residents of a large city.

Cost of Living	Rating: 4

 The cost of living in San Antonio is evaluated as follows:

- *Composite.* ACCRA data suggest that the composite cost of living in San Antonio is 7 percent below the national average.

- *Housing.* According to ACCRA, housing costs are about 10 percent below the national average. This makes San Antonio among America's least expensive big cities in which to own a home. Suburban areas to the north and east of the I-410 Loop, 10 to 20 miles out from downtown, are growing rapidly. New and resale single-family residences there are priced between $175,000 and $275,000. Housing in some excellent older San Antonio neighborhoods near Trinity University and Brackenridge and Basin Parks, and in Alamo Heights and Terrell Hills, is priced similarly.

- *Goods and Services.* Most categories of goods and services are priced below national norms. Groceries are especially cheap, at 22 percent below the national average. Transportation and utilities costs are about 12 percent below national norms whereas health care and miscellaneous goods and services are priced just below and just above their national averages.

- *Taxes.* The state and local tax burden is 7.8 percent of income compared to the U.S. average of 9.7 percent. Texas does not tax income and property taxes approximate the national average. Conversely, sales and excise taxes are higher than average.

Transportation	Rating: 5

San Antonio has excellent intracity and intercity transportation. The metropolitan area's outstanding street and freeway network encourages automobile use but VIA Trans, with 500 relatively new and clean buses, provides a handy alternative. You can easily access most destinations within the I-410 Loop and some beyond it by bus. Bus fares are low; seniors 62 and older can buy a monthly pass for $10. San Antonio International Airport, nine miles north of downtown, is a medium hub offering nonstop jet service to about 30 destinations including Dallas, Houston and Phoenix. Amtrak provides service three times a week east to Orlando and west to Los Angeles and daily service north to Chicago. Greyhound and Kerrville Bus Company provide frequent bus service to points in Texas and beyond.

Retail Services	Rating: 5

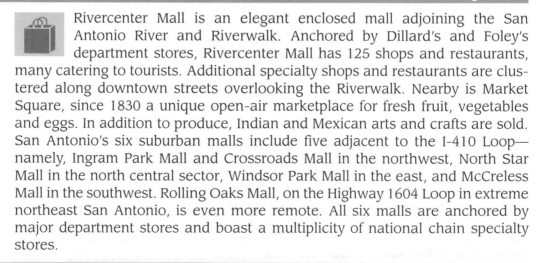

Rivercenter Mall is an elegant enclosed mall adjoining the San Antonio River and Riverwalk. Anchored by Dillard's and Foley's department stores, Rivercenter Mall has 125 shops and restaurants, many catering to tourists. Additional specialty shops and restaurants are clustered along downtown streets overlooking the Riverwalk. Nearby is Market Square, since 1830 a unique open-air marketplace for fresh fruit, vegetables and eggs. In addition to produce, Indian and Mexican arts and crafts are sold. San Antonio's six suburban malls include five adjacent to the I-410 Loop—namely, Ingram Park Mall and Crossroads Mall in the northwest, North Star Mall in the north central sector, Windsor Park Mall in the east, and McCreless Mall in the southwest. Rolling Oaks Mall, on the Highway 1604 Loop in extreme northeast San Antonio, is even more remote. All six malls are anchored by major department stores and boast a multiplicity of national chain specialty stores.

Health Care	Rating: 5

With 13 full-service general hospitals, several VA and military hospitals and a state psychiatric hospital, San Antonio provides comprehensive medical services consistent with its large population and regional centrality. South Texas Medical Center, located on a 700-acre site in northwest San Antonio, has an amazing assemblage of medical facilities. These include the University of Texas Health Science Center and Hospital, Southwest Texas Methodist Hospital, St. Luke's Baptist Hospital, two Humana Hospitals, Santa Rosa Hospital and several major clinics, laboratories, medical research, rehabilitation and nursing care units. Other major medical facilities including several hospitals operated by Christus Santa Rosa Health Care, Methodist Health Care Systems and Baptist Health System are scattered about the city.

Community Services   Rating: 4

 Basic public services such as fire and police protection, public transit, water supply, libraries, and parks and recreation facilities are excellent in San Antonio. Two major senior centers, several smaller ones, and more than 20 community centers provide social activities, information, arts and crafts classes and field trips for seniors. The Bexar County Area Agency on Aging and the Senior Information Center are helpful in providing information and locating services for seniors. Branches of national organizations such as AARP are also active locally.

Cultural and Educational Activities   Rating: 5

 The performing and visual arts are flourishing. Downtown's beautifully restored Majestic Theatre, formerly a vaudeville house, is now the home of the San Antonio Symphony and a venue for touring Broadway plays and guest artist concerts. In addition to formal classical performances, the symphony also performs chamber music, opera and pops series. Other resident ensembles include the Mid-Texas Symphony and the San Antonio Ballet. The Henry B. Gonzalez Convention Center Arena downtown is the scene of frequent jazz, pop and rock concerts, while the Theatre for the Performing Arts, next to the Majestic, hosts local and imported concerts, ballet, opera and theater. In nearby HemisFair Plaza, visiting dance and ballet troupes perform at Beethoven Hall and the Lila Cockerell Theatre. The respected San Antonio Little Theatre presents a varied program of comedies, drama and musicals at San Pedro Playhouse and Trinity University's drama department stages upwards of 10 productions annually in its Ruth Taylor Theater on campus. The San Antonio Museum of Art, which occupies a splendid site in the old Lone Star Brewery along the San Antonio River, features southwestern and American art, Mexican folk art, Chinese art and Greek and Roman antiquities. The McNay Art Museum is notable for French Post-Impressionist paintings, early twentieth century European art, modern American watercolors and Southwest folk art.

San Antonio has several fine universities and colleges. Largest of these is the University of Texas at San Antonio. Trinity University is much smaller yet ranks consistently as one of America's top liberal arts institutions. St. Mary's University and San Antonio (Community) College are also worth noting. Collectively these schools offer many courses of interest to seniors for enrollment or audit; additional choices are available through the city schools' adult education program. The San Antonio public library system, with more than two million books, is another important educational resource. The ultra-modern downtown central library is spectacular.

Recreational Activities Rating: 5

 San Antonio's subtropical climate and varied landscape favor outdoor sports and recreation. The city owns more than 6,800 acres of open space comprising 6 municipal golf courses, 135 parks and recreation centers, 22 swimming pools and one of the best zoos in the nation. More than 20 additional golf courses, including 10 operating on a daily fee basis, dot the metropolitan area. Tennis is played on more than 100 courts in the city, and bicycling and hiking are popular on many quiet roads and trails in northern residential areas and parks and in the nearby Texas Hill Country. The Hill Country is also popular for sightseeing, deer and turkey hunting, lake fishing and swimming.

Spectator sports, especially San Antonio Spurs NBA basketball and University of Texas Roadrunners NCAA basketball, bring out the crowds, as do the Riverwalk's shops, restaurants and nightspots. San Antonio also boasts more than 150 movie screens and countless excellent restaurants serving a good variety of American, Mexican, European and Asian cuisines in its regional malls and neighborhood shopping areas.

Work and Volunteer Activities Rating: 4

 San Antonio's economy has grown rapidly for a decade, generating an abundance of service jobs. Many of these, though, pay low wages and require fluency in English and Spanish. Demand for volunteers probably exceeds supply. Area hospitals, schools, libraries, places of worship and social organizations depend heavily on volunteers. United Way and the AARP help bring together volunteers and organizations needing them.

Crime Rates and Public Safety Rating: 2

 Crime rates are of continuing concern in San Antonio. For the metropolitan area as a whole, the violent crime rate is 30 percent above the national average while the property crime rate is 65 percent above the national norm. In general, areas of San Antonio south of downtown suffer disproportionately from crime, whereas the more affluent northern areas are much safer.

Conclusion

 Overall Rating 50 San Antonio is not perfect but it has much to offer retirees. Rush-hour traffic congestion getting in and out of downtown, high property crime rates and hot summers are all less than ideal. Yet despite recent growth, the city retains a unique ambiance and scores highly on most measures of desirability. You can live in San Antonio more cheaply than in most large cities and still enjoy exceptional intracity and intercity transportation, retail services, cultural options and medical care. San Antonio's historic sites and its art deco downtown, revitalized by the charming Riverwalk and tourist oriented commercial development, help define San Antonio as a special place offering a high quality of life. The air is clean much of the time and residential areas in the wooded and gently rolling landscape of the northern half of the city are pleasant and peaceful.

Very good community services, a fine selection of outdoor recreation and spectator sports and an easygoing way of life are other pluses. In summary, San Antonio should have special appeal to those seeking big-city amenities without big-city costs in a culturally stimulating, subtropical environment.

Kerrville, Texas and Fredericksburg, Texas

Kerrville and Fredericksburg, two delightful Texas Hill Country towns, are also worth considering for retirement. Situated in ruggedly beautiful terrain 65 miles northwest of San Antonio and 90 miles west of Austin, both places are a world apart from the traffic, crime and urban sprawl of these fast-growing south central Texas metropolitan areas. Yet both are within an hour's drive of San Antonio's rich cultural and recreational resources and excellent health care and transportation facilities and only a little farther from those of Austin.

Kerrville, population 21,000 and Fredericksburg, population 9,000, are only 25 miles apart and have generally similar physical environments. Both town centers are at an elevation of 1,700 feet but nearby hills rise several hundred feet higher. The surrounding countryside is park-like, with scattered live oaks separated by tall grass prairie. Summer weather is consistently hot and moderately humid, but in other seasons the weather can change drastically from day to day. Average high temperatures vary from the low 60s in winter to the low 90s in summer. Sunshine is abundant in all seasons and there is virtually no snow.

The quality of life is high in both towns although each has its own unique flavor. The oldest parts of Kerrville lie in the valley of the Guadalupe River, which meanders through the town center. Several riverside parks provide hiking, camping, fishing, swimming, boating and nature study. Outlying neighborhoods extend into the hills with some home sites offering splendid views of the lower town. Fredericksburg, on the other hand, occupies a gently rolling upland surface; a small creek runs through the town. Founded by German settlers in the 1840s, Fredericksburg still looks the part. Its wide main street is lined with buildings in German village style and most signage embodies Gothic script and German words. German is widely spoken here and the town is clean, orderly and well planned.

Kerrville and Fredericksburg will be most appreciated by those seeking a relatively tranquil retirement in a peaceful and friendly small town. The unspoiled natural environment, sunny subtropical climate, uncrowded streets and neighborhoods, low crime rates and lower-than-average living costs and taxes here are all highly desirable characteristics. On the other hand, both communities suffer from some of the limitations typical of small towns. Although you can get to and from San Antonio and Austin via intercity motor coach, there is no local bus service. Retail, health care and community services are modest in both towns but are growing to meet rising demand. For example, Fredericksburg's recently expanded hospital now has more than 60 physicians on staff. Cultural and recreational resources are also somewhat limited. Nonetheless, golf, swimming, tennis, bicycling, hiking and gardening can be enjoyed year-round in both communities so the outdoors oriented will find plenty to do.

The Southern Rockies Retirement Region

Climate: Semi-arid (steppe)

Place Description	Overall Rating	Page
Fort Collins, Colorado	48	199
Fort Collins is one of the most pleasant small towns in America and a good place for an active retirement in a rather relaxed setting.		
Boulder, Colorado	51	204
Boulder is one of the most sophisticated small cities in America and a wonderful place in which to lead an active retirement. Its physical and human environment is nearly ideal.		
Colorado Springs, Colorado	48	210
Colorado Springs is one of the most attractive medium-sized cities for retirement. Its physical site at the foot of Pikes Peak is scenic and its sunny, semi-arid climate with four distinct seasons appeals to many.		
Santa Fe, New Mexico	44	215
Santa Fe is a sophisticated small city and a delightfully stimulating place in which to lead an active retirement. Its physical and human environment is close to ideal.		

The Southern Rockies Retirement Region extends for 400 miles from Fort Collins, Colorado to Santa Fe, New Mexico. Snug against the spectacular Front Range of the Rocky Mountains, the Colorado Piedmont cities of Fort Collins, Boulder and Colorado Springs are becoming increasingly popular for retirement, as is Santa Fe, New Mexico, nestled at the foot of the scenic Sangre de Cristo Range.

The region is physically and culturally appealing. Catastrophic environmental problems are unlikely; hurricanes are unknown this far inland and earthquakes and tornadoes are extremely rare. All four cities provide an impressive list of amenities and services and offer easy access to the myriad recreational choices of the mountains. Although each community has its own unique character, all share a delightful, dry, sunny four-season climate and all rank among the best, if not the least expensive, upscale retirement towns.

Fort Collins, Colorado

Originally an army post on the western frontier and, for a time, merely a local market town for high plains farms and ranches, Fort Collins emerged in the late twentieth century as one of Colorado's principal educational, commercial and industrial centers and a pleasant residential community. Located only 60 miles north of Denver, 40 miles south of Cheyenne, Wyoming and 3 to 4 miles from the foothills of the Rocky Mountains, Fort Collins lies at the northern extremity of a rapidly growing complex of Colorado Piedmont cities stretching 140 miles southward through Denver to Colorado Springs. It has easy

Fort Collins, Colorado

CLIMATE					RATINGS					
Month	Average Daily Temperature High	Low	Daily Rel. Humidity Low	Average Monthly Precipitation	Category	poor	fair	good	very good	excellent
	F		**%**	**Inches**		**1**	**2**	**3**	**4**	**5**
January	42	15	50	0.4	Landscape				●	
February	47	20	45	0.4	Climate			●		
March	54	27	41	1.4	Quality of Life					●
April	61	34	36	2.1	Cost of Living			●		
May	70	43	39	2.6	Transportation				●	
June	81	52	36	2.0	Retail Services				●	
July	86	57	35	1.9	Health Care				●	
August	84	55	36	1.4	Community Services				●	
September	75	46	34	1.4	Cultural Activities					●
October	64	35	36	1.0	Recreational Activities					●
November	50	24	49	0.8	Work/Volunteer Activities				●	
December	43	17	52	0.5	Crime			●		

Annual Averages

Total Days		Total Inches	
Clear	110	Precipitation	15.8
Partly Cloudy	128	Snowfall	51.0
Cloudy	127		

Total Points: 48

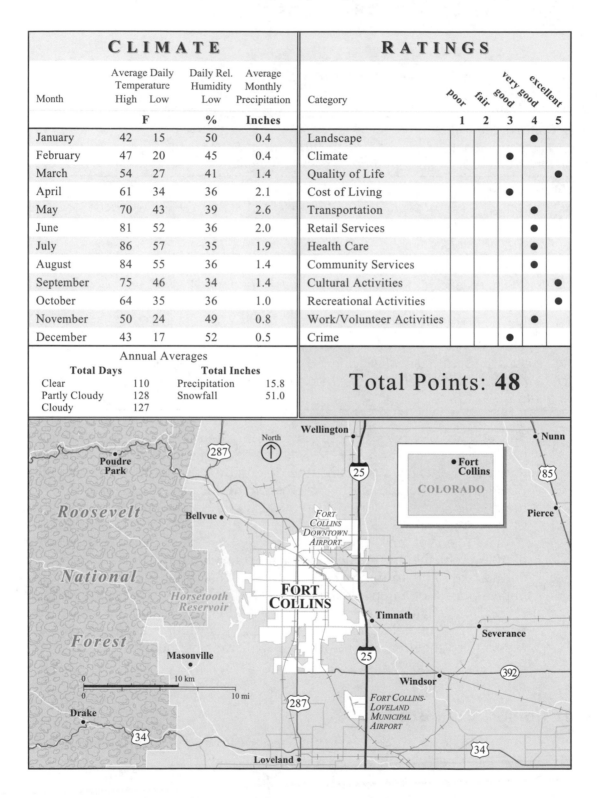

access via I-25 to the urban amenities of neighboring cities and via other routes to the limitless outdoor assets of Rocky Mountain National Park and other Front Range parks and recreation areas. With a population of 105,000 plus 24,000 Colorado State University students, Fort Collins has a relaxed atmosphere that reflects its residents' preference for a less frenetic lifestyle than found in some other Colorado Piedmont cities.

Landscape   Rating: 4

 Fort Collins is located in north central Colorado at an elevation of 5,000 feet. The city stretches across a gently sloping plain, which rises westward toward the foothills of the Rocky Mountains. Only 35 miles to the southwest the spectacular peaks of Rocky Mountain National Park grace the horizon. The natural landscape of the high plains is semi-arid with grassland grading into rather dry coniferous woodland in the foothills. In town and in nearby agricultural areas, though, irrigation water obtained from streams emanating from the mountains creates a lush landscape more typical of humid, eastern U.S. locales than of the Great Plains.

Climate   Rating: 3

 Fort Collins has a fairly severe four-season semi-arid climate characterized by light precipitation, ample sunshine and dramatic seasonal and day-to-day changes in the weather. About 70 percent of the normal annual precipitation of 15.8 inches falls between April and September. Although an average of 51 inches of snow falls annually, snow seldom lasts more than two consecutive weeks on the ground because daytime temperatures typically rise well above freezing except during winter cold waves. Summer afternoons are warm but quite comfortable owing to low relative humidity; summer evenings are pleasantly cool. Spring and autumn weather is changeable with average daytime highs ranging from the low 50s to the low 70s. Winters are cold with frequent and sometimes drastic departures from the average conditions documented on the climatic table. Fort Collins is sunny about 66 percent of the time and enjoys a frost-free season of about 150 days.

Quality of Life   Rating: 5

The quality of life is excellent in Fort Collins. With no major airport and with I-25 skirting the city on the east, noise pollution is minimal. However, the EPA recently designated Fort Collins as a "basic non-attainment area" for air quality, which means that the city is minimally out of compliance with current air quality standards. Although the air is clean much of the time, Fort Collins occasionally experiences light smog. Low population density, satisfactory land use planning and good transportation infrastructure combine to minimize crowding and traffic congestion. Even rush-hour traffic moves fairly smoothly and parking is abundant and inexpensive or free. The city lacks major polluting industries and dilapidated neighborhoods; residential areas are typically well maintained and treed. The city appears well managed; the beautifully restored historic downtown is delightful. Unfortunately, urbanization pressures in the Fort Collins–Loveland corridor are so great that even the best efforts of the Larimer County Open Lands Program seem likely to preserve from development only a few of the remaining farms separating the two cities. On a happier note, the people of this major college town appear friendly, well educated and appreciative of their community's high quality of life.

The cost of living in Fort Collins is evaluated as follows:

- *Composite.* ACCRA data for Fort Collins show that the composite cost of living approximates the national average.

- *Housing.* Average housing costs are about two percent above the national average according to ACCRA. This is consistent with a local realtor's estimate of an average sale price of $190,000 for a single-family residence. Quite a variety of housing is typically available in Fort Collins and the ambiance of most neighborhoods and the quality of the housing stock makes housing a good buy.

- *Goods and Services.* ACCRA data show health care, groceries and transportation costs to be 7 to 8 percent above national norms, whereas miscellaneous goods and services costs are at the national average. Utilities are priced 10 percent below average.

- *Taxes.* The state and local tax burden in Fort Collins is 8.8 percent of income compared to the U.S. average of 9.7 percent. State income taxes are a little above the national average but property and sales and excise taxes are lower than average.

Transportation   Rating: 4

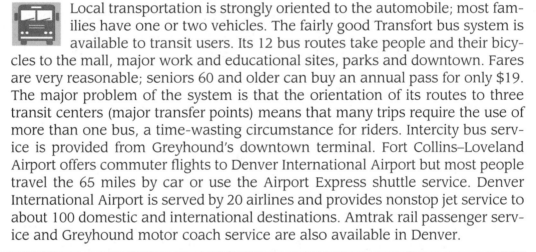 Local transportation is strongly oriented to the automobile; most families have one or two vehicles. The fairly good Transfort bus system is available to transit users. Its 12 bus routes take people and their bicycles to the mall, major work and educational sites, parks and downtown. Fares are very reasonable; seniors 60 and older can buy an annual pass for only $19. The major problem of the system is that the orientation of its routes to three transit centers (major transfer points) means that many trips require the use of more than one bus, a time-wasting circumstance for riders. Intercity bus service is provided from Greyhound's downtown terminal. Fort Collins–Loveland Airport offers commuter flights to Denver International Airport but most people travel the 65 miles by car or use the Airport Express shuttle service. Denver International Airport is served by 20 airlines and provides nonstop jet service to about 100 domestic and international destinations. Amtrak rail passenger service and Greyhound motor coach service are also available in Denver.

Retail Services   Rating: 4

Foothills Fashion Mall, located on College Avenue three miles south of downtown, is the major enclosed mall. Foleys, Mervyn's, JCPenney and Sears department stores anchor its 123 stores, restaurants and services. Nearby on College Avenue are Kmart, Target and Wal-Mart discount stores. More interesting, perhaps, is Fort Collins' beautifully revitalized historic downtown along College Avenue and at Old Town Square just east of College. A great place to walk and people watch, the historic area features one-of-a-kind specialty shops, art galleries, restaurants and brewpubs.

Health Care   Rating: 4

Poudre Valley Hospital, a medium-sized facility with 281 beds, is the area's major medical center. It offers the usual wide variety of medical services provided by regional medical centers including 24-hour emergency and intensive care, cardiac care, stroke management, oncology and radiology, among others. Much larger facilities with a greater range of medical services are only an hour away in Denver.

Community Services   Rating: 4

Fort Collins, Larimer County, Colorado State University and local community and religious organizations offer a fine array of services. The well-equipped Fort Collins Senior Center hosts day trips to nearby attractions, offers classes in arts and crafts, computers, dance, swimming and yoga, and provides a wellness program featuring free health screenings and flu shots.

Cultural and Educational Activities   Rating: 5

Fort Collins has much to offer culturally and educationally. Colorado State University, with 24,000 students and 1,500 faculty members, is the state's second-ranking public university. Its regular academic programs are open to all, whereas the Learning in Retirement Institute targets those 55 and older with programs of special interest to seniors. The university also hosts special lecture series, musical and theatrical events at the CSU Theatre and art exhibits at its two galleries. Front Range Community College regularly offers credit and noncredit courses on academic and applied topics on weekday, evening and weekend schedules. Lincoln Center, conveniently located downtown, is the city's principal center for the performing arts. This elegant facility includes a 1,180-seat auditorium, a 220-seat mini-theater, galleries, meeting rooms and a banquet hall. The excellent Fort Collins Symphony Orchestra, Canyon Concert Ballet, several resident chamber music, chorale, operatic, and theatrical companies and more than 100 touring artist bookings make Lincoln Center a busy place throughout the year. Also of interest is the Sundance Bluegrass Festival and Chili Cook-off, an all-day live band and food extravaganza, held annually on a September Saturday. On summer evenings Old Town Square comes alive with weekly free concerts featuring rock and roll, bluegrass, country, jazz and swing musical styles.

Recreational Activities   Rating: 5

Abundant recreational opportunities are found in and around Fort Collins. Golf enthusiasts can choose among six golf courses in town, all with reasonable greens fees. The city's complement of parks and playground facilities is exceptional. City Park has an outdoor pool, a lake with boat rentals, tennis courts, playing fields, playgrounds, trails and picnicking facilities. Indoor pools are found at the Senior Center, at the Mulberry Pool Recreation Center and at Eldora Pool and Ice Center. Numerous other parks, large and small, dot the landscape; no neighborhood is far from one. Bicycling enthusiasts will appreciate Fort Collins' more than 75 miles of bikeways that enable people to bike, walk or roller blade through scenic areas of the city without encountering motorized traffic. Horsetooth Reservoir and adjacent Lory State Park, just west of town in the Rocky Mountain foothills, offer boating, fishing, biking, horseback riding, hiking, rock climbing and camping.

In winter, Lory State Park's trails, roads and hills provide excellent surfaces for cross-country skiing. Downhill skiers need to travel a little farther; two resorts are within two hours by car with several others a little more distant. The Cache la Poudre River, which flows out of its canyon and into Fort Collins at the northwestern edge of town, is an exceptional trout-fishing stream and well suited to whitewater rafting. A one-hour drive takes you to the Estes Park entrance of Rocky Mountain National Park. The park's Trail Ridge Road is one of the great alpine highways of North America. Open from about Memorial Day through mid-October, this 50-mile scenic drive provides breathtaking views of the mountains on its way to a peak elevation of 12,183 feet above sea level. Back in Fort Collins, fitness buffs can join Colorado State University's adult fitness program, which provides fitness guidelines and assessment and access to the university's indoor track, pool and exercise equipment. Others might prefer to attend intercollegiate basketball or football games at the university, or movies at one of Fort Collins' six multi-screen cinema complexes. Everyone can enjoy an occasional meal at one of the city's gourmet or casual restaurants, many of which are clustered in the vibrant historic downtown.

Work and Volunteer Activities   Rating: 4

 The local service and high-tech economy is doing well, so opportunities for work and volunteerism are plentiful. Most part-time jobs are in the service sector, while volunteer work is available in many public facilities and community service organizations.

Crime Rates and Public Safety   Rating: 3

 The crime situation in Fort Collins is satisfactory. The overall property crime rate is about 10 percent above the national average. This total is largely a result of the city's high larceny–theft rate; rates of burglary and auto theft, the other property crime components, are below their respective national averages. The violent crime rate is 30 percent below the national average and the city feels quite safe as one walks its streets.

Conclusion

Overall Rating 48 Fort Collins is one of the most pleasant small towns in America and a good place for an active retirement in a rather relaxed setting. Its physical and human environment is very good. Its site on an irrigated plain near the Rocky Mountain foothills and within view of the snow-capped peaks of Rocky Mountain National Park is scenic. Its sunny, semi-arid, four-season climate is a bit too cold in winter for some, but few would criticize the excellent quality of life of the community. The city has very good transportation facilities including good public transit and an excellent network of bike paths. Its retail, medical and community services are very good, as are opportunities for work and volunteerism. Its cultural and recreational offerings are notable for their excellence, and the cost of living approximates the national average. All in all, Fort Collins ranks highly as a place for a low-key but active retirement.

Boulder, Colorado

First settled in 1858, Boulder has matured from its early role as a center for cattle ranching on the plains and a base for gold prospecting in the Rocky Mountains to its present status as an exquisite small city offering virtually

Boulder, Colorado

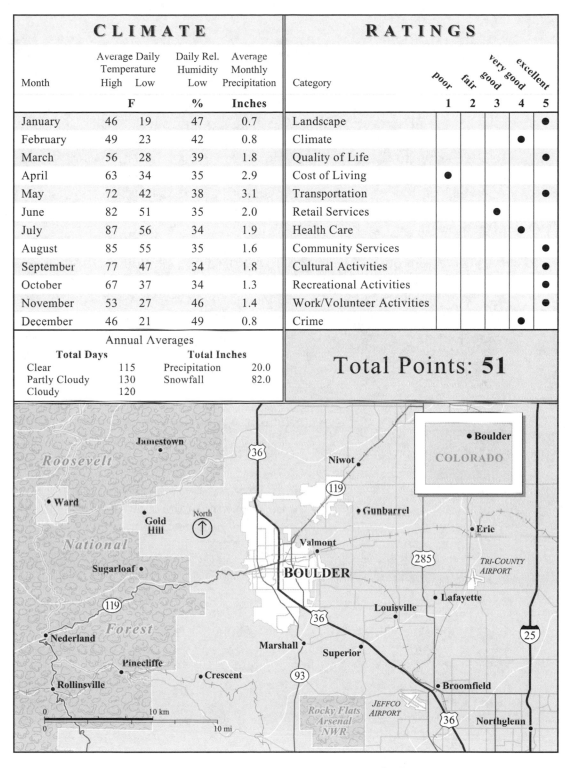

CLIMATE

Month	Average Daily Temperature High	Average Daily Temperature Low	Daily Rel. Humidity Low	Average Monthly Precipitation
	F		%	Inches
January	46	19	47	0.7
February	49	23	42	0.8
March	56	28	39	1.8
April	63	34	35	2.9
May	72	42	38	3.1
June	82	51	35	2.0
July	87	56	34	1.9
August	85	55	35	1.6
September	77	47	34	1.8
October	67	37	34	1.3
November	53	27	46	1.4
December	46	21	49	0.8

Annual Averages

Total Days		Total Inches	
Clear	115	Precipitation	20.0
Partly Cloudy	130	Snowfall	82.0
Cloudy	120		

RATINGS

Category	poor 1	fair 2	good 3	very good 4	excellent 5
Landscape					●
Climate				●	
Quality of Life					●
Cost of Living	●				
Transportation					●
Retail Services			●		
Health Care				●	
Community Services					●
Cultural Activities					●
Recreational Activities					●
Work/Volunteer Activities					●
Crime				●	

Total Points: 51

everything required to retire in style. With a population nearing 100,000 in the city and 320,000 in Boulder County, Boulder has carefully managed growth in order to preserve its excellent quality of life.

Located only 30 miles from downtown Denver, Boulder offers easy access to Denver's many amenities while remaining just far enough away to avoid many of the environmental and social problems of the metropolis. Those who want to live an active lifestyle in a rich cultural and gorgeous physical environment at the foot of the Rocky Mountains will find Boulder's many advantages compelling.

Landscape   Rating: 5

Boulder is situated at an elevation of 5,400 feet on a gently sloping plain at the foot of the Flatiron Range, the craggy foothills of the Front Range of the Rocky Mountains. Most of the city is built on a relatively flat surface but some charming older neighborhoods west of the University of Colorado and the downtown area slope up to the very base of the mountains. Boulder's site is spectacular from almost any vantage point. From the eastern part of town out on the plains there is a great view of the snow-capped 14,000-foot peaks of Rocky Mountain National Park, whereas from points closer to the mountains you will be captivated by the forests and unique flatiron-shaped rock formations of the foothills.

Boulder is located in a semi-arid environment with steppe (grassland) natural vegetation. But nature has been improved upon in Boulder. With an excellent municipal water supply available from the city-owned Arapahoe Glacier, Boulder supplements natural precipitation with enough irrigation water to create an appealing landscape of lawns, flowers and trees.

Climate   Rating: 4

Boulder has an invigorating four-season semi-arid climate characterized by modest precipitation, abundant sunshine, and marked day-to-day and seasonal changes in weather. About two-thirds of the normal annual precipitation of 20 inches falls between April and September. Although an average of 82 inches of snow falls annually, snow seldom lasts more than two consecutive weeks on the ground as daytime temperatures generally rise well above freezing even in winter. Summer afternoons are generally in the 80s and low 90s yet are fairly comfortable thanks to low relative humidity, and summer evenings are pleasantly mild. Spring and autumn weather is highly changeable from day to day but is normally pleasant. Winter is normally cool to cold with sunny weather interrupted by occasional winter storms. On average, Boulder is sunny about 70 percent of the time and enjoys an average frost-free period of 160 days.

Quality of Life   Rating: 5

Boulder offers residents an excellent quality of life. There is little noise pollution except immediately adjacent to the busiest thoroughfares. The EPA recently designated Boulder as a "basic non-attainment area" for air quality, which means that the city is minimally out of compliance with current air quality standards. Boulder experiences occasional light smog in all seasons. Low population density, careful land use planning and good road infrastructure combine to minimize crowding and traffic congestion, although parking is often scarce downtown and near the university. The community is affluent so there are many pleasant neighborhoods, including older historic districts adjacent to downtown and the university and newer tract developments on the periphery. Despite strong growth pressures, the city and county of Boulder tightly controls land use, which has prevented the city from sprawling outward. Other niceties of Boulder's well-designed human landscape include well-treed streets, beautiful parks and greenways, the vibrant Pearl Street Mall and the exceptionally beautiful University of Colorado campus. Happily, Boulder's affluent and educated populace appreciates its exceptional quality of life and seems determined to preserve it by effectively managing inevitable economic and population growth.

Cost of Living
Rating: 1

 The cost of living in Boulder is evaluated as follows:

- *Composite.* ACCRA data for Boulder show a composite cost of living about 17 percent above the national average.

- *Housing.* According to ACCRA, housing costs are about 60 percent above the national average. Data from the Boulder County Assessor confirm the high cost of Boulder housing. The average single-family residence now sells for about $350,000 in the city and $250,000 in the county. Condominiums are about half as expensive in both city and county. Housing prices can be expected to remain high in Boulder because of anti-growth policies that restrict the rate of new construction.

- *Goods and Services.* Costs of health care and groceries are about 4 percent and 12 percent, respectively, above national norms. Transportation and miscellaneous goods and services are priced 8 percent above and 3 percent below their national averages. Utilities are a bargain at a cost about 25 percent below average.

- *Taxes.* The state and local tax burden in Boulder is 8.8 percent of income compared to the U.S. average of 9.7 percent. State income taxes are a little above the national average but property and sales and excise taxes are lower than average.

Transportation
Rating: 5

 As is true in most affluent communities, the private automobile dominates local transportation. However, unlike the situation in most small cities, public transit is a reasonable and popular alternative here. The Regional Transportation District (RTD) operates 10 local (Boulder) routes and 11 regional routes connecting Boulder with other parts of the Denver–Boulder Consolidated Metropolitan Area. In addition, the city of Boulder operates 6 shuttle bus lines that provide frequent service on several routes in Boulder. Buses are clean, efficient and inexpensive to ride. Substantial discounts are available to seniors. Denver International Airport, 42 miles away, is the major commercial aviation facility. Denver International is served by 20 airlines and provides nonstop jet service to about 100 domestic and international destinations. From Denver Amtrak provides service eastbound to Chicago and westbound to Oakland and Seattle. Greyhound provides service to many points.

Retail Services
Rating: 3

The Pearl Street Mall, Boulder's revitalized historic downtown, is the heart and soul of the community. Easily reached by automobile, bicycle or public transit, this beautifully landscaped brick-surfaced pedestrian mall is a great place to shop, eat, or just stroll and people watch. Crossroads Mall, formerly Boulder's major enclosed shopping mall, closed in

February 2004 and the city and mall owner have yet to reach an agreement to redevelop it. Meanwhile, Boulder residents must travel nine miles south along U.S. 39 to Flatiron Crossing Shopping Center, in Broomfield, for mall shopping. Flatiron Crossing Shopping Center is anchored by Dillard's, Foley's, Lord & Taylor and Nordstrom department stores and features more than 180 specialty stores and services.

Health Care   Rating: 4

 Boulder Community Hospital, a medium-sized facility with 197 beds, is the city's major medical center. With more than 425 physicians, it offers a wide variety of medical services including 24-hour emergency care, intensive and cardiac care and nearly 40 other full-care services. Much larger facilities with a greater range of medical services are only 30 minutes away in Denver.

Community Services   Rating: 5

 The city and county of Boulder, the University of Colorado and local religious and community organizations offer an amazing array of services. For example, Boulder Senior Services, run by the City of Boulder Department of Housing and Human Services, operates two senior centers—one in the western part of town and one in the eastern part of town. Senior Services provides day and overnight travel programs, hikes, sports and social activities, a variety of classes from fitness to computers and a wellness program.

Cultural and Educational Activities   Rating: 5

 The culturally and educationally inclined will never want for things to do in Boulder. The schedule of musical, theatrical, and visual arts events and educational opportunities is so full that only a hint of its richness can be conveyed here. Historic Chatauqua Auditorium is the venue for a summer season of concerts and talks from early June through mid-September. The auditorium also hosts the Colorado Music Festival, which features a chamber music series and an orchestral series in July and August. Another summer highlight is the Colorado Shakespeare Festival, staged at the outdoor Mary Rippon Theatre and the indoor University Theatre on the University of Colorado campus. The university's Imig Music Building is the site for operas and musicals courtesy of the College of Music. The Boulder Philharmonic Orchestra is also worthy of note, as are several museums including the Boulder Museum of Contemporary Art and the University of Colorado Museum. With 25,000 students and 150 fields of study, the University of Colorado is a first-rate academic institution with one of the most beautiful campuses in the country. The university's continuing education division offers a bonanza of credit and noncredit classes and workshops of interest to all age groups.

Recreational Activities   Rating: 5

An amazing assortment of recreational opportunities exists in and around Boulder. The city has nearly 1,000 acres of parkland, 30,000 acres of open space and 200 miles of trails. The city's parks and three recreation centers are well equipped and staffed. Whether your interests are walking, running, hiking, biking, fishing, swimming, inline skating, tennis, volleyball, rock climbing or golfing, Boulder can accommodate you. You can even water-ski at Boulder Reservoir on the northern edge of town or white-water canoe or kayak on Boulder Creek. Boulder has one public and one private golf course with six more in neighboring communities. Alpine and Nordic skiing are locally available at Eldora Mountain Resort, 20 miles west of Boulder, and at nine other ski areas within a radius of 110 miles. If spectator sports are your preference, you can enjoy varsity basketball and football locally at the University of Colorado and Denver Broncos and Colorado Rockies professional football and baseball in Denver. Also nearby are the spectacular scenic and recreational resources of Eldorado and Golden Gate Canyon State Parks and Rocky Mountain National Park.

Whatever your taste in food or preference in restaurant style, your needs are apt to be met in Boulder. The city's 300 restaurants run the gamut from informal sidewalk cafes downtown, specializing in sandwiches and desserts, to five-star dining at Flagstaff House, which overlooks the city from its perch high in the Flatiron Range.

Work and Volunteer Activities   Rating: 5

Boulder's economy has boomed in recent years and unemployment rates are low so opportunities for work and volunteerism are plentiful. Most part-time jobs are in the service sector, while volunteer work is found at parks and recreation centers, the hospital and public library, the chamber of commerce and in many community service organizations. Boulder Senior Services can give good advice on where to look.

Crime Rates and Public Safety   Rating: 4

Boulder's crime situation has improved in recent years. The property crime rate is now slightly below the national average and largely reflects a high larceny–theft rate; other property crime rates are low. Significantly, Boulder's violent crime rate is fully 50 percent below the national average and most residents do not hesitate to walk its streets day or night.

Conclusion

Overall Rating 51 Boulder is one of the most sophisticated small cities in America and a wonderful place in which to lead an active retirement. Its physical and human environment is nearly ideal. Its site on an irrigated plain at the foot of the Flatiron Range, within view of the 14,000-foot peaks of Rocky Mountain National Park, is spectacular. Its sunny, semi-arid climate provides four genuine seasons, yet few days in the year are severely cold or hot. The quality of life is excellent, a tribute to sound land use and transportation planning by the municipality and to the environmental awareness of Boulder residents. The city has excellent transportation facilities including an excellent bus system and one of the best bike path networks in the nation. Medical services are very good and community services, cultural and recreational offerings, and work and volunteer activities are excellent. The principal drawbacks to retirement in Boulder are the recent closure of the Crossroads Mall, formerly the city's major shopping center, and a cost of living about 17 percent above the national average. That said, Boulder ranks as one of America's best places for an active and sophisticated retirement.

Colorado Springs, Colorado

William J. Palmer founded Colorado Springs at the foot of Pikes Peak in 1871. Palmer planned to develop a resort city linked by road to the supposedly curative waters at Manitou Springs six miles to the west. Within a few years a well-planned small settlement with wide streets, irrigated cottonwood trees, parks and buildings existed on the formerly barren site. As predicted, lured by spectacular mountain scenery, Manitou Springs waters, the tourist facilities being built and the hope of getting rich by speculating in gold mining in the Colorado Rockies, newcomers began to pour into the city. In later years, huge military bases including the Air Force Academy, high-tech industries and the growing service economy have combined to spur economic and population growth. With a population nearing 380,000 in the city and 550,000 in El Paso County (the metropolitan area), Colorado Springs is and seems likely to remain Colorado's second largest city. It is only 70 miles south of Denver via I-25 and is highly accessible to the mountains via Highway24. Its beautiful setting at the foot of the Front Range and its many amenities make it an attractive place for retirement.

Landscape · Rating: 5

Colorado Springs is located at an elevation of 6,000 feet on a gently rolling plain in the shadow of 14,110-foot Pikes Peak. Much of the city—including the downtown and older residential areas—is built on a relatively flat surface, but some newer neighborhoods extend up a steepening slope to the base of the mountains. Colorado Springs' site is spectacular. From the eastern part of town you get a superb view of snow-capped Pikes Peak, whereas from most points west of downtown the forested foothills, quite beautiful themselves, eclipse the larger mountain. The cityscape is well wooded, especially in the older neighborhoods, despite the rather dry environment. Plenty of irrigation water keeps the city green.

Climate · Rating: 3

Colorado Springs is cool for its latitude because of its high elevation. Its moderately severe four-season climate features light precipitation, plenty of sunshine and dramatic day-to-day and seasonal changes in weather. About 80 percent of the normal annual precipitation of 17 inches falls between April and September. Although an average of 42 inches of snow falls annually, snow seldom lasts more than two consecutive weeks on the ground because daytime temperatures usually rise well above freezing except during severe winter cold waves. Summer days are pleasantly warm; summer evenings are comfortably cool, with low relative humidity. Spring and autumn weather is quite changeable but is dominantly sunny with cool to warm temperatures. Winters are cold, dry and occasionally stormy. The city is sunny about 70 percent of the time and enjoys a frost-free season of 150 days.

Quality of Life · Rating: 4

The quality of life is generally good but there are a few problems. Some areas suffer jet noise from military and commercial aviation and the city seems very automobile dependent. I-25 runs through the center of town and traffic noise impacts a narrow corridor adjacent to the freeway. In most other neighborhoods traffic noise is not a serious problem.

Colorado Springs, Colorado

CLIMATE				
Month	Average Daily Temperature High Low	Daily Rel. Humidity Low	Average Monthly Precipitation	
	F	%	Inches	
January	42	15	46	0.3
February	45	18	40	0.4
March	52	24	38	1.1
April	59	31	34	1.6
May	68	41	36	2.4
June	79	50	34	2.3
July	84	55	39	2.9
August	82	54	42	3.5
September	74	45	37	1.2
October	63	34	35	0.9
November	50	23	45	0.5
December	42	16	51	0.4

Annual Averages

Total Days		Total Inches	
Clear	127	Precipitation	17.4
Partly Cloudy	120	Snowfall	42.4
Cloudy	118		

RATINGS					
Category	poor 1	fair 2	good 3	very good 4	excellent 5
Landscape					●
Climate			●		
Quality of Life				●	
Cost of Living			●		
Transportation				●	
Retail Services				●	
Health Care				●	
Community Services				●	
Cultural Activities					●
Recreational Activities					●
Work/Volunteer Activities				●	
Crime			●		

Total Points: 48

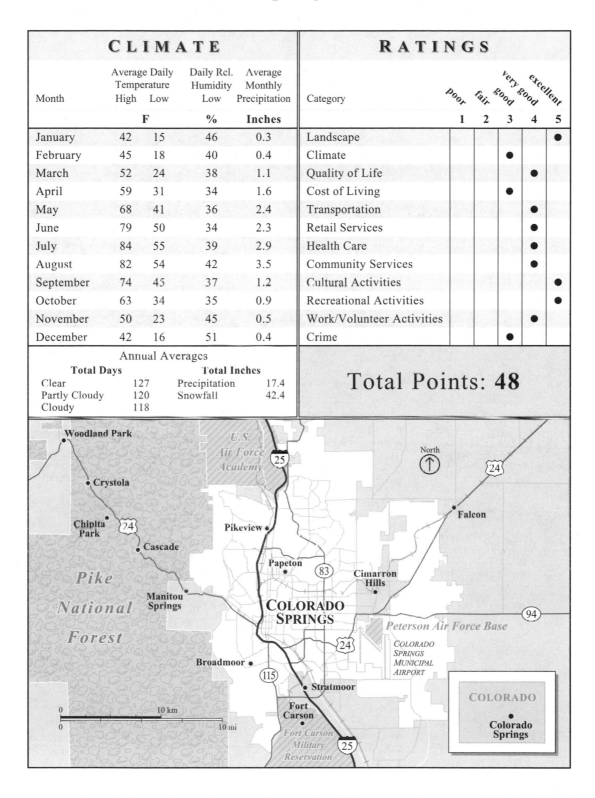

The city has clean air. Crowding and traffic congestion are minimized by the low population density and good road infrastructure. Parking is plentiful in the city center and at the main malls. The community's housing stock is excellent. Neighborhoods near downtown are remarkably attractive, with nicely maintained older houses of great individuality located along shady tree-lined streets. Great pride of home ownership is evident there and in newer manicured suburban areas as well. Colorado Springs' striking physical setting and its excellent parks—including the internationally known "Garden of the Gods"—also contribute to its high quality of life.

Cost of Living   Rating: 3

 The cost of living in Colorado Springs is evaluated as follows:

- *Composite.* ACCRA data for Colorado Springs show a composite cost of living near the national average.

- *Housing.* According to ACCRA, housing costs approximate the national average. Hundreds of charming Victorian and early twentieth century homes, large and small, are found just north of downtown, and suburban areas offer a great diversity of newer houses. Housing prices can be expected to remain affordable, as Colorado Springs is quite growth oriented and new construction is rampant.

- *Goods and Services.* Groceries and health care costs are 8 and 13 percent above their national averages whereas utilities are priced 20 percent below average. Transportation and miscellaneous goods and services costs are near national norms.

- *Taxes.* The state and local tax burden in Colorado Springs is 8.8 percent of income compared to the U.S. average of 9.7 percent. State income taxes are a little above the national average but property and sales and excise taxes are lower than average.

Transportation   Rating: 4

Local transportation is strongly dominated by the private automobile. Public transit is utilized mostly by the transit dependent. The city of Colorado Springs operates Springs Transit, whose 19 routes provide access to most parts of town except on Sundays and major holidays. Springs Mobility, a door-to-door service for the handicapped, also provides local transportation. Intercity bus service is provided by TNM&O, a regional carrier that connects with Greyhound Lines national routes. Colorado Springs Airport Shuttle provides convenient access to Colorado Springs Airport and to Denver International Airport, 100 miles north. Colorado Springs Airport is served by 9 airlines and provides nonstop jet service to 20 cities including Dallas, Denver and Phoenix. Denver International is served by 20 airlines and provides nonstop jet service to about 100 domestic and international destinations. Amtrak rail passenger service and Greyhound bus service are available in downtown Denver, 70 miles north.

Retail Services   Rating: 4

Colorado Springs offers very good shopping even though retailing is largely absent downtown. Major malls include the Citadel in the east central part of the city and Chapel Hills Mall and the Shops at Briargate in the north. The Citadel is anchored by Dillard's, Foleys, JCPenney and Mervyn's department stores and includes more than 170 specialty retailers. Its tropically foliated, sky-lit Food Court is unusually attractive with restaurants on two levels and seating on three. A Wal-Mart Supercenter is located just south of the mall across Platte Avenue. Chapel Hills Mall, with 140 stores and restaurants, is only slightly smaller than the Citadel. It is anchored by JCPenney, Joslin's, Mervyn's and Sears department stores. The Shops at Briargate is an architecturally interesting, open-air center that allows storefront shopping at upscale, national specialty retailers.

Health Care   Rating: 4

 Medical services are a bit thin relative to population in rapidly growing Colorado Springs. Although the city has five hospitals with a total of more than 1,000 beds, only two of them are large general hospitals. Memorial Hospital, with 467 beds, offers a wide variety of medical services including 24-hour emergency care, critical and cardiac care, oncology and surgery. Penrose Hospital, with 300 beds, is part of Penrose–St. Francis Health Services; it specializes in cardiac care, oncology and internal medicine but also offers the usual array of primary care medical services. Larger facilities with a wider range of medical specialties are only an hour away in Denver.

Community Services   Rating: 4

 The city, El Paso County, Pikes Peak Community College and local religious and community organizations offer a great variety of services to seniors and the general public. The Colorado Springs Senior Center organizes social activities, screens seniors for medical problems and offers numerous academic and applied classes in concert with the community college. The Pikes Peak Area Agency on Aging provides information and referral services for seniors.

Cultural and Educational Activities   Rating: 5

Colorado Springs is one of America's best small cities for cultural and educational activities. Downtown's Pikes Peak Center is the principal venue for major musical events. The Colorado Springs Symphony Orchestra performs its winter season there from September through May. The orchestra also performs a summer season of free concerts in area parks. In late July the Colorado Opera Festival is held at the Center. During the winter season, the Colorado Dance Theatre hosts the Colorado Ballet and internationally acclaimed touring companies such as the Balletto di Toscana and the Bolshoi Ballet. The U.S. Air Force Academy Band presents free concerts at the Center in spring and at the Air Force Academy in summer.

The Colorado Springs Fine Arts Center, the Iron Springs Chateau and Playhouse, the Broadmoor International Center and Colorado College are also important centers for the arts. The Fine Arts Center houses collections of Native American and Hispanic art, an art school and a 450-seat theater. The theater hosts performances by the Civic Music Theater, as well as legitimate theater, concerts, dance productions and a classical film series. The Broadmoor International Center features nationally known touring performers in concerts and theatrical productions. Dinner theater is popular at the Iron Springs Chateau and Playhouse and plays may also be seen at Colorado College. Colorado College, the Continuing Education Department of the University of Colorado at Colorado Springs and Pikes Peak Community College all offer courses on academic and applied subjects of interest to seniors. Some courses are offered for nominal fees at the Senior Center.

Outdoor recreation is plentiful in and around Colorado Springs. Golfers can choose among three 18-hole public courses in the city and several others in county territory. The city's supply of parks and playgrounds is exceptional. The Parks and Recreation Department manages 156 public areas totaling 10,762 acres. Most city parks have tennis courts, sports fields, playgrounds, biking and hiking trails and picnicking facilities. Swimming is possible at three indoor pools.

Palmer Park and the justifiably famous Garden of the Gods Park at the foot of Pikes Peak are special gems of the park system. Towering red sandstone formations intricately carved by forces of erosion are the trademark of the 1,300-acre Garden of the Gods, but the park also offers foot and horse trails and picnicking areas. Palmer Park is a 740-acre site located in the newer northeastern part of town. Much of the park is a rocky, wooded and relatively wild area providing a spectacular view westward to the mountains from its sandstone bluffs. Other attractions of the park include hiking trails, picnicking areas and ball diamonds. Other city parks, large and small, dot the urban landscape so no location is far from one.

County parks add an additional 2,800 acres of metropolitan area parkland. El Paso County operates seven regional and neighborhood parks, one recreation area and trailheads accessing 48 miles of regional and park trails. Just west of town is Pikes Peak (elevation 14,110 feet) and the 1.1 million-acre Pike National Forest. The summit can be reached by highway, cog railway or via the 12-mile long Barr National Recreation Trail. Pike National Forest is known for its scenic drives, camping, fishing, hunting and cross-country skiing. There are no major downhill ski resorts near Colorado Springs but the great ski resorts of central Colorado, including Aspen, are only about 150 miles away. Fans of spectator sports can enjoy intercollegiate basketball, football, baseball and hockey at the Air Force Academy; professional baseball and football games can be attended in Denver. Movies can be seen at 10 cinema complexes in Colorado Springs. Area restaurants purvey a remarkable variety of cuisines in casual to formal settings.

 The Colorado Springs economy, based heavily on the military, high-tech industries, service activities, tourism and construction, has boomed in recent years so jobs and volunteer positions are available. Most part-time jobs are in the service and tourism industries, while volunteer work is found in public facilities, community service and nonprofit organizations.

 The Colorado Springs crime situation is somewhat mixed. The city's violent crime rate approximates the national average but the property crime rate exceeds the national norm by about 30 percent. Local police officers report that much of the crime occurs near the Fort Carson military base in the southern part of town and that central and northern neighborhoods of the city are comparatively safe.

Overall Rating 48 Colorado Springs is one of the most attractive medium-sized cities for retirement. Its physical site at the foot of Pikes Peak is scenic and its sunny, semi-arid climate with four distinct seasons appeals to many. The air is clean and there are no serious environmental problems. The city has an adequate road infrastructure that is continually being upgraded and residents rely heavily on the private automobile for transportation. Even so, public transit is available and the quality of life is very good. Just north of downtown along Nevada Avenue and in the blocks between it and the freeway are historic districts containing hundreds of beautiful Victorian homes. Mixed among them and concentrated just east of Nevada Avenue are hundreds of smaller 1,000- to 1,500-square-foot frame craftsman-style houses, most of which—whether modernized or not—seem in excellent condition and reflect considerable pride of ownership. The city's retail, health care and community services and work/volunteer opportunities are very good, and its cultural and recreational offerings are excellent. About the only drawbacks to retirement in Colorado Springs are the above-average incidence of property crime, a winter season that might not appeal to all, and—for those with heart, circulatory or respiratory problems—the 6,000-foot elevation and resultant thin air.

Santa Fe, New Mexico

First settled by the Spanish in 1607, 13 years before the Pilgrims set foot in America, Santa Fe was designated capital of the province of New Mexico by the newly appointed governor Don Pedro de Peralta only three years later. It has remained a vital center of New Mexican political and cultural life ever since, whether the flag atop the Palace of the Governors on the north side of the Plaza was Spanish, Mexican, Confederate or American. Today the self-styled City Different revels in the diversity of its Native American, Spanish and Anglo cultures and in its historical, architectural, cultural and environmental amenities. With a population of nearly 65,000 in the city and 140,000 in Santa Fe County, Santa Fe is large enough to meet the needs of residents yet small enough to manage growth and resources effectively and preserve its unique character and high quality of life. Located only 60 miles from Albuquerque, Santa Fe has convenient access to that city's transportation facilities and attractions yet is far enough away to avoid its social and environmental problems. Those desiring an active lifestyle in a rich cultural and beautiful high plateau and mountain environment may find Santa Fe attractive indeed.

Landscape   **Rating: 4**

 Santa Fe is located at an elevation of 7,000 feet in a transition zone between northern New Mexico's high plateaus and the foothills of the Sangre de Cristo Mountains, the southernmost range of the Rocky Mountains. The western part of town is quite flat; the eastern part is hilly. Nearby peaks reach elevations of 12,000 feet, providing a scenic backdrop to the city. Local natural vegetation varies from stunted pinion pine/juniper woodland in lower, drier areas to a more luxuriant coniferous forest in the wetter foothills. The city is well treed as precipitation is supplemented by irrigation.

Santa Fe, New Mexico

CLIMATE

Month	Average Daily Temperature High	Low	Daily Rel. Humidity Low	Average Monthly Precipitation
	F		%	Inches
January	43	16	51	0.6
February	49	21	46	0.5
March	56	26	40	0.8
April	64	32	30	0.7
May	73	40	27	1.3
June	83	49	20	1.3
July	86	54	38	2.3
August	83	53	42	2.1
September	77	46	37	1.7
October	66	35	36	1.3
November	52	24	43	1.1
December	44	16	51	0.7

Annual Averages

Total Days		Total Inches	
Clear	167	Precipitation	14.2
Partly Cloudy	111	Snowfall	35.3
Cloudy	87		

RATINGS

Category	poor 1	fair 2	good 3	very good 4	excellent 5
Landscape				●	
Climate				●	
Quality of Life					●
Cost of Living	●				
Transportation				●	
Retail Services				●	
Health Care				●	
Community Services				●	
Cultural Activities					●
Recreational Activities					●
Work/Volunteer Activities		●			
Crime		●			

Total Points: 44

Climate **Rating: 4**

Santa Fe enjoys an invigorating semi-arid, four-season climate characterized by modest precipitation, abundant sunshine and marked day-to-day and seasonal changes in weather. About 70 percent of the normal annual precipitation of 14 inches occurs between May and October. Although an average of 35 inches of snow falls annually, snowfalls seldom persist more than a week or so on the ground as daytime temperatures typically rise well above freezing even in winter. Summer afternoons are generally warm to hot yet fairly comfortable thanks to low relative humidity. Summer evenings are pleasantly cool. Spring and autumn weather is changeable but usually dry, with temperatures in the cool-to-warm range. Winter weather tends to be cool and generally sunny and dry. Occasionally, though, a winter storm brings a blanket of snow followed by severely cold temperatures for a few days. Even so, the city enjoys a frost-free period of about 170 days and, with sunny days 75 percent of the time throughout the year, is one of America's sunniest locations.

Quality of Life   Rating: 5

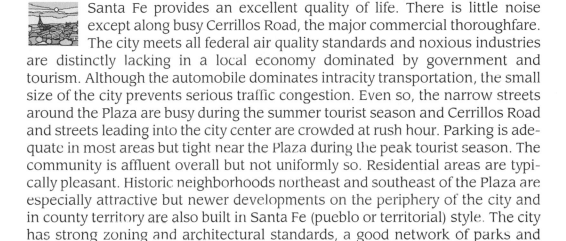

Santa Fe provides an excellent quality of life. There is little noise except along busy Cerrillos Road, the major commercial thoroughfare. The city meets all federal air quality standards and noxious industries are distinctly lacking in a local economy dominated by government and tourism. Although the automobile dominates intracity transportation, the small size of the city prevents serious traffic congestion. Even so, the narrow streets around the Plaza are busy during the summer tourist season and Cerrillos Road and streets leading into the city center are crowded at rush hour. Parking is adequate in most areas but tight near the Plaza during the peak tourist season. The community is affluent overall but not uniformly so. Residential areas are typically pleasant. Historic neighborhoods northeast and southeast of the Plaza are especially attractive but newer developments on the periphery of the city and in county territory are also built in Santa Fe (pueblo or territorial) style. The city has strong zoning and architectural standards, a good network of parks and recreational facilities, and appears well planned and run. The cozy narrow streets that wind through much of the city are a pleasant contrast to the unappealing commercial-strip development along Cerrillos Road.

Cost of Living   Rating: 1

The cost of living in Santa Fe is evaluated as follows:

- **Composite.** ACCRA data for Santa Fe show a composite cost of living about 17 percent above the national average.

- **Housing.** According to ACCRA, housing costs are 50 percent above the national average and local sources suggest that the median price of a house is around $300,000. In reality, prices vary substantially from neighborhood to neighborhood. On average the most expensive housing is found in the southeastern quadrant of the city and to the northwest, northeast and southeast of town in unincorporated county territory. Median prices for single-family residences range upward from $400,000 in all these areas. In contrast, in blue-collar southwestern Santa Fe prices average around $200,000.

- **Goods and Services.** ACCRA data show health care to be fairly expensive at about 20 percent above the national average. Groceries, transportation and miscellaneous goods and services are priced only slightly above their national averages, while utilities costs approximate the national average.

- *Taxes.* The state and local tax burden in Santa Fe is 10 percent of income compared to the U.S. average of 9.7 percent. Property and state income are below national norms but sales and excise taxes are well above average.

Transportation   Rating: 4

Local transportation, long the almost exclusive domain of the private automobile, is now nicely supplemented by public transit. Santa Fe Trails, the city of Santa Fe bus system, provides excellent service throughout the city via 10 routes focused on downtown's Sheridan Transit Center, just off the Plaza. The city also provides van and taxi service for the elderly and disabled. Intercity rail service is provided by Amtrak's Southwest Chief whose westbound (to Los Angeles) and eastbound (to Chicago) trains stop daily in Lamy, 18 miles south. The Lamy Shuttle connects the city center with the train station. Greyhound and TNM&O intercity buses stop at the Santa Fe bus station on St. Michael's Drive. Commercial airline service is available at Albuquerque International Airport, 60 miles south. Albuquerque International is served by 9 airlines and provides nonstop jet service to more than 30 destinations including hubs at Dallas, Denver and Phoenix.

Retail Services   Rating: 4

Because of its status as a major tourist destination, Santa Fe has a much stronger retailing base than do most cities of its size. Streets fronting the Plaza and just off it are lined with distinctly upscale shops and restaurants. These charming and rather expensive facilities attract tourists and affluent locals alike. Villa Linda Mall, in a suburban location just off Cerrillos Road, is a fairly typical but not unattractive enclosed mall. Anchored by Dillard's, JCPenney, Mervyn's and Sears department stores, Villa Linda Mall houses more than 80 shops and restaurants. Many of the usual national chain stores and a few locally owned businesses are present here.

Health Care   Rating: 4

Santa Fe offers very good medical care. St. Vincent Hospital, a non-profit, non-affiliated hospital with 268 beds and 250 staff physicians representing 22 medical specialties, is the city's only general hospital. St. Vincent possesses state-of-the-art diagnostic services including CT scanning, magnetic resonance imaging, radiology and ultrasound. Cardiac and intensive care units, a trauma center and a comprehensive cancer unit, among other specialized facilities, are available at St. Vincent. Additional good health care services are available in Albuquerque, only an hour's drive away.

Community Services   Rating: 4

The city, Santa Fe County, local colleges and area religious and community organizations offer a fine variety of services. Particularly notable is the Santa Fe Senior Citizens Program, which oversees more than 20 programs for seniors. Senior centers offering recreational activities such as dancing, games, sports and arts and crafts are found in Santa Fe itself and in several outlying communities. The centers also provide health screenings free or at minimal cost, meals and transportation for seniors.

Those inclined toward culture and education will find plenty to do in Santa Fe. Santa Fe is the arts capital of the Southwest with more than 200 art galleries, marvelous museums and a world-class performing arts scene. Santa Fe's galleries claim to specialize in 16 different categories of art and to house one million pieces in a square mile. Downtown museums include the Georgia O'Keefe Museum, which possesses the world's largest permanent collection of her works, the Museum of Fine Arts and the Palace of the Governors. Within a few miles south of the city center are the excellent Museum of Indian Arts and Culture, the Wheelwright Museum of the American Indian and the Museum of International Folk Art.

The city's schedule of the performing arts is also impressive. The world renowned Santa Fe Opera now performs its two-month season in July and August in its remodeled outdoor theater a few miles north of town. After an extensive restoration, the old Lensic Theater in downtown Santa Fe reopened in the spring of 2001 as the Lensic Performing Arts Center. The Center seats 835 and hosts in fine style many of Santa Fe's leading arts ensembles, guest artists and distinguished speakers. The Santa Fe Symphony Orchestra and Chorus is now resident there and the Santa Fe Pro Musica performs chamber music at the Center, Loretta Chapel and other venues. The Festival of Chamber Music and Jazz, held every summer, is a special highlight. New Mexico's only professional vocal ensemble, the Desert Chorale, presents a six-week summer season as well as Christmas concerts. In addition to the resident ensembles, the Santa Fe Concert Association presents an impressive number of nationally and internationally known guest artists each year.

Theater, dance and formal education are well represented in Santa Fe. Santa Fe Stages now offers summer and winter seasons at the College of Santa Fe's Greer Garson Theatre. Other professional theater groups include Theater Grottesco and Theaterwork, while the popular Santa Fe Playhouse presents amateur theater. Professional dance productions are staged in summer by the Maria Benitez Teatro Flamenco and the Santa Fe Festival Ballet. Santa Fe Community College offers several hundred continuing education courses each semester, many of interest to seniors. St. John's College, in addition to its regular course offerings, schedules special readings and discussions for the wider community, while the local campus of the University of New Mexico offers a special peer learning program for seniors.

 Outdoor recreation galore exists in and near Santa Fe. The city recreation department's many assets include a new Municipal Recreation Complex with 9-hole and 18-hole golf courses, 4 heated pools, 44 tennis courts and numerous small parks and playgrounds. The 18-hole public golf course at Cochiti Lake and the private fairways of the Santa Fe Country Club are also open much of the year, as are several other public golf courses. For its size the city boasts an adequate complement of movie theaters, with upwards of 16 screens in all, and an excellent array of restaurants that offer good food in all price ranges with an emphasis on quality cuisine of the Southwest. The Santa Fe National Forest, Pecos Wilderness, Bandelier National Monument and several New Mexico state parks include more than three million acres of forested public lands. Here are wonderful places for sightseeing, hiking, backpacking, horseback riding, hunting, fishing, rafting, rock climbing and cross-country and downhill skiing. Only half an hour from town, the Santa Fe Ski Area boasts terrain between 10,350 and 12,000 feet elevation, more than 200 inches of snow in a typical winter, 7 lifts and 39 downhill trails. Although not a large ski area, it offers some of the best skiing in America.

Work and Volunteer Activities   Rating: 2

Part-time work opportunities for seniors are severely limited. The local economy is heavily dependent on tourism and state government for jobs, and wages for part-time work are low relative to the cost of living. Acute competition for jobs exists with those of normal working age, many of whom commute into the city from rural areas where living costs are low and work scarce. Prospects for volunteer work are more favorable. A host of social clubs and service organizations offer openings ranging from trail maintenance in Santa Fe National Forest to providing assistance to teachers, the sick, elderly and visitors.

Crime Rates and Public Safety   Rating: 2

Santa Fe's crime situation is complex but not particularly threatening. In recent years the city has experienced a violent crime rate 30 percent above the average for U.S. urban places and a property crime nearly double the national average. The assault rate, nearly three times the national average, is problematic. Significantly, most assaults occur among a small, economically disadvantaged segment of the population; few happen in areas lived in or frequented by middle class retirees. Among the property crimes, burglary and larceny–theft rates exceed their national averages but automobile theft rates are low.

Conclusion

Overall Rating 44
Santa Fe is a sophisticated small city and a delightfully stimulating place in which to lead an active retirement. Its physical and human environment is close to ideal. Its physical site, where the high plateaus of northern New Mexico run up against the foothills of the Sangre de Cristo Range, is beautiful. Its sunny, semi-arid climate with four distinct seasons and relatively few severely cold or hot days is delightful. Its quality of life is excellent thanks to its manageable size and to sound planning by the city. Santa Fe greatly improved its transportation facilities a few years ago by complementing its adequate road network with an excellent bus system. Retail and medical services are very good and community services, cultural and recreational offerings, and volunteer opportunities are good to excellent. The principal drawbacks to retirement in Santa Fe are above-average crime rates, minimal opportunities for part-time employment and a cost of living perhaps 17 percent above the national average. The city's elevation of 7,000 feet may also be of concern to those with cardiovascular, lung or asthma problems. That said, for many people Santa Fe ranks as one of America's premier locales for an active and stimulating retirement.

10 The Desert Southwest Retirement Region

Climate:
Semi-arid (steppe): Prescott, Carson City, Reno
Desert: Tuscon, Boulder City, Las Vegas, St. George

Place Description	Overall Rating	Page
Tucson, Arizona	**46**	**222**

Tucson is not utopia but it does have a lot going for it. Although the urban area is growing rapidly, it is still quite livable and should remain so for some time.

Prescott, Arizona	**40**	**228**

Because of its location, moderate elevation and underlying geology, Prescott enjoys a mild sunny, four-season climate and is at low risk of earthquakes and severe storms.

Boulder City, Nevada	**46**	**232**

Boulder City ranks highly as a retirement town. Although officially part of the Las Vegas metropolitan area, it is quite unlike the city and its sprawling suburbs. It is an oasis according to both meanings of the term.

Las Vegas, Nevada	**46**	**237**

Las Vegas ranks highly on most standard measures of suitability for retirement but it is not without problems. Its greatest strengths are in cultural and recreational activities, retail services and health care.

Carson City, Nevada	**40**	**243**

Carson City ranks highly as a place for retirement, especially for those seeking a laid-back lifestyle in an unspoiled, beautiful mountain and high desert environment.

St. George, Utah	**46**	**248**

St. George is one of the best retirement towns in the Desert Southwest. Because of its location, moderate elevation and geology, the city experiences a warm, sunny four-season climate and is spared serious environmental hazards.

Reno, Nevada	**not rated**	**252**

Although it suffers from a high cost of living and occasional air pollution, Reno offers exceptional recreation, very good transportation and health care, and a good quality of life.

The Desert Southwest Retirement Region is large in area and varied in its physical geography. Stretching 700 miles from Carson City and Reno in northwestern Nevada to Tucson in southeastern Arizona, the Desert Southwest is walled off from the moisture and moderating influence of the Pacific Ocean by California's Sierra Nevada and Coast Ranges. As a result, the entire region is sunny and dry although not uniformly so. Precipitation and temperatures vary from place to place owing to differences in elevation and latitude. Rugged mountains, plateaus and canyons not only provide gorgeous vistas but also influence local weather. High desert locales in the north like Carson City and Reno and high plateau cities like Prescott are distinctly more pleasant in summer but colder in winter than low desert cities like Las Vegas and Tucson. And, contrary to conventional wisdom, summer nights are not pleasantly cool in summer in low desert cities; they are very warm.

Rapidly growing Tucson and Las Vegas are stereotypical Sunbelt cities. A flood of retirees has been attracted to them for their superior services, health care and mild winters. Unfortunately, these mid-sized cities suffer from fairly high crime rates. The smaller cities and towns of the region, though, most notably Carson City, Boulder City, Prescott and St. George, boast low crime rates, a high quality of life and gorgeous physical environments. The tradeoff for these benefits is a more modest availability of services and health care here than in larger places.

Tucson, Arizona

With a population exceeding 530,000 within its city limits and around 950,000 in the metropolitan area, Tucson is one of few cities of its size that can be recommended for retirement. So far, its explosive growth of recent decades has not seriously damaged its environment or quality of life. Although increasingly varied ethnically, its Mexican heritage is strongly felt in typical pueblo and territorial style adobe buildings with their flat-tiled roofs and in living cultural monuments like Mission San Xavier del Bac. For those seeking a stimulating, amenity-rich lifestyle in a warm, sunny and scenic desert and mountain environment, Tucson has much to offer.

Landscape	Rating: 5

Tucson is located at an elevation of 2,400 feet in the Tucson Basin, part of the Southwest's Basin and Range landform region, in southeastern Arizona. Most of the city stretches across a relatively flat desert plain but newer residential areas have expanded beyond the city limits and up the alluvial slope to the foothills of the Santa Catalina Mountains. Tucson's site is attractive with four distinct mountain ranges—the Santa Catalina to the north, the Rincon to the east, the Santa Rita to the south and the Tucson Mountains to the west—providing a scenic backdrop to the city. Deep sedimentary deposits underlying the urban area contain a historic aquifer (water-bearing material), which is gradually being depleted as demand for water increases with the area's population growth. Central Arizona Project water, brought by canal from the Colorado River, is now being injected into the aquifer to augment the local water supply. The city water department estimates that with careful conservation Tucson's water supply will be sufficient for the projected area population of 1.7 million in the year 2050.

Although located in a true desert, the natural vegetation of the area is unusually lush, certainly much more so than in the Colorado Desert of southeastern California and southwestern Arizona. Indeed, higher parts of the city border Saguaro National Park, where a luxuriant growth of giant saguaro cacti and other exotic Sonoran Desert plants dominate the landscape. In the city itself, drought-resistant trees, shrubs and cacti, mostly of local origin, are characteristic plantings along streets, in parks and on private properties. Because of local constraints on water use and a preference for natural-looking southwestern landscapes, green lawns are much less a feature of the scene in Tucson than in Phoenix or Palm Springs.

Tucson, Arizona

CLIMATE

Month	Average Daily Temperature High	Average Daily Temperature Low	Daily Rel. Humidity Low	Average Monthly Precipitation
	F		%	Inches
January	65	39	32	1.0
February	68	42	27	0.9
March	73	45	23	0.8
April	82	51	16	0.3
May	90	59	13	0.2
June	100	68	13	0.2
July	100	74	28	2.1
August	97	72	33	2.3
September	94	68	27	1.5
October	84	57	25	1.2
November	72	45	28	0.7
December	65	39	34	1.0

Annual Averages

Total Days		Total Inches	
Clear	195	Precipitation	12.2
Partly Cloudy	90	Snowfall	1.3
Cloudy	80		

RATINGS

Category	poor 1	fair 2	good 3	very good 4	excellent 5
Landscape					●
Climate			●		
Quality of Life			●		
Cost of Living			●		
Transportation				●	
Retail Services				●	
Health Care					●
Community Services				●	
Cultural Activities					●
Recreational Activities					●
Work/Volunteer Activities				●	
Crime	●				

Total Points: 46

Climate	Rating: 3

Tucson's climate is true desert characterized by long, hot, sunny summers and mild, sunny winters. Average daily high temperatures exceed 90 degrees on most days from May through September, but they are generally bearable because of low relative humidity. Spring and autumn temperatures are nearly ideal with warm days and cool nights. Winter high temperatures average in the 60s but vary considerably from day to day, with frosts occurring occasionally at night.

Tucson is unusual among American desert locations in that it experiences winter and summer rainy seasons. Nonetheless, the city is one of the sunniest locations in the United States and has a high skin cancer rate to match. Clearly, the outdoors oriented need to cover up with loose-fitting clothing and use protective sunscreen in order to minimize skin damage in this sunny environment.

Quality of Life   Rating: 3

 Tucson measures up quite well in quality of life, especially for a moderate-sized city. Noise pollution from military aircraft and, to a lesser degree, from commercial aviation is somewhat annoying. However, noise from automobiles is not severe as the major freeway, I-10, skirts the city and does not run through its center. The freeway and major streets are getting busier year by year but still remain relatively free of congestion compared to larger cities. With a rather low population density and with development spread over a large area, parking tends to be plentiful where needed. Remarkably, Tucson—unlike Phoenix and most California cities—is in full compliance with all federal air quality standards.

Tucson is not rich; there are more modest neighborhoods than upscale ones in the city proper. Still, there are few really tacky areas, and the suburbs in the Catalina Foothills are lovely. The planted desert vegetation of the city blends nicely into the remaining natural vegetation of the surrounding area, while many beautifully landscaped parks and playgrounds dot the landscape. Overall, the urban area seems fairly well planned, although the enormous strip development along Oracle Road is visually unappealing. With its great diversity of population and income levels, it is not surprising that Tucson is not uniformly peaceful or upscale in character. However, its better neighborhoods, especially those in the northern half of the urban area and just east of the University of Arizona, are very nice indeed.

Cost of Living   Rating: 3

 The cost of living in Tucson is evaluated as follows:

- *Composite.* According to ACCRA, the composite cost of living in Tucson is about three percent below the national average.

- *Housing.* ACCRA data show housing costs to be about 20 percent below the national average. Housing costs in Tucson are kept down by the low-to-moderate incomes of much of the population and by the rapid construction of new housing. Growth controls are unknown in Tucson. Most of the political city is characterized by unpretentious housing priced between $125,000 and $150,000, but several outstanding neighborhoods where typical prices exceed $300,000 also exist. The suburban Catalina Foothills area tends to offer newer, nicer and pricier housing than is typical for Tucson.

- *Goods and Services.* Grocery costs are about 16 percent above the national average and transportation and health care costs are about 10 percent above their national norms. Costs of utilities and miscellaneous goods and services approximate their national averages.

- *Taxes.* The state and local tax burden in Tucson is 9.3 percent of income compared to the U.S. average of 9.7 percent. Sales and excise taxes are a little above average whereas state income taxes and property taxes are below average.

Transportation   Rating: 4

For a medium-sized city, Tucson has remarkably good public transportation. Sun Tran, the municipal transit agency, provides excellent bus service along major streets throughout the city, especially on weekdays. Unfortunately, except for a few express lines that extend into the suburbs, bus service is confined to the city of Tucson. Suburbanites in neighboring cities and in unincorporated areas like Catalina Foothills are heavily automobile dependent. Bus fares are reasonable but monthly passes, priced at around $12 for seniors and the disabled, are an even better deal. Tucson International Airport, located only six miles from the city center, offers good commercial airline service. Sixteen destinations including Dallas, Los Angeles and Phoenix are reached by nonstop jet service. Amtrak provides limited service to points east and west like New Orleans and Los Angeles via the Sunset Limited/Texas Eagle train. The combined train currently makes six weekly departures from Tucson, three in each direction. Intercity bus service to most major cities is available from the downtown Greyhound Bus station.

Tucson has endeavored successfully to keep freeways out of much of the city. Since the I-10 freeway skirts the city on the south, most local travel is along major north–south and east–west boulevards. These tend to become moderately congested at rush hour but traffic delays are not yet severe.

Retail Services   Rating: 4

Tucson provides an excellent range of retail services. Three major enclosed shopping malls dominate the metropolitan area retailing structure. The central business district (downtown) is weak. Newly remodeled Tucson Mall, located on Oracle Road in the northwestern part of town, is Tucson's largest retail complex. Anchored by Dillard's, JCPenncy, Macy's, Mervyn's, Robinsons–May and Sears department stores, the mall has 200 smaller shops, restaurants and service establishments. In east central Tucson, two major malls are found along Broadway. El Con Mall is now undergoing a major renovation. It is anchored by Home Depot, JCPenney, Robinsons–May and Target department stores and is temporarily down to about 20 specialty stores and a cinema complex. Park Place, located a little to the east, was completely renovated a few years ago and is now anchored by Dillard's, Macy's and Sears. This shopping complex has about 120 stores and a 20-screen cinema. Retailers are also found in smaller shopping centers and in freestanding locations along major Tucson boulevards. Larger stores and warehouse operations widely scattered around the urban area include Costco, Kmart, Sams Warehouse, three Wal-Marts and four Targets. Like the latter stores, movie theaters tend to locate as standalone complexes along major boulevards. Finally, all major malls and retail complexes have abundant parking, and all those within the city limits are served by Sun Tran buses on a frequent basis.

Health Care Rating: 5

 Tucson offers exceptional health care. University Medical Center, located on the University of Arizona campus near downtown, is a major teaching hospital offering the widest possible range of medical services and specialties. Tucson Medical Center, Carondelet St. Joseph's Hospital and Carondelet St. Mary's Hospital are among the community's other large and excellent medical facilities. Several smaller general hospitals, numerous clinics and a Veterans Administration medical center are also present.

Community Services Rating: 4

 Tucson has a great variety of services of interest to retirees. The Senior Resource Network provides information about programs for seniors, and four senior centers offer a plethora of recreational and social activities including games, sports, classes and field trips.

Cultural and Educational Activities Rating: 5

 Many cultural and educational resources, including the University of Arizona Theatre, the Arizona Theatre Company and the University Museum of Art, are found on campus. The nearby Civic Center boasts an arena, a convention center and two concert halls. Among the city's excellent resident ensembles are the Arizona Opera, Southern Arizona Light Opera, Ballet Arizona and Tucson Symphony Orchestra. Frequent visits by well-known touring groups are hosted in Tucson's excellent facilities and nicely round out the theatrical and musical scene. The Tucson Museum of Art, located downtown, and the DeGrazia Gallery in the Sun, in Catalina Foothills, are among the city's leading art museums and galleries. Only 14 miles west of downtown, in Tucson Mountain Park, is the Arizona–Sonora Desert Museum where more than 300 animal species and 1,300 plant species indigenous to the Sonoran Desert are displayed in their natural settings. You will want to visit this jewel of a museum again and again.

Recreational Activities Rating: 5

 The Tucson area abounds in recreational opportunities. Renowned for golf, Tucson has more than 30 courses including seven relatively inexpensive public facilities. Spectator sports include Pacific Coast Conference football and basketball games hosted by the University of Arizona Wildcats and Greyhound racing at Tucson Greyhound Park. Tucson's many municipal parks offer endless choices for recreation. Centrally located Reid Park is the city's largest and most varied in its attractions. With its tall trees, grassy areas, picnicking and sports facilities and zoo, it is the park of choice for many Tucsonans. Residents remote from Reid Park have a wide choice among smaller playground-type parks, which typically offer tennis, swimming, ball playing and picnicking. Camping, hiking and sightseeing choices are almost endless in nearby foothill and mountain areas. Sabino Canyon, in the Santa Catalina Mountains 17 miles northeast of downtown, is easily accessed by shuttle bus or on foot. Swimming and picnicking are permitted there, but for most visitors the basic attraction is walking along the road or trails in a gorgeous mountain and canyon environment. Tucson Mountain Park and Saguaro National Park, just west of the city, and the Catalina Mountains, just to the north, also offer camping, hiking and sightseeing. High up in the Catalina Mountains at Mount Lemmon, one can even ski downhill or cross country for at least a few weeks each winter at America's southernmost ski area. In town, you can bicycle until your heart's content on Tucson's excellent bike path and bike lane network.

If all this exercise makes you hungry, you might consider lunch or dinner at one of Tucson's fine restaurants. Reflecting the area's varied ethnic mix, the city's eateries feature a wonderful variety of cuisine at reasonable prices. Mexican restaurants are everywhere, serving unique Tucson-style dishes in addition to standard Mexican fare found elsewhere in the Southwest. You might also like to try some of the sandwich shops adjacent to the university. Their specialties are excellent and inexpensive.

Work and Volunteer Activities   Rating: 4

Opportunities for paid and volunteer work are numerous. The booming local economy has generated many jobs in recent years including a good number of part-time service openings of interest to seniors. Unfortunately, in many economic sectors wages are low because of acute competition for jobs among long-time residents, newcomers and students. For those preferring to contribute to the community through volunteerism, the local Volunteer Bureau is helpful in placing seniors in interesting positions as docents, for example, at the Arizona–Sonora Desert Museum or the Tucson Botanical Gardens, or in countless other activities.

Crime Rates and Public Safety   Rating: 1

Anyone contemplating relocating to Tucson should review the city's crime rates. In Tucson proper, crime rates are well above the national average; indeed Tucson ranks among the most crime-ridden of American retirement towns. Closer examination of crime data on a geographical basis, though, reveals marked spatial variations in potential exposure to crime across the urban area. Crime rates are worse in the city than in more affluent suburbs outside the city limits. Thus Catalina Foothills in unincorporated Pima County territory north of town is a comparatively safe area. Furthermore, many violent crimes are gang related and tend to occur primarily in the poorer southern part of the city. That said, and although much of Tucson doesn't feel like a high crime area, the statistics are probably not lying. So choose your retirement site carefully. You would probably feel more secure in the suburbs or in one of the better urban neighborhoods near the university than in one of the ordinary neighborhoods south or east of downtown.

Conclusion

Overall Rating 46

Tucson is not utopia but it does have a lot going for it. Although the urban area is growing rapidly, it is still quite livable and should remain so for some time. Careful land use and transportation planning are probably vital, though, if Tucson is to avoid urban ills such as air pollution and traffic congestion that generally accompany long-term population growth. Fortunately, the city is generally spared serious environmental hazards. Tornadoes, hurricanes and serious earthquakes are unknown here, and the Tucson region is blessed by a beautiful landscape, a warm sunny climate and a generally good quality of life. The city has very good transportation and very good to excellent ratings for medical, retail and community services. Cultural, educational and recreational offerings are plentiful and of excellent quality. And all these amenities are available in the context of a below-average cost of living. If you like a desert climate and landscape and the vibrancy of a major city, give Tucson a careful look.

Prescott, Arizona

First settled by gold prospectors in 1864 and capital of the Arizona Territory from 1863 to 1867 and again between 1877 and 1889, Prescott has gradually evolved to its present status as a pleasant resort and retirement community. With a population of around 40,000 in Prescott and 30,000 in adjoining Prescott Valley, the urban area suffers none of the serious environmental and quality of life problems that plague Phoenix 96 miles to the southeast. Thanks to the concern of its citizens for the town's historic legacy, much of its past has been preserved in its architecture. The downtown Courthouse Square, adjacent Whiskey Row, the first territorial governor's residence and hundreds of Victorian homes in the historic district, all lend a note of authenticity to its western frontier image. For those desiring a high quality of life in a historic town in a mild, sunny, and scenic plateau and mountain area, Prescott has much to offer.

Landscape	Rating: 4

Prescott is situated at an elevation of 5,500 feet on the gently rolling surface of the Colorado Plateau in central Arizona. Several hills including Thumb Butte rise above the general level, adding interest to the landscape and providing good vantage points from which to view the city and its surroundings. As a result of its moderate elevation, Prescott receives more precipitation than do low-desert cities like Phoenix and Tucson.

Natural moisture levels are just adequate to support a drought-resistant ponderosa pine forest that almost completely surrounds the populated area. Watson Lake and the towering, strangely shaped rock formations of the Granite Dells are just north of town along U.S. 89. More distant but still within day-trip range are better known wonders of the Colorado Plateau such as Sedona's red rock monoliths and Oak Creek Canyon, Flagstaff's snow-capped San Francisco Mountains and the incomparable Grand Canyon.

Climate	Rating: 4

Prescott has a moderate four-season climate as a result of its mile-high elevation and southerly location. Indeed, at 34 degrees north latitude, it is about the same distance from the equator as subtropical Los Angeles. Prescott is considerably cooler in all seasons than Phoenix and is a favorite refuge of southern Arizonans from the scorching temperatures of low-desert locales. Afternoon temperatures are warm to hot in summer but marked overnight cooling makes for temperatures pleasant for sleeping. Winters are brisk, with mild days and cold nights. Spring and autumn are delightful seasons with generally mild days and cool nights. Although the city receives an annual average of 19 inches of rain and 24 inches of snow, Prescott is mostly sunny and dry with low-to-moderate relative humidity readings. The frost-free period is about 150 days, extending from early May through early October, so gardening is mostly a summertime endeavor. Gardeners and others enjoying the outdoors need to protect exposed skin against the area's strong and persistent sunshine. The combination of low latitude and moderately high elevation leads to high ultraviolet index values in summer.

Prescott, Arizona

CLIMATE				
	Average Daily Temperature		Daily Rel. Humidity	Average Monthly Precipitation
Month	High	Low	Low	
	F		**%**	**Inches**
January	51	23	44	1.6
February	54	26	38	1.9
March	58	30	35	1.9
April	65	35	26	0.8
May	74	43	22	0.6
June	85	51	17	0.4
July	88	59	32	2.9
August	86	57	36	3.3
September	81	50	32	2.1
October	71	39	31	1.3
November	60	29	38	1.3
December	52	23	46	1.3

RATINGS	poor 1	fair 2	good 3	very good 4	excellent 5
Landscape				●	
Climate				●	
Quality of Life					●
Cost of Living			●		
Transportation		●			
Retail Services			●		
Health Care			●		
Community Services			●		
Cultural Activities			●		
Recreational Activities				●	
Work/Volunteer Activities			●		
Crime			●		

Annual Averages

Total Days		Total Inches	
Clear	180	Precipitation	19.2
Partly Cloudy	95	Snowfall	24.1
Cloudy	90		

Total Points: 40

Quality of Life — **Rating: 5**

Prescott provides an excellent quality of life. With no freeways, no heavily traveled highways and no major airports in the local area, intrusive noise is minimal. Although traffic on streets and highways is increasing steadily, especially during the summer tourist season, traffic congestion is seldom encountered and parking is more than adequate on streets and at shopping malls. The air is pristine and the community is in full compliance with federal air quality standards.

Despite the fact that per capita income levels are somewhat lower than the national average, the city has an aura of modest prosperity. While neighboring Prescott Valley has somewhat of an urban sprawl character, Prescott itself appears well planned. Its generally pleasant neighborhoods are so well treed that from some points it is difficult to discern where the city ends and the forest begins.

Cost of Living   Rating: 3

 The cost of living in Prescott is evaluated as follows:

- *Composite.* ACCRA data show that the composite cost of living in Prescott is about 3 percent above the national average.

- *Housing.* According to ACCRA, housing costs in Prescott–Prescott Valley are about 8 percent below the national average. In Prescott itself, though, I estimate housing costs to be somewhat above the national average. Housing of varied styles from California ranches to Santa Fe adobes to traditional frame Victorians is typically on the market. New tract developments are found mostly outside the city limits whereas attractive, older resale homes are found in Prescott itself.

- *Goods and Services.* Grocery and health care costs are about 17 percent above the national average and miscellaneous goods and services are priced about 8 percent above the national norm. Utilities and transportation costs approximate the national average.

- *Taxes.* The state and local tax burden in Prescott is 9.3 percent of income compared to the U.S. average of 9.7 percent. Sales and excise taxes are a little above average whereas state income taxes and property taxes are below average.

Transportation   Rating: 2

A small private bus company provides daytime service to shopping centers and medical complexes, while local shuttles connect the city with Sky Harbor International Airport in Phoenix, about 100 miles distant. Sky Harbor is served by 21 airlines and offers excellent commercial airline service including nonstop jet service to about 105 destinations including Chicago, Las Vegas and Los Angeles. Taxi and dial-a-ride service, the latter for seniors and the disabled, are available in Prescott but, as is typical in many small towns, nearly everyone but the transit dependent prefers to drive.

Retail Services   Rating: 3

The historic downtown, especially the blocks fronting on Courthouse Square, has a nice mix of specialty and antique shops, restaurants and bars. With its charming Old West atmosphere, this district, including Whiskey Row, is a great hit with tourists. Most locals, though, shop at malls and shopping centers. Prescott Gateway Mall is anchored by Dillard's, JCPenney and Sears department stores and features approximately 80 specialty stores and services and a 6-screen theater. Frontier Shopping Village includes Home Depot, Wal-Mart and Target stores and a Costco is nearby.

Health Care   Rating: 3

 Prescott provides adequate day-to-day medical care. Yavapai Regional Medical Center, with 135 beds, is a nonprofit community hospital. It offers services typical of smaller hospitals including emergency room services, cardiac and lung care, oncology services and wellness programs. Also present in Prescott is the large Prescott VA Medical Center; it provides a large number of medical specialties to veterans. A greater variety of medical services and facilities can be found in Phoenix, less than 100 miles southeast.

Community Services   Rating: 3

 The Adult Center of Prescott makes available classes in Spanish, computers and various crafts and organizes field excursions, dances and card games, among other activities. It also runs a popular wellness clinic.

Cultural and Educational Activities   Rating: 3

Prescott has many cultural and educational assets. Yavapai Community College (YCC) and Sharlot Hall Museum are centers of cultural life for residents and visitors. YCC now enrolls more than 8,000 students and makes available to seniors a wide range of academic and applied courses at reduced fees. The Performance Hall at YCC is a state-of-the-art 1,130-seat facility that hosts major concerts. The Phoenix Symphony performs seven concerts with major soloists here each year. Performance Hall has also hosted the National Symphony and its community concert series has highlighted stars such as Willie Nelson, Mel Torme and Doc Severinsen. The Prescott Bluegrass Festival is held here each June and the college fields annually the largest Elderhostel program in the country. Sharlot Hall Museum, a nine-building complex with a research library, explores the regional heritage of the American Southwest through festivals, living history and changing exhibits. Its annual highlights include a Folk Arts Fair, Folk Music Fair, Indian Art Market and the popular Cowboy Poets Gathering.

Prescott's beautiful Courthouse Plaza is the historic core of the city and is the principal venue for summer weekend arts and crafts shows, which draw exhibitors from throughout the West and visitors from all over Arizona. Prescott College, which enrolls 700 students in a non-traditional format emphasizing environmental studies and outdoor recreation, is another center of culture and education. Their adult undergraduate and graduate programs are popular.

Recreational Activities   Rating: 4

 Countless recreational activities are available locally and nearby. Prescott has 14 movie theaters, 14 lighted tennis courts, four 18-hole golf courses, three swimming pools, a roller skating rink and a small zoo. With 900 acres of parkland within the city and Prescott National Forest adjacent, places for picnicking, camping, horseback riding and rock climbing abound. Several small lakes are within 10 miles of downtown and the old Santa Fe rail route, which passes Prescott's spectacular Granite Dells, has been converted to a rails-to-trails hiking and biking path. More remote but within day trip range by car are some of Arizona's outstanding historic and scenic attractions. Worth visiting are Jerome—an old mining town and present-day art colony on the steep eastern slope of Mingus Mountain—the gorgeous red rock landscape of Sedona and Oak Creek Canyon, Flagstaff's San Francisco Mountains where you can ski in winter and Grand Canyon National Park. In town you can enjoy thoroughbred horse racing during the summer racing season, Memorial Day through Labor Day, and round out the day savoring food and drink at one of the historic restaurants on Courthouse Square.

Work and Volunteer Activities   Rating: 3

Work is sometimes hard to find and wages are lower than in Phoenix. But the volunteer work force is huge; hospitals and public schools employ thousands. Opportunities for volunteer work also exist at the Adult Center of Prescott, various social organizations, public library and visitor bureau, among other nonprofit sites.

Crime Rates and Public Safety   Rating: 3

Prescott feels like a safe city and for the most part it is. The city's violent crime rate is 20 percent below the national average but its property crime rate, at 50 percent above the national average, is less satisfactory. The principal crime locally is larceny–theft, which is annoying but not life threatening. Rates of burglary and auto theft, the more serious property crimes, are near their national averages. Violent and property crime rates are somewhat lower in Prescott Valley than in the city of Prescott.

Conclusion

Overall Rating 40 Prescott is not perfect but it is a pleasant small town in a scenic and unspoiled part of the Desert Southwest. Because of its location, moderate elevation and underlying geology, the city enjoys a mild sunny, four-season climate and is at low risk of earthquakes and severe storms. Many people from large cities appreciate the peaceful ambiance and excellent quality of life of Prescott. Those attracted to the great outdoors will doubtless enjoy the natural beauty of the city's wooded hilly site and the ease of visiting some of the geologic and historic wonders of the American West via relatively short automobile trips. Although a little above the national average, the cost of living remains affordable and health care, retail and community services, cultural and educational options, and volunteer opportunities are good. Prescott's has few serious weaknesses. Public transit is inadequate so a car is a virtual necessity and it is a long shuttle ride to Phoenix Airport. All in all, though, Prescott measures up quite well among smaller places as a retirement haven. It is worth a careful look.

Boulder City, Nevada

Founded in 1931 by the federal government to house workers constructing Hoover Dam, Boulder City is today a beautiful little oasis in the desert of southern Nevada. Only 8 miles from Hoover dam and 24 miles from downtown Las Vegas and technically part of the Las Vegas metropolitan area, Boulder City has little but its desert setting and climate in common with Las Vegas. With 15,000 residents, a well-planned urban structure and a controlled growth ordinance that limits the number of building permits issued each year to about 3 percent of existing development, this well-run city is determined to do

Boulder City, Nevada

CLIMATE

Month	Average Daily Temperature High	Average Daily Temperature Low	Daily Rel. Humidity Low	Average Monthly Precipitation
	F		%	Inches
January	53	38	33	0.7
February	59	42	27	0.8
March	65	46	23	0.9
April	73	53	17	0.3
May	83	62	15	0.2
June	94	71	14	0.1
July	99	77	18	0.6
August	98	75	20	0.9
September	90	69	19	0.6
October	78	58	21	0.3
November	62	46	28	0.5
December	53	38	33	0.5

Annual Averages

Total Days		Total Inches	
Clear	212	Precipitation	6.3
Partly Cloudy	82	Snowfall	1.0
Cloudy	71		

RATINGS

Category	poor 1	fair 2	good 3	very good 4	excellent 5
Landscape				●	
Climate			●		
Quality of Life					●
Cost of Living	●				
Transportation				●	
Retail Services				●	
Health Care				●	
Community Services				●	
Cultural Activities				●	
Recreational Activities					●
Work/Volunteer Activities			●		
Crime					●

Total Points: 46

whatever is necessary to preserve its high quality of life. To that end Boulder City has never allowed gambling within its city limits and has recently increased its size from 34.5 square miles to 200 square miles. The annexation of 165.5 square miles of desert stretching south of town is intended to protect the natural environment and prevent Las Vegas suburbs from eventually engulfing the community.

Landscape   Rating: 4

Boulder City is located on a gently sloping upland surface at an elevation of 2,500 feet. A low range of hills separates it from the urban sprawl and frenzied pace of Las Vegas and adds scenic interest to its setting. High mountains in the distance frame dramatic views of Lake Mead from the hilltop park and civic center complex in the heart of the historic district. The natural vegetation of the area is low desert scrub but the heavily irrigated urban landscape is lush indeed. As in Las Vegas, green lawns, flowers and exotic tree species including palms—rather than drought-resistant desert plants—are favored locally. Fortunately, Boulder City, unlike Las Vegas, has a large enough allocation of water from Lake Mead to meet its needs for the foreseeable future.

Climate   Rating: 3

Boulder City's climate is true desert with long, hot, sunny summers and cool, sunny winters. Among American desert locations, Boulder City, like Las Vegas, is unusually dry. It receives an average of only 6.3 inches of precipitation annually. Measurable precipitation falls on an average of only 13 days per year. Average daily high temperatures exceed 95 degrees and overnight temperatures are rather warm in summer. Spring and autumn are most pleasant with generally warm days and cool nights. Winters are fairly cool with normal highs in the upper 50s. Snowfall is insignificant and the frost-free season is nearly 300 days long on average, with light frost occurring frequently at night from December through February. The city is sunny about 85 percent of the time and is one of America's sunniest locations; use of a good sunscreen is essential.

Quality of Life   Rating: 5

The overall quality of life is excellent. McCarren International Airport is 20 miles away in Las Vegas, no freeway approaches the city limits and the U.S. 93 truck route bypasses the center of town. As a result there is little noise from road traffic or commercial aircraft. Like neighboring Las Vegas, Boulder City is now classified by the EPA as a "basic non-attainment area" for air quality, which means that the city is minimally out of compliance with current air quality standards. Although the air is clean much of the year, light smog occurs on many summer days. The city's small size, low population density, lack of major commercial development and location on the fringe of the Las Vegas urban region prevent crowding and traffic congestion. Parking is plentiful and free, even in the downtown area, and no heavy industries or garish gambling casinos blight the landscape. Residential neighborhoods, whether in the historic district around the civic center or in new areas on the periphery, are well maintained with green lawns or desert gardens fronting on clean tree-shaded streets. The city's beautifully landscaped small parks, plazas and playgrounds add additional notes of peaceful ambiance to the community.

The cost of living in Boulder City is evaluated as follows:

- *Composite.* ACCRA data are unavailable for Boulder City but local sources admit that costs there are significantly higher than in Las Vegas. I estimate that the overall cost of living is probably 20 percent above the national average.

- *Housing.* Housing costs are well above the national average in part because the housing supply in Boulder City has been limited since the late 1970s by a controlled growth ordinance. Other factors driving up house prices include the well-known ambiance of the community and the influx of equity-rich Californians who tend to bid up prices in the most desirable parts of the Las Vegas region. According to the city manager, Boulder City housing costs are about 30 percent higher than in Las Vegas. Small construction era homes in the historic district are priced between $150,000 and $200,000, while at the other extreme new, large homes near Lake Mead are priced at more than $400,000. Typical single-family residences in average neighborhoods are available for prices between $220,000 and $350,000.

- *Goods and Services.* Extrapolating from ACCRA data for Las Vegas, I estimate that local cost of health care is about 25 percent above the national average, whereas groceries, transportation and miscellaneous goods and services prices are about 10 percent above their national norms. Utilities, priced about 10 percent below average by the municipality, are a comparative bargain.

- *Taxes.* The state and local tax burden in Boulder City is 6 percent of income compared to the U.S. average of 9.7 percent. Nevada does not tax income, and property taxes and sales and excise taxes are well below average.

Transportation   **Rating: 4**

Citizen's Area Transit (CAT) provides local bus service and connects Boulder City with Las Vegas. Fares are reasonable; seniors 62 and older pay $15 for a monthly pass. The Southern Nevada Transport Coalition provides dial-a-ride service for seniors. McCarran Airport, only 24 miles away in Las Vegas, can be reached via the Boulder City Shuttle Service or by car. As noted more fully in the Las Vegas discussion, McCarran provides excellent jet service to numerous domestic and international locations.

Retail Services   **Rating: 4**

The historic downtown shopping district is quaint but oriented mainly to tourists. Residents shop locally at a small shopping center on Nevada Highway on the south side of town. A supermarket and several specialty stores are found there. The nearest major shopping mall is the Galleria at Sunset in Henderson, 18 miles away. There you will find Dillard's, Galyan's, JCPenney, Mervyn's and Robinsons–May department stores and more than 130 specialty shops, restaurants and service establishments. The immense retailing resources of Las Vegas' three other regional malls are only a few miles more distant.

Health Care   Rating: 4

Boulder City Hospital, a community nonprofit facility, and its staff of 100 doctors provide routine medical care. Facilities and services at the 67-bed hospital include a 24-hour emergency unit, clinical laboratory, intensive care unit, radiology department, CT and MRI scanners and nuclear medicine. Larger facilities with a greater range of medical specialties and services are only half an hour away in Las Vegas (see the Las Vegas Health Care discussion for details).

Community Services   Rating: 4

The municipality, places of worship and more than 50 community organizations offer an exceptional range of services to residents. Of special interest to retirees are the many activities and services provided by the Boulder City Senior Center. Social activities include playing pool in the center's fully equipped poolroom, card games, bingo, chess, horseshoes and croquet. Arts and crafts, movies, live theater and concerts are among the many attractions and entertainment available. The center provides assistance with legal problems, income tax preparation and social security applications and offers a number of onsite health services including physical examinations, nutrition education and blood pressure and vision screenings. The center also serves appetizing weekday lunches and delivers Meals on Wheels on request.

Cultural and Educational Activities   Rating: 4

Boulder City is a little too small, too protective of its residential ambiance and too close to Las Vegas to develop a strong cultural identity of its own. However, it has on its eastern side a branch campus of the Community College of Southern Nevada and several art galleries downtown. It even hosts numerous art shows including the annual "Art in the Park Festival," and its Boulder City "First Nighters" is the oldest amateur theater group in southern Nevada. The beautiful new city library in Adams Boulevard Community Park has more than 66,000 books and periodicals, 4,200 CDs and 1,200 video items.

Those seeking more advanced education or more sophisticated popular or classical culture need only travel the 24 miles to Las Vegas to have their needs met (see the Las Vegas Cultural and Educational Activities discussion for details). There is never a shortage of cultural events in Las Vegas.

Recreational Activities   Rating: 5

Recreational assets abound locally and nearby. The city's 34 acres of landscaped park and plaza areas offer facilities for picnicking, community events, shuffleboard, tennis, basketball and baseball. The downtown Boulder City Recreation Center features year-round indoor swimming and racquetball, and the Fitness Center in ABC Park is equipped to help you keep in shape. The Boulder City Parks and Recreation Department now operates the 18-hole Boulder City Golf Course and the new 27-hole Boulder Creek Golf Club. Other recreational facilities in town include a movie theater, bowling alley and a BMX bicycle track. Just outside of town is Lake Mead, created by impounding the Colorado River at Hoover Dam. The Lake Mead National Recreation Area, an element of the National Parks System, has 500 miles of shoreline and is a mecca for water sports enthusiasts and fishermen, as well as for campers, bikers, hikers and sightseers. Those seeking an even greater variety of recreation need only travel to Las Vegas where there are golf courses, parks, participant and spectator sports and restaurants galore (see the Las Vegas Recreational Activities discussion for details).

Work and Volunteer Activities   Rating: 3

Opportunities for employment and volunteerism are somewhat limited by the small size of Boulder City. Even so, some part-time jobs exist in the service sector. Volunteer work is available at the hospital, senior center, public library, chamber of commerce, National Parks Service and local service organizations. Individuals willing to travel to Las Vegas will find additional employment and volunteer opportunities.

Crime Rates and Public Safety   Rating: 5

Boulder City is one of America's safest communities. Recent FBI data show that the city's violent crime rate is about 25 percent below the national average, while its property crime rate is 60 percent below the national norm. The town's geographic isolation from Las Vegas, its relatively stable, affluent and alert population, excellent city government and police, and the absence of casinos and large-scale commercial development all help make Boulder City an enviably peaceful and safe place.

Conclusion

Overall Rating 46

Boulder City ranks highly as a retirement town. Although officially part of the Las Vegas metropolitan area, it is quite unlike the city and its sprawling suburbs. It is an oasis according to both meanings of the term. It is an area of the desert made fertile by the presence of water and, more importantly, it is a quiet, peaceful place in the midst of turbulent surroundings. At the same time it is close enough to Las Vegas for its residents to enjoy easy access to the many amenities of that lively city.

Boulder City is fortunate in its physical and human environment. Its site overlooking Lake Mead and the surrounding desert and mountains is striking and its climate is varied enough to offer four distinct seasons. Those seeking to escape from big city stresses will find Boulder City's excellent quality of life attributes and low crime rates attractive. The city is well planned and run and offers its residents high-quality public services including, among others, excellent parks and recreation facilities and a fine police department. Taking into account the fact that Boulder City residents can easily supplement local resources with those of nearby Las Vegas and Henderson, the community's ratings in transportation, retail services, health care, community services, and cultural and recreational activities are very good. Admittedly, all these benefits come at the price of a cost of living perhaps 20 percent above the national average. But that premium is a small price to pay for the privilege of living in Boulder City.

Las Vegas, Nevada

Las Vegas, with a population exceeding 520,000 in the city and 1.7 million in the metropolitan area, is fast becoming one of America's most popular retirement locales. Explosive economic and population growth is so much the norm that hotels along the Strip, only 20 or 30 years old, are replaced in record

Las Vegas, Nevada

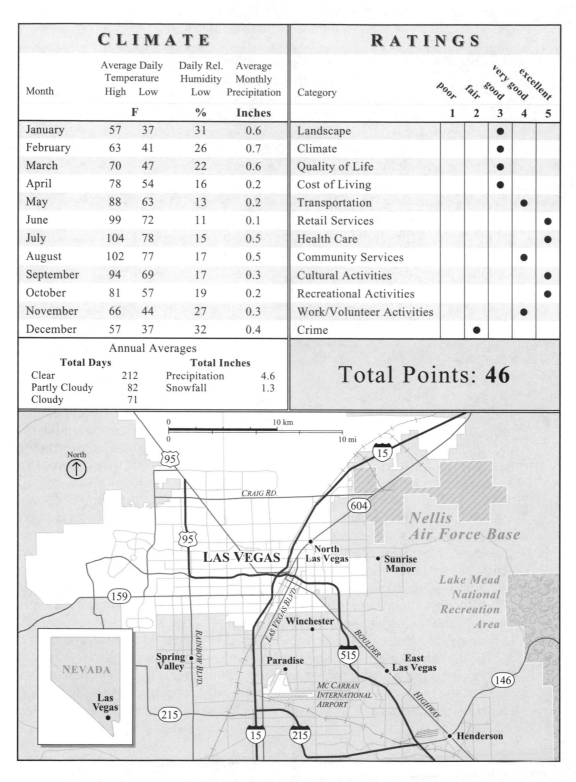

CLIMATE

Month	Average Daily Temperature High	Low	Daily Rel. Humidity Low	Average Monthly Precipitation
	F		%	Inches
January	57	37	31	0.6
February	63	41	26	0.7
March	70	47	22	0.6
April	78	54	16	0.2
May	88	63	13	0.2
June	99	72	11	0.1
July	104	78	15	0.5
August	102	77	17	0.5
September	94	69	17	0.3
October	81	57	19	0.2
November	66	44	27	0.3
December	57	37	32	0.4

Annual Averages

Total Days		Total Inches	
Clear	212	Precipitation	4.6
Partly Cloudy	82	Snowfall	1.3
Cloudy	71		

RATINGS

Category	poor 1	fair 2	good 3	very good 4	excellent 5
Landscape			●		
Climate			●		
Quality of Life			●		
Cost of Living			●		
Transportation				●	
Retail Services					●
Health Care					●
Community Services				●	
Cultural Activities					●
Recreational Activities					●
Work/Volunteer Activities				●	
Crime		●			

Total Points: 46

time by larger and more luxurious ones. But Las Vegas is far more than the famous hotels and gambling casinos of the Strip and downtown. Outside these dynamic and intensely developed areas, you will find a relatively low population density city, not unlike the newer suburban areas of many other mid-sized American cities. A suburban lifestyle in a sunny, warm, desert environment within a few miles of exciting Las Vegas attractions appeals to many people, young and old. Every month thousands of people move here.

Landscape   Rating: 3

Las Vegas sprawls across a flat desert basin in southern Nevada at an elevation of 2,500 feet. Although the city's site is uninteresting, nearby Mt. Charleston and the Spring Mountains, which are high enough to be snow-capped in winter, add interest to the surrounding terrain. The natural vegetation of the area consists of low desert scrub but this is not apparent amidst the greenery of the heavily irrigated city. Continuing drought in the Colorado River Basin, though, combined with rapid population growth in the metropolitan area, has recently induced the Southern Nevada Water Authority to enforce strict water conservation measures. More and more, green lawns and flowers are being replaced by Tucson-style desert plantings. Even so, present per capita water use is unsustainable and additional conservation will be needed.

Climate   Rating: 3

The Las Vegas climate is true desert characterized by long, hot, sunny summers and cool, sunny winters. Even among desert cities Las Vegas is unusually dry; it receives on average only five inches of precipitation annually as a result of its location in the rain shadow of high mountains to the west. Average daily high temperatures exceed 98 degrees during the summer and are typically pleasantly warm in spring and autumn. Winter is much cooler with normal highs in the upper 50s. Snowfall is insignificant but frosts occur on an average of 30 nights per year, mostly in December, January and February. In contrast, summer nights are very warm as a result of the "thermal heat island effect" typical of large cities. Overnight lows average 78 degrees in July. On average, the city is sunny 85 percent of the time and ranks with Tucson as one of America's sunniest cities. Careful use of sunscreen is essential to minimize damage to skin.

Quality of Life   Rating: 3

The overall quality of life is good but significant variation occurs locally depending on proximity to the airport and to busy streets, freeways and commercial areas. Neighborhoods away from tourist attractions tend to be relatively quiet, except for occasional noise from automobile traffic and commercial or military aircraft. The EPA now designates Las Vegas as a "basic non-attainment area" for air quality, which means that the city is minimally out of compliance with current air quality standards. Smog levels are light but the atmosphere is not entirely clear; some reduction in visibility occurs as a result of the mixing together of dust and locally generated pollution from the region's large automobile fleet. The city and the state of Nevada have aggressively built a high-capacity street and freeway network to accommodate the burgeoning car population. Two major freeways, I-15 and I-515, crisscross the metropolitan area and connect with most major east-west and north-south boulevards. Regrettably, as elsewhere, improvements in road infrastructure in Las Vegas appear to contribute to additional low density urban sprawl, longer average motor trips, greater total travel and, ultimately, to increased traffic congestion. To date, though, heavy traffic congestion remains largely a rush hour phenomenon, except on Las Vegas Boulevard (the Strip), which is nearly always busy. Plenty of parking is available where needed.

Ideally, urban growth on the massive scale that is occurring in Las Vegas would seem to mandate careful physical planning and zoning in order to preserve the present good quality of life. Unfortunately, the political will to constrain or guide development seems to be lacking with the result that Las Vegas is rather quickly developing into a smaller version of Los Angeles. Its older, pleasant inner city neighborhoods are becoming lost in a sea of quite decent but all-too-similar, newer tract homes.

Cost of Living	Rating: 3

 The cost of living in Las Vegas is evaluated as follows:

- **Composite.** ACCRA data show that the composite cost of living in Las Vegas is 2 percent below the national average.

- **Housing.** Average housing costs are just below the national average. Since growth controls are unknown and housing is being built at a rapid pace, housing costs should remain reasonable despite the massive influx of new residents. At present, a typical single-family home sells for around $200,000 but many larger, upscale homes on the suburban fringe sell at considerably higher prices.

- **Goods and Services.** ACCRA data show health care to be priced about 25 percent above the national average, while groceries and transportation costs are 10 percent above average. Costs of miscellaneous goods and services exceed the national average by 5 percent and utilities are a bargain at a price 10 percent below average.

- **Taxes.** The state and local tax burden in Las Vegas is 6 percent of income compared to the U.S. average of 9.7 percent. Nevada does not tax income, and property taxes and sales and excise taxes are well below average.

Transportation	Rating: 4

 The transportation infrastructure of Las Vegas is being expanded steadily in order to keep up with rising demand. Citizen's Area Transit (CAT) operates more than 300 buses and carries about 150,000 passengers daily on its 49 scheduled routes. Twenty-four-hour service is provided downtown and along the Strip but hours and frequency of service are less elsewhere. Fares are reasonable; seniors 62 and older pay $15 for a monthly pass. The Las Vegas Monorail, a privately developed elevated train system that connects major hotels and the Las Vegas Convention Center along a four-mile route, went into service in the summer of 2004. Officials hope that it will lighten traffic along the Strip and reduce air pollution. Even so, in such a sprawling city most people are wedded to their cars and leave public transit to the transit dependent. McCarran Airport, located just southeast of the Strip and only six miles from the city center, is currently the nation's tenth busiest airport. A major hub, McCarran offers nonstop jet service to numerous domestic and international locations. New terminals, gates and a 9,700-foot runway have recently been added and no end is in sight for the airport's expansion. Those preferring to stay on the ground can reach many destinations from the downtown Greyhound bus station.

Retail Services — Rating: 5

Greater Las Vegas offers an enormous variety of retail services to residents and visitors. Four major enclosed regional malls dominate the area's retailing structure but more than 100 smaller shopping centers are also present. The central business district is comparatively weak in retailing. Boulevard Mall, located on Maryland Parkway in the southern part of town, is the largest retail complex and is anchored by Dillard's, JCPenney, Macy's, Marshalls and Sears. Meadows Mall, at 4300 Meadows Lane, is only slightly smaller. Its anchor stores are Dillard's, JCPenney, Macy's and Sears. Fashion Show Mall, on the Strip at Las Vegas Boulevard and Spring Mountain Road, has Dillard's, Macy's, Neiman Marcus, Nordstrom, Robinsons–May, and Saks Fifth Avenue as principal tenants. The million-square foot Galleria at Sunset is located at 300 W. Sunset in suburban Henderson. Its anchor stores include Dillard's, Galyan's, JCPenney, Mervyn's and Robinsons–May. In addition to the major malls, retailers are found in several outlet malls, in smaller shopping centers and in freestanding locations along major boulevards. Warehouse operations and larger stores are scattered across the urban area.

Health Care — Rating: 5

Las Vegas offers comprehensive medical care, although at prices well above the national average. University Medical Center, affiliated with the University of Nevada School of Medicine, is a county-operated complex that provides a wide range of medical services. It was the first hospital in Nevada to develop an organ transplant program and it offers special health programs for Nevada's senior population. Other large general hospitals include Sunrise Hospital and Medical Center, Mountain View Hospital, Desert Springs Hospital, Lake Mead Hospital, St. Rose Dominican Hospital, Summerlin Hospital Medical Center and Valley Hospital Medical Center. Several smaller specialty hospitals and numerous clinics are also present. A new military and veteran's hospital opened in 1994.

Community Services — Rating: 4

The metropolitan area's more than 15 neighborhood senior centers are a major resource. These offer a variety of recreational facilities including gymnasiums, swimming pools, libraries, exercise rooms, billiard tables and shuffleboard courts. Many of the centers also offer meals, preventive health care, skills training, workshops, public service programs, field trips, and games and social activities of great variety.

Cultural and Educational Activities — Rating: 5

Significant cultural and educational resources are available to all age groups at the University of Nevada, Las Vegas (UNLV) and the Community College of Southern Nevada (CCSN). Now 45 years old, the university currently enrolls 25,000 students on its 337-acre campus. UNLV's excellent theatre arts department stages modern plays and the classics on campus at the Judy Bayley Theatre on Maryland Parkway. The Nevada Dance Theater also performs here regularly. Also on campus is the Artemus W. Ham Concert Hall, a principal venue for performances by the Las Vegas Civic Symphony, the Nevada Symphony and the Nevada Opera Theatre. Popular music and jazz performances are also scheduled here. CCSN, with three main campuses and 50 extension centers, is highly accessible to its 35,000 students. Its 2,500 courses in the academic and applied arts, scheduled seven days a week in daytime and evening, should appeal to nearly every taste.

Las Vegas hotels and casinos host an enormous variety of popular entertainment. Big-room shows typically feature a star performer and orchestra, supported by a vocalist or comedian; lounge shows feature a main performer and supporting acts. If art museums are your preference, the Las Vegas Art Museum and the University Art Gallery are worth visiting. The Las Vegas Public Library, with more than 1.5 million books in its eight branches, is also a useful resource.

Recreational Activities   Rating: 5

 Recreational opportunities are abundant locally. More than 40 golf courses, most open to the public on a daily fee basis, dot the landscape. More than 30 municipal parks offer some combination of ball fields, courts for basketball, tennis and volleyball, as well as playgrounds and picnic areas. Snow skiing facilities on Mount Charleston, water sports sites on Lake Mead, and the spectacularly eroded red sandstone cliffs of Valley of Fire State Park are within an hour's drive. A little farther afield but still reachable by one- or two-day car trips are Death Valley, Grand Canyon and Zion National Parks. In town, spectator sports enthusiasts can enjoy Las Vegas Wranglers professional ice hockey, as well as varsity basketball and football played by UNLV's Runnin Rebels. Las Vegas has many fine restaurants to enjoy after the game. Whether your preference is fine French or Continental dining in a semiformal setting or the more casual ambiance of American, Italian or other ethnic restaurants, the choices are almost infinite.

Work and Volunteer Activities   Rating: 4

Many opportunities exist for post-retirement work and volunteerism. Rapid growth of tourism and the gaming industry creates countless full-time and part-time jobs, some of which might be of interest to retirees. Those wishing to contribute through volunteerism may take advantage of the AARP community service employment program to find their niche in one of the city's numerous service organizations.

Crime Rates and Public Safety   Rating: 2

The metropolitan area suffers from an overall violent crime rate 33 percent above the national average; the homicide rate is nearly twice the national norm. On a more positive note, the property crime rate, although 15 percent above the national average, is not inordinately high. Indeed, considering that 30 million visitors come to Las Vegas annually, the threat of crime to a particular individual, resident or nonresident, is less than FBI crime data imply. Even so, you would be wise to choose your retirement site carefully in one of the better neighborhoods. There are many to choose from.

Conclusion

Overall Rating 46 Las Vegas ranks highly on most standard measures of suitability for retirement but it is not without problems. Its greatest strengths are in cultural and recreational activities, retail services and health care. It is also strong in transportation, community services, and work and volunteer activities. Despite tremendous recent population growth, much of the urban area still rates fairly highly in quality of life factors. However, if such rapid growth persists for another 20 years as seems almost certain, air quality and traffic congestion could worsen and per capita water use might need to be further curtailed. Luckily, environmental hazards except for smog are virtually unknown in southern Nevada. Unfortunately, serious crime is not. It is a potential threat that can be minimized but not entirely avoided by choosing an upscale neighborhood. Finally, it must be admitted that the newness and relative uniformity of much of the urban landscape may be unsatisfying to some. There are no charming historic neighborhoods and the various malls cannot entirely make up for the lack of a vibrant downtown. Nonetheless, for those well suited to a suburban lifestyle in a dynamic, new, exciting city full of cultural and recreational attractions, Las Vegas might be a good and economical choice.

Carson City, Nevada

From its humble origins as a commercial and industrial center serving the silver miners of nearby Virginia City in the late 1850s, Carson City has blossomed into one of the country's most beautiful state capitals. Located only 14 miles east of Lake Tahoe, 30 miles south of Reno, and 130 miles east of Sacramento, California, it offers easy access to countless outdoor recreational pursuits in the Lake Tahoe and the Sierra Nevada regions. The shopping, cultural and educational attractions, and gaming establishments of Reno are also nearby. Carson City, with a population around 60,000, is less than one-third the size of Reno and retains a laid-back atmosphere that reflects a preference for tranquility and a high quality of life over rapid growth. The local economy, owing to the city's role as capital of Nevada, is strongly service oriented and relatively stable.

Landscape	Rating: 5

Carson City is situated in northwestern Nevada at an elevation of 4,700 feet on a gently sloping plain at the foot of the Sierra Nevada, a massive mountain range separating the Central Valley of California from the desert and semi-arid areas of Nevada. Lying just east of the Sierra Nevada and in its rain shadow, Carson City occupies a pleasant and scenic site. Its low-profile, irrigated, well-treed urban landscape is framed by the forested Sierra Nevada to the west and by desert to the north, east and south. Although the natural vegetation of the area is semi-arid grass and shrub, the city and bordering farmland are well watered and spectacularly green in summer. Local water supplies are not unlimited, however, and the municipality mandates water conservation. Water use may need to be restricted further if population growth continues.

Climate	Rating: 4

Carson City experiences an invigorating four-season semi-arid climate characterized by modest precipitation, abundant sunshine and marked day-to-day and seasonal changes in weather. As in neighboring California, the precipitation regime is Mediterranean with about two-thirds of the normal annual precipitation of 10 inches occurring during the rainy season between November and March. Snowfall averages about 26 inches in a normal winter, but snow seldom persists on the ground for more than a week

Carson City, Nevada

Month	Average Daily Temperature High	Average Daily Temperature Low	Daily Rel. Humidity Low	Average Monthly Precipitation
	F		**%**	**Inches**
January	46	22	50	1.8
February	51	25	39	1.7
March	57	30	33	1.3
April	63	33	28	0.4
May	72	40	25	0.5
June	81	46	22	0.4
July	89	51	18	0.2
August	88	49	20	0.3
September	80	42	22	0.5
October	69	33	27	0.7
November	55	26	42	1.3
December	46	21	51	1.3

CLIMATE

Annual Averages

Total Days		Total Inches	
Clear	159	Precipitation	10.4
Partly Cloudy	93	Snowfall	26.2
Cloudy	113		

RATINGS

Category	poor 1	fair 2	good 3	very good 4	excellent 5
Landscape					●
Climate				●	
Quality of Life					●
Cost of Living			●		
Transportation		●			
Retail Services			●		
Health Care			●		
Community Services			●		
Cultural Activities		●			
Recreational Activities				●	
Work/Volunteer Activities			●		
Crime			●		

Total Points: 40

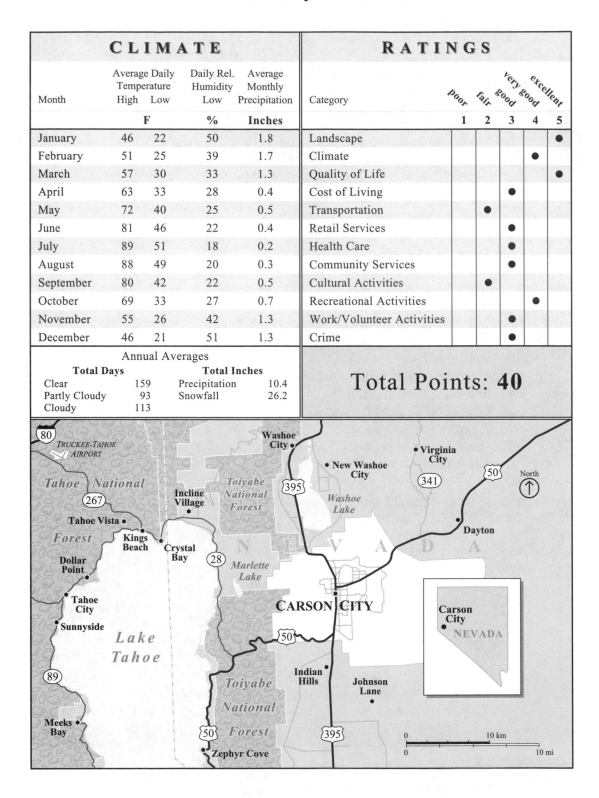

or so because daytime temperatures usually rise well above freezing, even in mid-winter. Summer afternoons are warm to hot but are fairly comfortable owing to low relative humidity. Marked cooling occurs soon after sunset as a result of the high elevation and clear dry air, so a sweater or jacket is required for summer evening walks. Spring and autumn weather is pleasant with cool to warm days and cold nights. Winters are cool with average high temperatures around 50 degrees and average low temperatures around 20 degrees. The frost-free period averages only 120 days. The city is sunny about 90 percent of the time in summer and 65 percent in winter.

Quality of Life   Rating: 5

 The overall quality of life is excellent. With no freeway or major airport and only moderate street traffic, noise levels are minimal. The city easily meets federal air quality standards. The city's small size, low population density and modest commercial and industrial development give the community an uncrowded, almost rural feeling. Plenty of parking is available at local malls and in the small central business district. Most residential neighborhoods, whether in the old core just west of Nevada Highway (U.S. 395) or in newer areas, are pleasant. Several newer subdivisions on the edge of town feature large homes, many of which look westward across a pastoral landscape toward the mountains. The city seems decently planned and inhabited by an educated, moderately affluent population appreciative of its high quality of life.

Cost of Living   Rating: 3

The cost of living in Carson City is evaluated as follows:

- **Composite.** ACCRA data for nearby Reno and local information suggest that the composite cost of living in Carson City is about 4 percent above the national average.

- **Housing.** Housing costs modestly exceed the national average. Recently the average price of a typical single-family residence ranged from $200,000 to $275,000. Although relatively few houses are for sale at any particular time in the small Carson City market, the city offers quite a variety of housing types, from apartments and manufactured homes at the low end of the market to large, custom-built single-family homes at high end.

- **Goods and Services.** Health care, groceries, utilities and miscellaneous goods and services are priced only 2 to 5 percent above national norms. Transportation costs, at 15 percent above the national average, are rather high.

- **Taxes.** The state and local tax burden in Carson City is 6 percent of income compared to the U.S. average of 9.7 percent. Nevada does not tax income and property taxes, and sales and excise taxes are well below average.

Transportation   Rating: 2

The city is automobile oriented and, until recently, entirely lacked public transit. Now, Carson City Community Transportation (CCCT) provides dial-a-ride service to the general public. Seniors 60 and older may ride free but are encouraged to make a $2 donation. Carson City has a general aviation airport but the nearest commercial aviation facility is Reno/Tahoe International Airport in Reno. Reno/Tahoe is served by 10 airlines and provides nonstop jet service to numerous destinations including Los Angeles, Las Vegas, Phoenix and San Francisco. Amtrak service eastbound to Chicago and westbound to Oakland is available daily from Reno.

Retail Services — Rating: 3

Most shopping is done at eight shopping centers, two of which—Carson City Mall and Southgate Mall—are small enclosed malls. Gottschalks anchors the Carson City Mall, whereas JCPenney and Mervyn's California department stores anchor the Southgate Mall. A free-standing Kmart is found on Carson Street, the city's major commercial thoroughfare, and a Wal-Mart Supercenter is located along U.S. 395 south of town.

Health Care — Rating: 3

Carson Tahoe Hospital, a public nonprofit community facility, is the principal medical center. With 128 beds and a medical staff of more than 180 physicians representing 25 specialties, the hospital provides good medical care to Carson City and vicinity. Major services offered include 24-hour emergency care, geriatric and psychiatric care, nutrition counseling, CPR and wellness programs, home health and hospice care, rehabilitative and physical therapy, cardiac care and catheterization. A new regional medical center approximately 2.5 times the size of the present building is scheduled to open late in 2005. Additional facilities with a wider range of medical services are only 30 minutes away in Reno.

Community Services — Rating: 3

The city, county and religious and community organizations offer the usual array of services to residents. A senior citizens' center hosts sports, games, social and educational activities and a wellness program. A seniors volunteer program helps retirees find their niche in community service.

Cultural and Educational Activities — Rating: 2

Western Nevada Community College, the Brewery Arts Center and the Community Center are Carson City's principal artistic venues. The college, a two-year public institution enrolling about 5,000 students, offers 50 Associate of Arts degrees and certificate programs and a variety of community service classes. The Brewery Arts Center schedules numerous arts and crafts classes and hosts a variety of visual and performing arts displays and programs. The Nevada Artists Association's gallery resides in the center, and the Procenium Players Community Theatre Company, Carson City Chamber Orchestra, Carson Chamber Singers and the Community Band perform there as well as at the Community College and Community Center. Several museums including the State Railroad Museum, the Stewart Indian Cultural Center, the Capitol Museum and the State Museum (housed in the old United States Mint of silver coinage days) are well worth visiting.

Individuals desiring additional educational and cultural opportunities can find them in Reno, only 30 miles north. The University of Nevada, Reno, in addition to offering a wide range of undergraduate and graduate academic courses and programs, is a center for the arts. Theatrical productions are staged in the university's Church Fine Arts Theatre, whereas concerts are performed in the Nightingale Music Hall.

Recreational opportunities are plentiful in and around Carson City. Five challenging public golf courses are found locally, with four others nearby. Golf is played in all seasons even though winter mornings can be freezing. The city has three major parks and several neighborhood parks with a total area of 600 acres. Park facilities include an aquatic center with indoor and outdoor pools, a community center with a gymnasium and theater, an equestrian center, exercise courses, lighted sports fields and tennis courts and a nature area. The parks department provides recreation programs for all age groups throughout the year. Other recreational facilities in town include casinos, bowling alleys, movie theaters and restaurants. Within an hour's drive are world-class ski resorts at Lake Tahoe, the Lake Tahoe fishery, hiking trails galore in the Sierra Nevada and excellent trout fly-fishing in the Carson and Walker rivers. Virginia City, a lively ghost town, is less than 15 miles away via scenic route SR-341. Its downtown has been lovingly restored to the way it looked in 1870 at the height of the Comstock Lode silver boom. Another 20 miles travel north along Highways 341 and 395 brings you to Reno, the self-styled "Biggest Little City in the World." Although its downtown hotel and casino district has lost some of its luster as a consequence of increased competition from legalized gambling throughout the country, Casino Row on Virginia Street is still a fun place to be 24 hours a day. Alternatives to gambling include visiting the Fleishmann Planetarium, the National Automobile and Nevada Historical Society museums, or one of the city's parks or riverside walks. Shopping is also quite good in Reno, offering a broader selection of goods and services than is available in the smaller Carson City market.

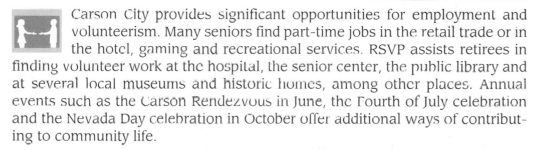 Carson City provides significant opportunities for employment and volunteerism. Many seniors find part-time jobs in the retail trade or in the hotel, gaming and recreational services. RSVP assists retirees in finding volunteer work at the hospital, the senior center, the public library and at several local museums and historic homes, among other places. Annual events such as the Carson Rendezvous in June, the Fourth of July celebration and the Nevada Day celebration in October offer additional ways of contributing to community life.

 Carson City is not as safe as it was a few years ago. Its violent crime rate is now about 20 percent above the national average whereas the property crime rate is 10 percent below the national norm. Among the violent crimes, homicides and robberies are rare but rates of rape and aggravated assault are above average.

Conclusion

 Overall Rating 40 Carson City ranks highly as a place for retirement, especially for those seeking a laid-back lifestyle in an unspoiled, beautiful mountain and high desert environment. Located on a flat plain in the shadow of the Sierra Nevada only 14 miles east of Lake Tahoe and 30 miles south of Reno, Carson City offers residents a high quality of life in a stimulating climate with four clearly defined dry and sunny seasons. Air pollution, tornadoes and hurricanes are unknown locally, although there is a significant long-term threat of earthquakes. The community offers excellent parks and recreation facilities, as well as at least adequate retailing, health care and work and volunteer opportunities. Only in transportation and culture is Carson City, like many small cities, below par. Fortunately, the greater assets of nearby Reno are readily available. Finally, although slightly above the national average, the cost of living in Carson City is distinctly affordable, especially taking into account the excellent quality of life in one of America's most beautiful natural settings.

St. George, Utah

Founded in 1861 by Mormon settlers sent south by Brigham Young, St. George was still only a quiet village of 7,000 residents in 1970. Thereafter, its isolation in the southwestern corner of Utah broken by completion of I-15, St. George has grown at an accelerating pace to become the attractive city of 60,000 people that it is today. Located only 40 miles west of Zion National Park and within a few hours' drive of Bryce Canyon and Grand Canyon National Parks, St. George has long been a gateway to these parks and a winter resort for retirees. Increasingly, attracted by the city's red rock setting, leisure activities, peaceful ambiance and warm sunny climate, visitors are returning in droves to St. George for permanent residence. In so doing they are emulating a choice made by Brigham Young in the 1870s when he bought a second home there in order to spend his winters in comfort.

Landscape	Rating: 5

St. George is located in the Virgin River Valley of southwestern Utah at an elevation of 2,800 feet. The city occupies a small basin near the western edge of the Colorado Plateau, in a gorgeous red rock canyon and mesa landscape. Lying east and in the rain shadow of California's high mountains, the area has an arid to semi-arid natural vegetation complex with desert shrub dominating the lower areas and steppe grasses higher up. Along the river and in the well-irrigated city, though, native riverbank trees like cottonwood and exotic deciduous trees lend a pleasing green contrast to the reds and browns of the surrounding desert. Local water supplies, mostly derived from the diminutive Virgin River, are adequate for now, but continued growth may require strict water conservation measures in the future.

Climate	Rating: 4

St. George enjoys a four-season, high-desert climate characterized by low precipitation and humidity, abundant sunshine and marked seasonal weather changes. The normal annual precipitation of nine inches falls mainly as rain. Three inches of snow falls in an average winter but it seldom remains on the ground for more than a day. On average, the city is sunny about 80 percent of the time, with winter being nearly as sunny as summer. Summer afternoons are hot but the heat is not oppressive as the relative humidity is low. Because of the clear air and moderate elevation, overnight low temperatures in summer average in the mid-60s, providing a pleasant contrast from the daytime heat. In spring and autumn, weather is more variable but most days are warm and nights are cool. Winters are pleasant with generally sunny, cool days and clear, cold nights. The average frost-free season of 217 days allows outdoor gardening from early April through early November.

St. George, Utah

CLIMATE

Month	Average Daily Temperature High	Low	Daily Rel. Humidity Low	Average Monthly Precipitation
	F		%	Inches
January	55	29	33	1.3
February	61	33	27	1.1
March	69	39	23	1.2
April	77	46	17	0.5
May	87	55	14	0.4
June	98	63	12	0.2
July	103	70	16	0.6
August	100	68	18	0.8
September	93	60	18	0.6
October	81	47	20	0.7
November	65	35	28	0.8
December	55	29	33	0.6

Annual Averages

Total Days		Total Inches	
Clear	200	Precipitation	8.8
Partly Cloudy	88	Snowfall	3.0
Cloudy	77		

RATINGS

Category	poor 1	fair 2	good 3	very good 4	excellent 5
Landscape					●
Climate				●	
Quality of Life					●
Cost of Living				●	
Transportation			●		
Retail Services			●		
Health Care			●		
Community Services					●
Cultural Activities		●			
Recreational Activities				●	
Work/Volunteer Activities				●	
Crime				●	

Total Points: 46

[Map of St. George, Utah area showing: Gunlock, Dixie National Forest, Zion National Park, Leeds, Toquerville, Virgin, La Verkin, Hurricane, Virgin River, Shivwits, Paiute Indian Reservation, Ivins, Santa Clara, Washington, St. George Municipal Airport, ST. GEORGE, Bloomington, Virgin River; highways 18, 15, 17, 9, 59; inset map of UTAH with St. George; UTAH / ARIZONA border; scale 0–10 km, 0–10 mi; North arrow]

Quality of Life   Rating: 5

St. George offers residents an excellent quality of life. Noise pollution is minimal except adjacent to I-15. There is no air pollution; the city easily meets federal air quality standards. Owing to its small size and low population density, the community has an uncrowded and nearly rural character. Plenty of parking is available at local malls and along St. George Boulevard downtown; traffic congestion is unknown. Residential neighborhoods, whether in the old central core or in outlying sections like Bloomington and Bloomington Hills, are pleasant in an understated way. Thanks to intensive tree planting and irrigation, long Mormon traditions in this desert environment, older neighborhoods are particularly well shaded, a blessing in the heat of summer. Mormon values are also reflected in the careful physical planning of the city, in its attractive and varied parks and recreation facilities, and in its peaceful ambiance. Its prosperous and well-educated population seems determined to preserve its high quality of life while accommodating inevitable growth.

Cost of Living   Rating: 4

 The cost of living in St. George is evaluated as follows:

- *Composite.* ACCRA data for St. George reveal a composite cost of living 8 percent below the national average.

- *Housing.* According to ACCRA, housing costs are 25 percent below the national average. An average 1,500-square foot home with three bedrooms and two bathrooms sells for around $140,000 in the St. George area. In fact, a good supply of housing of varied sizes, styles and prices is generally available. Construction of new housing appears to be keeping up with demand so prices should remain reasonable for some time.

- *Goods and Services.* Goods and services are priced near national norms. Miscellaneous goods and services, transportation and groceries are all priced between 1 and 5 percent above their national averages, whereas health care and utility costs are 9 and 15 percent below national norms.

- *Taxes.* The state and local tax burden in St. George is 10.8 percent of income compared to the U.S. average of 9.7 percent. State income and sales and excise taxes are above their national averages, but property taxes are well below the national norm.

Transportation   Rating: 3

Like most small cities in the west, St. George depends heavily on the automobile. Nonetheless, SunTran, the city's new bus system, is a welcome addition to the St. George scene. Buses run on three routes that serve major destinations hourly, Monday through Friday. Seniors can buy a monthly pass for $15. St. George Shuttle provides service to Las Vegas International Airport and Salt Lake International Airport. Greyhound offers intercity motor coach service along I-15 to Salt Lake City, Las Vegas and to points beyond these cities. St. George-based SkyWest Airlines connects St. George with major air transport hubs in Salt Lake City, Las Vegas and Los Angeles.

Retail Services   Rating: 3

Downtown, which stretches along St. George Boulevard and Bluff Street, has a number of quite varied specialty shops and restaurants. Red Cliffs Mall, located just off I-15, features about 70 national chain stores and restaurants and is the largest shopping center in southwestern Utah.

It is anchored by Dillard's, JCPenney and Sears department stores and Red Cliffs Cinemas. Zion Factory Stores and Promenade, also just off I-15, boasts major national chain stores and restaurants. Costco, Home Depot, Lowes, Target and two Wal-Mart Superstores have opened in St. George in recent years.

Health Care   Rating: 3

 Dixie Regional Medical Center (DRMC)—part of Intermountain Health Care (IHC), a private nonprofit hospital system based in Salt Lake City—is the principal medical complex in southwestern Utah. Like the other 24 IHC hospitals, it provides quality care to those with medical needs regardless of their ability to pay. In autumn of 2003, DRMC opened a new hospital with 132 patient rooms, a routine diagnosis center, a 31-bed emergency department and 8 operating suites. After renovation, the old hospital will offer women's care, behavioral medicine, cancer care, same-day surgery, imaging services and a diabetic clinic.

Community Services   Rating: 5

 City, county, religious and civic organizations offer a rich assortment of services. The St. George Leisure Services Department provides dozens of activities for residents and visitors. Senior citizen centers are operated throughout Washington County. They provide a great variety of programs including Meals on Wheels, shuttle service, free health screening, games such as pool, bingo and horseshoes, ballroom dancing and educational classes. More than 60 civic organizations give almost unlimited opportunities for community and charitable involvement.

Cultural and Educational Activities   Rating: 2

 Dixie College, a four-year college enrolling 7,000 students, is St. George's premier educational and cultural center. The college offers liberal arts and humanities, sciences, health sciences, elementary education and business and technology programs, among others. Its Institute for Continued Learning is run by and for retirees and its popular Elderhostel Program offers one-week noncredit classes featuring special events, field trips and other group activities for those 60 and older. The college's musical and theatrical programs are popular with all age groups. Dixie Center on campus is the principal venue for the Dixie College Celebrity Concert Series and the Southwest Symphony Orchestra. The summer concert series at the Tanner Amphitheater attracts residents and visitors alike, as do locally produced plays.

Recreational Activities   Rating: 4

Recreational activities to suit many tastes are available locally. Relative to population, St. George probably offers more golf than all but a few Sunbelt locations. Of the area's 12 golf courses, 4 are city owned and operated by St. George Leisure Services, which also runs the 19 city parks. Greens fees at St. George Public golf courses are reasonable, especially for residents. Leisure Services also provides activities such as arts and crafts, photography and framing, computing, cooking, bridge and dance. Free day hikes and historical lectures are sponsored on Saturdays throughout the year. Each year a marathon race and an arts festival are hosted. Other recreational facilities in town include bowling alleys, movie theaters and restaurants of varied culinary styles.

Some of America's greatest natural wonders are within a few hours' drive. The incomparable Zion National Park lies only 42 miles east of town. Cedar Breaks National Monument, a smaller version of Bryce Canyon, is 75 miles distant, while Bryce Canyon National Park itself is only 126 miles away. The North Rim of Grand Canyon National Park, which is higher, cooler and much less overrun with tourists than the South Rim, is only 140 miles from St. George. There is excellent downhill skiing at Brian Head, 80 miles northeast. Add to these national treasures two ghost towns, Snow Canyon State Park and Quail Creek Reservoir—all of which are within 20 miles of town—and it is obvious that there is no better base in the country than St. George from which to set off on day trips to sightseeing and hiking paradise.

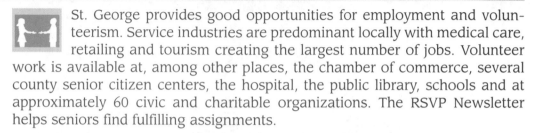

Work and Volunteer Activities — Rating: 4

St. George provides good opportunities for employment and volunteerism. Service industries are predominant locally with medical care, retailing and tourism creating the largest number of jobs. Volunteer work is available at, among other places, the chamber of commerce, several county senior citizen centers, the hospital, the public library, schools and at approximately 60 civic and charitable organizations. The RSVP Newsletter helps seniors find fulfilling assignments.

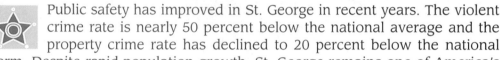

Crime Rates and Public Safety — Rating: 4

Public safety has improved in St. George in recent years. The violent crime rate is nearly 50 percent below the national average and the property crime rate has declined to 20 percent below the national norm. Despite rapid population growth, St. George remains one of America's safest retirement towns.

Conclusion

Overall Rating 46 — St. George is one of the best retirement towns in the Desert Southwest. Because of its location, moderate elevation and geology, the city experiences a warm, sunny four-season climate and is spared serious environmental hazards. The air is clean, urban stress is largely lacking and the quality of life is excellent. Devotees of the great outdoors will undoubtedly enjoy St. George's beautiful setting amidst the mountains, canyons and mesas of southwestern Utah and appreciate the fact that some of America's greatest national parks are nearby. With a cost of living significantly below the national average and good to very good ratings in transportation, retail services, health care, public safety, recreation and work and volunteer activities, St. George has great appeal. An absence of major cultural attractions is a minor weakness and one that can be easily remedied by a two-hour drive to Las Vegas attractions. All things considered, St. George measures up very well for retirement and merits careful consideration.

Reno, Nevada

Reno, Nevada is also worth considering for retirement. Situated on a high desert plain just east of the Sierra Nevada, Reno enjoys a spectacular setting and an invigorating, four-season semi-arid climate similar to that of nearby Carson City. Self-styled "The Biggest Little City in the World," Reno has long been known as the gambling and entertainment capital of northern Nevada and as a gateway to the Lake Tahoe region. With a population of 180,000 in Reno and 350,000 in Washoe County, the metropolitan area is large enough to offer many of the services and amenities sought by retirees.

Only above-average crime rates and occasional air pollution episodes that cause the city to exceed the federal air quality standard for particulates detract from Reno's desirability for retirement. The city offers exceptional recreation, very good transportation and health care and a good quality of life. Golf, tennis, horseback riding and hiking are popular summer pursuits; cross-country and downhill skiing and ice skating are popular in winter. Nearby Lake Tahoe and the Sierra Nevada offer excellent camping, hiking, boating and fishing in summer and some of America's best downhill skiing in winter. Reno has good public transit and excellent intercity air, motor coach and rail passenger service. The city's four hospitals provide very good medical care and retail and community services are more than adequate. Reno is alive with the performing and visual arts. It has its own ballet, opera and philharmonic orchestra and numerous theaters and galleries. The University of Nevada, Reno (UNVR) is a major educational, cultural and recreational asset. Reno residents love to watch UNVR Wolfpack basketball and football. Last, but not least, the city has low unemployment and provides many opportunities for paid and volunteer work.

11 The California Retirement Region

Climate:
Desert: Palm Springs–Palm Desert
Mediterranean: San Luis Obispo, Chico

Place Description	Overall Rating	Page
San Luis Obispo, California	**45**	**256**
Just far enough inland to escape coastal fog and far enough from Los Angeles and San Francisco to avoid metropolitan pressures, San Luis Obispo is a near-perfect little college town offering a fairly quiet yet amenity-rich lifestyle.		
Chico, California	**39**	**261**
Chico is a world apart from the sprawling metropolitan areas of central and southern California. For the most part it has escaped the serious social and environmental problems that limit their appeal as retirement places.		
Palm Springs–Palm Desert, California	**not rated**	**267**
Lying 120 miles east of Los Angeles at the base of 10,804-foot Mount San Jacinto, these low desert cities and neighboring Coachella Valley communities have enjoyed an economic boom in recent years that has restored their distinction as a world-class resort and retirement area.		

The California Retirement Region occupies the greater part of America's most physically appealing and culturally diverse state. Long a favorite region for retiree relocation thanks to its mild, sunny climate; lovely coastal, mountain and desert landscapes; abundant services; and cultural and recreational opportunities, the Golden State has lost some of its luster as a retirement haven in recent decades. Rampant population growth and urban sprawl have stressed the natural environment, pushed public services to the limit and overwhelmed the urban transportation infrastructure. Even though California has the toughest smog controls in the nation, smog persists as a health and aesthetic problem not only in Los Angeles and the San Francisco Bay Area but also throughout much of the state. Meanwhile, traffic congestion has reached epic proportions and the cost of housing has risen so high in Los Angeles and the Bay Area that home ownership is out of the question for people of moderate means.

As a result of these problems, few California cities now provide a high quality of life and an amenity-rich lifestyle at affordable prices. That said, San Luis Obispo and Chico—two delightful cities along the central California coast and in the Sacramento Valley, respectively—remain attractive for retirement. Both offer a gentle pace of life, sunny weather, clean air and amenities and services typical of small college towns. Also worth considering is Palm Springs–Palm Desert, a resort and retirement area in southern California. None of these places is inexpensive but each offers better value than the large coastal metropolitan areas of the state.

San Luis Obispo, California

Blessed by a year-round water supply, fertile soil and a mild, sunny climate, the beautiful valley of San Luis Obispo seemed an ideal site for settlement when Father Junipero Serra established Mission San Luis Obispo de Tolosa on the banks of San Luis Creek in 1772. Even so, the settlement surrounding the mission grew rather slowly until the isolation of the community was broken by the arrival of the Southern Pacific Railroad in 1894. Subsequent growth, owing in part to the city's location halfway between and more than 200 miles from San Francisco and Los Angeles, has proceeded at a modest pace. This has allowed San Luis Obispo to retain a nostalgic early-California ambiance, unique in a state characterized by frenzied growth. More than 20 percent of the local labor force is employed by government, with others working mostly in retail, tourist and miscellaneous services. California Polytechnic State University, San Luis Obispo (Cal Poly), with more than 17,000 students and 2,700 faculty and staff, is a vital economic and cultural force making the community younger and livelier than most cities with populations of around 45,000. Along with Mission San Luis Obispo and Mission Plaza, adjacent San Luis Creek, the charming downtown shopping district and the city's attractive and varied residential neighborhoods, the university makes San Luis Obispo a special place well worth considering for upscale retirement.

Landscape	Rating: 5

 The town occupies a splendid site at an elevation of 315 feet in a gently rolling lowland between a string of extinct volcanic foothills and the Santa Lucia Mountains. The Pacific Coast is only five to ten miles away at Port San Luis and Morro Bay. Oak parkland, a mix of drought-resistant grasses and trees, is the dominant natural vegetation but a greater variety of local and exotic trees, shrubs and flowering plants is grown in the city with the help of irrigation. The hill and valley setting of the town and the Cal Poly campus, buttressed by the towering Santa Lucia Range on the east, is strikingly beautiful whether colored in winter's green or summer's collage of green, gold and brown.

Climate	Rating: 5

San Luis Obispo enjoys a cool-summer variant of the Mediterranean climate. Proximity to the cool waters of the Pacific Ocean and relatively low latitude and elevation make for a very mild climate with few storms or drastic changes in weather. There are really only two seasons here. A mild, fairly wet winter is balanced by a warm, dry summer. More than 90 percent of annual precipitation falls from November through April. Because it is several miles inland, San Luis Obispo is somewhat warmer in summer and sunnier in all seasons than places right on the coast. The town is sunny more than 70 percent of the time, with only modest variations from month to month. The frost-free period averages 320 days and frosts are rarely severe enough to damage gardens or citrus.

Quality of Life	Rating: 5

 The quality of life is excellent in San Luis Obispo. The air is clean and significant noise pollution is limited to a narrow stretch along the U.S. 101 freeway. The small size and low population density of the city

San Luis Obispo, California

CLIMATE

Month	Average Daily Temperature High	Average Daily Temperature Low	Daily Rel. Humidity Low	Average Monthly Precipitation
	F		%	Inches
January	65	42	60	5.3
February	66	44	60	5.4
March	67	45	63	4.5
April	71	45	60	1.3
May	73	48	60	0.5
June	78	51	60	0.1
July	80	53	62	0.0
August	82	53	57	0.1
September	82	53	56	0.4
October	79	50	58	1.0
November	72	46	59	2.2
December	66	42	59	3.6

Annual Averages

Total Days		Total Inches	
Clear	176	Precipitation	24.4
Partly Cloudy	110	Snowfall	0.0
Cloudy	80		

RATINGS

Category	poor 1	fair 2	good 3	very good 4	excellent 5
Landscape					●
Climate					●
Quality of Life					●
Cost of Living	●				
Transportation			●		
Retail Services				●	
Health Care			●		
Community Services				●	
Cultural Activities				●	
Recreational Activities				●	
Work/Volunteer Activities			●		
Crime				●	

Total Points: 45

translate into little crowding or traffic congestion. Parking is adequate downtown, at suburban malls and on campus. Heavy industries and neglected neighborhoods are unknown and the urban landscape is well planned and maintained, with parks and playgrounds well distributed across the city.

Municipal authorities and downtown business interests have carefully preserved and enhanced the charming and historic central business district, which in many ways is the heart and soul of San Luis Obispo. Residents are typically well educated and friendly and their town exhibits the peaceful ambiance of a former and almost forgotten California era.

Cost of Living — Rating: 1

 The cost of living in San Luis Obispo is evaluated as follows:

- *Composite.* ACCRA data are unavailable for San Luis Obispo; therefore, cost of living estimates are based on my research in the local area. I estimate that the composite cost of living is about 20 percent above the national average.

- *Housing.* Higher-than-average family incomes and growth controls cause housing to be relatively expensive. Housing in San Luis Obispo is priced at least 50 percent above the national average. The local chamber of commerce estimates a median price of $350,000 for a single-family home. Field research indicates that homes priced between $300,000 and $400,000 are modest by national standards. Condominiums offer better value if present cost rather than potential appreciation is the buyer's primary concern.

- *Goods and Services.* Groceries, utilities, transportation and health care are all priced between 10 and 15 percent above national norms. Miscellaneous goods and services costs are 5 percent above the national average.

- *Taxes.* The state and local tax burden is 9.4 percent of income compared to the U.S. average of 9.7 percent. Sales and excise taxes are a little above average whereas state income taxes and property taxes are slightly below average.

Transportation — Rating: 3

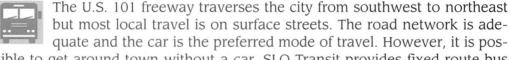 The U.S. 101 freeway traverses the city from southwest to northeast but most local travel is on surface streets. The road network is adequate and the car is the preferred mode of travel. However, it is possible to get around town without a car. SLO Transit provides fixed route bus service throughout the city and the Regional Transit Association links central coast communities from San Simeon to Santa Maria. The city trolley provides free service around a downtown loop. Ride-On Transportation offers door-to-door travel seven days a week on a reservation basis. Intercity travel is possible by air, bus and rail. San Luis Obispo Airport, three miles south, provides nonstop commuter service to Los Angeles, San Francisco and Phoenix. Greyhound offers frequent scheduled service north to San Francisco and south to Los Angeles. Amtrak provides one train northbound and two trains southbound daily, plus several additional southbound trains via connecting motor coach service to Santa Barbara.

Retail Services — Rating: 4

Madonna Plaza and adjacent SLO Promenade, located along U.S. 101 on the south side of town, have been remodeled recently and constitute the area's largest shopping complex. Madonna Plaza now has Mervyn's and Sears department stores, a Ralph's supermarket and Best Buy store, specialty shops and services. SLO Promenade features a Gottshalks department store, several large stores including Bed Bath & Beyond, Cost Plus World Market, a Staples Superstore and numerous smaller specialty shops and restaurants. A Home Depot is located on Los Osos Valley Road. The quaint downtown business district features scores of unique shops, restaurants and theaters, many located in historic buildings. Downtown Center, between Higuera and Marsh Streets, is a relatively new complex with national chain specialty retailers, a wide variety of small shops and restaurants and a seven-screen cinema. Additional stores and restaurants are scheduled to open downtown in 2005.

Health Care   Rating: 3

 For a city of its size, San Luis Obispo offers unusually good health care. Two rather small acute-care hospitals, Sierra Vista Regional Medical Center and French Hospital Medical Center, with a total of about 300 beds and 150 physicians on staff, meet the everyday medical needs of local residents. A greater variety of sophisticated medical care is available 200 miles away in Los Angeles and San Francisco.

Community Services   Rating: 4

 Very good public services, including some of special interest to seniors are available. The San Luis Obispo Senior Center, located downtown in Mitchell Park, is open five days a week. Popular activities there include an exercise class, bridge and other card games, arts and crafts, reading in the small library and socializing. Each month the center hosts a luncheon and a free legal advice session with a local lawyer. Meeting rooms are available for special events including meetings of the local chapter of AARP.

Cultural and Educational Activities   Rating: 4

Cal Poly is a major community asset in terms of its course and program offerings and as the site of the spectacular new Performing Arts Center of San Luis Obispo. Cal Poly and Cuesta Community College field courses of interest to seniors. Fees for California residents are low at the university and nominal at the college. The 1,350-seat Harman Concert Hall at the Performing Arts Center is reputed to be acoustically outstanding. It is the principal venue for major artistic performances including classical and pop concerts by the San Luis Obispo Symphony and modern dance, theater, opera and ballet by resident and visiting companies. The 500-seat Cal Poly Theater also schedules musical, dance and theatrical events. Performances by the university's Chamber Orchestra, Choir, and Jazz and Wind Orchestras and recitals by faculty and students are frequent occurrences throughout the academic year. The San Luis Obispo Mozart Festival is held annually in July and August at several venues on campus and around town.

Resident ensembles perform professional ballet, opera and theater, as well as amateur theater. The Civic Ballet of San Luis Obispo is known especially for its December staging of *The Nutcracker*. The Pacific Repertory Opera stages two operas per year plus several light operas. Center Point Theater Group emphasizes contemporary works and San Luis Obispo Little Theater performs a variety of productions from classical to contemporary all year long.

The San Luis Obispo Art Center, located downtown, is the focus of the visual arts scene. The Center presents a diverse mix of traditional and contemporary arts exhibits throughout the year and offers classes in basic artistic techniques and art appreciation, as well as hands-on experiences in contemporary and multicultural art forms.

Recreational Activities   Rating: 4

 San Luis Obispo's near-perfect climate favors year-round outdoor recreation. Sixteen city parks, playgrounds and recreation centers scattered around town collectively provide a good selection of facilities. Sinsheimer Sports Complex, with its swim center, tennis courts and sports fields, is especially well equipped. Additional tennis courts and pools open to the public are found at Cuesta College and Cal Poly. Laguna Lake Park and Open Space, toward the western edge of town, is ideal for water sports like canoeing, windsurfing and fishing. Hiking is also popular there. The considerably larger Lopez, Nacimiento and Santa Margarita Lakes, known for their bass, catfish and bluegill fishing, are within 45 miles of the city. At Lopez and Nacimiento Lakes one can also camp, picnic, boat, water-ski and swim. Boating and ocean fishing are available at nearby Port San Luis and Morro Bay but Central California beaches and waters are a little chilly for sunbathing and swimming.

Golf is played in comfort year-round at six 18-hole courses and two 9-hole courses open to the public in and around San Luis Obispo. Bicycle routes lead to coastal communities and hiking trails lead to vantage points offering stunning views of the Pacific Ocean and valley and mountain terrain. Quiet country roads provide access to some of America's most beautiful agricultural landscapes, which produce everything from organic fruits and vegetables to milk, grapes and fine wines. Wine tasting at the many excellent and hospitable wineries near San Luis Obispo has become popular in recent years.

Cal Poly individuals and teams compete in many varsity sports. The university's NCAA Division 1 football and women's basketball teams are local favorites. College students, city residents and visitors support a good selection of movie theaters and restaurants. Clustered downtown are multiplex movie theaters and an eclectic mix of eateries serving everything from American sandwiches to exotic Asian dishes. Several restaurants offer outdoor dining on terraces overlooking San Luis Creek. The San Luis Obispo Farmers Market, located on a blocked-off section of Higuera Street, downtown, is a special highlight every Thursday evening. Now a revered local tradition, the market offers everything from fresh produce to barbecued ribs and plenty of live entertainment and community fellowship.

Work and Volunteer Activities   Rating: 3

 Growth controls that resulted in part from drought-caused water rationing in the early 1990s and a shortage of building lots in the city have slowed economic growth. The population is only a little higher now than in 1990. There is little unemployment but there is acute competition among college students, seniors and the general public for jobs in the strongly service-oriented economy. Many opportunities exist, though, for volunteers in senior and community organizations, schools, hospitals, libraries and museums. Active chapters of RSVP and the United Way help place volunteers where they are most needed.

San Luis Obispo continues to be one of America's safer small college towns. The violent crime rate in the city is 30 percent below the national average, whereas the property crime rate is now 20 percent above the national norm. Homicides are almost unknown locally and all parts of town from the Cal Poly campus to the busy downtown have a safe and secure feel about them.

Conclusion

Overall Rating 45
Just far enough inland to escape coastal fog and far enough from Los Angeles and San Francisco to avoid metropolitan pressures, San Luis Obispo is a near-perfect little college town offering a fairly quiet yet amenity-rich lifestyle. Its lovely physical setting between California's spectacular central coast and the Santa Lucia Mountains, its mild sunny climate and its excellent quality of life—absent the smog and traffic characteristic of many California cities—are perhaps its greatest assets. But San Luis Obispo has other strengths as well. Thanks to Cal Poly, civic musical, theatrical and arts associations, and numerous parks and recreation facilities located in town, along the nearby coast and in the Santa Lucia Mountains, the community boasts a very good selection of cultural, educational and recreational activities and community services. Despite a daily influx of students, workers and visitors, the city is relatively free of serious crime. Transportation, retail services, health care and opportunities for volunteer work are quite good for a small town. Except for a moderately high cost of living, there is little to criticize about life in San Luis Obispo. Those already living there obviously think it is worth the price; perhaps you will too.

Chico, California

Chico was founded in 1860 by John Bidwell, who had made a fortune in the California Gold Rush. Attracted to the area by cheap land, a warm, sunny climate and a year-round water supply from streams flowing into the Sacramento Valley from the mountains to the east, Bidwell became Chico's largest landowner and its principal booster. In 1887, the fortunes of the small, agriculturally based town took a significant turn when a state teachers college was established in downtown Chico on land donated by Bidwell. In 1905, Annie Bidwell, wife of the town's founder, donated an additional 2,300 acres of the Bidwell ranch to the city of Chico in order to establish Bidwell Park. The park has since grown to 3,600 acres, making it the third largest municipal park in the United States. Meanwhile, the original teachers college has evolved into California State University, Chico (Chico State) with around 16,000 students and 900 faculty members. The university makes Chico younger and livelier than most cities of 70,000 people (there are about 105,000 in the urban area and 215,000 in Butte County). The park, the university, the traditional downtown with its shops, restaurants and delightful City Plaza, and the city's varied and attractive residential neighborhoods define Chico as a unique place well worth considering for quality retirement.

California **261**

Chico, California

CLIMATE				
Month	Average Daily Temperature High / Low	Daily Rel. Humidity Low	Average Monthly Precipitation	
	F	**%**	**Inches**	
January	54 / 35	59	5.2	
February	60 / 39	51	4.5	
March	65 / 42	44	4.3	
April	72 / 45	35	1.6	
May	80 / 51	28	0.9	
June	88 / 57	23	0.5	
July	93 / 61	19	0.1	
August	92 / 59	20	0.2	
September	88 / 55	22	0.6	
October	79 / 47	32	1.3	
November	63 / 40	50	3.5	
December	54 / 35	61	3.6	

Annual Averages

Total Days		Total Inches	
Clear	180	Precipitation	26.2
Partly Cloudy	75	Snowfall	0.2
Cloudy	110		

RATINGS	poor 1	fair 2	good 3	very good 4	excellent 5
Landscape				●	
Climate				●	
Quality of Life					●
Cost of Living			●		
Transportation			●		
Retail Services			●		
Health Care			●		
Community Services			●		
Cultural Activities			●		
Recreational Activities			●		
Work/Volunteer Activities		●			
Crime			●		

Total Points: 39

Vina
99
Stirling City
Forest Ranch
70
10 km
10 mi
CALIFORNIA
32
CHICO MUNICIPAL AIRPORT
Magalia
Plumas National Forest
Nord
Hamilton City
32
Paradise
Concow
CHICO
North ↑
Chico
CALIFORNIA
Lake Oroville
Durham
99
James
70

Landscape	**Rating: 4**

 Chico is located toward the eastern edge of the Sacramento Valley in northern California. The oak-studded foothills of the Sierra Nevada and Cascade Range lie immediately east and northeast and provide a scenic backdrop to the city. Located far inland from the cool, foggy California coast, Chico lies in a hot Mediterranean environment typical of interior, northern California. However, its riparian site along Chico Creek only a few miles east of the Sacramento River allows growth of luxuriant natural vegetation including large valley oaks. Some of these survive in town and especially in Bidwell Park but many exotic trees and shrubs have been planted throughout the city. Shade provided by the leafy canopy is much appreciated on scorching summer afternoons.

Climate — Rating: 4

 Chico experiences the hot-summer variant of the Mediterranean climate with four distinct seasons. Because it is so far inland, Chico is much warmer in summer and somewhat cooler in winter than coastal California locations at the same latitude. Summer days are hot, sunny and extremely dry. Less than an inch of rain falls during each of the five months from May through September. Fortunately, marked cooling typically drops overnight temperatures into the 50s or low 60s in mid-summer. Winter weather is mild and moderately rainy with many cloudy or foggy days. Spring and autumn are delightful intermediate seasons with typically warm days, cool nights and a good deal of sunshine. Chico is sunny more than 90 percent of the time in summer, 70 percent in spring and autumn, and a little less than 50 percent in winter.

Quality of Life — Rating: 5

 The quality of life is excellent in Chico. The EPA recently designated Chico as a "basic non-attainment area" for air quality, which means that the city is minimally out of compliance with current air quality standards. Although the air is relatively clean much of the year, Chico experiences light smog on many summer days. Traffic noise is mostly confined to the busiest commercial streets. Downtown streets and those adjacent to the university are busy at rush hour but congestion levels are modest compared to those in larger cities. The road infrastructure appears satisfactory for present demand and parking is generally adequate, although it can be tight at Chico State. The lovely, tree-shaded grounds and collegiate architecture of the university campus enhance the downtown. Chico's varied neighborhoods are typically well treed and nicely maintained. Several small neighborhood parks add to the general ambiance and Bidwell Park, a jewel among American urban parks, is an enormous asset to the entire community.

Cost of Living — Rating: 3

 The cost of living in Chico is evaluated as follows:

- *Composite.* ACCRA data are unavailable for Chico. Data from various published and unpublished sources indicate that the composite cost of living in Chico is about 5 percent above the national average.

- *Housing.* Chico housing is priced at or a little above the national average. A good supply of single-family residences and condominiums is usually available. The average price of a single-family residence is around $200,000 and condominiums are considerably cheaper. Many small houses cost little more than $150,000 but these are modest places by national standards.

- *Goods and Services.* Groceries, health care and utilities are all priced about 10 percent above their national norms. Miscellaneous goods and services costs are about 5 percent above average whereas health care costs approximate the national average.

- *Taxes.* The state and local tax burden in Chico is 9.4 percent of income compared to the U.S. average of 9.7 percent. Sales and excise taxes are a little above average whereas state income taxes and property taxes are slightly below average.

Transportation — Rating: 3

The CA-99 freeway traverses the eastern fringe of Chico but most travel within the city is on surface streets that are generally adequate for present traffic flows. The car is the preferred mode of travel but many students bike around the campus community. Chico Area Transit System (CATS) provides minimal transit service on 10 routes serving the Chico urban area during daytime hours, Monday through Saturday. Chico Clipper Service furnishes dial-a-ride transportation for the elderly and disabled, seven days a week. Intercity travel is possible by air, bus and rail. Chico Airport offers limited commuter air service to hub airports at San Francisco and Sacramento. Greyhound provides daily service to San Francisco and Sacramento, among other California locations, and Butte County Transit connects communities within the county. Amtrak's Coast Starlight train provides daily service north to Portland and Seattle and south to Oakland and Los Angeles.

Retail Services — Rating: 3

Chico Mall, located just south of downtown and east of CA-99, is the largest regional mall in Butte County. It is anchored by Gottschalk's, JCPenney and Sears department stores and features about 80 specialty stores, restaurants and services, mostly branches of regional or national chains. Scattered about Chico in smaller shopping centers and along commercial streets are other retailers including Costco, Home Depot, Kmart, Mervyn's and Wal-Mart. Chico's charming downtown is home to a wonderful traditional hardware store, numerous quaint galleries, cafes and specialty shops and is an interesting place to walk about. Farmers' markets boasting an excellent selection of local produce are open on Wednesday mornings, June through October at North Valley Plaza Mall and Saturday mornings, year-round, downtown.

Health Care — Rating: 3

For its size, Chico offers good medical care. Two general hospitals serve Chico proper; two others are located in other Butte County communities. Countywide there are 700 hospital beds and about 300 physicians. Enloe Memorial Medical Center and Chico Memorial Hospital are the principal hospitals in town. Enloe Memorial is designated a Level II Trauma Center for a six-county area. Its specialties include cancer and cardiac care, home and hospice care, neuro-trauma care, occupational therapy and orthopedic services. Chico Community Hospital is noted for its emergency and acute care facilities and specialized respiratory center.

Passages Adult Resource Center, a program of the California State University, Chico Research Foundation, serves as a source of information on community resources, government benefits and volunteer opportunities and as an advocate for seniors' health care and consumer rights. Persons age 50 and older may participate in Chico Area Recreational Park District (CARD) Senior Programs. The CARD Recreation Center, located just east of downtown adjacent to Bidwell Park, provides health screenings, tax assistance and recreational activities including pool, card games, dances and yoga and fitness programs.

Cultural and Educational Activities   **Rating: 3**

California State University, Chico is a major educational and cultural asset. Its beautiful campus, which occupies 119 acres next to downtown Chico, is a lively activity center. The university's diverse offerings include 128 majors and 51 graduate and professional programs. Known for its commitment to the liberal arts and sciences, the university also fields strong programs in agriculture, business administration, computer science, nursing and teacher training. Classes of particular interest to seniors are provided by the continuing education program at the university and by Butte Community College, located 12 miles south of town. Fees for California residents are low at the university and college.

Numerous cultural events are held in the two theaters and the recital hall of Chico State's Performing Arts Center and at several other venues in town. Live performances of classical music, dance, jazz and musical theater ensembles, including those by the Chico City Light Opera and Chico Symphony Orchestra, are well supported. Downtown Chico's City Plaza is a perfect place for lunch and relaxation. Free concerts are performed at its gazebo every Friday evening, May through September. Amateur theater is produced by Chico Children's Theater and Chico Community Theater. Popular music and dance programs are provided by the Chico Community Band, the Chico International Folkdancers and the Bidwell Generals Chorus.

The visual arts are showcased at the Janet Turner Print Gallery, the Third Floor Gallery and the University Art Gallery at Chico State. The works of local area artists can be seen at several commercial studios and galleries, downtown. The Chico Art Center, an art school and gallery operated by local artists, is especially noteworthy.

Recreational Activities   **Rating: 3**

Chico's warm, sunny climate, excellent municipal parks and the town's proximity to the mountains all favor year-round outdoor recreation. Bidwell Park, which occupies more than five square miles and extends from the valley floor into the foothills of the Sierra Nevada, is the crown jewel of the Chico park system. Each of its three major sections has its own unique character. Lower Park is a vehicle-free area—its roads and paths, winding among oak groves, are reserved for walkers, runners, cyclists and roller skaters. Children's playgrounds, picnic areas and natural swimming areas are the principal attractions. Middle Park is open to motorized traffic and provides a perfect venue for outdoor cultural events such as Shakespeare in the Park and the Chico World Music Festival. Middle Park also features ball fields, picnic areas, the World of Trees Walk (which is accessible to the physically challenged)

and the Chico Creek Nature Center. Upper Park remains largely undeveloped, with much of its hill and canyon terrain approaching wilderness status. A mecca for mountain bikers, equestrians and hikers, Upper Park has 35 trails, 25 of which are open to cyclists. Swimming holes along Chico Creek offer some of the best swimming in northern California.

Golf is played all year at four 18-hole and two 9-hole courses in and around Chico. Two of the 18-hole courses are private; the rest are open to the public. The warm, sunny climate and bicycle-friendly transportation planning encourage bicycle use. Bike lanes on city streets, quiet country roads leading to scenic orchard and ranch landscapes and the trails of Bidwell Park provide safe and interesting places to cycle. Farther afield but within a 100-mile radius are several scenic wonders and recreation sites in the Sierra Nevada and Cascade Range. Plumas National Forest is directly east of Chico; Lassen National Forest and Lassen Volcanic National Park lie to the northeast. Plumas National Forest comprises more than one million acres of forest and wilderness including the 93-mile long Middle Fork of the Feather River, a federally designated wild and scenic river. Spectacular canyons, rapids and waterfalls are scenic highlights here. Camping, hiking, fishing, and canoeing and tubing in designated areas are popular activities. Lassen National Forest's 1.4 million acres of rugged terrain includes several lakes. Summer visitors enjoy camping, hiking, fishing, sailing, swimming and water-skiing; cross-country skiing is popular in winter. Lassen Volcanic National Park is a 106,000-acre mini-Yellowstone. The park is a bizarre wonderland of volcanic features including Lassen Peak (10,457 feet), lava flows, boiling springs and mudpots. Camping, hiking, fishing, nature walks and sightseeing are popular activities in summer while cross-country skiing is a winter highlight. Water sports of all kinds are enjoyed at Lake Oroville State Recreation Area, 30 miles south of Chico. One can camp, bike, hike and picnic here but most people come for boating, fishing, swimming, water-skiing and windsurfing.

Perhaps because outdoor recreation is so compelling in and near Chico, indoor recreational assets are modest. For its size, Chico is underendowed with movie theaters, bowling alleys and good restaurants. Steak and seafood and traditional American cuisine are local favorites.

Work and Volunteer Activities   Rating: 2

 Like many other interior California cities, Chico has not shared in the economic boom of coastal metropolitan areas. Unemployment remains stubbornly high at about seven percent of the labor force. Competition for jobs in the service sector among college students, seniors and the general population is acute and wages are correspondingly low. Volunteer opportunities, though, are plentiful in senior and community organizations, children's services, hospitals, libraries, parks and recreation, schools and visitor services.

Crime Rates and Public Safety   Rating: 3

 Crime rates are declining in Chico and the overall crime rate in the city now approximates the national average. The property crime rate is slightly above the national norm but violent crime is well below average. Crime rates for the city are skewed upward by the large student population because most students do not count as residents of Chico yet they can be victims and perpetrators of crime. Crime rates for Butte County, which has an older demographic profile than the city of Chico, are lower than the rates for Chico and the nation.

Overall Rating 39 Chico is a world apart from the sprawling metropolitan areas of central and southern California. For the most part it has escaped the serious social and environmental problems that limit their appeal as retirement places. In many ways, Chico is a throwback to a more innocent age when small, neighborly communities, built at a human scale, offered a pleasant, laid-back and affordable lifestyle. Chico's ratings for cost of living, transportation, retail services, health care, community services, culture, recreation and crime are all good. Only in opportunities for paid work is the community below average. Its greatest strengths are the beautiful landscapes of the town and adjacent areas, the Mediterranean climate with four distinct yet fairly mild, sunny seasons and an excellent quality of life. Chico neighborhoods, the Chico State campus, Bidwell Park and the nearby Sierra Nevada and Cascade Range all offer a unique, tree-shaded ambiance that is especially appreciated on hot, summer afternoons. There is little traffic noise or congestion, the earthquake risk is relatively low and housing is affordable. Few California retirement places offer so much at such modest cost.

Palm Springs–Palm Desert, California

Palm Springs–Palm Desert is also worth considering for retirement. Lying 120 miles east of Los Angeles at the base of 10,804-foot Mount San Jacinto, these low desert cities and neighboring Coachella Valley communities have enjoyed an economic boom in recent years that has restored their distinction as a world-class resort and retirement area. Only high living costs, above-average crime rates, scorching summer heat and serious air pollution (largely from Los Angeles) keep these cities off the list of Top 50 Retirement Places.

Palm Springs and Palm Desert, each with populations nearing 45,000, are anchor cities of a rapidly growing urban complex with a population exceeding 250,000 residents. When visitors are added, the area houses more than 400,000 people at the height of the winter tourist season. This affluent population supports a wide range of services and amenities that make the Desert Cities desirable. Medical care is excellent; Eisenhower Medical Center is nationally known for the variety and quality of its services. Recreation and culture abound in this desert playground. Both cities boast several well-equipped parks and recreation centers. Civic Center Park in Palm Desert, with its volleyball, basketball and tennis courts and baseball fields, playgrounds, skating area, amphitheater, date grove and picnicking pavilions, is especially notable. There are more golf courses here than anywhere else in the world. One can play golf or tennis on a winter morning, then take the Palm Springs Aerial Tram to the 8,500-foot level of Mount San Jacinto and cross-country ski in the afternoon. The upper part of the mountain offers limitless hiking, picnicking and sightseeing in summer amidst spectacular mountain scenery. Musical and theatrical events take place at the McCallum Theater for the Performing Arts and shopping is good in downtown Palm Springs, along El Paseo, an upscale shopping and entertainment street in Palm Desert, and at Westfield Shoppingtown Palm Desert. Palm Springs–Palm Desert also boasts good public transit and intercity transportation and lively senior centers. It is among California's best and most popular retirement places.

12 The Pacific Northwest Retirement Region

Climate:
Mediterranean: Medford–Ashland, Victoria
Semi-arid (steppe): Bend, Vernon, Kelowna
Marine: Eugene, Portland, Olympia,
Bellingham

The Pacific Northwest Retirement Region is a Garden of Eden jealously guarded by environmentalists bent on preserving its nearly pristine environment. In the 1970s, Oregon Governor Tom McCall went so far as to urge tourists to enjoy their visits to his state and then "please go home." Similar sentiments persist to this day among many residents of the region. Nonetheless, attracted by gorgeous coastal, valley and mountain scenery, clean air and water, mild weather and livable cities boasting plentiful services and outstanding cultural and recreational amenities, Californians and residents of other states and provinces continue to migrate to the Pacific Northwest to live, work and retire in style.

The best retirement towns are found in a 500-mile corridor along I-5 and in southwestern British Columbia. Just inside Oregon you encounter Medford–Ashland amidst the orchards and ranches of the beautiful Rogue River Valley. An additional 150 miles brings you to Oregon's Willamette Valley, a fertile agricultural area bounded by the Cascade Range on the east and the Coast Range on the west and site of our recommended cities of Eugene and Portland. Each of these cities has a unique style and is attractive for retirement. About 125 miles after crossing the Columbia River you enter Olympia, the lovely little Washington State capital at the southern end of Puget Sound. Traveling another 150 miles north, skirting the shores of Puget Sound and within view of the Cascade and Olympic Mountains, you reach Bellingham, a charming seaside college town.

Continuing northward or westward a few miles by road or ferry brings you to beautiful British Columbia, Canada's westernmost province and a favorite retirement destination. Victoria, the lovely provincial capital and Canada's climatically mildest major city, lies 50 miles (80 kilometers) southwest of Bellingham across Georgia Strait. A trip of 150 miles (250 kilometers) in the opposite direction takes you to the Okanagan Valley. This 120-mile (200-kilometer) long valley, sheltered from Pacific storms by the Coast Mountains and Cascade Range, boasts several attractive small, affordable cities set among scenic lakes, orchards and vineyards. Vernon is our top choice here but Kelowna is also worth considering. Another Pacific Northwest locale worth considering is Bend, Oregon, an all-season resort and retirement town on the sunny eastern slope of the Cascade Range. Californians are flocking there.

Medford–Ashland, Oregon

The Rogue River Valley of southern Oregon, site of present-day Medford and Ashland, was the preserve of the Rogue Indian tribe until the middle of the nineteenth century. The discovery of gold in 1852 brought in the first wave of white settlers, followed soon by farmers attracted by the valley's productive soils and mild climate. Today a new wave of migrants, especially retirees from California, is flooding into the Medford–Ashland area in search of the good life. Medford, with a population nearing 70,000, is the business, commercial and professional center of Jackson County. Just 12 miles south is Ashland, a quaint community of 20,000 that is home to the Southern Oregon University and the Oregon Shakespeare Festival, as well as the site of numerous excellent shops and restaurants. Medford–Ashland is sheltered by distance from the hustle and bustle of city life. Eugene, the nearest major city, is 170 miles north via I-5 and Portland is 115 miles farther.

Medford-Ashland, Oregon

CLIMATE

Month	Average Daily Temperature High (F)	Average Daily Temperature Low (F)	Daily Rel. Humidity Low (%)	Average Monthly Precipitation (Inches)
January	47	31	71	2.5
February	54	33	57	2.1
March	58	36	50	1.9
April	64	39	45	1.3
May	72	44	39	1.2
June	81	50	33	0.7
July	90	55	26	0.3
August	90	55	26	0.5
September	84	48	29	0.8
October	70	40	43	1.3
November	53	35	68	2.9
December	45	31	76	2.9

Annual Averages

Total Days		Total Inches	
Clear	117	Precipitation	18.4
Partly Cloudy	79	Snowfall	7.4
Cloudy	169		

RATINGS

Category	poor 1	fair 2	good 3	very good 4	excellent 5
Landscape					●
Climate				●	
Quality of Life					●
Cost of Living		●			
Transportation			●		
Retail Services			●		
Health Care				●	
Community Services				●	
Cultural Activities					●
Recreational Activities					●
Work/Volunteer Activities				●	
Crime			●		

Total Points: 47

Landscape   **Rating: 5**

Medford–Ashland is located just north of the California state line in southern Oregon's beautiful Rogue River Valley. Fruit and vegetable farms and the oak-studded grasslands of large livestock ranches surround both cities and several neighboring small towns. Medford occupies a gently rolling surface with gorgeous views of nearby hills and mountains. Ashland extends from the valley floor into the foothills of the Siskiyou Mountains from which one gets a bird's-eye view of the valley's park-like landscape, a scene reminiscent of oak parkland areas in California.

Climate — Rating: 4

 Sheltered by the surrounding Coast, Cascade and Siskiyou Mountains, the Rogue River Valley is unique in Oregon in having a Mediterranean climate similar to that found in some inland areas of northern California. Winters are cloudy and mild with many showery days; summers are sunny, hot and dry. Valley locations average only 18 inches of precipitation annually but mountain slopes a few thousand feet higher receive considerably more. About 75 percent of annual precipitation falls in the rainy season between October and March and only 4.8 inches falls during the dry season between April and September. Snow accumulation totals an average of 7.4 inches annually and seldom lasts on the ground for more than a few days at a time. Winter days are cloudy and mild, spring and autumn weather is quite variable from day to day, and summer weather is relatively steady with warm to hot days, cool nights, low relative humidity and ample sunshine. Medford–Ashland is sunny about 60 percent of the time, varying seasonally from about 35 percent in winter to more than 80 percent in summer. The frost-free period averages about 160 days with outdoor gardening possible from early May through mid-October.

Quality of Life — Rating: 5

 Medford and Ashland provide a very good to excellent quality of life. There is little serious noise pollution except along I-5, which skirts Ashland but bisects Medford. All federal air quality standards are currently met and smog testing of automobiles to keep the air clean is mandatory. The small population of the urban area (70,000 in Medford, 20,000 in Ashland and 190,000 in Jackson County) makes for minimal traffic congestion and no difficulties parking. Noxious industries are lacking and most residential neighborhoods, old and new, feature appealing but unpretentious frame dwellings. In Ashland, particularly, hundreds of beautifully maintained Victorian homes occupy choice sites near downtown and Southern Oregon University. Both cities are graced with numerous aesthetically appealing, well-equipped parks and woodland landscapes thanks to careful tree planting and frequent irrigation.

Unfortunately, Medford's historic downtown area, although marginally viable, has lost much of its retailing function to nearby Rogue Valley Mall. In contrast, downtown Ashland is a thriving and architecturally charming business district. The enormously successful Oregon Shakespeare Festival, which attracts thousands of visitors into central Ashland, deserves much credit for downtown's vitality.

The cost of living in Medford–Ashland is evaluated as follows:

- *Composite.* ACCRA data are unavailable for Medford–Ashland so statistics for Eugene, the closest economically comparable Oregon city, are utilized here. On that basis, the composite cost of living in Medford–Ashland is about 10 percent above the national average.

- *Housing.* Housing costs are perhaps 20 percent above the national average. According to local realtors, prices for comparable dwellings are significantly higher in Ashland than in Medford. In 2004, an average house with three bedrooms and two baths sold for $290,000 in Ashland and $160,000 in Medford. Despite the moderately high prices, area housing appears to offer good value considering its style and good quality.

- *Goods and Services.* ACCRA data suggest that transportation, groceries and health care costs are 7, 9 and 20 percent above their national averages, respectively. Utilities and miscellaneous goods and services are priced near their national norms.

- *Taxes.* The state and local tax burden in Medford–Ashland is 8.7 percent of income compared to the U.S. average of 9.7 percent. There is no sales tax in Oregon but the state's steeply graduated income tax rates largely compensate for this advantage. Property taxes approximate the national average, having declined sharply in recent years owing to property tax reform by the state.

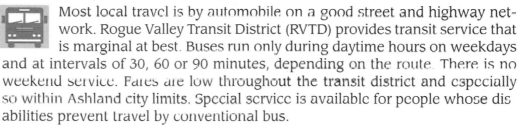 Most local travel is by automobile on a good street and highway network. Rogue Valley Transit District (RVTD) provides transit service that is marginal at best. Buses run only during daytime hours on weekdays and at intervals of 30, 60 or 90 minutes, depending on the route. There is no weekend service. Fares are low throughout the transit district and especially so within Ashland city limits. Special service is available for people whose disabilities prevent travel by conventional bus.

Intercity travel is possible by several modes. Greyhound provides motor coach service along I-5. Daily Amtrak service north to Portland and Seattle and south to Los Angeles is available in Klamath Falls, 80 miles east. Rogue Valley International Airport in Medford provides nonstop jet service to Portland, San Francisco and Seattle. Locals complain, though, that fares are high because of limited competition.

The downtown areas of Ashland and Medford provide an interesting contrast. Downtown Ashland's quaint galleries, shops and restaurants are prospering as a result of their proximity to Southern Oregon University and the Oregon Shakespeare Festival, a big tourist draw. Downtown Medford, although significantly revitalized in recent years, is more ordinary having lost much of the retail market to nearby Rogue River Mall. Anchored by JCPenney, Mervyn's, and Meier & Frank, the mall includes more than 120 specialty stores, services and restaurants. Medford also has standalone Wal-Mart and Sears stores.

Medford and Ashland have three hospitals between them with a total capacity of exceeding 500 beds and more than 270 resident physicians. Rogue Valley Medical Center in Medford, with approximately 305 beds and 150 doctors on staff, is the largest hospital in southern Oregon. It boasts cardiac and cancer treatment centers as well as the usual array of diagnostic and treatment services found in a major regional medical referral facility. Providence Medford Medical Center, a 168-bed hospital, is known particularly for its heart care and rehabilitation and a low-cost health-screening program for seniors. Ashland Community Hospital, with 37 beds, is affiliated with Rogue Valley Medical Center in Medford.

Community Services   **Rating: 4**

 Public and community services are very good in Ashland and Medford. Five senior centers and several additional senior clubs and community centers offer varied programs of interest to seniors. Medford Senior Center, the largest in the Rogue Valley Region, provides classes in crafts, Spanish, writing and painting as well as daily card games and pool. The center's travel club offers day trips to Oregon attractions and long-distance bus or air travel to destinations such as Reno, Branson and Puerto Vallarta. Various support services including daily luncheons, tax help, and monthly hearing and blood pressure checks are popular with Medford seniors. Similar social and recreational programs are available at senior and community centers in Ashland and in smaller towns including Central Point, Eagle Point and Rogue River.

Cultural and Educational Activities   **Rating: 5**

 Medford–Ashland's cultural and educational assets far exceed those normally found in small metropolitan areas. The nationally respected Oregon Shakespeare Festival, whose season runs from late February through October, stages eleven plays annually in its three Ashland theaters. Its theatrical calendar includes Shakespearean and other classic and contemporary plays. From mid-June through August, internationally known musicians present open-air concerts at Jacksonville's Peter Britt Festival. Jacksonville, a National Historic Landmark Town famous for a gold rush era downtown and historic homes, is only 5 miles west of Medford and 19 miles northwest of Ashland. The renovated, historic Craterian Ginger Rogers Theater in downtown Medford is the area's third major performing arts venue. It is home to the Rogue Valley Chorale and Rogue Opera and the site for performances of touring professional dance, operatic, orchestral and theatrical companies.

Southern Oregon University has much to offer seniors and the general public. Its Music Recital Hall is the Ashland home of the Rogue Valley Symphony, which also performs in Medford. University programs especially tailored to seniors include a Lectures and Lunches program, Southern Oregon Learning in Retirement (SOLIR) and Senior Ventures. The Lectures and Lunches program combines lunches and lectures on the Oregon Shakespeare Festival. SOLIR actively involves seniors in developing courses and selecting teachers. For an annual fee of $100 seniors can participate in a great variety of noncredit courses. Senior Ventures provides educational travel opportunities in the United States and abroad for reasonable fees.

The lovely landscape and mild climate of southern Oregon favor all kinds of outdoor recreation. Golfers of all skill levels can find suitable courses on which to play throughout the year. Four 18-hole and six 9-hole layouts are found locally with several others within 30 miles of Medford. Ashland, Medford and Jackson County all boast excellent park systems. Medford alone has more than 30 municipal parks ranging from small neighborhood picnic areas and playgrounds to large community parks featuring tennis courts, outdoor swimming pools and hiking trails. Lithia Park, which occupies 100 acres in downtown Ashland, is a magnificent resource for residents and visitors. Its walking trails, wooded areas, gardens, and sports and playground facilities are used heavily. Every Monday evening, June through August, the State Ballet of Oregon provides free performances at the outdoor amphitheater in the park. Among the more popular county facilities is Emigrant Lake Park, five miles southeast of Ashland. Regular activities there include swimming, boating, canoeing, fishing, camping, hiking and bird watching. A little farther afield in the Cascade, Siskiyou and Coast Mountains are several wonderful natural areas for exploration and recreation. The incomparable Crater Lake National Park, 80 miles north of Medford–Ashland, offers a unique volcanic landscape, summer camping, hiking and picnicking, and cross-country skiing much of the year. One can ski downhill between late November and April at Mount Ashland, 20 miles south of Ashland, and whitewater raft the Rogue River, bicycle the Bear Creek Greenway and take wine tours to several excellent area wineries much of the year. Indoor sports facilities in Medford include the YMCA swimming pool and racquetball courts, two bowling establishments, and roller skating and ice skating rinks.

For a small metropolitan area, Medford–Ashland has a good selection of movie theaters and many excellent restaurants. Menus available range from standard American and Italian fare to French, Japanese, Mexican, Russian and Middle Eastern cuisines.

Although the Jackson County unemployment rate remains stubbornly above the national average, the economy in Medford–Ashford has boomed in recent years. Part-time employment opportunities are plentiful in retailing and in other service industries. All kinds of volunteer work can be found, especially in tourist-oriented activities like the Shakespearean Festival, visitor centers, and local, state and federal parks. Oregon Shakespeare Festival alone has 850 volunteers in Ashland. Senior centers, hospitals, public libraries, the Salvation Army and the Red Cross also depend heavily on volunteers.

The metropolitan area (Jackson County) has low to moderate crime rates. Considering the massive influx of visitors this is not bad. The overall property crime rate approximates the national average whereas the violent crime rate is about 40 percent below the national norm. Crime rates are somewhat higher in Medford than in smaller communities like Ashland and Jacksonville.

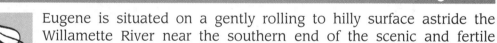

Overall Rating 47 Medford–Ashland is one of America's best places for an unhurried yet stimulating retirement. Its lovely oak-studded hill and valley landscape and mild Mediterranean climate make the area appealing. The quality of life is excellent. Air and water are clean and noise pollution is minimal except along I-5. Residential areas and parks are attractive and downtown Ashland is delightful. Cultural and educational opportunities are excellent in Medford, Ashland and the surrounding area, while health care, community services and work and volunteer activities are unusually good. Only the above-average cost of living, average property crime rate and somewhat limited transportation choices detract from the area's overall excellence for retirement. That said, Medford–Ashland ranks as a wonderful place to live if one is seeking small-town ambiance along with educational and cultural amenities typical of much larger cities.

Eugene, Oregon

Long primarily a place for wood processing and a market town for Willamette Valley farmers, Eugene has blossomed in recent decades into one of Oregon's principal educational, commercial and manufacturing centers and an attractive residential community. Home of the University of Oregon and Lane Community College, Eugene offers an unusually rich mix of services to residents, as well as easy access to the outstanding urban amenities of Portland and to the varied recreational assets of the Oregon shoreline and Coast and Cascade Mountains. With a population nearing 150,000 in Eugene proper and 340,000 in Lane County, Eugene retains much that is good in America's best small towns. It is a progressive, tolerant and welcoming community, supportive of the arts, education and environmental protection and determined to keep Eugene relaxed and livable despite inevitable pressures of growth.

Landscape   **Rating: 4**

Eugene is situated on a gently rolling to hilly surface astride the Willamette River near the southern end of the scenic and fertile Willamette Valley. The city site is attractive with high wooded hills like Spencer Butte overlooking the downtown area. Residential neighborhoods extend from flat terrain near the river up into the hills to the south where some home sites offer splendid views of the city, valley and distant mountains. The Oregon Coast Range lies 40 miles west with Pacific beaches 20 miles farther; the crest of the Cascade Range is 60 miles east. Thanks to its sheltered inland valley location, Eugene receives only two-thirds as much rain as coastal towns west of the Coast Range. Even so, Eugene is wet enough to support a luxuriant forest of coniferous and deciduous trees including Douglas fir, oak and maple. The city is nicely landscaped although not as heavily treed as one might expect. Eugenians prefer a mix of wooded and open terrain so that they can enjoy the sun whenever it shines.

Climate   **Rating: 3**

Eugene's climate is generally similar to but rainier than Portland's. Mild, cloudy, wet winters and warm, sunny, relatively dry summers are characteristic. Eugene receives an annual average of 51 inches of

Eugene, Oregon

CLIMATE				
Month	Average Daily Temperature		Daily Rel. Humidity Low	Average Monthly Precipitation
	High	Low		
	F		%	Inches
January	47	33	80	7.7
February	51	35	73	6.4
March	56	37	64	5.8
April	61	39	58	3.7
May	67	43	54	2.7
June	73	47	49	1.5
July	82	51	38	0.6
August	82	51	39	1.0
September	77	47	43	1.5
October	65	41	62	3.4
November	52	37	79	8.4
December	46	33	84	8.3

Annual Averages

Total Days		Total Inches	
Clear	75	Precipitation	50.9
Partly Cloudy	82	Snowfall	6.5
Cloudy	209		

RATINGS					
Category	poor	fair	good	very good	excellent
	1	2	3	4	5
Landscape				●	
Climate			●		
Quality of Life				●	
Cost of Living		●			
Transportation					●
Retail Services				●	
Health Care				●	
Community Services					●
Cultural Activities					●
Recreational Activities					●
Work/Volunteer Activities			●		
Crime		●			

Total Points: 46

precipitation, with nearly 80 percent of the total falling during the rainy season between October and March. During the drier half of the year between April and September, Eugene receives only 11 inches of precipitation on average. Annual snowfall totals less than seven inches and seldom lasts more than a few days on the ground. Winters are mild for the latitude. Spring and autumn weather is quite variable with cool to warm days followed by cool nights. Summers are typically delightful with warm, sunny days and cool nights. The frost-free season averages 190 days and skies are generally cloudy or partly cloudy, except in summer. On average, Eugene is sunny about 50 percent of the time, varying seasonally from about 25 percent in winter to 70 percent in summer.

Quality of Life   Rating: 4

 Eugene provides a very good quality of life. There is minor noise pollution alongside the I-5 and I-105 freeways and several major streets but the air is generally clean. Most industries—except for several wood-processing mills—are innocuous and traffic usually flows well, although it is worsening year by year. Parking is plentiful and the city's popular bike routes and public transit reduce demand for additional automotive infrastructure. Most neighborhoods, whether modest or affluent and central or suburban, are nicely treed, landscaped and well maintained. Eugene has an excellent inventory of parks and playgrounds and the University of Oregon adds to the ambiance of the city. Downtown has been renewed in the last 20 years and boasts the Hult Center, the focus of community cultural life, and a few interesting stores and restaurants. Unfortunately, major department stores, discount outlets and most national chain stores have fled from central Eugene to nearby regional malls.

Cost of Living   Rating: 2

 The cost of living in Eugene is evaluated as follows:

- *Composite.* According to ACCRA, the composite cost of living in Eugene is 9 percent above the national average.

- *Housing.* Housing costs are 18 percent above the national average yet offer good value. Eugene housing is plentiful, varied in style and well built. Attractive 1,600 square-foot homes with three bedrooms and two bathrooms are typically priced between $200,000 and $250,000 according to local sources. Larger suburban homes are generally priced higher; condominiums and small central city homes are generally priced somewhat lower.

- *Goods and Services.* ACCRA data suggest that groceries and transportation costs are about 8 percent above their national averages. Utilities and miscellaneous goods and services are priced near national norms, whereas health care is priced about 20 percent above average.

- *Taxes.* The state and local tax burden in Eugene is 8.7 percent of income compared to the U.S. average of 9.7 percent. There is no sales tax in Oregon but the state's steeply graduated income tax rates largely compensate for this advantage. Property taxes approximate the national average, having declined in recent years due to property tax reform by the state.

Transportation   Rating: 5

Most intracity travel is by car but buses and bicycles provide alternatives for many residents. Lane Transit District (LTD) furnishes excellent transportation throughout Eugene and neighboring Springfield and to several destinations outside the urban area. LTD's 60-route system is focused on the full-service downtown Eugene station, with routes radiating to smaller transit stations strategically located in or near major destinations in the metropolitan area. Schools, colleges, hospitals, parks, shopping malls and downtown, among other locations, are all easily reached via LTD. Fares are reasonable; seniors pay $17.50 for a monthly pass. Bicycling is also a rational transportation choice for many people owing to Eugene's excellent network of bicycle paths and lanes. More than 25 miles of off-street bike trails are available, some along the scenic Willamette River, as well as more than 300 miles of striped bike lanes on city streets.

Amtrak, Greyhound and several airlines provide intercity transportation. Amtrak runs four daily trains north to Portland and Seattle and one train south to Los Angeles. Greyhound service to these locations and other points is possible from the downtown Greyhound bus station. Eugene Airport, eight miles northwest of the city center, provides nonstop jet service to Denver, Portland and San Francisco and commuter service to several other western cities. Portland International Airport, 125 miles north via I-5, furnishes nonstop jet service to more than 45 destinations.

Retail Services — Rating: 4

Although downtown Eugene retains a colorful collection of shops, restaurants and galleries, major retailing is now concentrated in two enclosed regional malls. Valley River Center is located adjacent to the I-105 freeway just a mile and a half north of downtown. Anchored by Bon–Macy's, JCPenney and Meier & Frank, Valley River Center also includes about 140 specialty shops, services, restaurants and a cinema complex. Gateway Mall is located next to I-5 about three miles northeast of the civic center. This regional mall, anchored by Emporium, Sears and Target stores, features more than 80 specialty stores, 11 eateries and 12 movie screens.

Health Care — Rating: 4

Two major hospitals in Eugene and neighboring Springfield provide comprehensive medical care. Sacred Heart Medical Center, a 432-bed facility in Eugene, is the regional center for several specialties including the Oregon Heart and Vascular Institute Center and the Oregon Rehabilitation Center. McKenzie–Willamette Hospital in Springfield is a 106-bed acute care, surgical and outpatient facility providing a wide range of medical services. Area hospitals have state-of-the-art technology such as magnetic resonance imaging, CT scanning, nuclear medicine and ultrasound. With nearly 500 physicians in all, Eugene and Springfield have an excellent supply of general–family practitioners as well as medical and surgical specialists.

Community Services — Rating: 5

Eugene provides unusually varied and comprehensive public services. Both medical centers offer outreach programs and the city operates two outstanding senior centers. The Campbell Senior Center, located in a lovely riverfront park just north of downtown Eugene, provides an extensive list of excursions, outdoor activities, classes, drop-in activities and special services for seniors. Vans and buses take seniors to destinations such as coastal Oregon towns, Crater Lake, Salem museums and to jump-off points for rural hiking, bicycling and canoeing and rafting trips. Classes at the center are taught primarily by volunteers and fees are reasonable. Classes in several arts and crafts, computers, fitness and languages are offered regularly. Drop-in activities include card and table games, dancing, pool and woodworking. Special services include outreach programs to improve seniors' access to community resources, health and foot-care clinics and Wednesday luncheons. Broadly similar activities and programs are available at the Trudy Kauffman Senior Center, a few blocks west of the civic center.

Cultural and Educational Activities   Rating: 5

 Eugene is excellently endowed culturally and educationally, especially for a small city. Downtown's architecturally stunning Hult Center for the Performing Arts is Eugene's cultural focus. Its 500-seat Soreng Theatre is ideal for small-scale opera, dance, chamber music and film, while the magnificent 2,500-seat Silva Concert Hall hosts large-scale musical and theatrical productions. Major companies calling Hult Center home include the Eugene Symphony Orchestra, Eugene Ballet Company, Eugene Opera, Oregon Bach Festival, Oregon Mozart Players, Eugene Festival of Musical Theatre and Actor's Cabaret/Mainstage Theatre. In addition to the offerings of the Hult Center's excellent resident companies, the Center presents six or seven multi-disciplinary performing arts series annually. Ranging from early music to jazz, from modern dance to musical theater, from international music and dance to one-person portrayals of historical figures, Hult Center programs offer something for everyone. In summer, Eugene's cultural scene expands into the great outdoors. Following the Fourth of July performance by the Eugene Symphonic Band, the Washburn Park Classical Series provides 10 free Sunday evening light classics concerts from early July through mid-September. Free mid-week concerts offering varied musical fare are performed at other Eugene parks and recreation centers in July.

The University of Oregon and Lane Community College are strong assets for seniors as well as the community at large. The university has an excellent Elderhostel program each summer as well as continuing education programs for seniors 65 and older. Lane Community College, recognized since 1985 as one of the top community colleges in the United States, helps local residents develop talents, hobbies and leisure pursuits to better enjoy all that Oregon has to offer. Seniors may audit courses at the University of Oregon and at Lane Community College for nominal fees.

Recreational Activities   Rating: 5

 Eugene and its surrounding areas offer an abundance of recreational amenities. The city's 100-unit park and recreation system, covering more than 2,000 acres, is among the best in the country. Whatever your preference, be it viewing the roses, rhododendrons and azaleas of Owen Rose Garden or Hendricks Park; walking, jogging or biking the trails of Spencer Butte Park or those in the series of parks fronting the Willamette River; or playing tennis or golf at numerous locations, Eugene city parks have the facilities you need. Within a 15-mile radius of Eugene there are more than 10 golf courses and several rivers and reservoirs afford ample opportunities for rafting, canoeing and fishing. Fern Ridge Reservoir, just west of town, is especially popular for sailing. Several ski resorts in the Cascades including Mount Bachelor and the incomparable Crater Lake National Park and endless opportunities for sightseeing and fishing along the Oregon coast are also within easy driving distance.

For a small city, Eugene is well endowed with good restaurants and movie theaters. One can enjoy NCAA Division 1 basketball and football games played by the University of Oregon Ducks and travel to Portland to enjoy NBA basketball, minor league baseball and other recreational attractions.

Work and Volunteer Activities   Rating: 3

The Eugene and Lane County economy remains heavily dependent on service industries. Unemployment has risen to more than six percent, and although part-time jobs are available, college students compete aggressively for many of them. Many organizations provide volunteer opportunities through Eugene senior centers. Examples include hospitals, schools, the library, Hult Center, Meals on Wheels and Eugene Senior Services.

Crime Rates and Public Safety   Rating: 2

Although the city's overall property crime rate is 80 percent above the average for U.S. metropolitan areas, with larceny–theft being a particular problem, the violent crime rate is 35 percent below the national norm. And despite concerns expressed locally about a tiny, militant anarchist group, described as urban terrorists by the mayor, Eugene felt safe and comfortable as we walked its streets.

Conclusion

Overall Rating 46 Eugene is a particularly attractive college town. Its physical site on hilly terrain astride Oregon's Willamette River is beautiful and its mild, marine climate is quite agreeable. The local quality of life is very good even though there is some noise alongside busy streets and freeways.

Environmental quality is a high priority here as manifested in the excellent city parks, pleasant residential areas and excellent air quality. Transportation, community services and cultural and recreational activities are excellent, and retail services and health care are very good. Only the city's moderate cost of living, moderate crime statistics, and limited openings for paid part-time work detract from its excellence for retirement. Even so, Eugene ranks as one of America's best places for a relaxed yet sophisticated retirement.

Portland, Oregon

Thirty years ago no one would have forecast that Portland would be a wonderful place to live at the beginning of the twenty-first century. In the late 1960s the city was beset by several devastating trends that were most pronounced downtown and in the central city. Historic structures and housing were being lost to parking lots and new freeways, retail activity was dwindling and the Willamette River waterfront was blighted by industrial decline. Capital, jobs and families were fleeing to the suburbs, traffic congestion was developing and regional air quality was deteriorating. Today, thanks to three decades of careful planning and the cooperative efforts of state and local government, businesses and citizens, downtown Portland has been reborn as an attractive, dynamic, exciting and pedestrian-friendly center of the metropolitan area. In town and in outlying areas, development is now better planned, the environment better protected and pollution controlled than in previous decades. As a result, Portland, with a population of 550,000 within its city limits and around two million in the metropolitan area, is one of the few cities of its size that can be recommended for retirement.

Portland, Oregon

CLIMATE				
	Average Daily Temperature		Daily Rel. Humidity	Average Monthly Precipitation
Month	High	Low	Low	
	F		%	Inches
January	46	34	75	5.1
February	50	36	67	4.2
March	56	39	60	3.7
April	61	42	55	2.6
May	67	48	53	2.4
June	73	53	49	1.6
July	79	57	45	0.7
August	80	57	45	0.9
September	75	53	48	1.7
October	63	45	62	2.9
November	52	40	74	5.6
December	45	35	78	5.7

Annual Averages

Total Days		Total Inches	
Clear	69	Precipitation	37.1
Partly Cloudy	74	Snowfall	6.5
Cloudy	222		

RATINGS					
Category	poor	fair	good	very good	excellent
	1	2	3	4	5
Landscape					●
Climate				●	
Quality of Life					●
Cost of Living		●			
Transportation					●
Retail Services					●
Health Care					●
Community Services					●
Cultural Activities					●
Recreational Activities					●
Work/Volunteer Activities			●		
Crime	●				

Total Points: 51

Landscape   Rating: 5

Portland possesses an enviable site astride the Willamette River and within sight of Mount Hood and the Cascade Range. Much of the terrain west of the river is hilly and forested, with lower areas and gentler slopes occupied by upscale neighborhoods scattered among several of Portland's excellent parks. Some of these, most notably Washington Park, reach down from the hills almost into downtown. It is an easy walk or a short drive from the city center to Washington Park's zoo, gardens or picnic areas. East of the river the land is fairly flat with several high hills adding interest to the landscape. Oak and Douglas fir are the principal trees native to Portland, but many exotic broad-leafed tree varieties including magnolia are widely planted in the city and suburbs. Residential gardens often include rhododendrons and other flowering shrubs, flowers and lush green lawns.

Climate   Rating: 4

 Portland has a marine climate characterized by mild, cloudy, wet winters and warm, sunny and relatively dry summers. Portland is a little warmer in summer than Seattle as a result of its Willamette Valley location and its 60-mile distance from the cold waters of the Pacific Ocean. Portland averages 37 inches of annual precipitation with fully 27 inches falling during the rainy season between October and March. The six-month period between April and September gets 10 inches and is much sunnier. Nearly all precipitation occurs as rain; snow totals an average of less than seven inches annually and seldom persists more than a day or two on the ground because winter days are typically mild. Spring and autumn weather is variable with cool to warm days and cool nights. Summer is nearly ideal with warm days, cool nights, low relative humidity and abundant sunshine. The frost-free period is long for the latitude, averaging about 270 days annually. Cloudy to partly cloudy skies are more typical than clear skies except in summer. On average, Portland is sunny about 48 percent of the time, varying seasonally from about 26 percent in winter to 66 percent in summer.

Quality of Life   Rating: 5

 Portland offers residents an excellent quality of life, an unusually high rating for a medium-sized American city. There is some noise pollution adjacent to the freeways and near the airport but the city meets all federal air quality standards. Noxious industries are lacking and, although area freeways are busy at rush hour, traffic generally flows freely. Metropolitan Portland's excellent public transit system helps by diverting some travel from the private automobile. Parking is plentiful in suburban areas but is tight downtown because Portland utilizes traffic calming measures including low speed limits, wide sidewalks and reductions in street capacity and parking to favor walking and transit use. There are some rather uninspiring 1960s era neighborhoods in the eastern suburbs but much of the metropolitan area is attractive, well treed, well planned and dotted with community and regional parks. Residents are strongly environmentalist and devoted to Portland. They are now enjoying the fruits of downtown renewal, improved public transit, the transformation of the west bank of the Willamette from a freeway corridor into Tom McCall Waterfront Park and the cleaning up of the river, which is now fit for boating, fishing and water-skiing.

The cost of living in Portland is evaluated as follows:

- **Composite.** ACCRA data for Portland reveal a composite cost of living about 14 percent above the national average.

- **Housing.** According to ACCRA, housing costs are 20 percent above the national average. As elsewhere, housing costs vary drastically across the city and metropolitan region. Prime properties near Washington and Mountain Parks sell for upwards of $600,000 while nicely renovated older homes in excellent Portland neighborhoods east of the Willamette River cost upwards of $300,000. Suburban communities like Beaverton, Hillsboro and Gresham offer good values with many attractive homes selling between $200,000 and $250,000.

- **Goods and Services.** ACCRA data show health care to be priced about 30 percent above the national average, whereas transportation, groceries and miscellaneous goods and services are all priced around 12 percent above their national norms. Utilities are priced about 5 percent above average.

- **Taxes.** The state and local tax burden in Portland is 8.7 percent of income compared to the U.S. average of 9.7 percent. There is no state sales tax in Oregon but the state's steeply graduated income tax rates largely compensate for this advantage. Property taxes approximate the national average, having declined sharply in recent years owing to property tax reform by the state.

Portland has an excellent street and freeway network and most intracity travel is by car. That said, the bus and light rail services provided by Tri-Met, the metropolitan area public transit agency, provide alternative transportation to a broad cross section of residents, not just the transit dependent. Tri-Met's 160-route bus system, focused on the downtown transit mall and strategically located transit centers in Portland and suburban communities, links residential areas with schools, colleges, hospitals, malls and shopping centers, parks, the airport and the Amtrak station, among other destinations. Tri-Met's original MAX (Metropolitan Area Express) light rail line links the eastern and western suburbs of Gresham and Hillsboro via downtown Portland. Once intended specifically to reduce auto use and improve air quality, MAX has become so popular with riders that new MAX lines to Portland Airport and north Portland have recently come into service. Three additional north-south rail lines are now in the planning stage. Within a few years they will provide service to south central Portland and eastern and western suburbs.

Tri-Met is unusually user friendly for a big-city transit agency. All buses and trains are equipped with racks for bicycles and bike lockers are available at many transit centers, MAX stations and park-and-ride lots. All rides are free downtown and fares are reasonable elsewhere. Seniors pay only $17 for a monthly pass or $175 for an annual pass.

Amtrak, Greyhound and numerous airlines provide intercity transportation. Amtrak runs four trains a day north to Seattle and south to Eugene; one southbound train daily continues on to Los Angeles. Greyhound service to these locations and other points is possible from Greyhound's downtown terminal, adjacent to the Amtrak station. Portland International Airport, nine miles north-east of the city center, provides nonstop jet service to more than 45 locations.

Retail Services — Rating: 5

Downtown Portland has been revitalized in recent decades and is once again the physical, cultural and economic heart of the city. Pioneer Place, an upscale enclosed shopping center in the heart of downtown, is the major retailing complex. It hosts 50 specialty shops, upwards of 15 informal eateries and a Saks Fifth Avenue. Nordstrom and Meier & Frank stores are only two short blocks away, and dozens of specialty shops and restaurants line the streets of the downtown core.

Three large enclosed regional malls dominate retail trade outside downtown. Lloyd Center, located east of the Willamette River in Portland, is anchored by Marshalls, Meier & Frank, Nordstrom and Sears department stores. It also features more than 150 specialty shops and services, dozens of casual restaurants, a cinema complex and an ice skating rink. Clackamas Town Center, in suburban Clackamas, is anchored by JCPenney, Meier & Frank, Nordstrom and Sears department stores. It also boasts more than 150 specialty stores, a 22-unit food court, a cinema complex and an ice skating rink. JCPenney, Meier & Frank, Mervyn's, Nordstrom and Sears department stores anchor Washington Square, in suburban Tigard, which also features more than 120 specialty stores, 11 casual eating places and a movie theater complex.

Health Care — Rating: 5

Portland provides excellent state-of-the-art medical care. Site of the Oregon Health Sciences University, with its medical school and teaching hospitals, Portland has a total of 20 acute care hospitals that collectively offer virtually every medical specialty.

Community Services — Rating: 5

Portland offers excellent public services. The metropolitan area's more than 30 senior/community centers are of particular interest to retirees. These offer an enormous variety of recreational facilities and programs including tai chi and yoga; instruction in computers, arts and crafts, dancing, piano and golf; swimming, hiking and fitness programs; and local and regional field excursions. Some centers also provide outreach services, information and referrals, health screenings, and group and/or home-delivered meals.

Cultural and Educational Activities — Rating: 5

Portland is very strong culturally and educationally. The magnificent Portland Center for the Performing Arts in downtown's cultural district includes the Portland Civic Auditorium, Arlene Schnitzer Concert Hall and the New Theatre Building containing the Newmark and Dolores Winningstad Theatres. Performances by Portland's excellent Oregon Symphony, the Portland Opera and Oregon Ballet Theatre and local theater groups, jazz, baroque and chamber ensembles help make downtown a lively place. Several touring artist series featuring some of the world's best musical, dance, theatrical and comedic performances and ensembles round out the Performing Arts calendar of events. In summer, Portland performing arts offerings spill out of downtown into city parks. Free concerts are scheduled a minimum of three evenings a week at various locations all through July and August.

Portland State University, located downtown, is the city's largest university. Its more than 20,000 students can choose from a wide range of courses and programs at undergraduate and graduate levels. Ten other colleges and universities in the metropolitan area, including prestigious Reed College, offer undergraduate and/or graduate programs; the multi-campus Portland Community College offers a large number of academic and applied courses in Associate of Arts and continuing education programs at bargain prices. Also of general cultural and educational interest are downtown's Oregon History Center and Portland Art Museum; the Oregon Museum of Science and Industry is just across the Willamette River.

Recreational Activities   Rating: 5

 The Portland area is truly a paradise for outdoor recreation enthusiasts. Lush forests, sparkling waterways, awesome mountains and an abundance of well-designed and maintained parks offer something for everyone. Portland has 9,400 acres of parkland including Washington Park, nestled in the beautiful West Hills overlooking downtown. Washington Park is home to such attractions as the Oregon Zoo, International Rose Test Garden, Japanese Garden and the Hoyt Arboretum with its 10-mile network of hiking trails. Nearby Forest Park, with miles of hiking trails, is the largest urban wilderness park in the United States. All in all, the City of Portland has upwards of 250 parks of varying size and function. Collectively they offer a profusion of picnicking facilities, gardens and natural areas, playgrounds, sports fields, tennis courts, swimming pools, walking and jogging routes and golf courses.

Additional opportunities for the adventurous are found within a one- or two-hour drive of town. Camping, fishing, hunting, mountain hiking and climbing, boating, windsurfing, whitewater rafting, water- and snow-skiing and bike touring are widely available. During much of the year you can ski at Timberline Lodge on Mount Hood and play golf in the Willamette Valley on the same day. There are more than 30 golf courses, mostly 18-hole public or semi-public facilities, within 20 miles of downtown Portland.

Portland is less notable for popular indoor activities than for outdoor recreation. For its size it is somewhat underendowed with movie theaters, although the downtown Guild Theater, with its program of art and foreign films, does provide a welcome alternative to the mainstream movies screened in cinema complexes in the regional malls. The city is known for the tremendous variety and excellence of its restaurants, many of which are clustered downtown or in interesting upscale neighborhoods like the Belmont, Hawthorne and Nob Hill districts. Pro sports fans can enjoy Portland Trail Blazers NBA basketball and minor league baseball locally or travel 180 miles to Seattle for big league baseball, basketball and football.

Work and Volunteer Activities   Rating: 3

 The Portland economy has stagnated in recent years and unemployment now exceeds six percent. As elsewhere, the service sector generates the majority of full-time and part-time jobs and competition for them is keen. Senior citizens are in high demand for volunteer work in schools, hospitals, senior and community centers, and for providing transportation to the elderly and disabled. Several volunteer referral services including the Volunteer Center and RSVP can help you get involved.

Portland's crime situation is worse than average for American metropolitan areas. The property crime rate for the metropolitan area is approximately 30 percent above the national average but the violent crime rate is 20 percent below the national norm. On a more positive note, Portland's crime statistics have been improving in recent years and most parts of the city, including downtown, feel safe enough. In a city as large as Portland there are obviously considerable variations from place to place in potential exposure to crime, and here (as elsewhere), it would be wise to avoid high-crime areas.

Conclusion

Overall Rating 51

Portland is a special place. Its physical and human environment is close to ideal. Its location astride the Willamette River in the shadow of the Cascade Range is beautiful and its mild, marine climate is seldom severely hot or cold. Tornadoes and hurricanes are unknown and serious earthquakes are unlikely. Even the Cascades' famous volcanoes are too far away to pose a major threat. Portland's quality of life is excellent thanks to sound land use and transportation planning and heavy private and public sector investment that has revitalized and humanized downtown and greatly strengthened the metropolitan area public transit system. Environmental protection is high on the list of Portland priorities as reflected in the area's clean air and water, excellent parks and well-maintained neighborhoods. The city provides very good health care and work and volunteer opportunities. Its transportation, retail and community services are excellent, as are its vast array of cultural and recreational activities. The principal drawbacks to retirement in Portland are crime rates and a cost of living somewhat above national norms. That said, Portland ranks as one of America's best places for a lively and sophisticated retirement.

Olympia, Washington

European settlers first arrived at the southern end of Puget Sound in the 1840s. Their little community of Smithfield became the site of the first United States customhouse in the Pacific Northwest. Soon renamed Olympia for its spectacular view of the Olympic Mountains, Olympia became capital of the Washington Territory in 1853 and has managed to retain its status as capital of the State of Washington despite occasional challenges from Seattle, Tacoma and other cities. With a population of 44,000 in the city and 230,000 in Thurston County, Olympia retains a small-town atmosphere yet offers amenities typical of larger places. The city is rich in history and natural beauty and is prized for its high quality of life. Elegant old homes, tree-lined streets and a popular farmers' market add to its charm.

Olympia is located on the shores of Budd Inlet, the southernmost arm of Puget Sound, and Capitol Lake. Elevations rise from sea level to about 200 feet within the city limits but are slightly higher in neighboring Tumwater. Olympia is built on a gently rolling surface with many vantage points offering outstanding views of the snow-capped ridges of the

Olympia, Washington

CLIMATE

Month	Average Daily Temperature High	Low	Daily Rel. Humidity Low	Average Monthly Precipitation
	F		%	Inches
January	44	32	80	7.5
February	48	33	71	6.2
March	53	34	62	5.3
April	58	37	57	3.6
May	65	42	55	2.3
June	70	46	54	1.8
July	76	50	50	0.8
August	77	50	50	1.1
September	72	45	54	2.0
October	60	39	67	4.2
November	50	35	80	8.1
December	44	32	84	7.9

Annual Averages

Total Days		Total Inches	
Clear	53	Precipitation	50.8
Partly Cloudy	84	Snowfall	16.7
Cloudy	228		

RATINGS

Category	poor 1	fair 2	good 3	very good 4	excellent 5
Landscape				●	
Climate			●		
Quality of Life				●	
Cost of Living			●		
Transportation				●	
Retail Services			●		
Health Care				●	
Community Services				●	
Cultural Activities			●		
Recreational Activities				●	
Work/Volunteer Activities			●		
Crime			●		

Total Points: 42

Olympic Mountains on clear days. The city is only 60 miles from Seattle and 120 miles from Portland, Oregon. The natural vegetation of luxuriant coniferous forest is associated with the area's mild, wet climate but broad-leafed tree varieties, including magnolia, have been planted widely in town to add aesthetic variety. Residential gardens typically include rhododendrons, other flowering shrubs, seasonal flowers and vibrant green lawns.

Climate   Rating: 3

 Olympia has a mild marine climate broadly similar to, but somewhat rainier than, that of Seattle. Olympia averages 51 inches of annual precipitation with nearly 40 inches falling between October and March. The summer half of the year is much drier and sunnier. Most precipitation occurs as rain; snow totals an average of 17 inches annually and seldom lasts long on the ground because winter days are typically mild. Spring and autumn weather varies considerably from day to day with cool-to-warm daytime highs and cool to cold nights. Summer weather is generally pleasant with average highs around 75 degrees and lows around 50 degrees. The frost-free season averages 150 days. Overcast conditions are more typical than clear skies, especially in winter. Olympia is sunny about 40 percent of the time, varying seasonally from about 25 percent in winter to 60 percent in summer.

Quality of Life   Rating: 4

 Olympia offers residents a very good quality of life. Noise pollution is confined to a narrow corridor along I-5 and Highway 101 and local air quality is excellent. The city is uncrowded and there is adequate parking downtown, at the mall, at the university and at other activity centers. Traffic is generally light and free flowing even at rush hour. With its economy dominated by state government, retail services and education, Olympia lacks noxious industry and seems decently managed. Residents are generally liberal and progressive with a laissez-faire attitude that allows them to tolerate an odd mix of housing styles in some neighborhoods and the presence of a seemingly transient population in a downtown park in summer. Upscale neighborhoods, though, whether central like the South Capitol Historic District or on the several peninsulas stretching beyond the city limits far out into Puget Sound, are attractively designed, well treed and landscaped and moderately priced. A number of municipal and county parks, some largely undeveloped woodlands, others more activity oriented, add much to the general ambiance.

Cost of Living   Rating: 3

 The cost of living in Olympia is evaluated as follows:

- *Composite.* ACCRA data show that the composite cost of living in Olympia approximates the national average.

- *Housing.* According to ACCRA, housing costs are about 10 percent below the national average. Typical single-family residences are priced between $150,000 and $200,000. Condominiums are about $20,000 cheaper than comparable single-family home.

- *Goods and Services.* Health care, groceries and transportation are priced at 35 percent, 8 percent and 5 percent above their national averages, respectively. Miscellaneous goods and services are priced near the national average while utilities are a bargain at a price 13 percent below the national norm.

- *Taxes.* The state and local tax burden in Olympia is 10.4 percent of income compared to the U.S. average of 9.7 percent. There is no state income tax in Washington but property taxes are moderate and sales and excise taxes are high.

Transportation   Rating: 4

Although most residents drive, the comprehensive transit services offered by Intercity Transit (IT) provide a useful alternative. Intercity Transit's excellent fixed route bus system, focused on the downtown transit center, provides service to destinations throughout the city and county including schools, Evergreen State College, major area hospitals, Capital Mall and smaller shopping centers, the Amtrak station and most residential areas. Specialized transportation services are provided to those requiring door-to-door service. Fares are low. Seniors and the disabled pay only $12.50 for a monthly pass. Amtrak runs four trains daily north to Seattle and south to Portland; Greyhound provides service to these and other points from the Greyhound bus station downtown. Seattle–Tacoma International Airport, 45 miles northeast, provides flights to a large number of points including nonstop jet service to more than 60 destinations.

Retail Services   Rating: 3

Capital Mall, located two miles west of downtown, is the major enclosed regional mall. Anchored by Best Buy, Bon–Macy's, JCPenney and Mervyn's, the mall also features nearly 100 specialty shops, restaurants, services and a cinema complex. A large Target store is located adjacent to Capital Mall while Sears and an additional Mervyn's are found in South Sound Shopping Center in Lacey, a few miles east of Olympia. Historic Downtown Olympia has revived nicely in recent years and now boasts an interesting mix of specialty shops, galleries, restaurants and theaters. Just north of the city center and next to the harbor is an exceptionally good farmers' market that operates on Saturdays and Sundays, April through December.

Health Care   Rating: 4

Providence St. Peter Hospital and Capital Medical Center provide very good health care. Providence St. Peter, a 390-bed hospital with a medical staff of 450 primary care and specialist physicians, is the largest medical center in the southern Puget Sound Region. It offers a full range of acute care, specialty and outpatient services including 24-hour emergency care, outpatient surgery, and cardiac surgery and rehabilitation. A teaching hospital, Providence St. Peter is affiliated with the University of Washington Medical School and trains physicians in primary care. Capital Medical Center is a 110-bed facility that furnishes 24-hour emergency care, a diabetes wellness program, and community health lectures, among other services, and operates several family-practice clinics in Thurston County.

Community Services   Rating: 4

Senior citizens can give and get help, and stay active socially, in a variety of programs in Olympia and Thurston County. Olympia, Lacey, Tumwater and several other towns have senior centers. The Olympia Senior Activity Center offers classes in arts and crafts, history and politics, and languages and exercise, among others, and organizes day trips and longer tours. The center's wellness program provides medical tests, referrals and subsidized meals. Tumwater's senior program in Old Town Center provides another outlet for senior activities. During morning and early afternoon hours, much of the community center is given over to seniors for cards, classes, exercise programs, other social activities and meals. Senior Information and Assistance Services and RSVP provide additional resources for seniors.

Cultural and Educational Activities   Rating: 3

 For a small city, Olympia is well endowed culturally and educationally. Downtown's Washington Center for the Performing Arts is the principal venue for resident and touring music, dance and theater groups. Its season runs from early October through early May and recently included diverse fare from the Chicago Jazz Band, Seattle Symphony, Trinity Irish Dance Company and the Royal Winnipeg Ballet, among other visiting ensembles. Tickets are reasonably priced and discounts are available to seniors and those attending eight or more events. The Center is also home to the Olympia Chamber and Symphony Orchestras. In July and August, free outdoor concerts are scheduled in Sylvester Park, downtown and in Lacey. Cultural events at area colleges are also open to the public.

The Evergreen State College, ranked by Thomas Gaines in his seminal monograph *The Campus as a Work of Art* as one of the most beautiful college campuses in the country, is also notable for its experimental curriculum and its hospitality to seniors. Senior residents of the State of Washington may audit a maximum of two courses (eight quarter units) per term for a nominal fee. Courses at any level may be taken and range from culture, language and the expressive arts to environmental studies, social science and scientific inquiry. Lifelong learning classes are available inexpensively at South Puget Sound Community College and through the Olympia Parks and Recreation Department. Their offerings include computers, languages, yoga, karate and sailing, among others.

Recreational Activities   Rating: 4

 Outdoor recreation is abundant in Olympia and its beautiful surroundings but rainy-day alternatives are also available locally. Major league sports and other big-city attractions are only 60 miles away in Seattle. Percival Landing's 1.5-mile boardwalk skirting Budd Inlet at the downtown Olympia waterfront is a great place for a stroll. In addition to offering access to restaurants and the marina, it provides fine views of the capitol building and Olympic Mountains. You can watch for migrating salmon, in season, and you might see an occasional lost whale from the nearby Fourth Street Bridge. Another nice place to walk is Tumwater Falls Park, where one can watch salmon climb the fish ladder beside the falls during spawning season and also see the now-abandoned early incarnation of the famed Olympia brewery. Olympia's other parks—there are 14 within the city limits—vary from small neighborhood playgrounds to the large and complex Priest Point Park along Budd Inlet. Collectively they provide a comprehensive list of recreational facilities including nature trails, picnicking facilities, playgrounds and sports fields, tennis courts and boating. There are three 9-hole and six 18-hole golf courses within 20 miles of Olympia. Two ski areas, Crystal Mountain and White Pass, are less than a hundred miles away in the Cascade Range. Three unique and spectacular national parks are within two or three hours of Olympia by car—Mount Rainier National Park, which includes the towering ice-clad volcano for which it is named, lies 100 miles east of Olympia; Olympic National Park, with its luxuriant temperate rainforest and countless snow-capped peaks, is about 100 miles northwest; Mount St. Helens, which was reshaped by a 1980 explosion that blew the top 1,313 feet off the volcano, lies 100 miles south. Each park offers remarkable opportunities for hiking and sightseeing. Closer to town, you can sail and fish on Puget Sound or hike its shoreline.

Olympia's modest endowment of movie theaters, restaurants and other foul-weather attractions are easily supplemented by the much greater resources of Seattle. Seattle boasts a plethora of excellent restaurants, shopping facilities and recreational attractions of all kinds. For many, the city's big league baseball, basketball and football teams are of particular interest.

Work and Volunteer Activities   Rating: 3

 The local economy is dominated by government, education and service activities and has not shared in the high-tech boom and bust of metropolitan Seattle. Competition for jobs with the large college student population, though, limits part-time work opportunities for seniors. Volunteer jobs are plentiful. Senior citizens help in schools, hospitals, soup kitchens, senior centers, government facilities and animal shelters. In Lacey, the Lacey Senior Patrol assists the Police Department's crime prevention unit by performing non-hazardous duties such as fingerprinting, patrolling shopping areas and checking on empty houses.

Crime Rates and Public Safety   Rating: 3

 Olympia's crime situation is moderate. The property crime rate is approximately 60 percent above the national average. This largely reflects the high incidence of larceny–theft; burglary and auto theft rates are fairly close to national norms. In contrast, the incidence of violent crime is relatively low, with an overall rate about 35 percent below the national average. Outlying suburban areas of the county are significantly more crime free than Olympia itself.

Conclusion

Overall Rating 42 Located just 60 miles southwest of Seattle, Olympia is conveniently close to its amenities yet far enough away to avoid its rapid urbanization, high housing prices and increasing traffic congestion. Olympia's physical setting overlooking Budd Inlet and within sight of the Olympic Mountains is attractive. Its mild, four-season marine climate is seldom too hot or cold but the persistence of cloudy and showery weather during much of the year can wear thin. Olympia's quality of life is very good. Noxious industries are lacking, air and water are clean, there is little traffic noise or congestion and catastrophic environmental events are unlikely. Tornadoes and hurricanes are absent in this mild climatic zone but a moderate threat of earthquakes does exist in the Puget Sound region. The city has good transportation including excellent public transit, good intercity bus and rail service and reasonably convenient access to Seattle–Tacoma Airport. The housing stock is quite varied and affordable, especially when compared to that of Seattle. The city's health care, community services and recreational facilities are very good; its retail services, cultural life, opportunities for work and volunteer activities, and public safety situation are good. If you are seeking a small laid-back town with better-than-average amenities and easy access to one of America's most desirable large cities, Olympia might prove an excellent and economical choice.

Bellingham, Washington

Long the hunting and fishing grounds of the Lummi Indians, who flourished in the area for thousands of years before the arrival of Europeans, Bellingham is largely a creation of the twentieth century. Incorporated in 1902, the city of Bellingham became the county seat of Whatcom County and an important center of coal mining, salmon canning and saw milling. In recent decades these frontier industries have been largely replaced by a service economy based on retailing, government, education, tourism and retirement. With a population of 70,000 in Bellingham itself and 180,000 in the metropolitan area (Whatcom County), Bellingham is surrounded by the natural beauty of the Cascade Mountains, Bellingham Bay and the San Juan Islands. The city is small enough to offer the intimacy and friendliness of a small town while providing a good array of urban services and amenities. Additional attractions are nearby in Vancouver and Victoria, British Columbia and in Seattle.

Landscape   Rating: 5

Bellingham occupies a splendid site on the eastern shore of Bellingham Bay, an arm of the Strait of Georgia, in the northwestern corner of Washington State. Elevations in the city proper vary from sea level to around 500 feet but only 30 miles to the east, Mount Baker—a spectacular snow-capped volcano—towers to 10,778 feet. Bellingham is within sight of Washington's famous San Juan Islands, which, like nearby Victoria, are reached easily by inter-island ferries. The city is only 90 miles from Seattle and 60 miles from Vancouver, B. C. Bellingham is rather hilly with many home sites offering superb views of Bellingham Bay, the islands or the Cascades. In the surrounding area the natural vegetation consists of oak and Douglas fir forests, with the same species as well as many other mild-climate trees and shrubs including magnolia and rhododendron gracing the town.

Climate   Rating: 4

Bellingham enjoys a mild, marine climate similar to that of London, England or Seattle. Although rainy enough, Bellingham is significantly drier than many locations in the Pacific Northwest because of the sheltering (rain shadow) effect of the high Olympic Mountains to the southwest and the Vancouver Island Mountains, directly west. Bellingham averages 36 inches of annual precipitation, far less than the 80 inches or more received on the west side of the Olympic Peninsula. Even so, Bellingham is cloudy and wet in winter, with 24 inches of precipitation falling between October and March. In contrast, the summer half of the year gets only 12 inches. Most precipitation occurs as rain; average annual snowfall totals 14 inches and snow seldom persists on the ground for more than a few days at a time because of prevailing winter mildness. Spring and autumn weather is changeable with cool to mild days and cool nights. Summer days are generally sunny and warm with daytime highs around 70 degrees and overnight lows in the low 50s. The frost-free period averages around 200 days, allowing outdoor gardening from April through October. In summary, Bellingham's climate has four distinct seasons, with few severely cold

Bellingham, Washington

CLIMATE

Month	Average Daily Temperature High	Average Daily Temperature Low	Daily Rel. Humidity Low	Average Monthly Precipitation
	F		%	Inches
January	46	32	74	4.8
February	49	35	67	3.6
March	53	37	61	3.0
April	58	41	58	2.8
May	63	46	54	2.3
June	68	51	53	2.0
July	73	54	49	1.4
August	73	54	50	1.3
September	67	49	57	1.6
October	59	43	67	3.3
November	52	37	75	5.4
December	47	33	78	4.9

Annual Averages

Total Days		Total Inches	
Clear	71	Precipitation	36.3
Partly Cloudy	93	Snowfall	14.3
Cloudy	201		

RATINGS

Category	poor 1	fair 2	good 3	very good 4	excellent 5
Landscape					●
Climate				●	
Quality of Life					●
Cost of Living		●			
Transportation				●	
Retail Services			●		
Health Care			●		
Community Services				●	
Cultural Activities				●	
Recreational Activities					●
Work/Volunteer Activities			●		
Crime			●		

Total Points: 45

or excessively warm days and ample precipitation. Its principal negative is the cloudy and drizzly weather characteristic of all seasons except summer.

Quality of Life Rating: 5

 Bellingham provides an excellent quality of life. Noise pollution is insignificant except along a narrow strip paralleling I-5. Local air quality is excellent and the city appears clean and uncrowded with plenty of parking available downtown, at the mall, at the university and at other activity centers. Traffic is light and flows freely even at rush hour. The city seems well planned and managed; its traditional downtown is attractive and viable, as is the smaller historic Fairhaven business district toward the southern edge of town. Residential neighborhoods are typically well maintained and pleasantly landscaped, as are the numerous city and county parks and natural areas.

Cost of Living Rating: 2

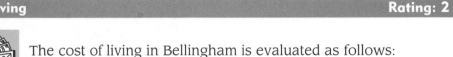 The cost of living in Bellingham is evaluated as follows:

- *Composite.* ACCRA data show that the composite cost of living in Bellingham is 7 percent above the national average.

- *Housing.* According to ACCRA, housing costs are about 10 percent above the national average. This estimate is consistent with the advertised prices of mid-priced homes seen in the area. A good variety of excellent housing is generally available.

- *Goods and Services.* Health care is priced about 20 percent above the national average. In contrast, groceries and miscellaneous goods and services are all priced about 10 percent above national norms, while utilities and transportation are available at approximately their national average costs.

- *Taxes.* The state and local tax burden in Bellingham is 10.4 percent of income compared to the U.S. average of 9.7 percent. There is no state income tax in Washington but property taxes are moderate and sales and excise taxes are high.

Transportation Rating: 4

 Although travel by car is easy in Bellingham, the varied transit services provided by the Whatcom Transportation Authority (WTA) offer convenient alternatives. WTA's excellent fixed-route bus system, focused on the downtown transit center, provides service to destinations throughout the city including schools, Western Washington University, the hospital, malls and shopping centers, the senior center and residential areas. Dial-a-ride and specialized transportation services are available to those needing door-to-door service. Fares are low. Seniors and the disabled pay $7 per month or $80 per year. At the Fairhaven Transportation Center in southwest Bellingham, one may choose among Amtrak and Greyhound service to Seattle and Vancouver, inter-island ferry service to the San Juan Islands and Victoria, or the Alaska Marine Highway service to coastal Alaska. Bellingham International Airport offers a modest level of commuter service, primarily to Seattle, but Seattle–Tacoma International Airport, 100 miles south, provides a much greater variety of flights including nonstop jet service to more than 60 destinations. Vancouver International Airport, 50 miles north, with more than 32 nonstop jet destinations including Los Angeles, is another convenient option.

Retail Services · Rating: 3

Bellis Fair, located at I-5 and Guide Meridian Road in the northern part of town, is the city's main retail center. Built in part to attract customers from the Greater Vancouver area, Bellis Fair is a very large mall for a small city. Anchored by Bon–Macy's, Mervyn's, JCPenney, Sears and Target stores, the enclosed mall also features more than 100 specialty shops, restaurants, services and a cinema complex. An unusually pleasant east-facing food court offers customers a gorgeous view of Mount Baker on clear days. Sunset Square, at I-5 and Sunset Drive in northern Bellingham, is anchored by a Kmart and includes a collage of unique shops and restaurants and Sunset Cinemas. Downtown Bellingham and the Fairhaven Historic District provide the traditional ambiance of old-fashioned central business districts. Both feature an interesting assortment of arts and crafts galleries, specialty stores and restaurants. Downtown also boasts the historic Mount Baker Theatre and a farmers' market on weekends, April through October.

Health Care · Rating: 3

St. Joseph Hospital is Bellingham's only full-service general hospital. With 253 beds and 270 physicians covering a fairly wide range of specialties, St. Joseph Hospital provides a full range of services including 24-hour emergency and trauma care, neurosurgery, joint replacement, oncology and cardiovascular care. Outstanding comprehensive medical care is less than 100 miles away in Seattle and Vancouver.

Community Services · Rating: 4

Local government and the private sector make available a fine assortment of services to seniors and the general public. The Bellingham Senior Activity Center, which may be reached via its own WTA bus line, is a centrally located, well-equipped and well-run facility. Bustling with activity, the center offers daily classes, a music and dance program, walking and hiking, day trips and multi-day tours, games and exercise programs. The center's wellness program provides a battery of medical tests, foot care and massage therapy, and information on health goals free or at nominal cost. Inexpensive hot lunches are available to those 60 and older.

Cultural and Educational Activities · Rating: 4

For a community of its size, Bellingham has remarkable cultural and educational assets. Western Washington University is a great resource. Its Performing Arts Center is a principal venue for music and theater. A summer highlight there is the Bellingham Festival of Music held from late July through mid-August. This series presents world- class music making by the American Sinfonietta, the festival's 40-member ensemble, at bargain prices. During the winter season (October through May), a Performing Arts Center Series featuring musical and dance performances by distinguished guest artists, and a theater arts series of drama and comedy, occupy much of the calendar. Downtown's historic Mount Baker Theatre provides another venue for classical and children's theater, ballet and musical entertainment. It is the home of the Whatcom Symphony Orchestra and nationally known entertainers perform there regularly. In summer, free outdoor evening concerts are scheduled in Boulevard, Big Rock Garden and Marine Heritage Parks.

Western Washington University is notable for high academic standards and generous treatment of seniors. Washington residents who are 60 years of age or older may register at no cost for a maximum of two courses per quarter on a space-available basis. Alternately, anyone may audit courses at nominal cost. Auditors, unlike regular students, do not write papers, take tests, complete class projects or receive credits

Recreational Activities   Rating: 5

Outdoor recreation reigns supreme in Bellingham and Whatcom County but major league spectator sports and other big-city attractions are only an hour or two away in Vancouver and Seattle. Bellingham and Whatcom County operate superb park systems that are well designed, equipped and maintained. Bellingham's award-winning parks system occupies 2,200 acres with 70 miles of trails. Hiking, biking and horseback riding are popular in many city and county parks, including the city's scenic 1,000-acre Lake Padden Park, which also offers fishing, swimming, wind surfing, tennis, playgrounds, ball fields and an 18-hole public golf course. Thirteen other golf courses, many providing spectacular views of Mount Baker, Georgia Strait and the San Juan Islands, are found within the county. The Civic Field Complex, near downtown, features facilities for football, soccer, track, softball, ice skating, year-round swimming and professional baseball.

Water sports enthusiasts will appreciate the Bellingham area for its numerous lakes, rivers and miles of shoreline. Opportunities for canoeing, river rafting, kayaking, scuba diving and whale watching are virtually endless. Snow skiing is available at Mount Baker Ski Area, 50 miles east of town. Also nearby are the cosmopolitan pleasures of Seattle and Vancouver and the quainter delights of Victoria. Seattle and Vancouver are especially notable for the excellence of their shopping facilities and restaurants. Both also field major league sports teams. Seattle boasts teams playing baseball, basketball and football while Vancouver has teams playing basketball, Canadian football and hockey. Varsity basketball and football are played in Seattle by the University of Washington Huskies.

Work and Volunteer Activities   Rating: 3

Bellingham has not shared in the high-tech boom and bust of the Seattle area but local unemployment rates remain above the state average. This fact, along with competition for jobs with college students, limits opportunities for the retired to work part time. Volunteer work, though, is plentiful and many placements are arranged through RSVP. The Bellingham–Whatcom County Convention and Visitors Center, city hall, the hospital and public library, public parks and recreation facilities, the senior center and the Women's Care Shelter all depend heavily on volunteer staff.

Crime Rates and Public Safety   Rating: 3

The crime situation is somewhat mixed. The property crime rate is twice the national average. This largely reflects the city's high larceny–theft rate. Other property crime rates are close to or below national norms. The good news is that the incidence of violent crime in Bellingham is enviably low with an overall rate 50 percent below the national average. Outlying parts of the metropolitan area are even safer.

Overall Rating 45 Situated between Seattle and Vancouver, British Columbia, Bellingham is close enough to each for residents to enjoy their amenities yet far enough away to avoid runaway urbanization, high prices and environmental deterioration. Its physical setting on Bellingham Bay, with the San Juan Islands and the Cascade Range within view, is splendid. Its mild, four-season marine climate with little snow appeals to many, although some may find its cloudy, rainy winters less than ideal. Its quality of life is excellent. Air and water are clean, there is little traffic noise or congestion and catastrophic environmental events are unlikely. The city has good transportation facilities including excellent public transit, a good network of bike lanes and trails and good intercity bus, rail and ferry service. Although housing is priced above the national average, it offers good value. Residential neighborhoods are typically attractive with well-maintained homes and lovely gardens, many offering views of Bellingham Bay, Whatcom Lake or the Cascade Range. Retail services and health care are good. Community services, cultural life, and parks and recreation assets are excellent and the overall cost of living is only slightly above the national average. All in all, Bellingham clearly ranks among America's best locales for quality retirement. It will appeal especially to those who would enjoy an active lifestyle in a charming seaside town.

Victoria, British Columbia

Capital of the province of British Columbia since 1868, Victoria has come a long way since its rowdy early days as a Hudson's Bay Company fort and port city connecting the wider world with the natural resources of Vancouver Island and mainland British Columbia. With a population of 75,000 in the core city and upwards of 330,000 in the metropolitan area, Victoria is more diverse demographically and economically than usually credited. Although Oak Bay remains a somewhat British-looking neighborhood, most parts of Victoria are quintessentially Canadian, reflecting the cultures of First Nation, European and Asian ethnic groups who now call Victoria home. The urban area is prosperous in an understated way with its economy especially strong in tourism, public administration, defense and retailing. The metropolitan area's strong economy, beautiful mountain and seashore landscape and mild climate continue to attract new residents, yet the city retains its essential charm and refined quality of life. In 1998, Conde Nast Traveler magazine rated Victoria as the top Canadian city for environment and ambiance.

Landscape   **Rating: 5**

Victoria occupies a splendid site on the Saanich Peninsula at the southeastern extremity of Vancouver Island. Several waterways to the west, including the Upper Harbour and Inner Harbour, separate Victoria from the naval port of Esquimalt. The Strait of Juan de Fuca to the south divides British Columbia from the state of Washington, while Haro Strait separates Victoria from the U.S. Gulf Islands. The rolling surface of the Saanich Peninsula is largely urbanized but patches of farmland and forested hillsides add interest to the landscape. The natural vegetation is predominantly coniferous forest but oaks are found in drier areas. Victoria is well landscaped with a variety of broad-leafed and coniferous trees and shrubs and is notable for the profusion of flowers that bloom there most of the year.

Victoria, British Columbia

CLIMATE							RATINGS					
Month	Average Daily Temperature High		Low		Average Monthly Precipitation		Category	poor 1	fair 2	good 3	very good 4	excellent 5
	F	C	F	C	in	mm						
January	44	6	34	1	5.4	137	Landscape					●
February	46	7	35	1	4.0	101	Climate				●	
March	51	10	37	2	2.8	71	Quality of Life					●
April	56	13	40	4	1.7	43	Cost of Living				●	
May	61	16	45	7	1.3	33	Transportation					●
June	66	18	50	10	1.2	30	Retail Services				●	
July	70	21	52	11	0.7	17	Health Care					●
August	70	21	52	11	0.9	22	Community Services					●
September	66	18	48	8	1.4	35	Cultural Activities				●	
October	57	13	43	6	3.1	78	Recreational Activities				●	
November	48	8	37	2	5.2	132	Work/Volunteer Activities				●	
December	44	6	35	1	5.7	144	Crime			●		

Annual Averages			
Precipitation		**Snowfall**	
Inches	33.3	Inches	4.9
Millimeters	845	Centimeters	12.5

Total Points: 52

Climate   Rating: 4

Victoria is unique in Canada for the mildness of its climate. Lying in the rain shadow of the Olympic Mountains to the south and the Vancouver Island Mountains to the west, Victoria has a cool Mediterranean climate somewhat similar to that of coastal central California. Winters are cloudy and mild with many showery days; summers are sunny, mild to warm, and dry. Annual precipitation is about 33 inches (84.5 centimeters) with nearly 80 percent of the total falling in the rainy season between October and March. Snow accumulation totals only 4.9 inches (12.5 centimeters) annually and seldom lasts on the ground more than a few days at a time. On average, Victoria is sunny about 50 percent of the time, varying seasonally from about 30 percent in winter to 70 percent in summer. The city enjoys a frost-free period of 240 days and frosts are seldom severe even in winter.

Quality of Life — Rating: 5

 Victoria is notable for its excellent quality of life. There is little noise from aircraft or motor vehicles. The airport is 15 miles (25 kilometers) north and no freeway penetrates the city. Victoria is peaceful, clean and uncrowded. Although heavy tourist traffic puts some pressure on local streets and parking lots in summer, the city's excellent public transit compensates somewhat. With its economy dominated by tourism, government, retail services and education, Victoria lacks noxious industry and boasts the cleanest air of major North American cities. Downtown Victoria, with its government buildings, museums, retail stores and restaurants is the vibrant core of the community. Several picturesque, historic neighborhoods including James Bay and Fairfield are adjacent to downtown; a little farther from the center, newer—but still attractive—housing is found. Neighborhoods are typically well landscaped and city parks, large and small, dot the landscape.

Cost of Living — Rating: 4

The cost of living in Victoria is evaluated as follows:

- *Composite.* ACCRA data are unavailable for Victoria. I estimate that the overall cost of living is 10 percent above the Canadian average and 10 percent below the American average.

- *Housing.* Housing costs are 20 percent above the Canadian average and near the American average. Greater Victoria prices for single-family residences average $380,000 ($280,000 U.S.). Condominiums and townhouses average around $240,000 ($180,000 U.S.). Housing in prime locations along the shore is considerably more expensive; modest housing in inland suburban areas is cheaper.

- *Goods and Services.* Goods and services are priced a little above Canadian norms but are 10 to 20 percent below U.S. averages. Utilities and medical care are particularly inexpensive by American standards.

- *Taxes.* The overall tax burden in Victoria approximates the Canadian average and is about 30 percent higher than the U.S. average for people of moderate means. Federal and provincial income tax rates are modestly higher than in the U.S., but the combined federal and provincial sales tax on goods and services is twice the U.S. average. These high rates are balanced somewhat by relatively low property taxes and by the low cost of medical care provided by BC Health Care.

Transportation

Victoria offers excellent intracity and intercity transportation. The city has one of the highest rates of non-automobile travel in Canada due to greater dependence on walking, bicycling and public transit than in other metropolitan areas. BC Transit's more than 200 buses provide excellent, inexpensive transportation throughout Victoria and the Saanich Peninsula 365 days a year. You can travel to points near and far by air, rail, bus and ferry. Victoria International Airport provides nonstop flights to Vancouver, Seattle, Portland, Kelowna, Calgary and Toronto. VIA Rail Canada offers daily passenger service on Vancouver Island between Victoria and Courtenay and transcontinental passenger service from Vancouver. Greyhound Canada and its affiliates provide motor coach service to points on Vancouver Island and across Canada and connect with Greyhound Lines in the United States. The BC Ferries fleet of 35 vessels provides service to 47 ports of call along the British Columbia coast including Vancouver and Victoria. Senior residents of the province enjoy free travel, Monday through Thursday.

Retail Services

Downtown Victoria is thriving. Its streets are lined with specialty stores of all kinds, art galleries and studios, restaurants and antique shops. Downtown's Bay Centre, an architecturally interesting five-level indoor mall, is a focal point of activity. Anchored by a large Hudson's Bay Company department store (The Bay), Bay Centre also features nearly 100 specialty shops, services, restaurants and fast-food eateries. Just north of downtown is Mayfair Shopping Centre, Greater Victoria's largest regional mall. It too is anchored by a large Bay department store and boasts 135 other shops, services, and restaurants and a large food court. Victoria is a collage of neighborhoods, many of which are advantaged by having a small shopping center consisting of several shops and a supermarket.

Health Care

The Vancouver Island Health Authority provides excellent health care through its seven hospitals and numerous clinics in Greater Victoria. Victoria General Hospital and Royal Jubilee Hospital are the largest acute care hospitals in the area. Both are tertiary referral centers for Vancouver Island, providing a complete range of specialty services. All in all there are more than 2,000 hospital beds and 900 physicians in Greater Victoria.

Community Services

Victoria provides excellent basic public services and others oriented specifically toward seniors. In addition to seven community centers, the city of Victoria has three senior centers—Fairfield New Horizons Seniors Activity Centre, James Bay New Horizons Seniors Activity Centre and Victoria Silver Threads Seniors Center. Activities offered include cards and games, billiards, carpet bowling, exercise programs, computer training and access, guest speakers, arts and crafts, movies and plays, parties, day trips and wellness programs.

The University of Victoria, with upwards of 18,000 students, is a major focus of culture and education. Its Division of Continuing Studies offers flexible programs to suit your schedule, with noncredit courses, study groups and seminars, educational study tours, independent study materials and distance education in a variety of subjects. The Music Department presents a nearly endless series of student and faculty recitals, and chamber musical, choral, symphonic and Big Band concerts are offered on campus at the Phillip T. Young Recital Hall and the Farquhar Auditorium throughout the academic year. The Theatre Department also contributes to the cultural life of campus and city. The works of students and faculty as well as visiting talent are showcased regularly at the Phoenix Theatre.

Numerous historic and modern venues host artistic events in town. The McPherson Playhouse, a restored theater, presents concerts and musical comedy. The Pacific Opera Society also performs there. The Royal Theatre is home to the Victoria Symphony Orchestra, which offers a pops and classical series September through April. Free outdoor musical events are presented at Centennial Square and in Beacon Hill Park from May through September. Comedy revues and music hall shows are performed frequently at the Belfry, Gladstone and Royal theatres, and the Memorial Arena hosts top-name entertainers and rock bands that draw large crowds. The biggest venue of all, though, is Victoria's Inner Harbour, which is transformed into a concert venue of gargantuan proportions for Symphony Splash, an all-day free concert held annually in August or September.

Victoria has several museums but the Royal British Columbia Museum, located next to the Parliament Buildings, merits special note. Two floors of displays tell the natural and human history of British Columbia. The province's First Nations are highlighted in Nisga'a and Haida exhibits and outside in Thunderbird Park several impressive Northwest Coast totem poles may be seen. A National Geographic IMAX Theater is on site at the museum.

Victoria's scenic coastal location and mild climate favor year-round outdoor recreation. The city and neighboring Saanich Peninsula communities have magnificent park systems that are supplemented by nearby provincial parks. Greater Victoria has more parkland than any other Canadian city and area residents put it to good use. Popular activities include sightseeing from coastal and hilltop vantage points; hiking, biking and horseback riding along coastal and mountain trails; camping, picnicking and participation in organized or casual sports. Twenty golf courses, many in spectacular locations, offer excellent playing conditions throughout the year. Several beaches and pools provide opportunities for swimming, although coastal waters and air temperatures are a bit chilly. If your preference is downhill skiing, you'll have to drive 120 miles (200 kilometers) north to Mount Washington Ski Area where natural snow is abundant every winter.

Water sports have obvious appeal in an island environment blessed with sheltered bays, inlets and harbors. Game fish including flounder, lingcod, rockfish and sole are caught in coastal waters. Surf fishing for salmon and sea bass is popular locally and clams and oysters can be harvested on shorelines of the Gulf Islands, accessible by ferry from Swartz Bay. Boating is enjoyed on the waters of Saanich Inlet and among the islands of Georgia Strait.

Owing in part to its popularity with tourists, Victoria is unusually well endowed with excellent restaurants. Whatever your preferences in cuisines and dining styles, they will be met here. The selection of movie houses, though, is rather limited and for major league sports you will have to make the short trip by ferry or air to Vancouver, Canada's west coast metropolis just across Georgia Strait.

Work and Volunteer Activities   Rating: 4

Victoria's service-based economy is among the healthiest in Canada and part-time jobs and volunteer assignments are readily available. Most part-time work is in the retail and tourism industries. The area's many parks and recreational centers, museums and performing arts venues, among other sites, offer plentiful opportunities for volunteers.

Crime Rates and Public Safety   Rating: 3

Crime rates vary significantly in different parts of Greater Victoria. In the city of Victoria violent and property crime rates are more than twice the national average. Yet Victoria is not particularly unsafe; its high crime rates are in part a statistical quirk resulting from two factors. Because it is a relatively small core city adjacent to politically and statistically separate suburbs and because the city is a major tourist destination, it has a large nonresident population subject to crime but not included in the population base on which crime rates are calculated. Not surprisingly, the suburban communities of the Saanich Peninsula have very low crime rates and those of Greater Victoria are near national norms.

Conclusion

Overall Rating 52 It is easy to understand why Victoria has long been one of Canada's favorite retirement destinations. It environment leaves little to be desired. Victoria's mild and virtually snow-free climate is a powerful draw for those seeking refuge from winter's rigors. The city's splendid site at the southeastern tip of Vancouver Island, with distant views of the snow-capped Olympic, Cascade and Coastal Mountains, is among the most beautiful urban settings in North America.

Victoria scores well on all criteria for upscale retirement. It earns top ratings for its beautiful landscape, quality of life, local and long-distance transportation, health care and community services. Its endowment of retail services, cultural, educational and recreational assets, and work and volunteer opportunities is very good, especially for a small city. Even Victoria's cost of living, although above the Canadian average, is reasonable compared to that of larger Canadian cities such as Toronto and Vancouver and is a little cheaper than the U.S. average.

In many ways, modern Victoria is reminiscent of several large Canadian cities before they were damaged by rampant growth in recent decades. Victoria has pristine air and remains a peaceful, clean and uncrowded refuge from the stresses of big city life. Yet it offers the many amenities demanded by present-day North Americans at a cost affordable by most. It is clearly one of North America's most desirable and livable cities.

Vernon, British Columbia

The beautiful Okanagan Valley of southern, interior British Columbia has long been popular as a retirement destination. Although Kelowna is the largest of several retirement places in the valley, for a variety of reasons Vernon is our top choice. Incorporated in 1892, Vernon is the largest city and the commercial center of the North Okanagan region. With a population of 35,000 in the city and 50,000 in the urban area, which includes neighboring Coldstream and a number of smaller population clusters, Greater Vernon is large enough to offer the amenities most people want yet small enough to retain small-town charm and low living costs.

Landscape   Rating: 5

Vernon rests at an elevation of 1,300 feet (383 meters) on the rolling surface of the Okanagan Valley. Embraced by Okanagan, Kalamalka and Swan Lakes and virtually surrounded by forested and snow-capped mountain peaks, the city has an idyllic setting. According to National Geographic, Kalamalka Lake is one of the 10 most beautiful lakes in the world. Owing to the dry climate, the natural vegetation of the valley floor is steppe grass but tree cover increases with elevation. The mountains are mantled in coniferous forest and the irrigated townscape is nicely treed by a variety of deciduous and coniferous species. Lawns and flowers are prominent in city parks and in residential areas in summer.

Climate   Rating: 3

Vernon enjoys an invigorating semi-arid, four-season climate characterized by modest precipitation, sunny summers, cloudy winters and marked day-to-day and seasonal changes in weather. About 40 inches (103 centimeters) of snow falls annually in the valley but nearby mountain slopes receive much more. Summer afternoons are warm and pleasant with low relative humidity and summer evenings are cool. Spring and autumn weather is quite changeable but fairly sunny. Winter weather tends to be cold and cloudy with occasional snow. The city enjoys a frost-free season of 150 days and is sunny 55 percent of the time. The climate is just mild enough to allow growing of hardier orchard fruits including apples and pears.

Quality of Life   Rating: 5

Vernon offers an excellent quality of life. There is little noise from vehicular or air traffic and the air is clean. Although the automobile dominates local transportation, there is no traffic congestion and parking is abundant. The community is not particularly affluent yet residential areas—modest or upscale—are typically nicely maintained. The urban area is well planned and managed and the recently revived and refurbished historic downtown is a delightful place in which to walk and shop. City parks and recreation facilities are impressive and the recently opened Vernon and District Performing Arts Centre attracts talent not normally seen in cities of this size.

Vernon, British Columbia

CLIMATE

Month	High F	High C	Low F	Low C	in	mm
	Average Daily Temperature				Average Monthly Precipitation	
January	28	-2	19	-7	1.3	33
February	36	2	25	-4	1.0	26
March	46	8	30	-1	1.1	27
April	57	14	37	3	1.1	28
May	66	19	45	7	1.6	40
June	73	23	52	11	1.7	42
July	79	26	55	13	1.5	38
August	79	26	55	13	1.3	34
September	68	20	48	9	1.3	33
October	54	12	39	4	1.1	27
November	39	4	28	-2	1.6	40
December	30	-1	21	-6	1.7	43

Annual Averages

Precipitation		Snowfall	
Inches	16.3	Inches	40.6
Millimeters	410	Centimeters	103

RATINGS

Category	poor 1	fair 2	good 3	very good 4	excellent 5
Landscape					●
Climate			●		
Quality of Life					●
Cost of Living					●
Transportation			●		
Retail Services			●		
Health Care			●		
Community Services				●	
Cultural Activities			●		
Recreational Activities				●	
Work/Volunteer Activities		●			
Crime		●			

Total Points: 42

The cost of living in Vernon is evaluated as follows:

- *Composite.* ACCRA data are unavailable for Vernon. I estimate that the overall cost of living approximates the Canadian average and is about 20 percent below the American average.

- *Housing.* Housing is a bargain in Vernon, averaging $170,000 ($128,000 U.S.) for a modest three-bedroom, two-bath single-family residence. Superior housing in upscale neighborhoods overlooking Kalamalka Lake is more expensive.

- *Goods and Services.* Goods and services are priced slightly above Canadian norms but generally below U.S. averages by 10 to 20 percent. Groceries and transportation are comparatively expensive whereas utilities and health care are cheap.

- *Taxes.* The overall tax burden in Vernon approximates the Canadian average and is about 30 percent higher than the U.S. average for people of moderate means. Federal and provincial income tax rates are modestly higher than in the U.S. but the combined federal and provincial sales tax on goods and services is twice the U.S. average. These high rates are balanced somewhat by relatively low property taxes and by the low cost of medical care provided by BC Health Care.

Transportation   **Rating: 3**

Travel is easy in Vernon. Most people drive but BC Transit buses provide a convenient and economical alternative to local destinations. Intercity travel is possible via Greyhound Canada buses and by air. Kelowna International Airport, 30 miles south, offers 30 nonstop departures a day to Seattle, Vancouver, Victoria, Calgary, Edmonton, Toronto and Hamilton.

Retail Services   **Rating: 3**

Colorful, historic downtown Vernon is a good place to savor the city's unique character. You can walk the self-guided Heritage Mural Tour to view Vernon's rich history as depicted by local artists on large, formerly blank walls. On route, you can sample the fare at coffee shops and restaurants and explore unique boutiques and specialty shops that offer everyday wares and one-of-a-kind treasures. Typical suburban shopping is available at Village Green Mall on the northern edge of town. Anchored by The Bay, Zellers and Winners department stores, the mall also features more than 60 specialty shops, services, restaurants and a food court.

Health Care   **Rating: 3**

Interior Health, a branch of BC Health Care, provides medical services to the Okanagan Valley through its clinics, labs and hospitals. Vernon Jubilee Hospital, with 161 beds, 55 general practitioners and about 40 medical specialists, meets the everyday health care needs of Vernon residents. Kelowna General Hospital, a 350-bed acute care facility, provides highly specialized services to the entire Okanagan Valley. It is only 30 minutes from Vernon via Highway 97.

Community Services   Rating: 4

 Like most Canadian cities, Vernon provides excellent basic public services including parks and recreation centers. Halina Seniors Centre, located in the Vernon Recreation Center in Becker Park, offers carpet bowling, cards, bingo and dances, among other social activities.

Cultural and Educational Activities   Rating: 3

 The visual and performing arts are well represented in Vernon. Almost everywhere you look in the downtown core, you'll encounter larger-than-life characters from Vernon's past displayed on 23 historic murals. The Vernon Public Art Gallery highlights works by local, national and international artists. Vernon Museum, located in the Civic Centre, presents North Okanagan history through streetscapes, dioramas and changing exhibits. Highlights include native and natural history artifacts, military displays and extensive archives. Several historic and modern venues host performing arts events. The Powerhouse Theatre, once the city power plant, is now the home of amateur theater. The Vernon and District Multiplex is a large arena that hosts major touring concerts. More intimate cultural events are held at the new Vernon and District Performing Arts Centre. This impressive 750-seat auditorium was designed specifically for music and drama. It is Vernon home of the Okanagan Symphony Orchestra and the Sunshine Theatre Company and has already attracted a number of quality visiting ensembles to Vernon.

Recreational Activities   Rating: 4

 Vernon's varied physical geography and four-season climate favor diverse outdoor recreation. Okanagan and Kalamalka Lakes have public beaches and boat launching ramps just minutes from downtown. Eight beach parks in the Vernon area provide a wealth of opportunities for water sports such as swimming, scuba diving, canoeing, kayaking, sailing, boating and fishing. Kalamalka Lake Provincial Park, 6 miles (10 kilometers) south of town, boasts miles of trails providing access to the park's natural features, viewpoints and beaches. Four golf courses in and around Vernon offer challenges to golfers of all skill levels. In winter, you can turn your attention to cross-country and downhill skiing. Nearby Silver Star Mountain has 65 miles (105 kilometers) of groomed trails and more are found in adjacent Silver Star Provincial Park. Silver Star Ski Resort, just 12 miles (20 kilometers) northeast of Vernon, boasts 108 downhill runs to challenge skiers of all abilities. With 2,500 feet of vertical drop and 2,725 acres of skiing terrain, Silver Star is skiers' heaven.

Work and Volunteer Activities   Rating: 2

 Unemployment rates are somewhat higher in the Okanagan Valley than in coastal British Columbia so job opportunities for seniors are somewhat limited. Most part-time work is in the retail and tourism sectors. The area's parks and recreation centers, museums, performing arts venues, visitor bureaus and several festivals offer many opportunities for volunteer work.

Vernon property and crime rates are well above national norms for Canada. As in Victoria, some of the "excess crime" may be attributable to the large transient population of visitors in the city both summer and winter and commuters year-round. Be that as it may, Vernon did not appear at all dangerous during our daytime and evening walks in the downtown area during our May 2004 visit.

Conclusion

Overall Rating 42 If you prefer a four-season climate, enjoy summer and winter outdoor recreation and appreciate small-town virtues, you may find life in Vernon very appealing. Located in the beautiful Okanagan Valley of British Columbia, surrounded by spectacular lakes and mountains, Vernon offers an excellent quality of life unspoiled by traffic congestion, pollution or excessive development. Downtown Vernon is the most attractive urban core found in any Okanagan Valley city and the community's public services and cultural and recreational assets are exceptional for a small town. Transportation, retail services and health care are good, and the cost of living is low. Only higher-than-average crime rates and limited opportunities for part-time employment detract from Vernon's high ranking. Fortunately, Vernon is growing fairly slowly so it should remain a highly desirable, unspoiled refuge from urban costs and stresses for years to come.

Kelowna, British Columbia

Kelowna, the largest city of the Okanagan Valley, is also worth considering for retirement. Situated on the shores of Okanagan Lake about 28 miles (48 kilometers) south of Vernon, Kelowna is a little warmer and drier than its northern neighbor but has a generally similar physical landscape. Blessed with spectacular mountain scenery, large and pristine lakes, sandy beaches and hillsides covered with orchards and vineyards, the Kelowna area is a vacationers' paradise and a good place to live. You can ski at the nearby Big White Ski Resort from late November to mid-April. And down in the valley 17 golf courses beckon you onto the links between March and November.

With a population of 100,000 and a rapidly growing economy, Kelowna has a lot to offer and a few problems. Its transportation, retail, health care and community services are good and its cultural and recreational assets are impressive. Nowadays you can even taste excellent wines produced at local wineries such as the renowned Mission Hill Family Estate, which occupies a spectacular site overlooking Okanagan Lake. Rapid growth, though, has brought some unpleasant side effects. Housing and living costs are rising rapidly and are approaching the U.S. average. A good deal of Harvey Drive (Highway 97) is paralleled by ugly retail strip development and the city has sprawled upslope to the edge of the forest where the fire danger is acute. Traffic is heavy, especially along Highway 97, and property crime rates are above average. All in all though, Kelowna remains one of North America's more desirable communities. It is justifiably a popular choice for a busy and fulfilling retirement.

Bend, Oregon

Bend, Oregon is also worth considering for retirement, especially by those who enjoy outdoor activities in all seasons. Bend is located in central Oregon just east of the Cascade Range. Lying in the rain shadow of the Cascades, Bend has a drier and sunnier climate than most Pacific Northwest locations. To the west the land slopes gradually upward to Mount Bachelor and The Three Sisters, which provide a spectacular backdrop to the town on clear days. Small and isolated from major cities, Bend offers residents a very good quality of life free of pollution and most urban ills. Residential neighborhoods are typically attractive and the old-fashioned downtown has been nicely refurbished and is an attractive place to walk, shop and dine.

With a population of 60,000 in the city and about 130,000 in Deschutes County, Bend is too small to rank highly in transportation, cultural amenities and part-time and volunteer work. There is no local public transit but CAC Transportation offers shuttle service to Portland (160 miles away) and Greyhound connects Bend with other cities. Surprisingly, Bend suffers from a property crime rate 60 percent above the national average. More importantly, the violent crime rate is nearly 50 percent below the national norm.

Bend's greatest assets are its scenic high desert and mountain landscape, high quality of life and wonderful outdoor recreation. The city has excellent parks and recreation facilities. In spring and autumn one can ski in the morning on Mount Bachelor and golf in the afternoon in town. Trout fishing is excellent on several streams emanating from the Cascades; hiking and horseback riding are popular on desert and mountain trails. Retail, health care and community services are more than adequate and the cost of living is only slightly above average. All in all, Bend is a quite desirable retirement place.

Epilogue:
Choosing Your Place to Retire in Style

People often ask, "Where is the best place to retire?" There is obviously no simple answer to this question. Indeed, there is no single best place in which to retire because individuals vary in their wants and needs. Only you can determine what you want, need and can afford. And only you can choose among the unique and special communities described in this book.

Remember that the point totals (overall ratings) are not meant to rank the retirement towns from best to worst. Rather, the ratings charts help you assess a community's overall resources for retirement and its relative strength in each of 12 criteria important to retirees. In this book, each criterion is weighted equally. You might want to weight them differently depending on your priorities.

But numbers cannot tell the whole story about a place. Each town and city has a unique character and ambiance, which I have tried to capture in the place descriptions. However, to fully appreciate the nuances that differentiate an irresistible place from a merely likable one, you must visit in person.

This book can help you narrow your choices to a few outstanding locales worthy of additional consideration. You can learn more about each by requesting information, mostly provided free of charge, from local chambers of commerce, visitors bureaus and economic development departments. Their postal addresses, telephone numbers and Internet addresses are listed following the Epilogue. If you are seriously contemplating relocating, you should visit your favorite cities and towns as I have done in the course of researching and writing this book. Ideally, you should visit the selected places for extended periods in summer and winter in order to get to know the places, people and their way of life. With a little luck, you will discover that special place where you can retire in style and lead a happy and fulfilling life during your golden years.

Sources of Relocation Information

Free or inexpensive information useful to those contemplating relocation is available in printed and/or digital form from a variety of sources. Chambers of commerce (CC), visitors bureaus (VB) and economic development departments (EDD) typically respond to inquiries from potential new residents with miscellaneous promotional brochures, cost of living data, economic statistics, maps and real estate information. A list of chambers of commerce, visitors bureaus and economic development departments contacted for this book's 60 top-rated retirement places follows.

Chambers of Commerce, Visitors Bureaus, and Economic Development Departments

Atlantic Canada

Halifax, Nova Scotia

International Visitor Centre
1595 Barrington Street
Halifax, NS
Canada B3J1Z7
halifaxinfo.com

Fredericton, New Brunswick

Fredericton Tourism
P O Box 130
Fredericton, NB
Canada E3B4Y7
(506) 460-2041
fredericton.ca

Charlottetown, P.E.I.

Island Info. Service
P O Box 2000
Charlottetown, PE
Canada C1A7N8
(888) PEI-PLAY
gov.pe.ca

Northeast Region

Burlington, Vermont

Lake Champlain Regional CC
60 Main Street, Suite 100
Burlington, VT 05401
(802) 863-3489
vermont.org

Ithaca, New York

Tompkins County CC
Ithaca-Thompkins County VB
904 East Shore Drive
Ithaca, NY 14850
(607) 272-1313
visitithaca.com

State College, Pennsylvania

Chamber of Business and Industry
 of Centre County
200 Innovation Blvd., Suite 201
State College, PA 16803
(814) 234-1829
cbicc.org

Pittsburgh, Pennsylvania

Greater Pittsburgh Convention and VB
Regional Enterprise Tower
425 Sixth Avenue, 30th Floor
Pittsburgh, PA 15219
(412) 281-7711
visitpittsburgh.com

Northeast Region continued

Kingston, Ontario

Kingston Tourism Information Office
209 Ontario St.
Kingston, ON
Canada K7L2Z1
(888) 855-4355
kingstoncanada.com

Owen Sound, Ontario

Owen Sound Visitor Info. Centre
1155 First Avenue West
Owen Sound, ON
Canada N4K4K8
e-owensound.com

Stratford, Ontario

Stratford EDD and Tourism
P O Box 818
Stratford, ON
Canada N5A6W1
(800) 561-SWAN
www.city.stratford.on.ca

London, Ontario

Tourism London, City Hall
300 Dufferin Avenue
London, ON
Canada N6B1Z2
(800) 265-2602
londontourism.ca

Hanover–Lebanon, New Hampshire

Hanover Area CC
P O Box 5105
47-53 South Main Street
Hanover, NH 03755
(603) 643-3115
hanoverchamber.org

Greater Lebanon CC
P O Box 97, 1 School Street
Lebanon, NH 03766
(603) 448-1203
lebanonchamber.com

Midwest Region

Madison, Wisconsin

Greater Madison Chamber of Commerce
P O Box 71
Madison, WI 53701
(608) 256-8348
madisonchamber.com

Bloomington, Indiana

Greater Bloomington CC
P O Box 1302
Bloomington, IN 47402
(812) 336-6381
www.chamber.bloomington.in.us

Upper South Region

Charlottesville, Virginia

Charlottesville–Albemarle CC
P O Box 1564, Fifth and Market Streets
Charlottesville, VA 22902
(804) 295-3141
www.cvillechamber.org

Lexington, Virginia

Lexington-Rockbridge County CC
100 E. Washington St.
Lexington, VA 24450
(540) 463-5375
lexingtonvirginia.com

Lexington Tourism Department
106 E. Washington St.
Lexington, VA 24450
(540) 463-3777

Chapel Hill, North Carolina

Chapel Hill–Orange County VB
501 West Franklin Street
Chapel Hill, NC 27516
(919) 968-2060
www.chocvb.org

Pinehurst–Southern Pines, North Carolina

Sandhills Area CC
P O Box 458
Southern Pines, NC 28387
(910) 692-3926
sandhillschamber.com

Pinehurst–Southern Pines VB
P O Box 2270
Southern Pines, NC 28388
(800) 346-5362
homeofgolf.com

Asheville, North Carolina

Asheville Area CC and VB
P O Box 1010
Asheville, NC 28802
(828) 258-6137
ashevillechamber.org

Hendersonville, North Carolina

Greater Hendersonville CC
330 North King Street
Hendersonville, NC 28792
(828) 692-1413
hendesonvillechamber.org

Brevard, North Carolina

Brevard–Transylvania CC and VB
35 West Main Street
Brevard, NC 28712
(828) 883-3700
brevardncchamber.org

Southeast Coast Region

Boca Raton, Florida

Greater Boca Raton CC
1800 North Dixie Highway
Boca Raton, Florida 33432
(561) 395-4433
bocaratonchamber.com

Naples, Florida

Naples Area CC
3620 Tamiami Trail North
Naples, FL 34103
(239) 262-6376
napleschamber.org

Sarasota, Florida

Greater Sarasota CC
1945 Fruitville Road
Sarasota, FL 34236
(941) 955-8187
sarasotachamber.org

Gainesville, Florida

Alachua County VB
30 East University Avenue
Gainesville, FL 32601
(352) 374-5231
visitgainesville.net

Tallahassee, Florida

Tallahassee Area CC
100 North Duval Street
P O Box 1639
Tallahassee, FL 32302
talchamber.com

Thomasville, Georgia

Thomasville–Thomas County CC
401 South Broad Street
Thomasville, GA 31799
(229) 226-9600
thomasvillechamber.com

Savannah, Georgia

Savannah Area CC
101 East Bay Street
Savannah, Georgia 31401
(912) 644-6400
savannahchamber.com

Covington, Louisiana

St. Tammany West CC
201 Holiday Boulevard
Covington, LA 70434
(985) 892-3216
sttammanychamber.org

Southeast Coast Region
continued

Fairhope, Alabama
Eastern Shore CC
327 Fairhope Avenue
Fairhope, AL 36532
(251) 928-6387
www.eschamber.com

Interior South Region

Oxford, Mississippi
Oxford–Lafayette County CC and
Economic Development Foundation, Inc.
P O Box 108
Oxford, MS 38655
(662) 234-4651
edf.oxfordms.com

Fayetteville, Arkansas
Fayetteville Chamber of Commerce
123 West Mountain
P O Box 4216
Fayetteville, AR 72702
(501) 521-1710
fayettevillear.com

Hot Springs, Arkansas
Greater Hot Springs CC
659 Ouachita Avenue
P O Box 6090
Hot Springs, AR 71902
(501) 321-1700
www.hotspringschamber.com

Heart of Texas Region

Austin, Texas
Greater Austin CC
P O Box 1967
Austin, TX 78767
(512) 478-9383
austinchamber.org

San Antonio, Texas
Greater San Antonio CC
P O Box 1628
San Antonio, TX 78296
(210) 229-2181
sachamber.org

Fredericksburg, Texas
Fredericksburg CC
302 East Austin Street
Fredericksburg, TX 78624
(888) 997-3600
fredericksburg-texas.com

Kerrville, Texas
Kerrville Convention and VB
2108 Sidney Baker
Kerrville, TX 78028
(800) 221-7958
kerrvilletexascvb.com

Southern Rockies Region

Fort Collins, Colorado
Fort Collins Area CC
225 South Meldrum
Fort Collins, CO 80521
(970) 482-3746
fortcollins.com

Boulder, Colorado
Boulder CC
2440 Pearl Street
Boulder, Co 80302
(303) 442-1044
boulderchamber.com

Colorado Springs, Colorado
Colorado Springs Convention and VB
515 South Cascade Avenue
Colorado Springs, CO 80903
(800) 888-4748
coloradosprings-travel.com

Santa Fe, New Mexico
Santa Fe CC
P O Box 1928
Santa Fe, NM 87504
(505) 988-3279
santafechamber.com

Santa Fe Convention and VB
P.O. Box 909
Santa Fe, NM 87504
(800) 777-2489
santafe.org

Desert Southwest Region

Tucson, Arizona

Tucson Metropolitan CC
465 W. St. Mary's Road, P O Box 991
Tucson, AZ 85701
(520) 792-1212
tucsonchamber.org

Prescott, Arizona

Prescott CC
117 W. Goodwin Street
Prescott, AZ 86303
(800) 266-7534
prescott.org

Boulder City, Nevada

Boulder City CC
465 Nevada Way
Boulder City, Nevada 89005
(702) 293-2034
bouldercitychamber.com

Las Vegas, Nevada

Las Vegas CC
3720 Howard Hughes Parkway
Las Vegas, NV 89109
(702) 735-2451
lasvegaschamber.com

Carson City, Nevada

Carson City Area CC
1900 S. Carson Street, Suite 100
Carson City, NV 89701
(775) 882-1565
carsoncitychamber.com

Reno, Nevada

Reno–Sparks CC
P O Box 3499
Reno, NV 89505
(775) 337-3030
reno-sparkschamber.org

St. George, Utah

St. George Area CC
97 E. St. George Blvd.
St. George, UT 84770
(435) 628-1658
stgeorgechamber.com

California Region

San Luis Obispo, California

San Luis Obispo CC
1039 Chorro Street
San Luis Obispo, CA 93401
(805) 781-2777
slochamber.org

Chico, California

Chico CC
300 Salem Street
Chico, CA 95928
(530) 891-5556
chicochamber.com

Palm Springs–Palm Desert, California

Palm Springs CC
190 W. Amado Road
Palm Springs, CA 92262
(760) 325-1577
pschamber.org

Palm Desert CC
73-710 Fred Waring Drive, Suite 114
Palm Desert, CA 92260
(760) 346-6111
pdcc.org

Pacific Northwest Region

Medford–Ashland, Oregon

Ashland Chamber of Commerce
110 E. Main Street
Ashland, OR 97520
(541) 482-3486
ashlandchamber.com

The Chamber of Medford–
Jackson County and
Medford Visitors and Convention Bureau
101 East 8th Street
Medford, Or 97501
(541) 779-4847
medfordchamber.com

Eugene, Oregon

Eugene Area CC
1401 Willamette
Eugene, OR 97440
(541) 242-2351
eugenechamber.com

Portland, Oregon

Portland Business Alliance
520 S. W. Yamhill Street, Suite 1000
Portland, OR 97204
(503) 224-8684
portlandalliance.com

Bend, Oregon

Bend Visitor and Convention Center
63085 N. Business 97
Bend, OR 977017
(541) 382-8048
visitbend.com

Olympia, Washington

Olympia–Thurston County VB
P O Box 7338
Olympia, WA 98507
(360) 704-7544
visitolympia.com

Bellingham, Washington

Bellingham–Whatcom CC & Industry
P O Box 958
Bellingham, WA 98227
(360) 734-1330
bellingham.com

Victoria, British Columbia

Victoria EDD
1 Centennial Square
Victoria, BC, Canada V8W1P6
(250) 361-0555
city.victoria.bc.ca

Vernon, British Columbia

Greater Vernon EDD
Third Floor, 3105 33rd Street
Vernon, BC, Canada V1T9P7
(250) 550-3662
greatervernon.com

Kelowna, British Columbia

Tourism Kelowna
544 Harvey Avenue
Kelowna, BC, Canada V1Y6C9
(250) 861-1515
tourismkelowna.org

Resources for Climatic Information

Climatic data are often included in chamber of commerce and visitors bureau mailings but can be misleading. The National Climatic Data Center (NCDC) in Asheville, North Carolina is the best source for comparative climatic data for American locations. The center's best-selling *Comparative Climatic Data for the United States*, published annually, was the primary source of climatic data for the larger places described in this book. It provides a wealth of information in 17 climatic tables for more than 270 American cities. It is free online and is available in book form for a nominal charge. Check the NCDC website (ncdc.noaa.gov) for complete information for ordering their data and products, or call them at (828) 271-4800 between 8:00 a.m. and 6:00 p.m. EST. Canadian climatic data are most easily found by performing an Internet search for "Canadian climatic normals 1971-2000." The Environment Canada website provides climatic data for an enormous number of places across Canada.

Resources for Cost of Living Information

Cost of living data for more than 300 American cities, including most of those covered in *Retire in Style*, are published by ACCRA (formerly called the American Chamber of Commerce Researchers Association). *The ACCRA Cost of Living Index*, published quarterly, provides a useful and relatively accurate measure of living cost differences among urban areas. Single copies of current or back issues cost $70 each or $140 for four consecutive issues. Order forms are available from the ACCRA Subscription Office at (703) 522-4980, or at accra.org.

Resources for Crime Rate Information

Crime rates for American cities and all but the smallest towns can be calculated from data in the FBI's annual publication, *Crime in the United States: Uniform Crime Reports*. Be sure to utilize city/town data whenever possible, as we did for *Retire in Style*. Countywide crime rates, reported in some retirement places books, are too generalized to give a clear picture of the crime threat in particular cities and towns within county boundaries. *Crime in the United States: Uniform Crime Reports* is available online at www.fbi.gov/ucr/ucr.htm and in hard copy in many libraries and may be ordered from:

> The U.S. Government Printing Office
> Mail Stop: SSOP
> Washington, DC 20402-9328

Detailed crime statistics for most Canadian cities are not published in hard copy but Juristat, the Canadian Centre for Justice Statistics at Statistics Canada, provides a broad range of crime data products online. For information, contact them at (800) 387-2231 or by email at ccjsccsj@statcan.ca.

If the town you are interested in is not listed in these American or Canadian sources, feel free to contact the municipal police chief or county sheriff. They are generally very helpful and willing to provide crime data for their communities.

Resources for Health Care Information

Health care information for American locations is available in a number of guidebooks, the best of which is probably the American Hospital Association's annual *Guide to the Health-Care Field*. Organized by state and city, this guide provides data on every hospital in the United States. Most importantly, it specifies which of more than 80 specialized facilities and services are available in each hospital. This is important information as small-town hospitals may lack one or more services potentially important to you. Check the reference department of your local public or college library to see if they have a copy.

There is no standard guidebook to health care in Canada. Web-based research to sites such as Health Canada, provincial health care systems and local hospitals provide information on general medicine and specialized medical services available in most localities.

Miscellaneous Resources on the Internet

A variety of retirement resources are available on the Internet. Here are a few, in alphabetical order, that are filled with useful information.

Boomercafe.com

Demko.com

Elderlawanswers.com

Realtor.org

Retirementcoachinstitute.com

Retirementliving.com

Seniorcitizens.com

Seniorjournal.com

Seniors-site.com

Senioryears.com

Index

NOTES

NOTES